Software Process Improvement

Reidar Conradi · Tore Dybå · Dag I.K. Sjøberg
Tor Ulsund (Eds.)

Software
Process
Improvement

Results and Experience from the Field

With 42 Figures and 56 Tables

 Springer

Editors

Reidar Conradi

Department of Computer and
Information Science
Norwegian University of Science
and Technology
7491 Trondheim, Norway
conradi@idi.ntnu.no

Tore Dybå

SINTEF Information and Communication
Technology
7465 Trondheim, Norway
tore.dyba@sintef.no

Dag Ingar Kondrup Sjøberg

Department of Software Engineering
Simula Research Laboratory
Post Box 134
1325 Lysaker, Norway
dag.sjoberg@simula.no

Tor Ulsund

Geomatikk AS
Otto Nielsens vei 12
7052 Trondheim, Norway
tore.ulsund@geomatikk.no

ISBN 978-3-642-06880-5   e-ISBN 978-3-540-32179-8

Springer is a part of Springer Science+Business Media
springer.com
© Springer-Verlag Berlin Heidelberg 2010
Printed in The Netherlands

Cover design: KünkelLopka, Heidelberg

Printed on acid-free paper   45/3100/SPI   5 4 3 2 1 0

Preface

Software process improvement (SPI) has for over a decade been promoted as an approach to systematically improving the way software is developed and managed, especially in large software companies. But does SPI work for small and medium sized enterprises, with fast changing environments and processes?

This book reports on results and experience from four Norwegian, industrial R&D projects on SPI, all supported by The Research Council of Norway in the period 1996-2005. The projects are SPIQ (project grant number 118206/221), PROFIT (137901/221), INTERPROFIT (extension of the former, 145207/221), and SPIKE (156701/220) – with emphasis on the latter. More than 70 individual industrial studies in 30 different companies have been carried out. Some related studies are also reported, all supported by The Research Council of Norway.

The target audience is software professionals, especially developers and middle managers, researchers and graduate students.

The book is organized in five sections, with totally 20 previously published papers. The five sections are:

Section 1: Software Process Improvement: general principles and methods, 5 papers.
Section 2: Knowledge Management for SPI, 5 papers.
Section 3: Process Modelling and Electronic Process Guides, 4 papers.
Section 4: Estimation Methods, 3 papers.
Section 5: Empirical Studies in OO and Component-based Systems, 3 papers.

Each section has a preface to motivate for and summarize the papers in the section.

Trondheim/Oslo
December 2005

Reidar Conradi, IDI, NTNU
Tore Dybå, SINTEF ICT
Dag. I. K. Sjøberg
Tor Ulsund

Contents

Section 4 Estimation Methods

Section 5 Empirical Studies in OO and Component-based Systems

Section 1

Software Process Improvement – General Principles and Methods

Software Process Improvement (SPI) is a systematic approach to improving software processes in order to improve software products. It borrows basic principles from Total Quality Management (TQM), e.g. the Plan–Do–Check–Act cycle and the emphasis on long-term commitment to customer quality by the entire development organisation.

Many so-called SPI frameworks have been proposed over the last years, like CMM (in many variants), SPICE, BOOTSTRAP, and partially ISO-9001. However, they are mostly useful for large and stable organisations, while most software companies are small and medium sized enterprises, so-called SMEs, that cannot undertake massive improvement efforts with uncertain future payoff.

This section contains six chapters on the experience with down-sizing such SPI frameworks to make them effective for SMEs:

1. *Conradi, R., Dybå, T., Sjøberg, D.I.K. and Ulsund, T., (2003)* "Lessons Learned and Recommendations from Two Large Norwegian SPI Programmes", in F. Oquendo (Ed.): *Software Process Technology, Ninth International Workshop, EWSPT'2003,* Helsinki, Finland, September 2–1, 2003, Proceedings – in conjunction with FSE/ESEC'2003, Springer Berlin Heidelberg New YorkLNCS 2786, ISBN 3-540-40764-2, pp 32–45
This chapter discusses the results from two Norwegian SPI programs.

2. *Dybå T. (2000)* "Improvisation in Small Software Organizations," *IEEE Software*, 17(5):82–87
This chapter argues that SMEs cannot have too stiff processes.

3. *Dybå T. (2005)* "An Empirical Investigation of the Key Factors for Success in Software Process Improvement," *IEEE Transactions on Software Engineering*, 31(5):410–424
This chapter explores the success factors in SPI.

4. *Dybå, T., Kitchenham, B.A., and Jørgensen M. (2005)* "Evidence-Based Software Engineering for Practitioners," *IEEE Software*, 22(1):158–165
This chapter advocates a systematic empirical paradigm for SPI.

5. *Sjøberg, D.I.K., Anda B., Arisholm, E., Dybå, T., Jørgensen, M,. Kara-hasanović, A., and Vokác M. (2003)* "Challenges and Recommendations when Increasing the Realism of Controlled Software Engineering Experiments," in Reidar Conradi and Alf Inge Wang (Eds.): *Empirical Methods and Studies in Software Engineering–Experiences from ESERNET project*, Springer Berlin Heidelberg New York LNCS 2765, ISBN 3-540-40672-7, pp. 24–38.
This chapter reports on the experience with running distributed, industrial experiments using a web-tool.

Lessons Learned and Recommendations from Two Large Norwegian SPI Programmes

R. Conradi, T. Dybå, D.I.K. Sjøberg, and T. Ulsund

Abstract: Software development is an experimental discipline, i.e. somewhat unpredictable. This suggests that software processes improvement should be based on the continuous iteration of characterization, goal setting, selection of improved technology, monitoring and analysis of its effects. This chapter describes experiences from the empirical studies in two large SPI programmes in Norway. Five main lessons were learned (1) It is a challenge for the industrial partners to invest enough resources in SPI activities; (2) The research partners must learn to know the companies; (3) they must work as a multi-competent and coherent unit towards them (4) Any SPI initiative must show visible, short-term payoff (5) establishing a solid baseline from which to improve is unrealistic. Based on these lessons, a set of operational recommendations for other researchers in the area are proposed.

Keywords: software process improvement, empirical studies, industrial collaboration

1.1 Introduction

Improving the software process, or the way and with what means we develop software, is recognized as a key challenge in our society – cf. the American PITAC report [1] and the European Union's framework programmes [2].

The first three authors of this chapter were responsible for the software process improvement (SPI) work jointly conducted by three research institutions in two successive, cooperative, industrial Norwegian SPI programmes, called SPIQ and PROFIT. The fourth author was the overall manager of both programmes. A dozen software-intensive companies, mostly small- and medium-sized enterprises (SMEs), participated in the programmes.

This article describes the main lessons learned from the seven years of experience in these two programmes from *the point of view of the authors*. We describe potential motivations for why companies and individuals take part in such a programme, and that many of these motivations may make the SPI work very hard. We also focus on requirements to the involved researchers for successful conduct of an SPI programme, e.g. they must familiarize themselves with each company, and work as a multi-competent and coherent unit towards the company. It is important to show visible, short-term payoffs, while complying with long-term business strategies and research objectives. Finally, we describe the importance of generating new understandings and new actions, in whatever order they evolve.

Based on these lessons learned, we propose a set of operative recommendations for other researchers in the area. We will also apply these recommendations ourselves in a new, successor SPI programme, SPIKE, that we have just started.

To make our general position on SPI more explicit, we will start by characteriz-ing some existing SPI approaches and their assumptions. In our view, SPI covers *process assessment, process refinement,* and *process innovation.* Typical im-provement approaches have involved SPI frameworks such as CMM [3], BOOTSTRAP [4], (Software Process Improvement and Capability dEtermination, SPICE ISO/IEC 15504) [5] and the Quality Improvement Paradigm (QIP) [6]. CMM has later been supplemented with the IDEAL improvement model and with Personal Software Process and Team CMM.

Most of these frameworks have become wellknown among practitioners and researchers. However, such frameworks implicitly assume rather stable and large organizations ("dinosaurs"?), and that software can be systematically developed in a more "rational" way – cf. the legacy of Total Quality Management (TQM) [7]. Frameworks in this category may indeed work well, if the focus is process refine-ment, as reported in success stories of using CMM in large companies like Hughes and Raytheon in the early 1990s and in more recent studies [8].

However, the opposite situation applies for small companies ("upstarts"?), rely-ing on knowledge-based improvization [9] to rapidly innovate new products for new markets. Even in the US, 80% of all software developers work in companies with less than 500 employees [10]; that is, in SMEs. Rifkin [11] blatantly claims that we have offered the "wrong medicine" to such companies, which have conse-quently failed in their SPI programs. In contrast to the mentioned CMM studies in the US, several European SPI studies have been performed about SMEs [12, 13]. These studies conclude that short-term priorities – combined with business and market turbulence – may severely prevent, hamper and even abort well-planned and pragmatic SPI efforts. Papers [14, 15] elaborate on some of these issues.

Our general position therefore has been to downscale and make applicable ap-proaches from several SPI frameworks, in particular QIP and TQM, and to apply these in concrete development projects called pilots. Organizational learning has been facilitated through various follow-up actions inside each company, as well as across companies through joint experience groups, shared programme meetings and seminars, technical reports and two pragmatic method books.

QIP assumes that software development is experimental (not quite predictable) and therefore needs to be conducted accordingly. QIP suggests that projects within an organization are based on a *continuous iteration* of characterization, goal set-ting, selection of improved technologies, project execution with changed technologies, monitoring of the effects, and post-mortem analysis and packaging of lessons learned for adoption in future projects. Furthermore, measurement is regarded essential to capture and to effectively reuse software experience. An effective and long-lasting cooperation between academia and industry is also necessary to achieve significant improvements. See [16] for a reflection on 25 years of SPI work at NASA.

In our SPI programmes, individual pilots were implemented according to the model of the European System and Software Initiative (ESSI) [17]. Here, an improvement project and a development project (pilot) are managed as two separate, but strongly connected parts – in a so-called Process Improvement Experiment (PIE).

The remainder of this chapter is organized as follows. Section 1.2 describes the mentioned Norwegian SPI programmes and the approaches taken. Section 1.3 describes the lessons learned. Section 1.4 presents some operational recommendations based on the lessons learned. Section 1.5 concludes and contains ideas for further work.

1.2 The Norwegian SPI Programmes

This section describes the SPIQ, PROFIT and SPIKE programmes for industrial SPI in Norway. SPIQ and PROFIT are finished, while SPIKE is upstarting.

1.2.1 General About the Norwegian SPI Programmes

The first programme, *SPIQ* or *SPI for better Quality* [18], was run for three years in 1997–1999, after a half-year pre-study in 1996. The successor programme, *PROFIT* or *PROcess improvement For IT Industry*, was run in 2000–2002. Both programmes were funded 45% by The Research Council of Norway and involved three research institutions (NTNU, SINTEF, and University of Oslo) and ca. 15–20 IT companies, both SMEs and large companies. More than 40 SPI pilot projects have been run in these companies. A follow-up programme, *SPIKE* or *SPI based on Knowledge and Experience*, is carried out in 2003–2005 with 40% public funding.

All three programmes were and are being coordinated and lead by one of the industrial partners, Bravida Geomatikk (previous part of Norwegian Telecom), which acts on behalf of one of the major Norwegian IT organizations, Abelia. The public support of ca. 1 mill. Euro per year is mostly used to pay 10–12 part-time researchers, travel expenses, administration and deliveries from the companies. The main annual contribution to a company is a fixed amount (now 12,500 €), plus 300–400 free researcher hours to help carry out a pilot project and thus improve each company. The companies may recently also be compensated extra for direct participation in concrete experiments (see Sect. 1.4). A total of six PhD students will be funded by these three programmes (three of which have already received their PhD), and over 30 MSc students have so far done their thesis related to these programmes.

The programmes provide networks of cooperation both between researchers and the IT industry, between researchers on a national and international level, and among the participating companies. Figure 1.1 below shows the principle cooperation and work mode.

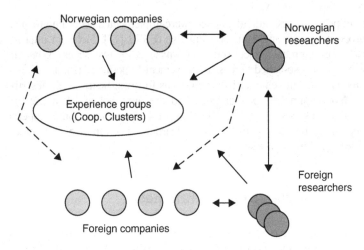

Fig. 1.1. Cooperation mode in the SPI programmes

Typical work in the industrial companies includes pilot projects to test out a given improvement technology, like novel inspection techniques, agile development methods, electronic process guides, or use of software experience bases for estimation (see later). There has been local planning and follow-up activities around each pilot project, involving one or two researchers and an industrial partner. There have also been monthly coordination meetings between the researchers and the programme manager, and two common technical meetings (seminars) per year. In addition comes researcher-lead experience groups (clusters) on subjects like experience bases and testing. A bi-monthly newsletter has been issued (on paper and web), and various technical reports written with industry as a targeted audience. International collaboration has in some cases also involved direct, inter-company exchanges.

Education has effectively been used to spread results. For instance, several revised and new courses have been extended with SPI-related topics and formal experiments around SPI. MSc and PhD students participate regularly in industrial case studies, and this has been highly appreciated by all parties.

This type of *shared collaboration programmes* over a sufficient number of years have proved advantageous in counteracting the volatility problems of SMEs and their priorities. *Learning* in our context therefore assumes *cross-company* activities, and thus willingness to share own experience, bad and good. Luckily, most companies have similar problems. That is, effective long-term SPI learning can take place as a joint endeavour by and for the IT industry. In this task, academia (the three research partners and their foreign contacts), the Abelia industrial association, and The Research Council of Norway act as initiating and coordinating bodies. Thus the *whole* IT industry can learn and improve, not only single and spurious companies (SMEs).

1.2.2 The SPIQ Programme in 1997–1999

We refer to the previous description of general work mode. The main result of SPIQ (www.geomatikk.no/spiq) was a first version of a pragmatic *method handbook* [19]. This handbook combined aspects of *TQM* and *QIP* including the latter's *Goal-Question-Metric* method [20] and *Experience Factory* concept [21]. SPIQ has furthermore, as mentioned, adopted the *ESSI* PIE model. An *incremental* approach was generally advocated, e.g. relying on action research [23]. Five *case studies* from the SPIQ companies were also documented.

1.2.3 The PROFIT Programme in 2000–2002

In PROFIT (www.geomatikk.no/profit), we applied the same overall work mode. We concentrated on improvement under change and uncertainty, learning organizations, and novel technologies like XP and component-based development. We also wrote a second, down-scaled and more accessible *method handbook* [24], issued by a Norwegian publisher.

Mostly in parallel with PROFIT, we are running an INTER-PROFIT add-on programme in 2001–2004 to promote international experience exchange and cooperation between Norwegian and European companies and researchers. Cooperation agreements are in effect between INTER-PROFIT and the CeBASE (www.cebase.org) project in 2000–2002 lead by University of Maryland, the ESERNET thematic network (www.esernet.org) in 2001–2003 lead by the Fraunhofer IESE in Kaiserslautern, and VTT in Finland. Several joint seminars and workshops have been arranged. All three research partners participate in the International Software Engineering Research Network ISERN (www.iese.fhg.de/ISERN).

1.2.4 The Upstarting SPIKE Programme in 2003–2005

We have just started a successor programme in 2003–2005, SPIKE (www.abelia.no/spike). The technical focus is adaptation and trials of "context-dependent" methods, i.e. finding out the "correct" application of, e.g. incremental methods, object-oriented analysis and design, electronic process guides, knowledge management, and estimation technologies. As in SPIQ and PROFIT, we support empirical studies, shared activities like experience groups and seminars, international cooperation, and PhD studies. See Sect. 1.4 on Operative Recommendations.

1.2.5 Some Industrial and Research Goals

In these SPI programmes, some overall *industrial goals* have been (examples):

1. At least half of the companies shall run an overall improvement program.

2. All the participating companies shall continually run an improvement project linked to a pilot development project.
3. All companies shall participate in at least one experience group, e.g. within:
   – SPI in changing environments (technical, organizational, and market).
   – Knowledge management and experience data bases.
   – Model-based development (often based on UML).
   – Project management and estimation.
4. All companies shall make presentations in national or international conferences.

Some *research goals* have similarly been (examples):

1. Develop methods and guidelines for process improvement with focus on experience and knowledge reuse techniques for environments with a high degree of change.
2. Document the results in articles and case studies.
3. Disseminate the results through a close cooperation with universities and colleges.
4. Dontribute to PhD and MSc theses, and an updated curriculum in software engineering and SPI.

1.2.6 Some Typical SPI Pilot Projects in SPIQ and PROFIT

Figure 1.2 shows nine typical SPI pilots with their companies and improvement themes. As mentioned, a total of 40 SPI pilots have been performed in SPIQ and PROFIT. This corresponds to about 10 pilots per year, as some went over two years.

1.2.7 Main Results from the SPIQ and PROFIT Programmes

The two programmes have achieved and reported results for many actors and in many directions:

1. For each participating company, e.g. improved methods and processes, and better process understanding
2. For the Norwegian IT industry, e.g. as experience summaries with revised process guidelines and lessons learned, and by establishing meeting places such as experience groups, seminars, and a web site
3. For the broader software community, e.g. as collections of published papers and international research cooperation
4. For the research partners, e.g. as revised educational programs and through MSc and PhD candidates
5. On a national level: creation of an SPI community between industry and academia, and internal in academia

- Fjellanger-Widerøe, Trondheim, 1998: Improving the inspection process

- TietoEnator, Oslo, 1998–1999: establishing an experience database for consulting

- Genera, Oslo, 1999–2000: improving development methods for web-applications

- Mogul.com, Oslo/Trondheim, 2000–2001: improving estimation methods for use cases

- Kongsberg Spacetec, Tromsø, 2001: establishing an experience database, using PMA

- NERA, Oslo, 2001–2002: SPI by incremental and component-based development

- Ericsson, Grimstad, 2002: improving design inspections by OO reading techniques

- ObjectNet, Oslo, 2002: Experimenting with XP to improve the development process

- Kongsberg-Ericsson, 2002: comparing UML with textual requirement formalisms

Fig. 1.2. Examples of companies and work themes

The main external results come from points 2 and 3, and comprise revised methods, lessons learned and recommendations in how to carry out SPI in small and medium sized IT-organizations [25, 26]. In addition, almost 100 refereed publications on related topics have been published, and three PhD theses defended as part of the SPIQ and PROFIT programmes.

1.3 Lessons Learned

Many empirical studies have been conducted in the Norwegian industry as part of these SPI programmes. This section describes the main lessons learned from the point of view of the research managers and the programme manager, that is, the authors.

Lesson 1: It is a Challenge for the Industrial Partners to Invest Enough resources in SPI Activities

The authors were research and programme managers of the two SPI programmes. In our opinion, the perhaps largest practical problem was to keep up the SPI activities within the companies. The performance of a company is closely related to the effort (person-hours) it is willing to spend on the SPI activities. There were several reasons for why many of the companies did not spend as much effort as they initially had planned. Understanding these reasons is important in order to achieve success in an SPI programme. This issue is closely related to the underlying *motives* of the companies and the individual contact persons for taking part in partially externally funded SPI programmes such as SPIQ and PROFIT. A company will ask itself *"what's in it for the company?"* Similarly, an individual will ask: *"what's in it for me?"* We have observed the following motives of a company:

- *Improving its software processes.* As seen from research councils that fund SPI programmes, this should be the main motivation of a company.
- *Increasing the level of competence and knowledge in certain areas.* Although a company is not particularly interested in SPI, it may be interested in using an SPI programme to increase the competence in certain technology areas.
- *Publicity.* Several companies use the collaboration with SPI researchers as a selling point.
- *Be present where things happen.* Even if a company is not genuinely interested in SPI, it may wish to participate in such SPI programmes, just to be present where interesting things possibly happen. The company will not risk to miss information or activities that might be considered important by their customers or competitors.
- *Networking and recruitment.* Connecting to companies, research institutes, and universities has proved a real motivation. For example, since many SPI researchers also teach at universities, they have indirectly been recruitment channels for the companies. The companies are also interested in collaborating with the other companies in the programmes on business issues (in addition to SPI activities).
- *Money.* The Research Council of Norway partially supports the companies' SPI activities.
- *Inexpensive consultancy work.* Some companies have work duties, that are not SPI activities, but which they believe they can use researchers in an SPI program to carry out. That is, they may consider researchers as cheap consultants.

The industrial people in the SPI programmes may also individually have various motives for taking part, amongst others:

- Supporting the motives of the company such as those described earlier. In particular, supporting the SPI activities of the company.
- Personal interest in SPI activities. This may be the case, even if SPI is not considered important within the company.
- Personal interest in research. This may be the case, even if research is not considered important within the company.
- Increased level of competence in certain technology areas. This may be the case, even if those areas are not considered important within the company.

– Internal status in the company. Holding a high profile and demonstrating a good personal network may increase the status and respect of one's colleagues.

The first two motives of a company are the ones that comply with the research councils' intention of the SPI programmes. Understanding the other companies and the motives of the participating individuals, make it easier for the research partners in the programmes to understand the behaviours a participating company and respond accordingly. Note, that even though the main motivations for taking part in an SPI programme are not the "ideal" ones, the company may still contribute positively to the programme. It is when a company does not contribute to a programme, the underlying motives should be revealed and appropriate actions taken.

Related to the problem of spending sufficient resources on SPI activities within a company, is not only the time of the people involved, but the ability and internal position of the contact persons. To have an impact on the SPI within the company, the peoples should have relevant competence, experience, respect, and position in the company [27]. We have experienced that several companies do not wish to allocate key technical persons to SPI work, because they are considered too important in ordinary business projects (this phenomenon is also seen in collaborative projects, in quality assurance work, and in standardization activities). Therefore, to save costs, the companies let junior or "less important" persons take part in the programmes. As a consequence, the SPI impact within the company is reduced.

Although tailored involvement is required by an organization for successful SPI, it is no precondition for successful *research*. We experienced in SPIQ and PROFIT several cases where data from a company gave interesting research results, although the SPI internal in the company was neglected.

Lesson 2: The Research Partners Must Put Much Effort in Getting to Know the Companies

The impact of an SPI programme does, of course, depend on the resources spent by the researchers, and their competence and enthusiasm. Another success factor is a humble attitude of the researchers towards the situation of the practitioners, and the interest and ability to learn to know the actual company. The researcher should help to solve concrete problems of an organization, cf. action research. For studies where a deep understanding of an organization and its processes is important, the researcher will gain much goodwill if he or she takes part in some of the organization's regular activities. That is, to give courses, to participate in social activities etc. The presentation of the research results to a company should be tailored towards different roles and needs, and answer "what's important in this study for me".

Another reason to learn in detail about a company, is that such information may be required to identify the kind of companies and contexts to which the results can be generalized. That is, where they are relevant and valid.

Lesson 3: The Research Partners Must Work as a Multi-Competent and Coherent unit towards the companies

After seven years of experience, we have learned that a research team for a successful SPI programme primarily must be *competent*. That is, it must cover the relevant technical areas in a convincing manner, e.g. testing, incremental development, component-based development etc. In addition comes knowledge of SPI-related methods, often coupled with insight in organizational science and data analysis. Likewise, the researchers should have adequate industrial experience and insight. e.g. putting fresh university candidates to "improve" seasoned developers is ill-advised, although junior researchers can grow into able assistants, often having ample time to work and familiarize with the practitioners.

The second main issue is that the team must cooperate well internally, i.e. be externally in line. There can and should be tough scientific and other discussions among the researchers themselves, but towards industry, the team should appear as a *coherent* unit. Within a company there are many stakeholders with different interests and agendas in the local SPI effort. The companies are openly reluctant to collaborate with a research team that disagrees on the approach and activities towards the company, simply because it complicates the already complex, local SPI effort even further.

To begin with, the SPIQ and PROFIT programmes were run by four research institutions. Due to internal problems of collaboration, which were partly visible to the collaborating companies, one of the research institutions had to leave the programme after two years. After seven years, the working environment among the remaining researcher institutions is very good. In other words, do not underestimate the time it takes to create a well-functioning SPI research team of a certain size (we have been from 10–15 researchers at any time).

Lesson 4: Any SPI Initiative Must Show Visible, Short-Term Payoff

The research community is used to think that improvement actions will have long-term payoff in terms of increased competitiveness, improved product quality, increased competence, etc. However, it is often the task of the SPI responsible within the individual company to visualize the payoffs of their investments in SPI. If they fail to do so, it may cause lack of confidence and support from management, which again is an important prerequisite for succeeding in SPI.

For instance, top management in a cooperating company said suddenly that they wanted to release the internal SPI responsible from his tasks, because they could not see that he had delivered the expected SPI results. The management had expected documentation of a new process model in the form of a printed handbook. The SPI responsible, on the other hand, had concentrated his effort on establishing company-wide motivation for the new SPI initiative and was planning extensive experience harvesting sessions to build the new process description. This had not been visible to the management; instead they saw a large consumption of human resources without any concrete results.

This story shows the importance of being open about the overall process from the very beginning, and to explain how the SPI activities eventually will lead to a worthwhile benefit. Even large companies will not embark upon five-year SPI plans.

Lesson 5: Establishing a Solid Baseline from Which to Improve is Unrealistic

The conventional way of thinking about SPI puts generation of new understandings and the associated actions in a *sequential* order, i.e. first understanding, then action. For example, in the early Japanese software factories, a strong emphasis was put on gathering data on existing processes, before changing or improving them [28]. QIP similarly advocates that we should first understand what we do, before we attempt to change it – in line with the Plan–Do–Check–Act loop in TQM.

SMEs face two main challenges with this approach: (1) an ever-changing environment (2) few projects running at any given point in time. As a consequence, they have few data, which they can analyze and use to build an understanding. In addition, collected data will soon be outdated and left irrelevant or – in the best case – uncertain. Taken together, this implies that SMEs need to utilize their data as soon as it is available, extract the important information for learning, and engage in expedite improvement actions. There is simply no opportunity to collect long time series or amass large amounts of data, needed for traditional improvement approaches such as TQM's Statistical Process Control.

A specific challenge involves balancing the refinement of the existing skill base with the experimentation of new ideas to find alternatives that improve on old ideas, see again [9]. Since the most powerful learning comes from direct experience, actions and understandings often need to be reversed. Therefore, the generation of new understandings and new actions, in whatever order they evolve, is fundamental to successful SPI. This matches research results from organizational science on combined working and learning, cf. the "storytelling" metaphor in Brown and Duguid's seminal study of the (poor) use of experience bases at Xerox [29].

1.4 Operational Recommendations

Based on our experiences, we have in the new SPIKE programme introduced the following pragmatic guidelines:

– *Agree on expectations.* In addition to a formal contract between the companies and the programme manager, the mutual expectations among the company and researchers should be clarified in a project plan.

– *Teams instead of individuals.* To ensure continuity, we will for each company co-operate with a team instead of a single contact person. The same applies on the research side.

– *Rapidly identify high risk companies.* If a company tends to show little interest (defers or cancels meetings, does not reply to emails, etc.), we will quickly confront the company with this behaviour. Since our experience is that people do not change behaviour in this area, we will try to replace passive contact persons with more enthusiastic ones.

- *Be flexible upon problems.* Flexibility and responsiveness are particularly important when things seem to be going badly, e.g. when people say they have insufficient time or resources for a task. In such cases we will do things differently, extend deadlines, compromise on the task, offer an extra pair of hands, and so on.

- *Provide timely and accurate feedback.* The real payoff from using data analysis in the organizational learning cycle comes when the data is fed back to the local teams, from which it was collected, and problem solving begins.

- *Picking a good topic ("killer application").* The ideal topic for an SPI programme is locally relevant, based on sound evidence, and able to demonstrate tangible benefits in a short time. Such a focus on small and immediately useful result may, however, not always go hand in hand with the researchers' needs and interests. Our solution is to offer direct payment for extra effort spent on long-term SPI work internally or on results that mostly are relevant to the research community or industry at large. This suggests that SPI programmes should focus both on short-term and long-term alignment of SPI goals with business goals and research objectives. An important challenge is thus to achieve a high degree of mutual understanding of current business objectives, as well as to align long-term SPI goals with business and research strategies.

- *Tailor payment for concrete activities.* The most active companies will naturally get the "lion's share" of the programme resources (i.e. free researcher support and direct payment). In SPIQ we bureaucratically requested that each company got a fixed sum for each finished report, such as an initial project plan, intermediate status reports, and a final report. The experience was that the company felt that writing formal reports did not contribute to the SPI effort of the company. The quality of such reports was also too poor for research purposes. In the following PROFIT, we therefore introduced a flat payment model, where each company was given 100,000 NOK (12,500 €) as long as they contributed with a minimum of activity. Since this model did not stimulate effort over a minimum, SPIKE allows to pay for extra, focused activities. For example, if a company wants to run a controlled experiment on a certain technology, we will also pay the company for the marginal extra effort involved, e.g. 10 employees each working 5 hours à 70 € per person-hour.

- *Tailor payment to those involved.* It is important that the payment is directed to those who actually perform the SPI work. Particularly in large companies, the payment may easily end up a "sink" with no gain for those who are involved. The money should benefit those involved at least at the departmental level. We have experienced that even small incitements can be effective. For example, in one company, we were successful in organizing a lottery where each interviewed person was given a ticket in a lottery where the prize was a hotel weekend in the mountains. In another case, we simply paid each individual 1,000 NOK (125 €) to fill in a questionnaire.

1.5 Conclusion and Future Work

In the Sect. 1.4 we have outlined some critical factors and lessons learned from the SPIQ and PROFIT programmes.

Some *national-level results* are:

– Many profitable and concrete process improvements in Norwegian IT companies, as well as a better understanding and learning of underlying needs and principles.
– An effective and consolidated cooperation network between researchers and IT industry. This expands a Norwegian tradition for cooperative R&D programmes.
– A fast, national build-up of competence in SPI and empirical methods, resulting in two method books (in Norwegian).
– Upgraded education in software engineering, and many MSc and PhD graduates.
– An extended cooperative network of international contacts.

Some *overall lessons for SPI methods and –programmes* are:

– Textbook methods and approaches to SPI must be fundamentally rethought and down-scaled to be effective in an IT industry with mostly SMEs and a generally high change rate.
– (Inter-)company and long-term learning for volatile SMEs can successfully be organized as a joint effort between companies and research institutions, with proper links to industrial associations and a founding research council. Such efforts must span at least five years – in our case three times three years.
– There should be a close coupling between working and learning e.g. experience bases and quality systems should be created, introduced, and maintained in a truly collaborative and incremental way [30, 31].

1.5.1 Future Work

This chapter has described the lessons learned from the point of view of the research managers and the programme manager. We conducted a small survey among the companies to identify their views. They generally seemed happy with the support from the programme, but in several areas the competence and behaviour of the researchers could obviously be improved. One reason for the sometimes low activity in the companies (cf. Lessons 1, Sect. 1.3), *might* be that the effort of the researchers was not felt sufficiently good. Future work could include interviews with the participants from the industry to identify their real opinions.

Acknowledgements

We thank our colleagues Letizia Jaccheri and Tor Stålhane from NTNU, Torgeir Dingsøyr, Geir Kjetil Hanssen, Nils Brede Moe, Kari Juul Wedde and Hans Westerheim from SINTEF, and Bente Anda, Erik Arisholm, Hans Gallis, Magne Jørgensen and Espen Koren from the Simula Research Laboratory/University of Oslo for their effort in the programmes. We would also like to thank all the companies that took part: Bergen Data Consulting, Bravida Geomatikk, Computas, EDB 4tel, Ergo Solutions, Ericsson, Firm, Fjellanger Widerøe, Genera (Software Innovation), Icon Medialab, Kongsberg Defence Communication, Kongsberg Ericsson Communication, Kongsberg Spacetec, MaXware, Mogul, Navia Aviation, Nera, Numerica Taskon, OM Technology, Siemens, Storebrand, Tandberg Data, Telenor Geomatikk, TietoEnator and TV2 Interaktiv. All programmes were funded by the Research Council of Norway.

References

[1] The President's Information Technology Advisory Committee (1998), *Advisory Committee Interim Report to the President*, August, pp. 66, See http://www.itrd.gov/ac/interim/

[2] European Commission, *Information Society Technologies: A Thematic Priority for Research and Development ... – 2003–2004 Work Programme*, p. 90. See http://fp6.cordis.lu/fp6

[3] Paulk, M.C., Weber, C.V., Curtis, B., and Chrissis, M.B. (1995) The Capability Maturity Model for Software: Guidelines for Improving the Software Process, *SEI Series in Software Engineering*, Addison-Wesley Reading, MA, p. 640

[4] Haase, V., Messnarz, R., Koch, G., Kugler, H.J., and Decrinis, P. (1994)BOOTSTRAP: Fine-Tuning Process Assessment, *IEEE Software*, July, 11(4), pp. 25–35

[5] *SPICE, Software Process Improvement and Capability dEtermination* (1998). See on-line version on http://www.sqi.gu.edu.au/spice/

[6] Basili, V.R. and Caldiera, G. (1995) Improving Software Quality by Reusing Knowledge and Experience, *Sloan Management Review*, 37(1), pp. 55–64, Fall

[7] Deming, W. (1986) *Out of the crisis*, MIT Center for Advanced Engineering Study, Cambridge, MA: MIT

[8] Curtis, B. (2000) The Global Pursuit of Process Maturity, *IEEE Software*, July/August, 17(4), pp. 76–78 (introduction to special issue on SPI results)

[9] Dybå, T.(2000) Improvisation in Small Software Organizations: Implications for Software Process Improvement, *IEEE Software*, September/October, 17(5), pp. 82–87

[10] Ward, R.P., Fayad, M.E., and Laitinen, M. Thinking Objectively: software process improvement in the small, *Comm. of ACM*, April. 44(4), pp. 105–107

[11] Rifkin, S. (1999) "Discipline of Market Leaders and Other Accelerators to Measurement, *Proc. 24th Annual NASA-SEL Software Engineering Workshop (on CD-ROM)*, NASA Goddard Space Flight Center, Greenbelt, MD, USA, 1–2 December, p. 6

[12] Stålhane, T. and Wedde, K.J. (1999) SPI – Why Isn't it More Used?, *Proc. EuroSPI'99*, Pori, Finland, 26–27 October, p. 13

[13] Cattaneo, F., Fuggetta, A., and Sciuto, D. (2001) Pursuing Coherence in Software Process Assessment and Improvement, *Software Process: Improvement and Practice*, 6(1), pp.3–22

[14] Arisholm, E., Anda, B., Jørgensen, M., and Sjøberg, D. (1999) "Guidelines on Conducting Software Process Improvement Studies in Industry", *Proc. 22nd IRIS Conference* (Information Systems Research Seminar In Scandinavia), Keuruu, Finland, 7–10, August, pp. 87–102

[15] Conradi, R. and Fuggetta, A. (2002) Improving Software Process Improvement, *IEEE Software*, 19(4), pp. 92–99

[16] Basili, V.R., McGarry, F.E., Pajerski, R., and Zelkowitz, M.V. (2002) Lessons Learned from 25 Years of Process Improvement: The Rise and Fall of the NASA Software Engineering Laboratory, *Proc. 24th Int'l Conference on Software Engineering*, Orlando, Florida, ACM/IEEE-CS PressMay 19–25, pp. 69–79

[17] Consolini, L. and Fonade, G. (1997) The European Systems and Software Initiative – ESSI: A Review of Current Results", Final Version, The European Commission's Directorate General III, Industry. See http://www.cordis.lu/esprit/src/stessi.htm

[18] Conradi, R. (1996) SPIQ: A Revised Agenda for Software Process Support, In Carlo Montangero, editor, *Proc. 4th European Workshop on Software Process Technology (EWSPT'96)*, Nancy, France, 9–11 October Springer, Berlin Heidelberg New York, LNCS 1149, pp 36–41

[19] Dybå, T. et al. (2000) SPIQ Metodebok for Prosessforbedring" (V3, in Norwegian), UiO/SINTEF/NTNU, 14. January 2000, ISSN 0802-6394, pp. 250, See also http://www.geomatikk.no/spiq

[20] Basili, V.R., Caldiera, G., and Rombach, H.-D. (1994) The Goal Question Metric Paradigm, In [22], pp. 528–532

[21] Basili, V.R., Caldiera, G., and Rombach, H.-D. (1994) The Experience Factory, In [22], pp. 469–476

[22] Marciniak, J.J., (1994) Editor, *Encyclopedia of Software Engineering – 2 Volume Set*, Wiley

[23] Greenwood, D.J. and Levin, M. (1998) *Introduction to Action Research: Social Research for Social Change*, Thousand Oaks, California, Sage

[24] Dybå, T., Dingsøyr, T., and Moe, N.B. Praktisk Prosessforbedring, Fagbokforlaget, ISBN 82-7674-914-3, pp. 116 (in Norwegian, the PROFIT method book). See also http://www.geomatikk.no/profit

[25] Dybå, T. (2000) An Instrument for Measuring the Key Factors of Success in Software Process Improvement, *Journal of Empirical Software Engineering*, 5(4):357–390, December

[26] Dybå, T. (2001) Enabling Software Process Improvement: An Investigation of the Importance of Organizational Issues, PhD Thesis, NTNU 2001:101, ISBN 82-471-5371-8, 5 November, p. 332, See http://www.idi.ntnu.no/grupper/su/publ/pdf/dybaa-dring-thesis-2001.pdf.

[27] El-Emam, K., Goldenson, D., McCurley, J., and Herbsleb, J. (2001) Modelling the Likelihood of Software Process Improvement: An Exploratory Study, *Journal of Empirical Software Engineering*, 6(3):207–229, September

[28] Cusumano, M.A. (1991) *Japan's Software Factories*, Oxford University Press

[29] Brown, J.S. and Duguid, P. (1991) Organizational Learning and Communities of Practice: Toward a Unified View of Working, Learning, and Innovation, *Organization Science*, Vol. 2, No. 1, February, pp.40–57

[30] Conradi, R., Lindvall, M., and Seaman, C. (2000) Success Factors for Software Experience Bases: What We Need to Learn from Other Disciplines, In Janice Singer et al., editors, *Proc. ICSE'2000 Workshop on Beg, Borrow or Steal: Using Multidisciplinary Approaches in Empirical Software Engineering Research*, Limerick, Ireland, 5 June, pp. 113–119

[31] Conradi, R. and Dybå, T. (2001) "An Empirical Study on the Utility of Formal Routines to Transfer Knowledge and Experience" In Gruhn, V. (Ed.): *Proc. European Software Engineering Conference 2001 (ESEC'2001)*, Vienna, 10–14, September 2001, ACM/IEEE CS Press, ACM Order no. 594010, ISBN 1-58113-390-1, pp. 268–276

2

Improvisation in Small Software Organizations

T. Dybå

Abstract: Improvisation can give valuable insights into the relationship between action and learning in small, software-intensive organizations. As this chapter describes, a specific challenge involves balancing the refinement of the existing skill base with the experimentation of new ideas to find alternatives that improve on old ideas.

Keywords: software process improve ment, software process assessment, improvisation, learning, Capability Maturity Model (CMM).

2.1 Introduction

We are witnessing an explosive growth in the size and complexity of problems that software can address. Software organizations and their environments – which includes their market conditions, customers, suppliers, and recruitment base for future employees – are also experiencing complex interactions, as well as the implications of rapid changes in technology. But there is an important distinction between acknowledging complex interactions and understanding or controlling them.

Unfortunately, researchers and managers within the software community tend to share a belief that success depends on the ability to predict changes in the environment and to develop rational plans to cope with these changes. Predictability, however, is a property of simple systems. Reality is different – an environment is not a simple system, is not predictable, is not entirely knowable, and is definitely not controllable by the software manager or software organization. As I will use this chapter to show, the sooner we admit this to ourselves, the sooner we can develop more useful models for improving software development.

2.2 Alice and the Croquet Game

To most small software organizations, their environment is like the croquet game in *Alice in Wonderland* – everything constantly changes around the player. In Alice's game, the croquet balls were live hedgehogs, the mallets were live flamingoes, and the arches were card soldiers. The players all played at once, without waiting for turns, and they had to fight the hedgehogs, which constantly crawled away, the flamingoes, which often twisted themselves around into the opposite direction, and the card soldiers, who frequently abandoned the game. As Alice did, small organizations face environmental turbulence. They require an improvement approach that recognizes

– The need for a dramatically shorter time frame between planning and action
– That planning an action does not provide all the details of its implementation
– That creativity is necessary to make sense of the environment

Improvisation is an improvement approach that can help us better understand the relationship between action and learning in small software organizations. For that reason, small software organizations should become more improvisational to survive in an increasingly turbulent and complex environment. Most research focuses on large organizations, but I'd like to explore the environmental turbulence that small organizations face. Software organizations should pay more attention to future demands and seek the opportunities that are inherent in experimenting. Improvisation links a strong skill base with such experimentations and could be a viable alternative for improvement in small software organizations.

2.3 Improvisation

Improvisation deals with the unforeseen. It involves continual experimentation with new possibilities to create innovative and improved solutions outside current plans and routines. The explorative nature of improvisation necessarily involves a potential for failure, leading to the popular misconception that improvisation is only of a spontaneous, intuitive nature that happens among untutored geniuses or in immature organizations. However, organizational improvisation does not emerge from thin air. Instead, it involves and partly depends on the exploitation of prior routines and knowledge. Paul Berliner asserted that "Improvisation involves reworking precomposed material and designs in relation to unanticipated ideas conceived, shaped, and transformed under the special conditions of performance, thereby adding unique features to every creation" [1].

Generally, there are different levels of improvisation, ranging from interpreting or minimally adjusting an already existing model (through embellishment and variation) to radically altering the original models [1].

Improvisational activities that fall under interpretation and minor adjustment depend on the models with which they start, while extreme improvisation depends more heavily on past experience and memory. Berliner explained the role experience and knowledge plays in jazz improvisation when he described good jazz improvisers as having large vocabularies, repertory storehouses, and a reservoir of techniques. Hence, improvisation mixes previously learned lessons with the current setting's contingencies. This mix, however, points to improvisation's core paradox (which is also at the heart of software process improvement (SPI)): Too much reliance on previously learned patterns tends to limit the explorative behavior necessary for improvisation. Yet too much risk-taking leads to fruitless experimentation and repeated failures.

2.4 Improvisation in Software Development

Today, the dominant perspective on software development is rooted in the rationalistic paradigm, which promotes a product-line approach to software development using a standardized, controllable, and predictable software engineering process. From this perspective, the software literature advocates discipline and replacing routinized human labor with mechanical routines and factory-like automation. As a result, a large part of the SPI community has promoted a rational, "best practices" approach to SPI (see the "Current Practices" sidebar). The Software Engineering Institute has advocated the use of *statistical process control* techniques (specifically control charts) in recent technical reports, and it has proposed changes for the CMM to explicitly support the use of rigorous statistical techniques.

But software development is not manufacturing. It is not a mechanical process with strong causal models appropriate for a passive improvement approach based on SPC. On the contrary, software development is largely an intellectual and social activity, requiring the ability to deal with change above the ability to achieve stability [2]. Therefore, we need to distance ourselves from the assumptions underlying the rationalistic, linear model of software engineering and admit that reality for most small software organizations is a nondeterministic, multidirectional flux that involves constant negotiation and renegotiation among and between the groups shaping the software.

2.4.1 Balance

We should not abandon discipline altogether – there needs to be a balance between discipline and creativity in software development [3]. This balance can be challenging, because losing sight of software work's creative, design-intense nature leads to stifling rigidity, but losing sight of the need for discipline leads to chaos. In software, as in jazz, discipline enables creativity [4].

A distinct characteristic of software development, as with all improvisational processes, is the fact that we cannot specify results completely at the outset of the work process. This means that we can only outline the planned software products. Therefore, improvisation differs from the rational approach in that there is no detailed plan and that planning and executing an action converge in time. This last point is particularly important because time to market often determines competitiveness.

Current Practices

Basically, there are three ways in which a software organization can improve its process capability using "best practice" models such as the CMM [1]: it can increase the average performance (the mean of the performance distribution), it can reduce the variance in performance (increase predictability), or it can use a combination of both. Increased average performance is a general feature of experiential learning, and it is clearly beneficial for competitive advantage. Reduced variance, however, is not necessarily an advantage. In fact, for most small software companies, competition can turn reduced variance into a major disadvantage.

To examine the best practice approach to improvement and its consequences for competitiveness in small software organizations, let's consider a simple model James March devised [2], which assumes that survival is based on comparative performance within a group of competing organizations. Furthermore, each single performance is drawn from a performance distribution specific to a particular organization. The mean of the distribution reflects the organization's ability level, and the variance reflects the organization's reliability.

For small software organizations, performance samples are also small. Relative position does not depend on ability alone but is a consequence of ability and reliability [3]. Moreover, the competitive environment of most small software organizations is such that only the best survive—and survival depends on having an extreme performance draw. Thus, improving average ability helps relatively little, and increasing reliability (reducing variance) can detrimentally affect survival.

In an extreme case, where the organization faces only one competitor, increases in average performance always pay off, whereas changes in variance have no effect on competitive advantage. However, when there are several competitors, increases in either the mean or the variance have a positive effect. As the number of competitors increases, the variance's contribution to competitive advantage increases. Ultimately, as the number of competitors goes to infinity, the mean performance becomes irrelevant [2].

The argument behind CMM's improvement approach is that as the organization standardizes software processes and the developers learn techniques, the time required to accomplish development tasks will reduce and productivity and the quality of task performance will increase together with the reliability of task performance [4]. March's model implies that if the increase in reliability comes as a consequence of reducing the performance distribution's left-hand tail (see Fig. 2.1a), the likelihood of finishing last among several competitors is reduced without changing the likelihood of finishing first. But, if process improvement reduces the distribution's right-hand tail, it might easily decrease the chance of being best among the competitors despite increases in the organization's average performance.

An improvement strategy that simultaneously increases average performance and its reliability is, therefore, not a guarantee of competitive advantage (see Figure 2.1a). The consequence of such a strategy is that it helps in competition to avoid relatively low positions, whereas it has a negative effect in competition, where finishing near the top is important. Thus, the price of reliability is a smaller chance of primacy.

If our main goal is to increase the competitive advantage of small software organizations, it's time to move away from the model-based, one-size-fits-all thinking of the 1990s. Instead, we should proceed to improvement strategies that focus on learning from our success to increase the performance distribution's right-hand tail while at the same time reducing the left-hand tail by learning from our failures (see Fig. 2.1b). Improvisation is thus a potential approach for such strategies to succeed.

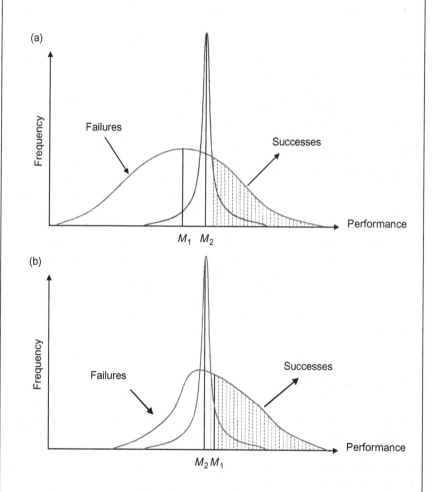

Fig. 2.1. The impact of ability and reliability on performance. M denotes the mean performance of the distributions. Shaded areas show where "improvising" organizations are more successful than "best practice" organizations

References

1. W.A. Florac and A.D. Carleton, *Measuring the Software Process: Statistical Process Control for Software Process Improvement*, Addison-Wesley, Reading, MA, 1999.
2. J.G. March, "Exploration and Exploitation in Organizational Learning," *Organization Science*, Vol. 2, No. 1, Feb. 1991, pp. 71–87
3. D.A. Levinthal and J.G. March, "The Myopia of Learning," *Strategic Management J.*, Vol. 14, Winter 1993, pp. 95–112
4. M.C. Paulk et al., *The Capability Maturity Model: Guidelines for Improving the Software Process*, Addison-Wesley, Reading, MA, 1995

2.4.2 Decisions

Improvisation in software development leads to an emphasis on how developers interpret the environment and on how we make choices in an open situation (where there is more than one possibility). We make such choices by selecting the aspects we consider relevant for modeling, making available modes of interaction with the computer, determining the system's architecture, and deciding how to use technical resources for system implementation. Moreover, we make choices when creating tools and constraints for users and other concerned parties. Ultimately, we choose how we conduct the development process itself.

Only a small part of these choices are made explicit in terms of predecided plans. Usually, they are implied by the course of action we take, or as Donald Schön argues: "Our knowing is *in* our action" [5]. Furthermore, each practitioner treats his or her case as unique and consequently cannot deal with it by applying standard theories or techniques. Also, our interactions with others constrain our choices. When seen in these terms, the task of software development clearly involves a large portion of improvisation, and thus social context and technological content are essential to a proper understanding of software development.

As in the case of a jazz band, close and sustained interaction between professionals stimulates creativity in such a way that the team performs better than its individuals could do alone [4]. The best teams are those that can honor the individualism of their members and at the same time act as a unit.

2.5 Implications for SPI

Having discussed the concept of improvisation and the consequences of CMM-based improvement (see the sidebar), let's now turn to the implications for SPI in small software organizations. There are many challenges for an improvisational approach to SPI to succeed. Two of the most important challenges are to sustain exploration and to learn from failure.

Table 2.1. Exploitation versus Exploration

exploitation	exploration
– refinement, routinizing and elaboration of existing ideas, paradigms, technologies, processes, strategies and knowledge.	– experimentation with new ideas, paradigms, technologies, processes, strategies and knowledge in order to find alternatives that improve on old ones.
– provides incremental returns on knowledge and low risk of failure.	– provides uncertain but potentially high returns on knowledge and carries significant risk of failure.
– requires personnel who are skilled in existing technologies.	– requires personnel who are skilled in emerging or innovative technologies.
– can generate short-term improvement results.	– often requires a long time horizon to generate improved results.

2.5.1 Exploitation and Exploration

Software organizations can engage in two broad kinds of improvement strategies. They can engage in exploitation – the adoption and use of existing knowledge and experience – or exploration – the search for new knowledge, either through imitation or innovation [6]. The basic balance problem is to undertake enough exploitation to ensure short-term results and, concurrently, to engage in exploration to ensure long-term survival [3]. A software organization that specializes in exploitation will eventually become better at using an increasingly obsolete technology, while an organization that specializes in exploration will never realize the advantages of its discoveries (see Table 2.1).

Improvisation requires both exploitation and exploration. Determining the appropriate balance is a complicated dynamic that involves considerations of both organizational size and environmental factors. Because exploitation generally generates clearer, earlier, and closer feedback than exploration, the most common situation is one in which exploitation tends to drive out exploration [7].To make improvisation possible for organizations operating in increasingly more complex and turbulent environments, it is therefore of vital importance that they can increase exploration while sustaining exploitation.

2.5.2 Survey

I studied the balance between exploitation and exploration in a survey of 120 software and quality managers representing whole organizations or independent business units within 55 Norwegian software companies. Specifically, I studied how organizational size and environmental turbulence affected balance. This was

done by comparing the effects of organizational size by contrasting large
organizations with small ones. I defined the groups such that large organizations
consisted of the upper third of the distribution (more than 200 developers) and
small organizations of the lower third (fewer than 30 developers). Similarly, I
examined the effects of environmental turbulence by contrasting the upper and
lower third of the operationalized environment distribution. (For further details
about the survey, contact me at tore.dyba@sintef.no.)

Results showed that small software organizations kept the same level of exploitation both in stable and turbulent environments. However, they engaged in
significantly more exploration in turbulent environments than they did in stable
environments. The increased level of exploration did not drive out exploitation. In
other words, we found support for the proposition that increased environmental
turbulence required increased levels of improvisation.

Similar to small organizations, large software organizations did not differ significantly in their level of exploitation between stable and turbulent environments.
In contrast to the small organizations, however, increased turbulence did not lead
to increased levels of exploration. On the contrary, the larger organizations
seemed to lower their levels of exploration during turbulent times (see Fig. 2.2).
Thus, the results showed that small software organizations engaged in significantly more exploration in turbulent environments than large software organizations. This supports the assertion that small software organizations in turbulent
environments require improvement strategies that are more closely aligned with
explorative behavior, while simultaneously promoting the exploitation of past experience. This is at the heart of an improvement strategy based on improvisation.

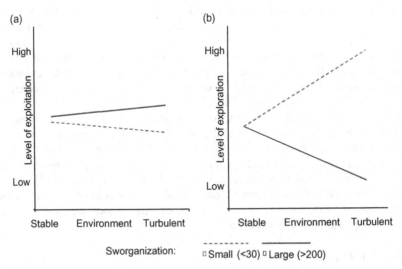

Fig. 2.2. Improvement strategy versus organizational size and environmental turbulence for (**a**) exploitation and (**b**) exploration in small and large organizations

Most software managers agreed that changes in their competitive environments are fast and increasingly unpredictable. However, managers of large software organizations still rely on learning from experience to prepare for the future rather than exploring new possibilities. They tended to generate the same responses even when the stimuli changed – they kept doing what they do well, rather than risk failure. One explanation for this, which is also a direct consequence of using improvement models such as the CMM, is institutionalized routines.

Large organizations tend to rely on formal routines for coordination – small organizations can coordinate their work through face-to-face communications and socializations to a much larger extent than large organizations can. In stable situations, such routinization can become an effective way of developing software, but it can also drive out the exploration of new alternative routines. The deeper these routines are grounded in the organizational culture, the more difficult they are to change and the more easily they can turn into an obstacle to improvement.

2.5.3 Learning Through Failure

Inherent in the rationalistic approach to software development is to consider failure as unacceptable. This is consistent with the goal of promoting stability and short-term performance, as is the case in exploitation. In this situation, success provides an excellent foundation for increased reliability. Hence, success tends to encourage the maintenance of the status quo – if it ain't broke, don't fix it. However, the absence of failure can result in decreased organizational competence when faced with changing and turbulent environments. Improvisation requires tolerance for failure, and failure is an essential prerequisite both for learning and for challenging the status quo.

In software development, we must be able to turn unexpected problems and failures into learning opportunities [8]. Rather than treat failure as unacceptable and stigmatizing, we should distinguish between failures that result from carelessness and those that are a result of intelligent efforts to experiment outside existing patterns [9]. In this way, we can draw attention to potential problems and stimulate the search for creative and innovative solutions when the environmental factors change. The paradox is that you have to experience failure to have success.

Successful improvisation is difficult because it requires both modes of learning – exploitation and exploration. I hope this article will trigger a fruitful debate on how small – and large – organizations can balance these modes and better learn to improvise to cope with their constantly changing and often unpredictable environments.

I plan to further develop the concept of improvisation and organizational learning processes in software organizations, based on survey data as well as several case studies that I have participated in. Also, because software organizations are social systems with people and activities that interact according to certain theories of action, we should pay more attention to the inherent tensions between discipline and creativity, diversity and consensus, and knowing and doing, to mention just a few. Improvisation is a good metaphor for describing the tension between exploration and exploitation. A better understanding of improvisation could, thus, lead to a better understanding of the other tensions in software development and SPI.

References

[1] Berliner, P.R. (1994) *Thinking in Jazz: The Infinite Art of Improvisation*, University of Chicago Press
[2] ChicagoOuld, M.A. (1996) CMM and ISO 9001, *Software Process: Improvement and Practice*, Vol. 2, No. 4, December, pp. 281–289
[3] Glass, R.L. (1995) *Software Creativity*, Prentice Hall, Englewood Cliffs, NJ.
[4] Humphrey, W.S. (1997) *Managing Technical People: Innovation, Teamwork, and the Software Process*, Addison-Wesley, Reading, MA,
[5] Schön, D.A. (1983) *The Reflective Practitioner: How Professionals Think in Action*, Basic Books, NY
[6] March, J.G. (1919) Exploration and Exploitation in Organizational Learning, *Organization Science*, Vol. 2, No. 1, February, pp. 71–87
[7] Levinthal, D.A. and March, J.G. (1993) The Myopia of Learning, *Strategic Management Journal*, Vol. 14, Winter, pp. 95–112
[8] Abdel-Hamid, T.K. and Madnick, S.E. (1990) The Elusive Silver Lining: How We Fail to Learn from Software Development Failures, *Sloan Management Review*, Vol. 32, No. 1, Fall, pp. 39–48
[9] Barrett, F.J. (1998) Creativity and Improvisation in Jazz and Organizations: Implications for Organizational Learning, *Organization Science*, Vol. 9, No. 5, pp. 605–622

3

An Empirical Investigation of the Key Factors for Success in Software Process Improvement

T. Dybå

Abstract: Understanding how to implement software process improvement (SPI) successfully is arguably the most challenging issue facing the SPI field today. The SPI literature contains many case studies of successful companies and descriptions of their SPI programs. However, the research efforts to date are limited and inconclusive and without adequate theoretical and psychometric justification. This chapter extends and integrates models from prior research by performing an empirical investigation of the key factors for success in SPI. A quantitative survey of 120 software organizations was designed to test the conceptual model and hypotheses of the study. The results indicate that success depends critically on six organizational factors, which explained more than 50% of the variance in the outcome variable. The main contribution of the paper is to increase the understanding of the influence of organizational issues by empirically showing that they are at least as important as technology for succeeding with SPI and, thus, to provide researchers and practitioners with important new insights regarding the critical factors of success in SPI.

Keywords: empirical software engineering, software process improvement, critical success factors, organizational issues, survey research.

3.1 Introduction

During the last decade, the software industry has been more and more concerned about software process improvement (SPI). Consequently, we have witnessed a proliferation of models and initiatives all claiming to increase the likelihood of succeeding with SPI initiatives, e.g. the Quality Improvement Paradigm (QIP) [7], the IDEAL model [70], the *ami* method [78], and SPICE [42]. The SPI literature is full of case studies and anecdotal evidence of successful companies and descriptions of their SPI programs, e.g. Alcatel [30], Hewlett-Packard [48], Hughes [57], Motorola [27], NASA [9], Philips [81], Raytheon [34], and Siemens [71]. Several authors repeatedly discuss the importance of certain success factors (e.g. [31, 43, 44, 47, 48, 79, 86, 87]. However, the research efforts to date are limited and inconclusive and without adequate theoretical and psychometric justification [35]. Even for commonly recognized factors such as management commitment and employee participation, no operational measures are available [2].

SPI has its roots in quality management and is closely related to "second generation" [46] organizational development approaches, specifically to organizational learning. Understanding the "quality revolution" is, therefore, an important prerequisite for understanding SPI.

The current state-of-the-art in quality management has more than anything else been shaped by quality gurus such as Deming [33], Juran [58], Crosby [25], and their quality frameworks. These and other authors (e.g., [3, 15, 77, 82, 97]) repeatedly discuss the importance of critical factors such as leadership involvement, employee participation, measurement, and process management to improve the quality performance in organizations.

Similarly, the current state-of-the-art in organizational learning has more than anything else been shaped by the works of Argyris and Schön, who made an important distinction between the concepts of *single-loop* and *double-loop* learning [5], Senge, who proposed five disciplines for creating a learning organization [84], and Nonaka, who discussed the conditions required of the "knowledge creating company" [74].

Humphrey [55, 56] and Basili [7, 8] have been the pioneers and leaders in the field of SPI, identifying the basic principles of software process change and improvement, goal-oriented measurement, and the reuse of organizational experience and learning. For a more detailed review of these and other studies of the facilitating factors of quality management, organizational learning, and SPI, see [35].

This paper extends and integrates models from prior research by performing an empirical investigation of the key factors for success in SPI. In the next section, we present our proposed model, which comprises six independent, one dependent, and two contextual variables, and the corresponding research hypotheses. In Sect. 3.3, we provide an overview of the population and sample, the variables and measures, the data collection procedure, the reliability and validity of the measurement scales, and the data analysis techniques. Section 3.4 presents the results of testing the hypothesis and exploring the relationships. Section 3.5 provides a discussion of the results, their implications, the limitations of the study, and suggests some directions for further research. Section 3.6 provides some concluding comments.

3.2 Conceptual Model and Hypotheses

The research model to be empirically tested in this study is depicted in Fig. 3.1. The model derives its theoretical foundations by combining prior research in quality management, organizational learning, and SPI with an explorative study of 54 managers, developers, and customer representatives in four software companies along with a detailed review by eleven SPI experts from academia and industry (see [35, 37]).

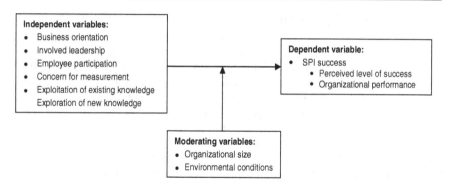

Fig. 3.1. Conceptual research model.

The model includes six facilitating factors: business orientation, involved leadership, employee participation, concern for measurement, exploitation of existing knowledge, and exploration of new knowledge, two moderating factors (organizational size and environmental conditions), and the dependent variable, SPI success. These are described next.

3.2.1 Business Orientation

Attaining business objectives is the ultimate target for any change program [10], and the role of process orientation and process improvement has long been recognized as essential factors to achieve business excellence and competitive advantage [46]. Consequently, a clearly defined SPI program driven by strategic business needs, have been suggested as a key factor for success in SPI (e.g. [13, 17, 48, 55, 78, 98]). Therefore, we would expect that a successful SPI program is one, in which SPI goals and policies have been clearly aligned with business goals, identifying the nature and direction of any SPI actions.

Furthermore, learning theorists [18, 63, 96] have rejected context-free transfer models that isolate knowledge from practice and developed a view of learning as social construction, putting knowledge back into the contexts in which it has meaning. In other words, we expect that successful SPI align improvement activities to the real needs of the individual business rather than the abstract expectations of context-free models of SPI.

Thus, *we define business orientation as the extent to which SPI goals and actions are aligned with explicit and implicit business goals and strategies.* Hence, we argue that business orientation is a key factor to facilitate a successful SPI program. Ceteris paribus,

Hypothesis 1. *SPI success is positively associated with business orientation.*

3.2.2 Involved Leadership

Major change requires leadership. Thus, a predominant theme in the quality management [3, 15, 77, 82, 97] and SPI literature [44, 47, 55, 86, 98] is the importance of leadership commitment and involvement in the implementation of improvement actions. Such involvement is of paramount importance to SPI since top executives often are committed to the status quo [50], and also because they ultimately determine the priority of the organization's SPI program.

Creating a vision is considered a key element in most leadership frameworks [56], and those leading the organization must take an active role in describing a desired future and energize commitment to moving toward it. However, traditional views on leaders as "heroes", who set the direction, make key decisions, and energize the troops, are changing [75, 84]. Creating vision is not enough; for assimilated learning to occur, leadership at any organizational level must engage in hands-on implementation of the vision. Thus, for building software organizations with learning capabilities, we need involved leadership at all levels that are committed to learning and SPI, and that take responsibility for enrolling others.

Accordingly, *we define involved leadership as the extent to which leaders at all levels in the organization are genuinely committed to and actively participate in SPI*. Hence, we argue that involved leadership is a key factor to facilitate a successful SPI program. Ceteris paribus,

Hypothesis 2. *SPI success is positively associated with involved leadership.*

3.2.3 Employee Participation

Employee participation, and the way people are treated, has been noted as a crucial factor in organizational management and development ever since Mayo's [68, 69] famous productivity studies at Western Electric's Hawthorne plant. The results of these studies started a revolution in management thinking, showing that even routine jobs can be improved if the workers are treated with respect. Besides, the Tavistock studies [92] reframed the view of organizational systems, proposing the *socio-technical system* (STS) in which the best match would be sought between the requirements of the interdependent social *and* technical system. Together, these studies showed that there were powerful alternatives to the pervasive views of Taylor's concept of scientific management [90] and Weber's description of bureaucracy [95]. STS also has a particularly strong position in Scandinavia and the UK, who has a long tradition for work-place democracy and participation. In fact, many of the early experiments of STS were pioneered in Norway [91].

Since then, participation and involvement has been one of the most important foundations of organization development and change. Participation is also one of the fundamental ideas of TQM, and has always been a central goal and one of the pillars of organizational learning.

With SPI becoming increasingly important, and people increasingly recognized as the principal source of competitive advantage, software organizations need to encourage and support collaboration in work groups and project teams, and engage in organizational learning [22, 31, 43, 47, 86]. Participation is also fundamental for creativity and innovation and for showing respect for the opinions of others and for the belief that learning and competitive advantage can result from an organizational climate that cultivates a diversity of ideas and opinions [67, 83].

Therefore, participation should be offered and managed in such a way as to allow all employees to improve their work and to feel a sense of contribution to the organization and its mission. In our view, then, SPI is neither top-down nor bottom-up – rather, it is participative at all levels. Hence, *we define employee participation as the extent to which employees use their knowledge and experience to decide, act, and take responsibility for SPI.* Consequently, we argue that employee participation is a key factor to facilitate a successful SPI program. Ceteris paribus,

Hypothesis 3. *SPI success is positively associated with employee participation.*

3.2.4 Concern for Measurement

Software measurement is widely recognized as an essential part of understanding, controlling, monitoring, predicting, and evaluating software development and maintenance projects [32, 45, 49, 93] and as a necessary part of any SPI or change program [7, 48, 55, 61].

This position is by no means unique to the software community. Measurement, and in particular; measurement of customer satisfaction, is at the heart of quality management and is also a major concern for related disciplines such as organization development [26], organizational learning [5], strategic planning [60], and business process reengineering [28, 52].

Measurement and analysis is not only an efficient means for identifying, recommending, and evaluating process change, it can also be of crucial importance for assisting and guiding ongoing change [73]. A major concern for a measurement program, therefore, is to provide opportunities for developers to participate in analyzing, interpreting, and learning from the results of measurements and to identify concrete areas for improvement. There is thus reason to believe that providing a constant flow of quality data from a variety of sources may lead to improved performance.

Hence, *we define concern for measurement as the extent to which the software organization collects and utilizes quality data to guide and assess the effects of SPI activities,* and argue that concern for measurement is a key factor to facilitate a successful SPI program. Ceteris paribus,

Hypothesis 4. *SPI success is positively associated with concern for measurement.*

3.2.5 Learning Strategy

A critical challenge facing software organizations is the dilemma of maintaining the capabilities of both efficiency and flexibility. This situation, which requires the management of both stability and change, has led researchers and practitioners to distinguish between the more modest, or evolutionary, efforts toward change and those that are more fundamental and, in a sense, revolutionary (e.g. [5, 64]).

In other words, software organizations can engage in two broad kinds of learning strategies. They can engage in *exploitation* – the adoption and use of existing knowledge and experience, and they can engage in *exploration* – the search for new knowledge, either through imitation or innovation [36]. Exploitation involves improving existing capabilities by refining, standardizing, routinizing, and elaborating established ideas, paradigms, technologies, strategies, and knowledge.

In contrast, exploration involves learning through discovery and experimenting with ideas, paradigms, technologies, strategies, and knowledge in hope of finding new alternatives and untapped opportunities that are superior to current practice.

Finding a good balance between exploration and exploitation is a recurrent problem of theories of adaptation [65], which talk about balancing search and action, variation and selection, change and stability, and diversity and unity. A basic problem is thus to engage in enough exploitation to ensure short-term results and, concurrently, to engage in exploration to ensure long-term survival.

Based on the preceding discussion we contend that exploitation and exploration are linked in an enduring symbiosis, and that each form requires the other in order to contribute effectively to a software organization's survival and prosperity. Consequently, *we define learning strategy as the extent to which a software organization is engaged in the exploitation of existing knowledge and in the exploration of new knowledge.* Hence, we argue that balancing the refinement of the existing skill base, with the experimentation of new ideas are important in order to find alternatives that improve on old ones. Ceteris paribus,

Hypothesis 5. *SPI success is positively associated with exploitation of existing knowledge.*

Hypothesis 6. *SPI success is positively associated with exploration of new knowledge.*

3.2.6 Joint Contribution of Facilitating Factors

So far we have discussed the possible independent contributions of business orientation, involved leadership, employee participation, concern for measurement, exploitation of existing knowledge, and exploration of new knowledge to SPI success. However, dependent variables such as organizational performance or other success measures, like the one used in this study, are rarely determined by one single independent variable. In addition to examining the independent contributions, therefore, we also want to examine the joint contribution of the independent variables to SPI success. Ceteris paribus,

Hypothesis 7 *The six independent variables of business orientation, involved leadership, employee participation, concern for measurement, exploitation of existing knowledge, and exploration of new knowledge will explain a large amount of the variance in SPI success.*

3.3 Research Method

3.3.1 Population and Sample

Software intensive organizations are considered as the target population for this study. This population includes companies of different sizes, developing either software or combined software and hardware products for a wide variety of markets.

A random sample of 154 software and quality managers in the Norwegian IT industry with corporate membership in the Association of the Norwegian Software Industry or the Norwegian IT Technology Forum, were contacted by telephone to request participation in the study prior to mailing the questionnaires. Since the unit of analysis in this study was the software organization, defined as a whole organization or an independent business unit within a larger company, the managers were asked to answer on behalf of their respective organizations.

We provided the respondents with self-addressed, stamped return envelopes. Also, by keeping the questionnaire as short as possible (a pilot study of the survey questionnaire showed that respondents needed about 10 minutes to complete it), we combined several well-proven techniques for improving the response rate of mailed questionnaires.

A total of 120 software and quality managers representing whole organizations or independent business units within 55 companies completed and returned the questionnaire. This is within the limits for both adequate statistical power and generalizability of the results in this study. Furthermore, this represents an effective response rate of 77.9%, which is well above the minimum norm of 40% for representatives of organizations and mid-level managers suggested for academic studies by Baruch [6]. Given the high response rate in this study, no further analysis was done on the differences between respondents and non-respondents. Table 3.1 shows the characteristics of the survey sample.

3.3.2 Variables and Measures

Based on the definitions of the factors identified in the conceptual model (see Fig. 3.1), one dependent, six independent, and two moderating variables were operationalized and used to collect the data in this study.

Table 3.1. Characteristics of the survey sample

characteristics of the respondents	mean	S.D.
average #years in the company	8.4	6.5
average #years with software development	11.4	7.4
highest completed education	Freq.	Percent
bachelor's degree	38	31.7
master's degree	74	61.7
doctoral degree	5	4.2
other	3	2.5
job function		
software manager	95	79.2
Quality manager	25	20.8
characteristics of the respondents' company		
number of software developers		
less than or equal to 30	45	37.5
between 30 and 200	31	25.8
more than or equal to 200	44	36.7
primary industry group		
public sector	7	5.8
banking/finance/insurance	12	10.0
manufacturing	21	17.5
IT sector	68	56.7
other	12	10.0
type of product business		
standard applications (shelfware)	31	25.8
tailor made solutions, external customers	84	70.0
tailor made solutions, internal customers	5	4.2
quality system in use		
yes	86	71.7
no	34	28.3

Independent variables. To measure the extent to which each of the six independent variables were practiced, we used multi-item, five-point, bipolar Likert scales that ranged from "strongly disagree" (1) to "strongly agree" (5) for all indicators. The item ratings were summarized to form a summated rating scale for each independent variable. Furthermore, since this is the first study of its kind within SPI, all items were written specifically for this study.

Dependent variable. We operationalized and measured SPI success based on two multi-item measures. Each manager was asked to rate, on five-point bipolar Likert scales, (1) the level of perceived SPI success and (2) the performance of their organization for the past three years with respect to cost reduction, cycle time reduction, and customer satisfaction. Two items were used to measure the level of perceived SPI success, while three items were used to measure organizational performance. As for the independent variables, all items were written specifically for this study. The ratings for the two performance dimensions were averaged to form a single measure of overall SPI success.

Moderating variables. Two moderating variables – *environmental conditions* and *organizational size* – were operationalized and included in the study to capture the most influential sources of variation in software organizations [36, 38]. Environmental conditions were measured using two semantic differential items, which were rated on a seven-point, bipolar, adjectival, graphic scale. The two items were stable vs. unstable environment and predictable vs. unpredictable environment. Organizational size was defined as the number of software developers in the organization.

The Appendix shows the summated rating scale items for the independent and dependent variables and the moderating variable environmental conditions along with the corresponding reliability measures (Cronbach's α).

3.3.3 Data Collection Procedure

The questionnaire consisted of two parts: the first part asked for managers' ratings of their software organizations with respect to factors of SPI success and organizational performance; the second part asked for general background information and an assessment of the environment.

In the first part, 36 separate items were used to measure the six factors of SPI success, while five items were used to measure the performance construct. Thus, each manager generated seven scores; one for each of the critical factors, and one for the success measure.

In the second part of the questionnaire, each manager assessed their organization's environment in addition to providing general background and demographic information.

3.3.4 Assessment of Reliability and Validity

Reliability refers to the consistency and stability of a score from a measurement scale. The reliability of the multiple-item measurement scales was evaluated by internal consistency analysis, using coefficient alpha [23] and detailed item analysis based on Nunnally's method [76]. We analyzed the correlation of items within each scale (item-item), the corrected item-to-total (item–scale) correlations, the effects of reliability if the item was deleted, and the item standard deviation scores to determine which items were candidates for deletion from the scale.

This analysis revealed that to obtain satisfactory values for coefficient alpha while retaining the domain coverage only required one item to be eliminated from the exploitation scale (marked with an asterisk in the Appendix). Table 3.2 reports the original sets of measurement items associated with the key factors, the items dropped from the original sets to increase alpha, and the reliability coefficients for the resulting scales. Furthermore, Table 3.2 shows that the reliability coefficients ranged from 0.78 to 0.87. Since reliability coefficients of 0.7 or higher are

Table 3.2. Reliability analysis

Independent variables	item numbers	number of items	items deleted	α
1. business Orientation	1–5	5	none	0.81
2. involved leadership	6–10	5	none	0.87
3. employee participation	11–17	7	none	0.80
4. measurement	18–23	6	none	0.81
5. exploitation	24–29	6	no. 29	0.78
6. exploration	30–37	8	none	0.85

considered satisfactory [76], all scales developed for this study were judged to be reliable. This is good for an instrument that is composed entirely of new scales, particularly since the scales do not contain large numbers of items.

Three kinds of validity are of special concern for this study; content validity, construct validity, and criterion-related validity. *Content validity* has to do with the degree to which the scale items represent the domain of the concept under study. Our procedure for ensuring content validity followed the general recommendations of Cronbach [24] and Straub [89], and included: (1) an exhaustive search of the literature for all possible items to be included in the scales; (2) an exploratory study in representative companies to find possible items and scales; (3) review of the proposed scales by experts of both psychological testing and SPI; and (4) pilot test of the scales on a set of respondents similar to the target population. Hence, we argue that our six measurement scales representing the facilitating factors of SPI success developed in this study have content validity since selection of measurement items was based on generally accepted procedures to obtain content validation [4].

Construct validity is an operational concept that examines whether the measurement scales represent and act like the attributes being measured. Assuming that the total score of a scale is valid, the extent to which an individual item measures the same thing as the total score is an indicator of the validity of that item. Hence, construct validity of the measurement scales was evaluated by confirmatory factor analysis.

The construct validity of the six measurement scales was evaluated by analyzing the items of each scale using principal components analysis with VARIMAX rotation. We used a combination of eigenvalues [59], cut-off points of the scree plots [19], and factor loadings [21] as a guide for interpreting the dimensionality of the scales. Table 3.3 shows the eigenvalues and item loading ranges for each scale. Analysis of the eigenvalues showed that five of the six scales formed a single factor. In the case of the exploration scale, two components seemed to emerge with eigenvalues greater than 1.0. However, the eigenvalue of the second factor was only slightly above this threshold (1.02). Furthermore, the scree plot showed a clear break after the first component. In addition, all item loadings for this component were greater than 0.6. This is in accordance with Stevens [88], who suggested that a reliable factor must have four or more loadings of at least 0.6 when the number of cases is below 150. These results indicate that all scales achieved a high degree of unidimensionality and, hence, construct validity.

Table 3.3. Summary of factor matrices for each construct

independent variables	eigen-value	item loading range	#items with loadings > 0.6
1. business Orientation	2.9	0.72–0.82	5 (out of 5)
2. involved leadership	3.3	0.78–0.89	5 (out of 5)
3. employee participation	3.2	0.62–0.72	7 (out of 7)
4. measurement	3.1	0.43–0.83	4 (out of 6)
5. exploitation	2.7	0.65–0.84	5 (out of 5)
6. exploration	3.9	0.61–0.78	8 (out of 8)

Criterion-related validity is concerned with the degree to which the scales under study are related to an independent measure of the relevant criterion.

The criterion-related validity of the measurement instrument was evaluated by computing the multiple correlation (R) between the measures of the six independent variables and SPI success. The multiple correlation coefficient was 0.76. Cohen [20] suggested that a multiple correlation coefficient of 0.14 corresponds to a small effect size, that coefficients of 0.36 correspond to a medium effect size, and that coefficients above 0.51 correspond to a large effect size. Thus, we conclude that the independent variables have a high degree of criterion-related validity.

All in all, then, the results of reliability and validity analyses showed that the instrument has desirable psychometric properties. A more detailed analysis and discussion of the validity and reliability of these variables is presented in [35].

3.3.5 Data Analysis Techniques

We used parametric statistics such as the Pearson product-moment correlation coefficient, the t-test, the F statistic, and multiple regression analysis to analyze the data in this study. Using such parametric tests for summated rating scales, which are not strictly interval, does not lead, except in extreme cases, to wrong statistical decisions [16, 76, 94]. An important prerequisite, therefore, is that the assumptions of these analyses be met.

The results of testing these assumptions showed that kurtosis, skewness, and the one-sample Kolmogorov-Smirnov tests for all variables were within the acceptable range for the normal distribution assumption. Also, the assumptions of homoscedasticity, linearity, and independence of the error terms were supported, and no influential observations were identified. Furthermore, investigations of collinearity and multicollinearity indicated no problems.

In other words, *there were no extreme violations to the basic assumptions underlying the chosen data analysis techniques* that could justify the use of less powerful non-parametric statistics. All quantitative analyses were conducted using SPSS.

Table 3.4. Item means, standard deviations, andcorrelations among the independent variables

independent variable (N=120)	Mean	S.D.	1	2	3	4	5	6
1. business orientation	3.27	0.66	1.00					
2. involved leadership	3.52	0.69	0.63***	1.00				
3. employee participation	3.49	0.52	0.39***	0.37***	1.00			
4. measure-ment	3.26	0.61	0.45***	0.41***	0.24**	1.00		
5. exploitation	3.34	0.62	0.57***	0.46***	0.47***	0.41***	1.00	
6. exploration	3.43	0.54	0.17*	0.11	0.46***	0.13	0.18*	1.00

Notes: $* p < 0.05$ $** p < 0.005$ $*** p < 0.0005$

1. All t-tests are one-tailed.

3.4 Results

Table 3.4 shows the means, standard deviations, and correlations among the independent variables. Out of 15 correlations between the independent variables, two have a correlation coefficient larger than 0.5. The highest correlation (0.63) is between involved leadership and business orientation.

3.4.1 Testing Individual Relationships

Hypotheses 1–6 consider the individual relationships between SPI success and each of the six independent variables. The testing of these hypotheses calls for the use of bivariate correlations. In addition to examine each independent variable's correlation with overall SPI success, we also examined the correlations with each of the two underlying success measures: perceived level of success and organizational performance. However, appropriate tests of the bivariate correlations require that the two contextual factors, environment and organizational size, be partialled from the analysis. Table 3.5 shows both the zero-order correlations and the partial correlations when the effects of the contextual variables have been removed between the independent variables and each of the SPI success measures.

The zero-order Pearson correlation results between exploration of new knowledge and overall SPI success showed a positive and significant correlation coefficient

Table 3.5. Tests of hypotheses H1 – H6

independent variable ($N = 120$)	overall SPI success		perceived level of success		organizational performance	
	R	pr	r	pr	r	pr
1. Business orientation	0.62***	0.61***	0.59***	0.59***	0.46***	0.44***
2. Involved leadership	0.55***	0.54***	0.58***	0.57***	0.34***	0.34***
3. Employee participation	0.55***	0.59***	0.49***	0.52***	0.43***	0.49***
4. Measurement	0.50***	0.48***	0.44***	0.44***	0.40***	0.38***
5. Exploitation	0.59***	0.59***	0.55***	0.56***	0.44***	0.44***
6. Exploration	0.21*	0.25**	0.15*	0.18*	0.20*	0.25**

Notes: $* p < 0.05$ $** p < 0.005$ $*** p < 0.0005$

1. All t-tests are one-tailed.

2. Partial r (pr) is the correlation between the success measure and the independent variable when the contextual factors (environment and organizational size) are held constant.

of 0.21 ($p < 0.05$). The zero-order correlations with perceived level of success ($r = 0.15$, $p < 0.05$) and organizational performance ($r = 0.20$, $p < 0.05$) were also positive and significant. Furthermore, all partial correlations were positive and significant, ranging from $pr = 0.18$ ($p < 0.05$) to $pr = 0.25$ ($p < 0.005$).

Similarly, all zero-order correlation results between the remaining five independent variables and overall SPI success showed *large positive* and *highly significant* correlations, ranging from $r = 0.50$ ($p < 0.0005$) to $r = 0.62$ ($p < 0.0005$). In addition, all zero-order correlations with perceived level of success and organizational performance were positive and highly significant, ranging from $r = 0.34$ ($p < 0.0005$) to $r = 0.59$ ($p < 0.0005$). Furthermore, all partial correlations with overall SPI success were positive and highly significant, ranging from $pr = 0.48$ ($p < 0.0005$) to $pr = 0.61$ ($p < 0.0005$). Finally, all partial correlations with perceived level of success and organizational performance were positive and highly significant, ranging from $pr = 0.34$ ($p < 0.0005$) to $pr = 0.59$ ($p < 0.0005$).

Taken together, all zero-order and partial correlations involved in testing hypotheses 1 through 6 were significant and in the hypothesized directions. This indicates support for the validity of all major measures used in this research. Thus, the findings in Table 3.5 support Hypotheses 1–6, along with the underlying assumption that SPI provides increased levels of performance to the organization.

3.4.2 Testing Overall Relationships

We examined the joint contribution of the independent variables to the explanation of SPI success as well as their contribution to the variate and its predictions in order to identify the critical factors for SPI success.

A "large" amount of the variance in SPI success was defined as a large effect size, $f^2 \geq 0.35$, according to Cohen's (1988) categorization, where

$$f^2 = \frac{R^2}{1-R^2} \tag{1}$$

Given this relationship between effect size (f^2) and the squared multiple correlation (R^2), a large effect size of $f^2 \geq 0.35$ corresponds to a squared multiple correlation of $R^2 \geq 0.26$ and a multiple correlation coefficient of $R \geq 0.51$.

In order to make inferences about the multiple correlation, we used Konishi's [62] extension of the Fisher r-to-Z transformation to test the exact hypothesis that the population value of R is large. That is, we tested the modified null hypothesis.

H7$_0$: $\rho < 0.51$, against the alternative
H7$_A$: $\rho \geq 0.51$

The test statistic, C_R, is referred to the normal distribution, and given by

$$C_R = \left\{ Z_R - \zeta_\rho - \frac{1}{2\rho(N-1)} \left(K - 1 + \rho^2 \right) \right\} \sqrt{N-1}$$

in which, Z_R is the Fisher Z value corresponding to the sample R value, ζ_ρ is the Fisher Z value corresponding to the population ρ value stated in the null hypothesis, K is the number of predictor variables, and N is the sample size.

The test statistic for the modified null hypothesis with $K = 6$ predictor variables, a sample size of $N = 120$, and a sample multiple correlation of $R = 0.76$ was $C_R = 4.26$. In a standard normal distribution, a value of 4.26 is highly significant and thus falls outside the acceptance region for the $\alpha = 0.05$ level. Hence, in light of the sample evidence we rejected the null hypothesis that the true value of the multiple correlation is less than 0.51, and accepted the alternate hypothesis that *the six predictor variables significantly* ($p < 0.00005$) *explain a large amount* ($\rho \geq 0.51$) *of the variance in SPI success.*

The contributions of each independent variable to the variate, however, differ substantially. As can be seen in Table 3.6, two of the independent variables – *involved leadership* and *exploration of new knowledge* – did not contribute significantly to the explanation of SPI success. Of the remaining four significant variables, *employee participation* seems to be associated with the highest explanatory power, since it achieved the highest standardized regression coefficient ($\beta = 0.297$, $t = 3.80$, $p < 0.0005$). Next came *business orientation* ($\beta = 0.245$, $t = 2.78$,

Table 3.6. Regression analysis of overall SPI success

independent variables	B	Std. error	beta	t-value
1. business Orientation	0.157	0.056	0.245	2.778**
2. involved leadership	0.076	0.050	0.125	1.526
3. employee participation	0.173	0.045	0.297	3.803***
4. measurement	0.115	0.041	0.200	2.828**
5. exploitation	0.121	0.055	0.177	2.201*
6. exploration	-0.019	0.034	-0.039	-0.559

Notes: $R = 0.76$ $R^2 = 0.58$ Adj. $R^2 = 0.56$ $(F = 25.95***)$
$*p < 0.05$ $**p < 0.01$ $***p < 0.0005$

$p < 0.01$), followed by *concern for measurement* ($\beta = 0.200$, $t = 2.83$, $p < 0.01$) and, finally, *exploitation of existing knowledge* ($\beta = 0.177$, $t = 2.20$, $p < 0.05$).

It is important to note, however, that the weights the independent variables carry in the multiple regression equation are always relative to the entire set of predictors employed. That is, the predictive strength that some independent variable seems to show for the dependent variable may differ if the set of remaining variables is altered.

The two contextual factors were added to the model to test the sensitivity of the variate to organizational size and environmental turbulence. The estimated coefficients of the independent variables of the original model were not significantly changed by the introduction of the contextual factors. *The results hold for small, as well as large, software organizations, and for organizations operating in stable as well as in turbulent environments.*

These results support the robustness of the original regression model results. Furthermore, the model with the two contextual factors added (R-square = 0.59, adjusted R-square = 0.56, $F = 19.60$, $p < 0.0005$) did not explain significantly more variance as compared with the original model (R-square = 0.58, adjusted R-square = 0.56, $F = 25.95$, $p < 0.0005$).

In conclusion, the multiple regression analysis did not support Hypotheses 2 and 6, provided that all hypotheses are considered as one set. In other words, considering both bivariate correlation analyses and the multiple regression analysis, we find strong support for Hypotheses 1, 3, 4, 5, and 7, and partial support for Hypotheses 2 and 6.

3.5 Discussion

A quantitative survey was performed to investigate the key factors of success in SPI. The results of the bivariate correlational and multiple regression analyses showed that SPI success depends critically on six organizational factors. In the following, we discuss the insights that can be gained for practitioners and researcher from these findings, the limitations of the study, and some suggestions for further research.

3.5.1 Practitioner and Researcher Insights

Organizational knowledge is created by ongoing experience and experimentation of organizational members. Without individuals who learn, there can be no improvement. The fundamental role of managers and leaders is, thus, to shape and create organizational contexts that are supportive of and conducive to organizational learning and SPI.

First of all, *business orientation*, that is, the extent to which SPI goals and actions are aligned with explicit and implicit business goals and strategies, was identified as one of the factors with the strongest influence on SPI success. This supports the hypothesis that SPI success is positively associated with business orientation.

This finding is important, and suggests that both *practitioners and researchers should direct significant effort toward understanding shared domain knowledge between software and business executives.* However, there are two basic conditions for establishing such connections and making communications between these groups effective. First, each group must respect the expertise of the other, and must acknowledge the relevance of that expertise to their own problems. Second, each group must have sufficient knowledge and understanding of the other groups' problems to be able to communicate effectively about them.

It is important to remember that experience has shown that such shared understandings are unlikely to occur unless a sufficient number of members of each group have had actual experience with the activities and responsibilities of the other group [85]. This suggests that the software organization should be active in creating the possibilities for such connections to be formed, for example through personnel rotation programs, and promotion and recruitment strategies.

The critical importance of a business orientation in SPI suggests that software organizations should focus on both short-term and long-term alignment of SPI goals with business goals. They should focus attention on how to achieve a high degree of mutual understanding of current objectives as well as on how to achieve congruence of long-term SPI goals with business strategies.

Thus, the importance of aligning SPI goals with business goals implies that if the SPI strategy is not kept in line with changes in the business strategy, there is a risk that the organization's software processes may end up as a burden rather than advance the business. Therefore, our results also suggest that understanding the business and organizational context is critical for achieving alignment between SPI activities and business strategy, which in turn is of paramount importance for the success of the SPI program. Similarly, by viewing the organization as a living organism, Zahran compared the introduction of a new process with transplanting a new organ [98]; if the new process is not aligned with the business strategy or does not match the organization's culture, it will be rejected by the "organizational" body.

Involved leadership – the extent to which leaders at all levels in the organization are genuinely committed to and actively participate in SPI – had a strong and highly significant correlation with overall SPI success, which supports the hypothesis that SPI success is positively associated with involved leadership.

A surprising result, however, was the insignificant importance of involved leadership in predicting SPI success. All the main studies on which this investigation is based share a strong belief in the importance of management commitment for the successful implementation of SPI. Furthermore, the quality management literature and the organizational learning literature also seem to share a strong belief in the importance of management commitment for improving organizational performance. With this background, it is surprising, both from a theoretical and practical perspective, that involved leadership, defined as the extent to which leaders at all levels in the organization are genuinely committed to and actively participate in SPI, is a non-significant predictor of SPI success. On the other hand, the results are in agreement with Abrahamsson's findings that many SPI initiatives do not require management commitment beyond obtaining the resources needed [1]. There could be several explanations for this seemingly surprising result.

First, there is no common understanding of the role of involved leadership or management commitment in SPI in terms of conceptual definitions and operationalized measures [2, 35]. Therefore, we cannot know what is actually meant by, e.g. management commitment in a particular study and it will be difficult (if not impossible) to compare the results of one study with those of another. So, until SPI researchers can agree upon the conceptual definitions used to describe the phenomenon under study, we cannot go beyond a face validity perspective and truly tell whether findings are comparable or not.

Second, we found that multicollinearity should not have a substantial impact on the estimated regression variate in this investigation. However, the results of the multiple regression analysis show that multicollinearity, nevertheless, does have an impact on the composition of the variate, and that correlations among the independent variables may make some variables redundant in the predictive effort. This is the case for involved leadership and also for exploration of new knowledge. However, this does not reflect their individual relationships with the dependent variable. Instead, it indicates that in a multivariate context, they are not needed together with the remaining set of four independent variables to explain the variance in SPI success. Therefore, we cannot determine the importance of involved leadership based solely on the derived variate, since relationships with the other independent variables may "mask" relationships that are not needed for predictive purposes, but represent substantive explanatory findings nonetheless.

Third, the role of management is often to ensure that SPI goals and actions are closely aligned with business goals and strategies, which is indicated by the highly significant correlation coefficient of 0.63 in Table 3.4 between business orientation and involved leadership. This suggests that involved leadership is important through business orientation. This is also in agreement with Grady's findings from his longitudinal studies in Hewlett-Packard that business aspects in the organization's SPI efforts had a strong influence on management commitment [48]. Furthermore, Debou and Kuntzmann-Combelles argued that management commitment implies business orientation and vice versa [29].

Finally, a large part of the published, and thus reviewed, studies on quality management, organizational learning, and SPI are from the United States. There are, however, important cultural differences between the United States and Europe in general [72] and between the United States and Scandinavia in particular [41]. The Norwegian Work Environment Act, for example, stipulates that the employer has to negotiate with the employees before making "major changes" in production. Also, in terms of Hofstede's model (see [14]), the relatively high degree of work-place democracy and socio-technical tradition in Scandinavian countries indicate that they might have a smaller power distance and a more collectivist culture than the United States. This suggests a higher importance of employee participation and a correspondingly minor importance of involved leadership in predicting SPI success in these countries. This is also indicated by the results of the multiple regression analysis that showed that together with business orientation, employee participation was the most important factor in predicting SPI success.

Thus, together with business orientation, *employee participation*, i.e. the extent to which employees use their knowledge and experience to decide, act, and take responsibility for SPI, was identified as the factor with the strongest influence on SPI success. This supports the hypothesis that SPI success is positively associated with employee participation. This is not surprising and it supports previous research on the role of employee participation in organizational management and development [26, 46].

Also, a multiple case study by Conradi and Dybå to explore the diffusion of knowledge and experience in software organizations [22], strongly support the importance of participation as a key factor for SPI success. Similarly, a multiple case study of tailor made assessments to focus software process improvement activities, showed that a structured process emphasizing participation in each and every step was a key factor for success [39].

This suggests that *people tend to support what they have participated in creating,* or to use Berger and Luckmann's words [11]: "it is more likely that one will deviate from programmes set up for one by others than from programmes that one has helped establish oneself." Thus, we learn a great deal more from our own experience than we do from those who are experienced.

Concern for measurement – the extent to which the software organization collects and utilizes quality data to guide and assess the effects of SPI activities – had a strong and highly significant correlation with overall SPI success. This supports the hypothesis that SPI success is positively associated with concern for measurement and suggests that *significant progress in software development depends on an ability to measure aspects of the process and the resulting artifacts, and to make analytical judgments based on the results of these measurements.* Thus, a lack of measurement leads to a lack of empirical validation of software techniques and ultimately to an inability of the organization to evaluate new (or old) ideas and to separate sound and useful practices from current fads.

Traditionally, measurement systems are used to provide upper management with data for decision making, and to assess the effects of organizational actions. Although this is still important, our concept of measurement not only includes these traditional uses; it also includes availability and feedback of data, and the use of data to guide SPI actions. So, while measurement in itself can have a significant effect on organizational behavior [73], our results suggest that the most effective use of data for organizational learning and SPI is to feed the data back in some form to the organization's members. Such feedback regarding actual performance not only motivates change in the behavior of individuals, groups, and organizations; it can also guide change in a specific direction. However, in order for feedback to change behavior through these mechanisms the data must be perceived as valid and accurate. Also, the conditions surrounding the feedback process must support the nonthreatening use of data for identifying and solving problems.

This suggests that without clear and consistent feedback to help monitor software teams' progress toward their goals and the effects of their actions, it is difficult to learn. Besides, our results demonstrate that measurement is meaningless without interpretation and judgment by those who will make decisions and take actions based on them. Within the context of SPI, therefore, *it is important that measurement systems are designed by software developers for learning, rather than by management for control.* Also, an important observation is that a few measures that are directly related to the software process are better than a multitude of measures that produce a lack of focus and confusion about what is important and what is not [40, 80].

Our findings thus suggest that data-based methods in general and feedback in particular are effective tools for the successful application of SPI, and that knowledge about *how things are* can be a potential force that moves software organizations toward *how things should be.*

Two fundamentally different learning strategies were identified as part of our investigation: *exploitation* of existing knowledge and *exploration* of new knowledge. Consequently, we defined learning strategy as the extent to which a software organization is engaged in the exploitation of existing knowledge and in the exploration of new knowledge. Both learning strategies had a significant correlation with overall SPI success, which supports the hypotheses that SPI success is positively associated with the exploitation of existing knowledge as well as with the exploration of new knowledge.

However, as in the case of involved leadership, exploration of new knowledge had an insignificant importance in *predicting* SPI success. We see two plausible explanations for this. First, as we explained with respect to involved leadership, relationships with the other independent variables may "mask" relationships that are not needed for predictive purposes, but represent substantive explanatory findings nonetheless. Therefore, we cannot determine the importance of exploration of new knowledge based solely on the derived variate.

Second, our concept of exploration includes issues such as innovation and creativity, questioning of "established" truths, flexibility, minimum critical specification, and diversity, which, within a socio-technical perspective, can be seen as closely related to conceptions of participation. This is also indicated by the highly significant correlation coefficient of 0.46 in Table 3.4 between employee participation and exploration of new knowledge, which suggests that exploration of new knowledge is important through employee participation.

With respect to the two contextual factors, we found that the general results hold for small, as well as large, software organizations, and for organizations operating in stable as well as in turbulent environments. Still, a closer examination of organizational size showed that large successful and small successful organizations differed fundamentally in their respective approach to SPI, specifically with respect to participation and their preferred mode of learning. Small successful organizations reported higher levels of employee participation and exploration of new knowledge than the larger organizations (see [38]). This suggests that both modes of learning are important for successful SPI. Moreover, it suggests that *software organizations should balance their learning efforts between exploitation and exploration.*

It is also interesting to note that there was no difference in the level of exploitation between small and large organizations regardless of the environment, while there was a marked difference in the level of exploration. The results showed that small software organizations engaged in significantly more exploration in turbulent environments than large software organization (see [36]), which suggests that *the main difference between small and large software organizations is the ways in which they react to unstable and changing stimulus situations.*

3.5.2 Limitations

Although we have discussed several implications of our results, the research reported here is not without its limitations. First, the results have been discussed as though the facilitating factors caused SPI success. However, the investigation was cross-sectional and these assumptions of causality are not technically justified. It is possible, for example, that there are complex feedback mechanisms by which performance in one time period is affected by performance in previous periods [66]. Both success and lack of success might very well be self-reinforcing. On the other hand, there could also be negative feedback mechanisms by which SPI success or failure creates countervailing tendencies. It is possible therefore that performance below target levels increases organizational efforts and, thus, the likelihood of subsequent success. Accordingly, success can also be seen as a trigger for adjustments in the opposite direction through decreased innovation or increased slack. Therefore, many of the facilitating factors that seem likely to influence SPI success can themselves be influenced by prior success or lack of success. Finding the "true" causal structure of SPI success based on incomplete information generated by prior experience is, therefore, problematic.

Second, although generally accepted psychometric principles were used to develop the measurement instrument, the variables were still measured on the basis of subjective performance definitions. Performance measures such as the return on investment, net present value, and payback periods are often regarded as objective measures. However, attempts to provide objective definitions of such measures may be as open to criticism as subjective definitions [12, 35], which points to a general problem of defining and measuring success in studies of SPI. The question, therefore, is not whether such measures are subjective or not, but what purpose they serve.

Finally, a further complication is that the independent variables were assessed using retrospective recall. This involves a risk for the introduction of retrospective bias. It is possible; therefore, that performance information itself colors subjective memories and perceptions of possible causes of SPI success or failure. Software organizations are constantly worried about their performance, and "common wisdom" has many explanations for good and poor performance. As a result, retrospective reports of independent variables may be less influenced by memory than by a reconstruction that connects common wisdom with the awareness of performance results [66].

Despite these limitations, this study contributes to the growing literature on empirical software engineering research and provides empirical support for the importance of organizational issues in SPI.

3.5.3 Future Work

SPI success measurement is a controversial issue and more research is needed to study it. Several levels of analysis are possible – e.g. individual, group, process, and organization – each with complex interactions with the others. Also, several, and possibly conflicting, dimensions (e.g. faster, better, and cheaper) and view-points (e.g. economic, engineering, organizational, and socio-technical) are relevant. Further research should be related to the study of new and improved measures of SPI success, comparison of measurement instruments, and validation of SPI success measures.

In addition, context variables, such as organizational size and environmental turbulence, did not play an important role in *predicting* SPI success in this study. However, under other circumstances, the independent variables of the present study could act as moderating or mediating variables in other studies. Further research is therefore needed to investigate the importance of such variables to several types of SPI problems and to validate the approaches proposed for solving them. Such studies should combine factor research with process research in order to provide satisfactory levels of external validity. This way, we can tailor software engineering methods and improvement strategies to better help software organizations succeed with their unique business of software.

There are certainly other directions for further research. However, the value of any such future work depends on the specific goals of each particular investigation.

3.6 Conclusion

The study focused on identifying the key factors for success in SPI by a quantitative survey. The results indicate support for all of the hypotheses in the proposed model and demonstrate the existence of important factors for SPI success. From a theoretical perspective, these findings add an important new dimension to empirical software engineering research in that they verify the importance of organizational factors for SPI success. From a practical perspective, this suggests that, rather than trying to imitate technical procedures, software organizations should focus their SPI efforts on creating an organizational culture within which these procedures can thrive. This differs substantially from that found in most of the existing SPI literature, which focuses almost entirely on software engineering tools and techniques. Overall, from both theoretical and practical perspectives, an important new insight from this research is that organizational issues are at least as important in SPI as technology, if not more so.

Appendix: Measurement Instrument

A more detailed analysis and discussion of the validity and reliability of the operationalized measures for the variables in this study can be found in [35]. Cronbach's alpha is shown in the parenthesis for each measure.

Business Orientation ($\alpha = 0.81$)

1. We have established unambiguous goals for the organization's SPI activities.

2. There is a broad understanding of SPI goals and policy within our organization.

3. Our SPI activities are closely integrated with software development activities.

4. Our SPI goals are closely aligned with the organization's business goals.

5. We have a fine balance between short-term and long-term SPI goals.

Leadership Involvement ($\alpha = 0.87$)

6. Management is actively supporting SPI activities.

7. Management accepts responsibility for SPI.

8. Management considers SPI as a way to increase competitive advantage.

9. Management is actively participating in SPI activities.

10. SPI issues are often discussed in top management meetings.

Employee Participation ($\alpha = 0.80$)

11. Software developers are involved to a great extent in decisions about the implementation of their own work.

12. Software developers are actively contributing with SPI proposals.

13. Software developers are actively involved in creating routines and procedures for software development.

14. We have an on-going dialogue and discussion about software development.

15. Software developers have responsibility related to the organization's SPI activities.

16. Software developers are actively involved in setting goals for our SPI activities.

17. We have an on-going dialogue and discussion about SPI.

Concern for Measurement ($\alpha = 0.81$)

18. We consider it as important to measure organizational performance.

19. We regularly collect quality data (e.g. defects, timeliness) from our projects.

20. Information on quality data is readily available to software developers.

21. Information on quality data is readily available to management.

22. We use quality data as a basis for SPI.

23. Our software projects get regular feedback on their performance.

Exploitation of Existing Knowledge ($\alpha = 0.78$)

24. We exploit the existing organizational knowledge to the utmost extent.

25. We are systematically learning from the experience of prior projects.

26. Our routines for software development are based on experience from prior projects.

27. We collect and classify experience from prior projects.

28. We put great emphasis on internal transfer of positive and negative experience.

29. To the extent we can avoid it, we do not take risks by experimenting with new ways of working.*

Exploration of New Knowledge ($\alpha = 0.85$)

30. We are very capable at managing uncertainty in the organization's environment.

31. In our organization, we encourage innovation and creativity.

32. We often carry out trials with new software engineering methods and tools.

33. We often conduct experiments with new ways of working with software development.

34. We have the ability to question "established" truths.

35. We are very flexible in the way we carry out our work.

36. We do not specify work processes more than what are absolutely necessary.

37. We make the most of the diversity in the developer's skills and interests to manage the variety and complexity of the organization's environment.

Organizational Performance ($\alpha = 0.76$)

1. Our SPI work has substantially increased our software engineering competence.

2. Our SPI work has substantially improved our overall performance.

3. Over the past 3 years, we have greatly reduced the cost of software development.

4. Over the past 3 years, we have greatly reduced the cycle time of software development.

5. Over the past 3 years, we have greatly increased our customers' satisfaction.

Environmental Conditions ($\alpha = 0.80$)

1. Stable   □ 1   □ 2   □ 3   □ 4   □ 5   □ 6   □ 7   Unstable
2. Predictable □ 1   □ 2   □ 3   □ 4   □ 5   □ 6   □ 7   Unpredictable

* Starred item is removed from the final instrument and should not be used.

Acknowledgment

This work was supported in part by the Research Council of Norway under Grant 118206/221. The author wishes to thank all respondents of the survey for their willingness to participate in the inquiries.

References

[1]   Abrahamsson, P. (2000) Is Management Commitment a Necessity after all in Software process Improvement? *Proc. 26th Euromicro Conf.*, Vol. 2, 5–7 September, pp. 246–253

[2]   Abrahamsson, P. (2001) Commitment Development in Software Process Improvement: Critical Misconceptions, *Proc. 23rd Int'l Conf. Software Eng. (ICSE 2001)*, IEEE Computer Society Press, pp. 71–80

[3]   Ahire, S.L., Golhar, D.Y., and Waller, M.A. (1996) Development and Validation of TQM Implementation Constructs, *Decision Sciences*, Vol. 27, No.1, pp. 23–56

[4]   Anastasi, A. and Urbina, S. (1997) *Psychological Testing*, Seventh Edition, Upper Saddle River, NJ: Prentice-Hall

[5]   Argyris, C. and Schön, D.A. (1996) *Organizational Learning II: Theory, Method, and Practice*, Reading, MA: Addison-Wesley

[6]   Baruch, Y. (1999) Response Rate in Academic Studies – A Comparative Analysis, *Human Relations*, Vol. 52, No. 4, pp. 421–438

[7]   Basili, V.R. and Caldiera, G. (1995) Improve Software Quality by Reusing Knowledge and Experience, *Sloan Management Review*, Vol. 37, No. 1, Autumn, pp. 55–64

[8]   Basili, V.R. and Rombach, H.D. (1988) The TAME project: Towards improvement-oriented software environments, *IEEE Transactions on Software Engineering*, Vol. 14, No. 6, pp. 758–773

[9]   Basili, V.R., McGarry, F.E., Pajerski, R., Zelkowitz, M.V. (2002) Lessons Learned from 25 Years of Process Improvement: The Rise and Fall of the NASA Software Engineering Laboratory, *Proc. 24th Int'l Conf. Software Eng. (ICSE 2002)*, IEEE Computer Society Press, pp. 69–79

[10] Beer, M., Eisenstat, R.A., and Spector, B. (1990) Why Change Programs Don't Produce Change, *Harvard Business Review*, Vol. 68, No. 6, pp. 158–166

[11] Berger P.L. and Luckmann, T. (1966) *The Social Construction of Reality: A Treatise in the Sociology of Knowledge*, Harmondsworth: Penguin Books.

[12] Berry, M. and Jeffery, R. (2000) An Instrument for Assessing Software Measurement Programs, *Empirical Software Engineering*, Vol. 5, No. 3, November, pp. 183–200

[13] Biró, M. and Tully, C. (1999) The Software Process in the Context of Business Goals and Performance, in R. Messnarz, and C. Tully (Eds.) *Better Software Practice for Business Benefit: Principles and Experience*, Los Alamitos, California: IEEE Computer Society Press, pp. 15–27

[14] Biró, M., Messnarz, R., and Davison, A.G. (2002) The Impact of National Cultural Factors on the Effectiveness of Process Improvement Methods: The Third Dimension, *ASQ Software Quality Professional*, Vol. 4, No. 4, pp. 34–41

[15] Black, S.A. and Porter, L.J. (1996) Identification of the Critical Factors of TQM, *Decision Sciences*, Vol. 27, No. 1, pp. 1–21

[16] Briand, L.C., El Emam, K., and Morasca, S. (1996) On the Application of Measurement Theory in Software Engineering, *Empirical Software Engineering*, Vol. 1, Issue 1, pp. 61–88

[17] Brodman, J.G. and Johnson, D.L. (1995) Return on Investment (ROI) from Software Process Improvement as Measured by US Industry, *Software Process Improvement and Practice*, Pilot Issue, pp. 35–47

[18] Brown, J.S. and Duguid, P. (1991) Organizational Learning and Communities of Practice: Toward a Unified View of Working, Learning, and Innovation, *Organization Science*, Vol. 2, No. 1, pp. 40–57

[19] Cattell, R.B. (1966) The Scree Test for the Number of Factors, *Multivariate Behavioral Research*, Vol. 1, pp. 245–276

[20] Cohen, J. (1988) *Statistical Power Analysis for the Behavioral Sciences*, Second Edition, Hillsdale, NJ: Laurence Erlbaum

[21] Comrey A.L, and Lee, H.B. (1992) *A First Course on Factor Analysis*, Second Edition, Hillsdale, NJ: Erlbaum

[22] Conradi, R. and Dybå, T. (2001) An Empirical Study on the Utility of Formal Routines to Transfer Knowledge and Experience, *Proceedings of the joint 8th European Software Engineering Conference (ESEC) and 9th ACM SIGSOFT International Symposium on the Foundations of Software Engineering (FSE)*, Vienna, Austria, 10–14 September, 2001

[23] Cronbach, L.J. (1951) Coefficient Alpha and the Internal Consistency of Tests, *Psychometrica*, Vol. 16, pp. 297–334

[24] Cronbach, L.J. (1971) Test Validation, in R.L. Thorndike (Ed.), *Educational Measurement*, Second Edition, Washington: American Council on Education, pp. 443–507

[25] Crosby, P.B. (1996) *Quality Is Still Free: Making Quality Certain in Uncertain Times*, NY: McGraw-Hill

[26] Cummings, T.G. and Worley, C.G. (2004) *Organization Development and Change*, Eight Edition, Cincinnati, OH: South-Western College Publishing.

[27] Daskalantonakis, M.K. (1992) A Practical View of Software Measurement and Implementation Experiences within Motorola, *IEEE Transactions on Software Engineering*, Vol. 18, No. 11, pp. 998–1010

[28] Davenport, T.H. (1993) *Process Innovation: Reengineering Work through Information Technology*, Boston, MA: Harvard Business School Press

[29] Debou, C. and Kuntzmann-Combelles, A. (2000) Linking Software Process Improvement to Business Strategies: Experience from Industry, *Software Process: Improvement and Practice*, Vol. 5, pp. 55–64

[30] Debou, C., Courtel, D., Lambert, H.-B., Fuchs, N., and Haux, M. (1999) Alcatel's Experience with Process Improvement, in R. Messnarz and C. Tully (Eds.), *Better Software Practice for Business Benefit: Principles and Experience*, Los Alamitos, CA: IEEE Computer Society Press, pp. 281–301

[31] Deephouse, C., Mukhopadhyay, T., Goldenson, D.R., and Kellner, M.I. (1996) Software Processes and Project Performance, *Journal of Management Information Systems*, Vol. 12, No. 3, pp. 187–205

[32] DeMarco, T. (1982) *Controlling Software Projects: Management, Measurement and Estimation*, New York: Yourdon Press.

[33] Deming, W.E. (1986) *Out of the Crisis*. Cambridge, Massachusetts: MIT Center for Advanced Engineering Study.

[34] Dion, R. (1993) Process Improvement and the Corporate Balance Sheet, *IEEE Software*, Vol. 10, No. 4, pp. 28–35

[35] Dybå, T. (2000) An Instrument for Measuring the Key Factors of Success in Software Process Improvement, *Empirical Software Eng.*, Vol. 5, No. 4, lpp. 357–390

[36] Dybå, T. (2000) Improvisation in Small Software Organizations, *IEEE Software*, Vol. 17, No. 5, pp. 82–87, Septembner-October

[37] Dybå, T. (2003) A Dynamic Model of Software Engineering Knowledge Creation, in A. Aurum, R. Jeffery, C. Wohlin, and M. Handzic (Eds.), *Managing Software Engineering Knowledge*, Springer Berlin Heidelberg New York, pp. 95–117

[38] Dybå, T. (2003) Factors of Software Process Improvement Success in Small and Large Organizations: An Empirical Study in the Scandinavian Context, *Proc. Joint 9th European Software Eng. Conf. (ESEC) and 11th SIGSOFT Symp. Foundations Software Eng. (FSE-11)*, pp. 148–157.

[39] Dybå, T. and Moe, N.B. (1999) Rethinking the Concept of Software Process Assessment, *Proceedings of the European Software Process Improvement Conference (EuroSPI'99)*, Pori, Finland, 25–27 October, 1999

[40] Dybå, T., Dingsøyr, T., and Moe, N.B. (2004) *Process Improvement in Practice: A Handbook for IT Companies*, The Kluwer International Series in Software Engineering, Boston: Kluwer Academic Publishers

[41] Ehn, P. (1992) Scandinavian Design: On Participation and Skill, in P.S. Adler and T.A. Winograd (Eds.), *Usability – Turning Technologies into Tools*, New York: Oxford University Press, pp. 96–132

[42] El Emam, K., Drouin, J.-N., and Melo, W. (Eds.) (1998) *SPICE: The Theory and Practice of Software Process Improvement and Capability Determination*, Los Alamitos, CA: IEEE Computer Society Press

[43] El Emam, K., Fusaro, P., and Smith, B. (1999) Success Factors and Barriers for Software Process Improvement, in R. Messnarz and C. Tully (Eds.) *Better Software Practice for Business Benefit: Principles and Experience*, Los Alamitos, CA: IEEE Computer Society Press, pp. 355–371

[44] El Emam, K., Goldenson, D.R., McCurley J., and Herbsleb, J. (2001) Modeling the Likelihood of Software Process Improvement: An Exploratory Study, *Empirical Software Engineering*, Vol. 6, No. 3, pp. 207–229

[45] Fenton, N.E. and Pfleeger, S.H. (1996) *Software Metrics: A Rigorous and Practical Approach*, London: International Thomson Computer Press

[46] French, W.L. and Bell, C.H. Jr. (1999) *Organization Development: Behavioral Science Interventions for Organization Improvement*, Sixth Edition, Upper Saddle River, NJ: Prentice-Hall

[47] Goldenson, D.R. and Herbsleb, J.D. (1995) *After the Appraisal: A Systematic Survey of Process Improvement, its Benefits, and Factors that Influence Success*, Technical Report, CMU/SEI-95-TR-009, Carnegie Mellon University, Software Engineering Institute

[48] Grady, R.B. (1997) *Successful Software Process Improvement*, Upper Saddle River, NJ: Prentice-Hall

[49] Grady, R.B. and Caswell, D. (1987) *Software Metrics: Establishing a Company-wide Program*, Englewood Cliffs, NJ: Prentice-Hall

[50] Hambrick, D.C., Geletkanycz, M.A., and Fredrickson, J.W. (1993) Top Executive Commitment to the Status Quo: Some Tests for its Determinants, *Strategic Management Journal*, Vol. 14, No. 6, pp. 401–418

[51] Hammer, M. (1996) *Beyond Reengineering: How the Process-Centered Organization is Changing Our Work and Our Lives*, London: HarperCollins

[52] Hammer, M. and Champy, J. (1993) *Reengineering the Corporation: A Manifesto for Business Revolution*, NY: Harper Business

[53] Hays, W.L. (1994) *Statistics*, Fifth edition, NY: Harcourt Brace

[54] Herbsleb, J.D. and Goldenson, D.R. (1996) A Systematic Survey of CMM Experience and Results, *Proceedings of the Eighteenth International Conference on Software Engineering (ICSE-18)*, IEEE Computer Society Press, pp. 323–330

[55] Humphrey, W.S. (1989) *Managing the Software Process*. Reading, MA: Addison-Wesley

[56] Humphrey, W.S. (1997) *Managing Technical People: Innovation, Teamwork, and the Software Process*. Reading, MA: Addison-Wesley

[57] Humphrey, W.S., Snyder, T., and Willis, R. (1991) Software Process Improvement at Hughes Aircraft, *IEEE Software*, Vol. 8, No. 4, pp. 11–23

[58] Juran, J.M. and Godfrey, A.B. (Eds.) (1999) *Juran's Quality Handbook*, Fifth Edition, NY: McGraw-Hill

[59] Kaiser, H.F. (1970) A Second Generation Little Jiffy, *Psychometrika*, Vol. 35, pp. 401–417

[60] Kaplan, R.S. and Norton, D.P. (1996) *The Balanced Scorecard: Translating Strategy into Action*, Boston, Massachusetts: Harvard Business School Press.

[61] Kitchenham, B.A. (1996) *Software Metrics: Measurement for Software Process Improvement*, Oxford, NCC Blackwell

[62] Konishi, S. (1981) Normalizing Transformations of some Statistics in Multivariate Analysis, *Biometrika*, Vol. 68, No. 3, pp. 647–651

[63] Lave, J. and Wenger, E. (1991) *Situated Learning: Legitimate Peripheral Participation*, Cambridge: Cambridge University Press

[64] March, J.G. (1991) Exploration and Exploitation in Organizational Learning, *Organization Science*, Vol. 2, No. 1, pp. 71–87

[65] March, J.G. (1999) *The Pursuit of Organizational Intelligence*, Malden, Massachusetts: Blackwell

[66] March, J.G. and Sutton, R.I. (1997) Organizational Performance as a Dependent Variable, *Organization Science*, Vol. 8, No. 6, pp. 698–706

[67] Martin, J. (1992) *Cultures in Organizations: Three Perspectives*, NY: Oxford University Press

[68] Mayo, E. (1933) *The Human Problems of an Industrial Civilization*, Boston: Harvard University Press

[69] Mayo, E. (1945) *The Social Problems of an Industrial Civilization*, Boston: Harvard University Press

[70] McFeeley, B. (1996) *IDEAL: A User's Guide for Software Process Improvement*, Handbook, CMU/SEI-96-HB-01, Carnegie Mellon University, Software Engineering Institute

[71] Mehner, T. (1999) Siemens Process Assessment Approach, in R. Messnarz and C. Tully (Eds.), *Better Software Practice for Business Benefit: Principles and Experience*, Los Alamitos, California: IEEE Computer Society Press, pp. 199–212

[72] Messnarz, R. (1999) Summary and Outlook, in R. Messnarz and C. Tully (Eds.) *Better Software Practice for Business Benefit: Principles and Experience*, Los Alamitos, CA: IEEE Computer Society Press, pp. 389–393

[73] Nadler, D.A. (1977) *Feedback and Organization Development: Using Data-based Methods*, Reading, MA: Addison-Wesley

[74] Nonaka, I. (1994) A Dynamic Theory of Organizational Knowledge Creation, *Organization Science*, Vol. 5, No.1, pp.14–37

[75] Nonaka, I. and Takeuchi, H. (1995) *The Knowledge-Creating Company: How Japanese Companies Create the Dynamics of Innovation*, NY: Oxford University Press

[76] Nunnally, J.C. and Bernstein, I.A. (1994) *Psychometric Theory*, Third Edition, NY: McGraw-Hill

[77] Powell, T.C. (1995) Total Quality Management as Competitive Advantage: A Review and Empirical Study, *Strategic Management Journal*, Vol. 16, No. 1, pp. 15–37

[78] Pulford, K., Kuntzmann-Combelles, A., and Shirlaw, S. (1996) *A Quantitative Approach to Software Management: The **ami** Handbook*. Wokingham, Addison-Wesley

[79] Rainer, A. and Hall, T. (2002) Key Success Factors for Implementing Software Process Improvement: A Maturity-based Analysis, *Journal of Systems and Software*, Vol. 62, No. 2, pp. 71–84

[80] Rifkin, S. (2001) What Makes Measuring Software So Hard?, *IEEE Software*, Vol. 18, No. 3, pp. 41–45

[81] Rooijmans, J., Aerts, H., and van Genuchten, M. (1996) Software Quality in Consumer Electronics Products, *IEEE Software*, Vol. 13, No. 1, pp. 55–64

[82] Saraph, J.V., Benson, P.G., and Schroeder, R.G. (1989) An Instrument for Measuring the Critical Factors of Quality Management, *Decision Sciences*, Vol. 20, No. 4, pp. 810–829

[83] Schein, E.H. (1996) Culture: The Missing Concept in Organization Studies, *Administrative Science Quarterly*, Vol. 41, pp. 229–240

[84] Senge, P.M. (1990) *The Fifth Discipline: The Art and Practice of the Learning Organization*, NY: Doubleday

[85] Simon, H.A. (1991) Bounded Rationality and Organizational Learning, *Organization Science*, Vol. 2, No. 1, pp. 125–134

[86] Stelzer, D. and Mellis, W. (1998) Success Factors of Organizational Change in Software Process Improvement, *Software Process – Improvement and Practice*, Vol. 4, No. 4, pp. 227–250

[87] Stelzer, D., Mellis, W., and Herzwurm, G. (1996) Software Process Improvement via ISO 9000? Results of Two Surveys among European Software Houses, *Proceedings of the 29th Hawaii International Conference on Systems Sciences*, January 3–6, 1996, Wailea, Hawaii, USA

[88] Stevens J. (2002) *Applied Multivariate Statistics for the Social Sciences*, Fourth Edition, Mahwah, NJ: Lawrence Erlbaum

[89] Straub, D.W. (1989) Validating Instruments in MIS research, *MIS Quarterly*, Vol. 13, No. 2, pp. 147–169

[90] Taylor, F.W. (1911) *The Principles of Scientific Management*, Newton Library Harper & Row

[91] Thorsrud, E., Sørensen, B., and Gustavsen, B. (1976) Sociotechnical Approach to Industrial Democracy in Norway, in R. Dubin (Ed.), *Handbook of Work Organization and Society*, Chicago: Rand McNally, pp. 648–687

[92] Trist, E. (1981) The Evolution of Socio-Technical Systems: A Conceptual Framework and an Action Research Program, *Occasional papers No. 2*, Toronto, Ontario: Ontario Quality of Working Life Center

[93] van Solingen, R. and Berghout, E. (1999) *The Goal/Question/Metric Method: A Practical Guide for Quality Improvement of Software Development*, London: McGraw-Hill

[94] Velleman, P.F. and Wilkinson, L. (1993) Nominal, Ordinal, Interval, and Ratio Typologies are Misleading, *The American Statistician*, Vol. 47, No. 1, pp. 65–72

[95] Weber, M., Wright Mills, C., and Gerth, H.H. (1958) *From Max Weber: Essays in Sociology*, Oxford: Oxford University Press

[96] Wenger, E. (1998) *Communities of Practice: Learning, Meaning, and Identity*, Cambridge: Cambridge University Press

[97] Yusof, S.M. and Aspinwall, E. (1999) Critical Success Factors for Total Quality Management Implementation in Small and Medium Enterprises, *Total Quality Management*, Vol. 10, Nos 4 & 5, pp. 803–809

[98] Zahran, S. (1998) Software Process Improvement: Practical Guidelines for Business Success, Harlow, Addison-Wesley

4

Evidence-Based Software Engineering
for Practitioners

T.Dybå, B.A. Kitchenham, and M. Jørgensen

Abstract: Software engineers might make incorrect decisions about adopting new techniques if they do not consider scientific evidence about the techniques' efficacy. They should consider using procedures similar to ones developed for evidence-based medicine.

Keywords: evidence-based software engineering, empirical software engineering, software process improvement.

4.1 Introduction

Software managers and practitioners often must make decisions about what technologies to employ on their projects. They might be aware of problems with their current development practices (for example, production bottlenecks or numerous defect reports from customers) and want to resolve them. Or, they might have read about a new technology and want to take advantage of its promised benefits. However, practitioners can have difficulty making informed decisions about whether to adopt a new technology because there's little objective evidence to confirm its suitability, limits, qualities, costs, and inherent risks. This can lead to poor decisions about technology adoption, as Marvin Zelkowitz, Dolores Wallace, and David Binkley describe:

> Software practitioners and managers seeking to improve the quality of their software development processes often adopt new technologies without sufficient evidence that they will be effective, while other technologies are ignored despite the evidence that they most probably will be useful [1].

For instance, enthusiasts of object-oriented programming were initially keen to promote the value of hierarchical models. Only later did experimental evidence reveal that deep hierarchies are more error prone than shallow ones.

In contrast, medical practice has changed dramatically during the last decade as a result of adopting an evidence-based paradigm. In the late 1980s and early 1990s, studies showed that failure to undertake systematic reviews of medical research could cost lives and that experts' clinical judgment compared unfavourably with the results of systematic reviews. Since then, many medical researchers have adopted the evidence-based paradigm, and medical practitioners are now trained in this approach [2]. Although *evidence-based medicine* (EBM) has its critics [3], it is generally regarded as successful and has prompted many other disciplines (for example, psychiatry, nursing, social policy, and education) to adopt a similar approach.

Software companies are often under pressure to adopt immature technologies because of market and management pressures. We suggest that practitioners consider *evidence-based software engineering* as a mechanism to support and improve their technology adoption decisions.

4.2 The Aim and Methodology of EBSE

EBSE aims to improve decision making related to software development and maintenance by integrating current best evidence from research with practical experience and human values [4]. This means we do not expect a technology to be universally good or universally bad, only more appropriate in some circumstances and for some organizations. Furthermore, practitioners will need to accumulate empirical research about a technology of interest and evaluate the research from the viewpoint of their specific circumstances.

This aim is decidedly ambitious, particularly because the gap between research and practice can be wide. EBSE seeks to close this gap by encouraging a stronger emphasis on methodological rigor while focusing on relevance for practice. This is important because rigor is necessary in any research that purports to be relevant. Moreover, because most SE research has not influenced industrial practice [5], there's also a pressing need to prevent SE research from remaining an ivory tower activity that emphasizes academic rigor over relevance to practice.

So, although rigor is a necessary condition for relevant SE research, it is not sufficient. Medical evidence is based on rigorous studies of therapies given to real patients requiring medical treatment; laboratory experiments are not considered to provide compelling evidence. This implies that SE should not rely solely on laboratory experiments and should attempt to gather evidence from industrial projects, using observation studies, case studies, surveys, and field experiments. These empirical techniques do not have the scientific rigor of formal randomized experiments, but they do avoid the limited relevance of small-scale, artificial SE experiments.

Furthermore, there are substantial problems with accumulating evidence systematically, and not only because accumulating evidence from different types of studies is difficult. A specific challenge in practicing EBSE is that different empirical studies of the same phenomenon often report different and sometimes contradictory results [6]. Unless we can understand these differences, integrating individual pieces of evidence is difficult. This points to the importance of reporting contextual information in empirical studies to help explain conflicting research results [7].

EBSE involves five steps:

1. Convert a relevant problem or information need into an answerable question.
2. Search the literature for the best available evidence to answer the question.
3. Critically appraise the evidence for its validity, impact, and applicability.
4. Integrate the appraised evidence with practical experience and the customer's values and circumstances to make decisions about practice.
5. Evaluate performance and seek ways to improve it.

However, EBSE is not a standalone activity. Much of what is needed to practice EBSE already exists in the concept of technology transfer [8] and software process improvement [9]. SPI involves several steps (each researcher and consultant has his or her own view of how many)–for example,

1. Identify a problem.
2. Propose a technology or procedure to address that problem.
3. Evaluate the proposed technology in a pilot project.
4. If the technology is appropriate, adopt and implement it.
5. Monitor the organization after implementing the new technology.
6. Return to step 1.

Thus, EBSE provides mechanisms to support various parts of SPI. In particular, EBSE focuses on finding and appraising an appropriate technology for its suitability in a particular situation. This is an area where SPI is usually rather weak. People often assume that finding a candidate technology is relatively easy and evaluating the technology is the hard part. However, we believe that selecting an appropriate technology is much more difficult than was previously assumed and is a critical element of good process improvement. The only step in SPI that EBSE doesn't support is technology infusion, which is supported by change management procedures and diffusion models.

4.3 Step 1: Ask an Answerable Question

EBSE does not propose a specific method to identify and prioritize problems. If you are using SPI, you should be monitoring your projects and so be in a position to identify process and product problems. Otherwise, problem identification relies on the expertise of individual staff members. Another form of help is the Goal-Question-Metric method [9] in which you derive questions from specific goals.

Asking the Right Question

Assume we want to ask, "Is pair programming useful?" According to what evidence-based medicine suggests, we should specify this question in more detail—for example, "Does pair programming lead to improved code quality when practiced by professional software developers?" Here, we've specified what intervention we're interested in (pair programming), what population we're interested in (professional software developers), and what effect we're looking for (code quality). Ideally, we should be even more specific regarding the intervention. In this example we presume a comparison with something, without specifying it. Any estimation of an effect size involves either a comparison or an association.

We could have clearly stated that we wanted to compare pair programming with "individual programming." Alternatively, we could compare it with "partner programming" (that is, the programmers work on different tasks on different computers but share the same physical office or workspace so that they can share ideas, thoughts, problems, and so forth). Regarding context, we could also have been more specific. We have, for example, not specified the software development organization's nature, the developers' skills and experience, or the software engineering environment being used.

However, searching for the keywords "pair," "programming," and "professional" in the abstracts of the nearly two million articles indexed in IEEE Xplore and the ACM Digital Library (see the "Useful Information Sources" sidebar) resulted in only four articles retrieved (search performed 22 Nov. 2004). Neither article examined pair programming using professionals as subjects. So, for software engineering problems, we might need to be less stringent in question formation, for these reasons:

- We have a much smaller body of empirical research than medicine has. We can't afford to restrict our searches too much, or we won't find any relevant studies.

- To support rational decision making, we're usually interested in all possible outcomes. For example, we might not want to adopt a technique that results in very fast time to market if a side effect is poor operational reliability. This implies that, in particular, we shouldn't restrict our questions too severely with respect to outcomes.

Once you've identified the problem, you need to specify an answerable question. Typical questions ask for specific knowledge about how to appraise and apply methods, tools, and techniques in practice. David Sackett and his colleagues suggest that well-formulated questions usually have three components [2]:

- The main intervention or action you are interested in
- The context or specific situations of interest
- The main outcomes or effects of interest

For medical problems, partitioning the question into intervention, context, and effect makes it easier not only to go from general problem descriptions to specific questions but also to think about what kind of information you need to answer the question.

In the SE context, factors to consider when deciding which question to answer first include these:

- Which question is most important to your customers?
- Which question is most relevant to your situation?
- Which question is the most interesting in the context of your business strategy?
- Which question is most likely to recur in your practice?
- Is the question possible to answer in the available time?

The main challenge in this step is, in other words, to convert a practical problem into a question that is specific enough to be answered but not so specific that you do not get any answers (see the "Asking the Right Question" sidebar).

4.4 Step 2: Find the Best Evidence

Finding an answer to your question includes selecting an appropriate information resource and executing a search strategy. However, you need to separate the question you want to answer, the question implemented in the search keywords, and the questions answered in the studies found.

There are several information sources you can use. You can, for example, get viewpoints from your customers or the software's users, ask a colleague or an expert, use what you have learned as a student or in professional courses, use your own experience, or search for re-search-based evidence, which is our main focus.

By research-based evidence, we mean reports, articles, and other documents that describe a study conducted and reported according to certain guidelines. The main source of such evidence is scientific journals. Additional sources include books, bibliographical databases, and the Internet. However, when you start searching for evidence, relevant evidence often is not as easy to find as you might wish. Several thousand software-related publications are published each year; even if you work in a rather specialized area, keeping up-to-date by reading all the journals is almost impossible. For most practitioners, reading important magazines such as the *Communications of the ACM, Computer, IEEE Software*, and *IT Professional* would probably be enough to get a general overview of the latest SE developments.

Keeping up to date is much easier when you can use sources that combine results from independent empirical studies of a particular phenomenon. Systematic reviews have clearly defined inclusion criteria and standardized indicators of individual and combined effect sizes. Such reviews summarize the available evidence regarding specific phenomena, showing where the studies correspond or contradict and uncovering gaps in your knowledge. However, *ACM Computing*

Surveys is the only SE journal dedicated to systematic reviews. So, you need to search for such reviews in other journals as well. The situation is quite different in medicine, where the Cochrane Collaboration (www.cochrane.org) publishes and updates systematic reviews of all important areas of healthcare online.

In addition, you will have to search for evidence in electronic databases on the Internet. By doing a literature search here, you get a more specific overview of the published research in your area of interest than is generally the case for magazines and systematic reviews (at least for the time being).

Many organizations index published articles in several databases; that is, they include bibliographic information such as author, title, and keywords. Such indexing simplifies searching for information regarding a problem area or finding an answer to a specific question. The "Useful Information Sources" sidebar gives exmples of such databases.

Useful Information Sources

- IEEE Xplore (http://ieeexplore.ieee.org) provides access to IEEE publications published since 1988 (and selected articles back to 1950) and to current IEEE standards. Access to abstracts and tables of contents is free. Access to full text requires IEEE membership, a subscription, or payment for individual articles.

- The IEEE Computer Society Digital Library provides access to 22 IEEE Computer Society magazines and journals and more than 1,200 conference proceedings. Access to full text requires Computer Society membership, a subscription, or payment individual articles (www.computer.org/publications/dlib).

- The ACM Digital Library (www.acm.org/dl) provides access to ACM publications and related citations. Full access requires ACM membership and possibly a subscription; nonmembers can browse the DL and perform basic searches.

- The ISI Web of Science (www.isinet.com/products/citation/wos) consists of databases containing information from approximately 8,700 journals in different research areas—for example, the Science Citation Index Expanded, Social Sciences Citation Index, and Arts & Humanities Citation Index. Users can perform searches, mark records, and link to full text.

- EBSCOhost Electronic Journals Service (http://ejournals.ebsco.com) provides access to over 8,000 e-journals. Users can view tables of contents and abstracts and can access the full text of the e-journals to which they subscribe.

- CiteSeer (http://citeseer.nj.nec.com), sponsored by the US National Science Foundation and Microsoft Research, indexes PostScript and PDF files of scientific research articles on the Web. Access is free.

> • Google Scholar (http://scholar.google.com) indexes scholarly literature from all research areas, including abstracts, books, peer-reviewed papers, preprints, technical reports, and theses. Users can find scholarly literature from different publishers, professional societies, preprint repositories, and universities, as well as articles posted on the Web.

4.5 Step 3: Critically Appraise the Evidence

Unfortunately, published research is not always of good quality; the problem under study might be unrelated to practice, or the research method might have weaknesses such that you cannot trust the results. To assess whether research is of good quality and is applicable to practice, you must be able to critically appraise the evidence.

For a nonscientist, evaluating an article's scientific quality can often be difficult (although for practitioners, evaluating the article's relevance to practice is often more important). Most journals use external referees to evaluate manuscripts before publication, which makes such manuscripts more trustworthy. This means that for research in non-refereed journals and conferences or on the Internet, the reader will need additional insight to evaluate the results and their relevance to practice. However, even in a reputable scientific journal, researchers might have difficulty agreeing about an experiment's rigor (see, for example, the discussion arising from a recent study of formal methods [10, 11]).

In EBM, the most convincing form of evidence is a systematic review of a series of double-blind randomized field trials. SE doesn't yet have many well-conducted replications of rigorous experiments, so our empirical studies are much less reliable scientifically. SE researchers could provide more help to practitioners if they undertook and published more systematic reviews of important SE topics. However, until this happens, practitioners must be prepared to summarize evidence themselves. When you have evidence from different types of studies, you need some way to assess each study's quality. Figure 4.1 presents a checklist of factors to consider when evaluating an empirical study. In addition, Australian National Health and Medical Research Council guidelines discuss the relative trustworthiness of different types of empirical studies [12].

4.6 Step 4: Apply the Evidence

To employ the evidence in your decision making, you integrate it with your practical experience, your customers' requirements, and your knowledge of the concrete situation's specific circumstances, and then you apply it in practice. However, this procedure isn't straightforward.

Active use of new knowledge consists of applying or adapting specific evidence to a specific situation in practice. This contrasts with traditional, passive modes of transmitting information through teachers, books, manuals, colleagues, or business partners. Although such transmission can help in arranging the conditions required

1. Is there any vested interest?
- Who sponsored the study?
- Do the researchers have any vested interest in the results?

2. Is the evidence valid?
- Was the study's design appropriate to answer the question?
- How were the tasks, subjects, and setting selected?
- What data was collected, and what were the methods for collecting the data?
- Which methods of data analysis were used, and were they appropriate?

3. Is the evidence important?
- What were the study's results?
- Are the results credible, and, if so, how accurate are they?
- What conclusions were drawn, and are they justified by the results?
- Are the results of practical and statistical significance?

4. Can the evidence be used in practice?
- Are the study's findings transferable to other industrial settings?
- Did the study evaluate all the important outcome measures?
- Does the study provide guidelines for practice based on the results?
- Are the guidelines well described and easy to use?
- Will the benefits of using the guidelines outweigh the costs?

5. Is the evidence in this study consistent with the evidence in other available studies?
- Are there good reasons for any apparent inconsistencies?
- Have the reasons for any disagreements been investigated?

Fig. 4.1. A checklist for appraising published studies

for learning to occur, it cannot substitute for learning through direct experience. So, to practice EBSE, a software developer must commit to actively engaging in a learning process, combining the externally transmitted evidence with prior knowledge and experience. What characterizes a software developer using EBSE is that he or she makes individual judgments in a given situation rather than simply conforming to approved standards and procedures.

In practice, the ease of applying evidence depends on the type of technology (method, tool, technique, or practice) you are evaluating. Some technologies apply at the level of the individual developer – for example, a developer can adopt evidence related to how best to comment programs. However, evidence related to the adoption of a computer-aided software engineering tool or a specific mathematically based formal method requires support from project and senior managers. Furthermore, even techniques that the individual developer can adopt and evaluate have little impact unless they lead to a project-wide or organizational-wide process change.

So, it is at this point that you need to integrate EBSE with SPI. SPI relies on a systematic introduction and evaluation of proposed process change and, as we mentioned before, is often supported by change management processes. EBSE should provide the scientific basis for undertaking specific process changes, while SPI should manage the new technology's introduction.

4.7 Step 5: Evaluate Performance

In EBM, the final step is for individual medical practitioners to reflect on their use of the EBM paradigm [2]. In SPI, the final step is usually to confirm that the process change has worked as expected. We believe both concerns are relevant for EBSE.

You need to consider how well you perform each step of EBSE and how you might improve your use of it. In particular, you should ask yourself how well you are integrating evidence with practical experience, customer requirements, and your knowledge of the specific circumstances.

Following SPI practice, you also must assess whether process change has been effective. However, environmental turbulence and rapid changes in technology often lead to the need to adapt and learn during projects. This involves a high degree of creativity and improvisation, which suggests that you cannot wait until a project's end to draw out the lessons learned [13].

After-action reviews [14], short meetings aimed at evaluating performance in the midst of action, are a simple way for individuals and teams to learn immediately from both successes and failures. All that is needed is a suitable task with an identifiable purpose and some metrics with which to measure performance. A typical AAR lasts for 10–20 min and answers four simple questions:

- What was supposed to happen?
- What actually happened?
- Why were there differences?
- What did we learn?

However, it is important not to overreact. One isolated bad result should not cause abandonment of a new method, unless strong grounds exist to believe that the bad result is intrinsic to the method itself rather than a chance effect resulting from the particular task and the particular engineering staff. Equally, a single good result should not mean that further monitoring is unnecessary. Barbara Kitchenham undertook a study of COCOMO in the early 1980s. The first two projects on which she collected data were an almost perfect fit to the intermediate COCOMO model. Thereafter, however, no other project exhibited effort values anywhere near the COCOMO predictions.

When the project, or a major part of it, is completed, SPI principles suggest you must confirm that the expected improvement has taken place. A simple way to do this is to arrange a *postmortem analysis* [15]. A PMA is similar to an AAR but is conducted in more depth. Instead of 10–20 min, a PMA typically lasts from a couple of hours to a full day. It aims to capture lessons and insights (both good and bad) for future projects by evaluating these questions:

- What went so well that we want to repeat it?
- What was useful but could have gone better?
- What were the mistakes that we want to avoid for the future?
- What were the reasons for the successes or mistakes, and what can we do about them?

A PMA results mainly in better evidence regarding the specific process or technology – evidence that you might reuse as guidelines for the future, in the form of experience notes, new or improved checklists, improved development models, and a general understanding of what works and what does not in projects in your organization. PMAs and, when available, organization-wide measurement programs provide the information needed to restart the EBSE cycle, letting you identify and prioritize product and process problems by collating experiences from different projects.

Evidence-Based Software Engineering Q&A

Is EBSE possible for ordinary practitioners?
Magne Jørgensen has obtained encouraging results from teaching EBSE principles to final-year university students. The results show that with relatively little effort, people can become better skilled at asking an answerable question, finding the best evidence by searching the literature and by asking experts (that is, practitioners and researchers), and critically appraising the available evidence.

Tore Dybå was external examiner of the reports that these students produced using EBSE principles to investigate a software engineering technology. In his opinion, the quality of these reports was at least as good as more conventional reports on software engineering topics.

Can we develop appropriate infrastructure?
Barbara Kitchenham has constructed guidelines for systematic reviews [1], which several groups are evaluating.

Does accumulation of evidence offer new insights?
Magne Jørgensen and Kjetil Moløkken performed a systematic review of the size of software cost overruns [2]. Their review showed that the results reported by the Standish Group's 1994 CHAOS report, the most influential study of the early 1990s, were out of step with the results of three other contemporary studies. (The CHAOS report showed cost overruns of 189% the other studies showed cost overruns of approximately 33%) Differences in cost overrun measurements between the CHAOS study and the other studies were

---

unable to explain this difference. A critical examination of the report revealed several problems, including these:

- The Standish Group reported in their 1998 CHAOS report an average cost overrun of 69% that is, an improvement from 189% to 69% overrun in about four years. This is hardly likely to have happened.

- The CHAOS report did not define how cost overrun was measured and described it inconsistently.

- The CHAOS report did not report how the included projects were selected. Formulations in the CHAOS report suggest that the Standish Group collected mainly failure stores in 1994. This explains the high cost overrun number but also means that the study results can't be used as indicators of the software industry in general.

So, evidence exists that project performance was never as bad as many people imagined and that subsequent "improvements" might be much smaller than many people have hoped. In addition, Jørgensen performed a systematic review of studies of expert effort estimation [3]. Although effort spent on developing cost estimation models is usually justified by the argument that human-based estimates are poor, Jørgensen found no evidence that models were superior to expert estimates. He identified a variety of conditions where expert estimates were likely to be superior and other conditions where models were likely to reduce situational or human bias.

References

1. B.A. Kitchenham, Procedures for Performing Systematic Reviews, tech. report SE0401, Dept. of Computer Science, Univ. of Keele, and tech. report 0400011T.1, Empirical Software Eng., National Information and Communications Technology Australia, 30 August. 2004.

2. M. Jørgensen and K. Moløkken, "How Large Are Software Cost Overruns? Critical Comments on the Standish Group's CHAOS Reports," Simula Research Laboratories, 2004; www.simula.no/publication_one.php?publication_id=711.

3. M. Jørgensen, "A Review of Studies on Expert Estimation of Software Development Effort," J. Systems and Software, Vol. 70, Nos. 1–2, 2004, pp. 37–60

4.8 Discussion

Although it is important for software practitioners to base their choice of development methods on available scientific evidence, this is not necessarily easy. EBM arose because medical practitioners were overwhelmed by the large number of scientific studies; in SE our problems are rather different. There are relatively few studies, as our pair-programming example (see the "Asking the Right Question" sidebar) showed. Furthermore, when evidence is available, software practitioners still have difficulty judging the evidence's quality and assessing what the evidence means in terms of their specific circumstances. This implies that given the current state of empirical SE, practitioners will need to adopt more proactive search strategies such as approaching experts, other experienced practitioners, and researchers directly.

Because a basic idea behind EBSE is to establish a fruitful cooperation between research and practice, a closer link should exist between research and practice so that research is relevant to practitioners' needs and practitioners are willing to participate in research.

You might have noticed that we have offered no evidence of EBSE's benefits. Although we have no examples of other practitioners using EBSE, the sidebar "Evidenced-Based Software Engineering Q&A" presents examples of our own use of EBSE. On the basis of this experience, and other ongoing industrial and educational initiatives in which we are engaged, we believe that evidence-based practice is possible and potentially useful for software practitioners.

However, evidence-based practice also places requirements on researchers. We recommend that researchers adopt as much of the evidence-based approach as is possible. Specifically, this includes being more responsive to practitioners' needs when identifying topics for empirical research. Also, it means improving the standard both of individual empirical studies and of systematic reviews of such studies. Researchers need to perform and report replication studies in order to accumulate reliable evidence about SE topics. Researchers also need to report their results in a manner that's accessible to practitioners.

Evidence-based practice works in medicine [2]. Furthermore, our experience from undertaking empirical studies, systematic reviews, and teaching students in EBSE gives us some confidence that it will also work in software engineering. So, to develop a more integrated approach to adopting research findings, we encourage both practitioners and researchers to develop coordinated mechanisms to support the continuing evolution of SE knowledge. This way, software organizations will be able to adopt good practice more quickly and with fewer risks, improve the quality of products, and reduce the risk of project failures.

References

[1] Zelkowitz, M.V., Wallace, D.R., and Binkley, D.W. (2003) Experimental Validation of New Software Technology, *Lecture Notes on Empirical Software Engineering*, World Scientific, pp. 229–263
[2] Sackett, D.L. et al. (2000) *Evidence-Based Medicine: How to Practice and Teach EBM*, 2nd ed., Churchill Livingstone
[3] Feinstein, A.R. and Horowitz, R.I. (1997) Problems with the 'Evidence' of 'Evidence-Based Medicine,' *Am. J. Medicine*, vol. 103, no. 6, pp. 529–535

[4] Kitchenham, B.A., Dybå, T., and Jørgensen, M. (2004) Evidence-Based Software Engineering," *Proc. 26th Int'l Conf. Software Eng.* (ICSE 2004), IEEE CS Press, pp. 273–281

[5] Potts, C. (1993) Software-Engineering Research Revisited, *IEEE Software*, Vol. 10, No. 5, 1993, pp. 19–28

[6] Pickard, L.M., Kitchenham, B.A., and Jones, P.W. (1998) Combining Empirical Results in Software Engineering, *Information and Software Technology*, Vol. 40, No. 14, pp. 811–821

[7] Kitchenham, B.A. et al. (2002) Preliminary Guidelines for Empirical Research in Software Engineering, *IEEE Trans. Software Eng.*, Vol. 28, No. 8, 2002, pp. 721–734

[8] Pfleeger, S.L. and Menezes, W. (2000) Marketing Technology to Software Practitioners, *IEEE Software*, Vol. 17, No. 1, pp. 27–33.

[9] Basili, V.R. and Caldiera, G. (1995) Improve Software Quality by Reusing Knowledge and Experience, *Sloan Management Review*, Vol. 37, No. 1, pp. 55–64.

[10] Berry, D.M. and Tichy, W.F. (2003) Comments on "Formal Methods Application: An Empirical Tale of Software Development," *IEEE Trans. Software Eng.*, Vol. 29, No. 6, pp. 567–571.

[11] Sobel, A.E.K. and Clarkson, M.R. (2003) Response to "Comments on 'Formal Methods Application: An Empirical Tale of Software Development,'" *IEEE Trans. Software Eng.*, Vol. 29, No. 6, pp. 572–575

[12] *How to Use the Evidence: Assessment and Application of Scientific Evidence*, Australian Nat'l Health and Medical Research Council, February 2000

[13] Dybå, T., Dingsøyr, T., and Moe, N.B. (2004) *Process Improvement in Practice: A Handbook for IT Companies*, Kluwer Academic

[14] Collison,C. and Parcell, G. (2001) *Learning to Fly: Practical Lessons from One of the World's Leading Knowledge Companies*, Capstone

[15] Collier, B., DeMarco, T., and Fearey, P. A Defined Process for Project Postmortem Review, *IEEE Software*, Vol. 13, No. 4, pp. 65–72

5

Challenges and Recommendations when Increasing the Realism of Controlled Software Engineering Experiments

D.I.K. Sjøberg, B. Anda, E. Arisholm, T. Dybå, M. Jørgensen, A. Karahasanović and M.Vokáč,

Abstract: An important goal of most empirical software engineering experiments is the transfer of the research results to industrial applications. To convince industry about the validity and applicability of the results of controlled software engineering experiments, the tasks, subjects and the environments should be as realistic as practically possible. Such experiments are, however, more demanding and expensive than experiments involving students, small tasks and pen-and-paper environments. This article describes challenges of increasing the realism of controlled experiments and lessons learned from the experiments that have been conducted at Simula Research Laboratory.

Keywords: empirical software engineering, technology transfer, controlled experiments

5.1 Introduction

The ultimate criterion for success in an applied discipline such as software engineering (SE) research is the widespread adoption of research results into everyday industrial practice. To achieve this, diffusion of innovation models requires the evidential credibility of software experiments, which depends on both the producer and the receiver of the results. Without a close tie between the experimental situation and the "real", industrial situation, practitioners may perceive the experiment as irrelevant and ignore the results.

Hence, there is an increasing understanding in the software engineering community that realistic empirical studies are needed to develop or improve processes, methods and tools for software development and maintenance [1, 2, 3, 4, 5, 6, 7].

Most of the studies in software engineering that have emphasized realism are case studies. However, a major deficiency of case studies is that many variables vary from one case study to another so that comparing the results to detect cause-effect relationships is difficult [8]. Therefore, controlled experiments should be conducted to *complement* case studies in empirical software engineering.

While the *raison d'être* for experimental research is to establish evidence for causality through *internal* logical rigor and control [9], this is not enough. It is also important to ensure *external* validity [8]. If an experiment lacks external validity, its findings may not be true beyond the experimental setting. An important issue, therefore, is whether the particular features of formal SE experiments are realistic. In particular, it is a challenge to achieve realism regarding experimental subjects, tasks and environment [10].

Controlled experiments in software engineering often involve students solving small pen-and-paper tasks in a classroom setting. A major criticism of such experiments is their lack of realism [11, 12], which may deter technology transfer from the research community to industry. The experiments would be more realistic if they are run on realistic tasks on realistic systems with professionals using their usual development technology in their usual workplace environment [13]. Generally, a weakness of most software engineering research is that one is rarely explicit about the target population regarding tasks, subjects and environments.

During the last couple of years the authors of this chapter have conducted 13 controlled experiments with a total of 800 students and 300 professionals as subjects. The purpose of this article is to describe some of the challenges and risks to be encountered when the realism of controlled experiments increases, and to give some recommendations based on our experience.

The remainder of this article is organised as follows. Sections 5.2–5.4 discuss challenges and lessons learned from our attempt of increasing the realism of respectively subjects, tasks and environment of controlled SE experiments. Section 5.5 addresses the logistics of conducting such experiments. Section 5.6 concludes.

5.2 Representative Subjects

A prerequisite for the discussion on realism is that we are conscious about the population we wish to make claims about [14]. Implicit in our discussion is that the interesting population is "representative" software builders doing "representative" tasks in "representative" industrial environments. Nevertheless, it is not trivial defining what "representative" means. For example, there may be many categories of professionals, such as junior, intermediate and senior consultants.

5.2.1 Target and Sample Population

As in all experimental disciplines involving people, two major challenges are:

– Identifying the population about which we wish to make claims and
– Selecting subjects who are representative of that population.

The similarity of the subjects of an experiment to the people who will use the technology impacts the ease of the technology transfer [15]. Unfortunately, few papers reporting controlled SE experiments are explicit on the target population. Usually, there is an assumption that the target population is "professional software builders". One should; however, be aware that this group may be very diverse. That is, the performance may differ significantly between various categories of professionals [16].

A common criticism of experiments in software engineering is that most of the subjects are students, which might make it difficult to generalise the results to settings with various kinds of professionals. To simplify the generalisation of experimental results to a realistic setting, one should attempt to sample subjects from the population of professionals that we wish to make claims about. However, students are more accessible and easier to organise, and hiring them is generally inexpensive. Consequently, experiments with students are easier to run than experiments with professionals and the risks are lower.

Student experiments should thus be used to test experimental design and initial hypotheses, before conducting experiments with professionals [17]. Experiments with students might have the goal of gaining an understanding of the basic issues without actually aiming for external validity. Conducting "unrealistic" experiments may be a first step in a technology transfer process, that is, to reduce risks and costs, one should start with a relatively small experiment with students, possibly with small tasks (see Sect. 5.3.2) and the use of pen and paper (see Sect. 5.4.1), and then increase the scale of realism if the first pilot experiments are promising.

5.2.2 Background Information about Subjects

Generally, papers describing SE experiments that involve professionals often do not characterise the professionals' competence, experience and educational background, and the authors seldom justify to what extent their subjects are representative of the software engineers who usually perform such tasks. This leads to several problems:

- The results may not be trustworthy, that is, the professionals may not be realistic for the actual experimental tasks. The sample recruited may be biased in some way, for example, a company may only be willing to let the software engineers who are least experienced or least in demand take part in an experiment.
- Comparing results from the original with replicated studies is difficult.
- Successful transfer of the results into industrial practice is less likely.

To generalise from experiments with a given group of subjects, we would need information about the ability and the variations among the subjects and the group of people to which the results will be generalised [18]. For professionals, depending on what we wish to study, it would be relevant to know the variations regarding competence, productivity, education, experience (including domains), age, culture/nationality (?), etc. (Some of this information may be highly controversial and should be carefully considered from an ethical point of view.) A challenge of measuring these attributes is to define good measures that can be used in practice. For example, how do we measure competence and productivity? In practice, we would have to find meaningful substitute measures for those we cannot measure directly. In an experiment on object-oriented (OO) design principles [16], we collected detailed information about:

- Age
- Education (number of credits in general, number of credits in computer science)
- General work experience
- Programming experience (OO in general, particular programming languages (Java, C++, etc.)
- Knowledge of systems developments methods and tools, and
- Subjective description of their own programming skills.

This background information can be used in several ways, for example, to determine

- The target population for which the results are valid, and
- To what extent the results of the treatments depend on the collected background information, e.g., that certain design principles might be easier to understand for experienced professionals than for novices.

It would also be interesting to identify the variations within the same company versus among companies, variations between in-house professionals versus consultants, etc. For example, in-house software development in Nokia, Ericsson, Bosch, etc. may differ from development projects run by consultancy companies. Nevertheless, knowledge about the effect of a certain technology among consultants or even students may still be useful in the lack of knowledge of the effect of the technology in a company's own environment.

5.2.3 How to Get Subjects?

Both students and professionals are used in SE experiments. For most university researchers it is relatively easy to use students as subjects in experiments. One can organise an experiment as follows:

1. The experiment is considered a compulsory part of a course, either as part of the teaching or as an exercise [19, 20].
2. The experiment is not compulsory; it is voluntary, but is still regarded relevant for the exam [21]. (In practice, students may feel obliged to take part to show their teacher that they are enthusiastic students.)
3. The students are paid, that is, the experiment is not considered as part of the course (but it may still be relevant) [22, 23, 24].

In our research group, we have experienced that the organisation indicated in alternative (3) is usually the easiest one. We then do not have the time constraint of the ordinary classes, the students are motivated and there seems to be few ethical problems [25, 26]. (One might argue that it is unethical if some students have been using a technology that proved better than the technologies being used by others students, that is, some students have learned better technologies than other students. However, when the experiment is voluntary and they are paid, this is hardly a problem). In any case, if practically possible, we inform the students about the results of the experiments.

The lack of professionals in software engineering experiments is due to the conception of high costs and large organisational effort. Harrison [10] puts it this way:

> Professional programmers are hard to come by and are very expensive. Thus, any study that uses more than a few professional programmers must be very well funded. Further, it is difficult to come by an adequate pool of professional developers in locations that do not have a significant software development industrial base. Even if we can somehow gather a sufficiently large group of professionals, the logistics of organizing the group into a set of experimental subjects can be daunting due to schedule and location issues.

Fenton claims that "generally, such [formal] experiments are prohibitively expensive and technically infeasible to set up properly" [27]. He then refers to an experiment conducted with MSc students that was criticised for the claim that these students were representative of trainee programmers in industry.

To alleviate these problems, we have applied alternative incentives to conduct experiments with professionals:

− Offer the organisation tailored internal courses and, for example, use the course exercises as experiments
− Have a part time job in the company and advocate the experiment as useful for the company [28]
− Involve some of the employees in the research and offer them co-authorship of the resulting research paper
− Offer the organisation a network of people from other organisations with relevant experience
− Pay the company directly for the hours spent on the experiment [29]

The first and the last alternative have proved most successful. Regarding the last alternative, we thought that it would be most effective to use our personal network to get people to take part in our experiments on their spare time and pay them individually. However, it turned out that a much better approach is to phone the switchboard of a major consultancy company and request a specific service.

This way, one can get a sample of different categories of professionals (junior, intermediate, senior) from different companies as subjects in one experiment. In the OO design experiment [16], 130 professionals from nine companies took part.

They were easy to get. It was considerably more difficult to get subjects to take part in another experiment on design pattern [30], because that experiment was held for a period of three given days, whereas the length of the OO design experiment was only one day, and the day was chosen by the participating companies themselves (within a certain interval).

When we hire people from consultancy companies to take part in our experiments, we are treated professionally like any ordinary customer (although several consultants say that they find our experiments more exciting than most other projects). We agree on a contract and they internally define a project with a project leader, budget, etc. Of course, one must have the resources to do research this way.

5.3 Realistic Tasks

When conducting controlled experiments in software engineering, one should consider the realism and representativeness of the tasks regarding the size, complexity and duration of the involved tasks. Specification, implementation and verification methods also vary considerably between domains, such as accounting software versus flight-control systems. In our opinion, some experimental tasks bear little resemblance to actual tasks in software engineering; others are very similar to actual tasks [31]. In between there is a continuum. Larger development tasks may take months, while many maintenance tasks may take only a couple of hours.

Most experiments in software engineering seem simplified and short-term: "the experimental variable must yield an observable effect in a matter of hours rather than six months or a year" [10]. Such experiments are hardly realistic given the tasks of building and maintaining real, industrial software, particularly since many of the factors we wish to study require significant time before we can obtain meaningful results.

5.3.1 Collecting Information about "Typical" Tasks

A systematic way to define representative tasks according to a given application area in a given context, is to collect information about the kinds and frequencies of tasks in the actual environment and then create "benchmark tasks", i.e., a set of tasks that is a representative sample of tasks from the population of all tasks. An example use of such benchmark tasks is described in [32]. In that study, the maintenance benchmark tasks were derived from another study of 109 randomly sampled maintenance tasks [33].

In yet another study, we collected information about all the maintenance tasks in a tool vendor company through a Web interface during a period of six months [34].

5.3.2 Longer Experiments

Generally, to increase the realism of SE experiments, the duration of the experimental tasks should be increased. As far as we have observed, the tasks carried out in student experiments take only up to three-four hours – most of them are shorter to fit with the time schedule of a university class. In the experiment on object-oriented (OO) design principles [16], the subjects spent one day each on five experimental tasks; whereas in the design pattern experiment [30] the subjects spent three days (including a course on design patterns the second day).

We have conducted one longer-term (35 h), one-subject explorative study [35], that is, an "*N*=1 Experiment" [10]. The longer duration of this study allowed a wider spectrum of tasks to be carried out. The system on which the tasks were performed was also larger in size and complexity than usual in most experiments. Another positive effect of the longer duration was that the pressure from the experimental situation put on the subject was less, that is, more realistic, than what we have experienced in the controlled experiments we have run. In the student experiments, most students felt as if they were in an exam situation. "How did I do?" they asked after the experiment.

Another example of an experiment with high realism of tasks is our ongoing study on uncertainty in the estimation of development effort. In that experiment we pay an organization to evaluate three estimation processes. The organization now estimates one third of their incoming projects respectively according to the first, second and third estimation process.

Increasing the duration of the experiments enables more realistic tasks to be carried out. We have tried several means to achieve longer experiments; some of them with success (see Sect. 5.4.2). Of course, our tasks may still be small compared with many actual tasks. We are therefore planning an experiment where an application system that is actually needed by Simula Research Laboratory, will be developed by 4–5 different project teams (each consisting of 4–5 persons) from different consultancy companies. It should be possible to develop the system in a couple of months. This would then be a very realistic development task. Of course, the number of subjects (here teams) is too small to conduct hypothesis testing, but we still have some control. Nevertheless, there are many challenges to such an experiment.

5.3.3 Methodological Challenges Regarding Quality and Time

Time is often a dependent variable in SE experiments. Usually, we want the subjects to solve the tasks with satisfactory quality in as short time as possible, as most software engineering jobs put a relatively high pressure on the tasks to be done. However, if the time pressure put on the participatory subjects is too high, then the task solution quality may be reduced to the point where it becomes meaningless to use the corresponding task times in subsequent statistical analyses. A challenge is therefore to put a realistic time pressure on the subjects. How to best deal with this challenge depends to some extent on the size, duration and location of the experiment. For smaller experiments where the subjects are located in the same physical location (e.g., a classroom), we have applied the following strategies:

- All subjects receive a fixed honorarium for their participation. This eliminates potential problems of subjects speculating in working slowly to get higher payment.
- The subjects work for the same amount of time (e.g., 3 h), finishing as many tasks as they can. This prevents faster subjects from disturbing the slower subjects. At the finishing time, everyone has to leave.
- The subjects are informed that they are not all given the same tasks. This (combined with the fixed time on the tasks) reduces the chances that the "slow" subjects deliver solutions with inadequate quality (faster than they should) in an attempt to appear smart in front of their peers; most persons would find it embarrassing to be the last to complete the tasks.
- The last task of the experiment is a large task that we a priori do not expect the subjects will be able to complete. This assumption should be tested in a small pilot experiment. Unknown to the subjects, this extra task is not included in the analysis. The extra task puts sufficient time pressure also on the fast subjects. It also reduces threats to validity caused by "ceiling effects", that is, the adverse effect of having too much or too little time towards the end of the experiment, since this extra task is not included in the analysis.

We applied all of these strategies in the pen-and-paper version of the OO design experiment [16]. Since nobody finished the extra task, there was sufficient time pressure. Everyone left at the same time (after three hours). Hence, there was no disturbance and it was fair that everybody received a fixed honorarium. Furthermore, there was no reason to speculate in working slowly (to increase their payment), or to work faster than they should (to look good).

In our more work-intensive experiments, the tasks would typically take one day or more to complete. Furthermore, the experiment may be located in different physical locations, e.g., in their usual work environment (Sect. 5.4). In these cases, the fixed honorarium and fixed time strategies seem less appropriate since many subjects will have to be present without doing any sensible work for a longer time and disturbance is less of an issue. In these cases we have applied the following strategies:

- Instead of a "fixed" honorarium, we estimate the work to (say) 5 h, and then say that the subjects will be paid for those 5 h independently of how long they would actually need. (Note that we wish the subjects to finish as soon as possible; we would discourage people to speculate in working slowly to get higher payment.) Hence, the subjects who finish early (e.g., 2 h) are still paid for 5 h. However, in practice, we tell the subjects when the 5 h have passed, that they will be paid for additional hours if they finish their tasks.
- The subjects are allowed to leave when they finish.

- As for fixed time, smaller scale "classroom" experiments, the subjects are still informed that they are not all given the same tasks to reduce the chances that they for competitive reasons work "faster" than they should with resulting low quality of the delivered task solutions.
- As for fixed time, smaller scale "classroom" experiments, the experiment should preferably still include an extra, last task not to be included in the analysis. Although the benefit of an extra task is probably not as large as for fixed time, fixed honorarium experiments, our results suggest that the last task nevertheless may exhibit ceiling effects and therefore should not be included in the analysis. The potential benefits of an extra, last task may justify the added duration and costs of the experiment.

We applied these alternative strategies for the professionals participating in the replicated OO design experiment [16]. Our experiences suggest that these strategies work fairly well, although each strategy provides different advantages and disadvantages in terms of threats to validity, practical issues and costs. For example, restrictions imposed by an existing experiment design might make it difficult to include an "extra task", like the experiment reported in [30].

In another experiment on UML design processes with 53 students [36], we combined the strategies described above. The experiment was run in a classroom setting and was scheduled for three hours. However, due to the need for extra time caused by the use of a CASE tool (see Sect. 5.4.1); many students had not finished after the three hours. Those students were then encouraged to stay longer and finish their tasks by being offered additional payment. This way, we managed to collect more data points than if everybody had left after the scheduled time.

5.4 Realistic Environment

While our focus is on controlled experiments, this does not mean that we are only concerned with laboratory, or in vitro, experiments. Controlled experiments can also be conducted in vivo, in a more realistic environment than is possible in the artificial, sanitized laboratory situation [3]. However, the realistic environment can also be a weakness, because it may be too costly or impossible to manipulate an independent variable or to randomize treatments in real life. Thus, the amount of control varies through a continuum, and prioritizing between the validity types is an optimization problem, given the purpose of the experiment. Nevertheless, external validity is always of extreme importance whenever we wish to generalize from behaviour observed in the laboratory to behaviour outside the laboratory, or when we wish to generalize from one non-laboratory situation to another non-laboratory situation.

5.4.1 System Development Tools

Even when realistic subjects perform realistic tasks, the tasks may be carried out in an unrealistic manner. The challenge is to configure the experimental environment with an infrastructure of supporting technology (processes, methods, tools, etc.) that resembles an industrial development environment. Traditional pen-and-paper based exercises used in a classroom setting are hardly realistic for dealing with relevant problems of the size and complexity of most contemporary software systems. Recently, we have replicated three experiments where we have replaced pen and paper with professional system development tools:

- In the OO design principle experiment [16], a variety of Java development environments were used (JBuilder, Forte, Visual Age, Visual J++, Visual Café, etc.). This is a replication of the experiment described in [23].
- In the OO design pattern experiment [30], a C++ environment was used. This is a replication of the experiment described in [37].
- In the experiment on UML design processes [36], 27 subjects used a commercially available OO development CASE tool (Tau UML Suite), while 26 subjects used pen and paper. This is a replication of the experiment described in [38].

Our experience from these experiments is that using system development tools requires proper preparation:

- Licences, installations, access rights, etc. must be checked
- The subjects must be or become familiar with the tools
- The tools must be checked to demonstrate acceptable performance and stability when many subjects are working simultaneously. In one experiment, several subjects had to give up because the tool crashed.

Other researchers who plan experiments using professional tools should take into account that our results show that the time spent to solve the same tasks took 20–30% longer when using tools than when using pen and paper [16, 30, 36]. Note also that the variance also increases considerably when tools are used. This may influence the time allocated to the experiment.

Regarding quality, there are, as expected, *fewer syntactical* errors when tools are used. More surprising is that there seem to be *more logical* errors. More analysis is needed to investigate this issue into further depth. In particular, the relationships among the three realism dimensions (subjects, tasks and environment) need to be investigated, for example, regarding scalability: a professional development tool will probably become more useful the larger and more complex the tasks and application system become.

5.4.2 Experimental Procedure in a Realistic Environment

Many threats to external validity are caused by the artificial setting of the experiment. For example, because the logistics is simpler, a classroom is used instead of the usual work place. Conducting an experiment on the usual work site with professional development tools implies less control of the experiment than we would have in a classroom setting with pen and paper. Thus, there are many challenges when conducting experiments with professionals in industry. We have learned the following lessons:

- Ask for a local project manager of the company who should select subjects according to the specification of the researchers, ensure that the subjects actually turn up, ensure that the necessary tools are installed on the PCs, and carry out all other logistics, accounting, etc.
- Motivate the experiment up-front: inform the subjects about the purpose of the experiment (at a general level) and the procedure (when to take lunch or breaks, that phone calls and other interruptions should be avoided, etc.).
- Ensure that the subjects do not talk with one another in breaks, lunch, etc.
- Assure the subjects that the information about their performance is kept confidential (both *within* company and *outside*).
- Assure the company that its general performance is kept confidential.
- Monitor the experiment, that is, be visible and accessible for questions.
- Give all the subjects a small training exercise to ensure that the PC and tool environment are working properly.
- Assure the company and subjects that they will be informed about the results of the experiment (and do it).
- Provide a proper experiment support environment to help set up and monitor the experiment, and collect and manage the experimental data (see Sect. 5.2).

5.5 Supporting the Logistics of Controlled Experiments

Our experience from the experiments we have run with both students and professionals is that all the logistics around the experiments is work intensive and error prone: general information and specific task documents must be printed and distributed, personal information (bank account, etc.) and background information must be collected, all solution documents must be collected and then punched into an electronic form, etc. This may in turn lead to typing errors, lost data [39], and other problems.

We realised that if we were to scale up our experiments, and particularly run experiments with professionals in industry using professional development tools, that is, make our experiments more realistic, we would need electronic tool support. Hence, we searched for suitable tools and found several Web tools developed

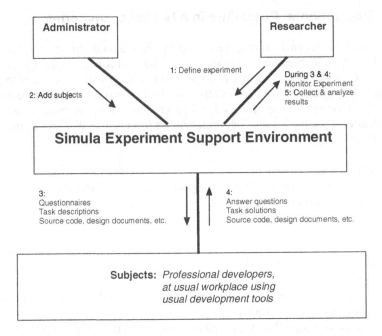

Fig. 5.1. Web-based experiment support environment

to support surveys, most of them designed by psychologists (e-Experiment[1], Psy-chExperiments[2], Survey Pro 3[3], S-Ware WWW Survey Assistant[4], Wextor[5]). Those tools basically distribute questionnaires to the respondents who fill them in online. Then the results are stored in a local database or sent via emails to the re-searchers. However, to conduct the kind of experiments that we were interested in, we needed a more sophisticated tool. Therefore, in collaboration with a software company that develops solutions for Human Resource Management, we developed (and are still extending and improving) the Web-based Simula Experiment Sup-port Environment (SESE). SESE is built on top of the company's standard com-mercial human resource management system. Fig. 5.1 illustrates the way SESE supports an experiment:

Step 1: The researcher defines a new experiment (SESE can manage an arbitrary number of experiments simultaneously) with the required questionnaires, task descriptions, files to be downloaded etc.

Step 2: The administrator creates a user-id and password for each person that will take part in the experiment, and emails that information to the person.

Step 3: The user (subject) fills in questionnaires (personal and background information) and downloads task descriptions and other required documents (design models, source code, etc.).

Step 4: The user carries out the tasks, answers questions along the way and uploads the finished documents. Timestamping is done continuously (when were the task descriptions downloaded and task solutions uploaded, when a break started and stopped, etc.).

Step 5: When a subject has finished the tasks, his or her results are stored in the (relational) database of SESE. When all the subjects have finished, the researcher can start analysing the data.

The OO design experiment was run at 10 different sites using SESE via the Web. The experiences from using SESE are positive. SESE enables us to run distributed experiments – both in location and time – instead of only "big-bang" experiments. If acceptable from a methodological point of view, one should avoid "big-bang" experiments to reduce risks. For example, in our design pattern experiment, a fibre cable breakdown far beyond our control forced us to send 44 consultants home and defer the experiment to start on the next day. This accident caused a lot of frustration and a direct loss of 20,000 €. Also in the UML experiment we had serious problems. The day before the experiment, there was a hacker break-in into the computer network of Oslo University where the experiment was to be run. All the 52,000 passwords of the university had to be changed by the systems department and all accounts were closed at the exact same time as our experiment was supposed to start. Fortunately, we managed to get a deal with the systems department to treat the accounts of our subjects as special cases.

Future extensions of SESE may include detailed logging of the way a task is performed or a technology is used. This may include window operations, keystrokes, mouse operations and movements logged with timestamps [40]. SESE and the experiences from using it are more fully described in [41].

5.6 Summary

This article focused on the need for conducting more realistic experiments in software engineering. Using a large experiment on OO design alternatives and other experiments conducted by our research group as examples, we described how increased realism can be achieved, particularly along the dimensions subjects, tasks and environment. A Web-based experiment supporting tool was also described briefly.

We discussed several extra challenges and larger risks that must be taken into account when conducting more realistic experiments. Based on our experiences, we described lessons learned and recommendations for tackling the challenges and reducing the risks, amongst others:

– Be explicit about your target and sample population, possibly divided into subpopulations (e.g., junior, intermediate and senior consultants).

- Record background information about subjects.
- Using professional system development tools in an experiment increases the realism, but requires careful planning, risk analysis and more resources.
- To get subjects to take part in experiments, consider the various kinds of "award" proposed.
- To help tackle the tradeoffs between quality of the tasks to be conducted in an experiment and the time spent on solving them, consider the proposed techniques.
- Apply the described guidelines on the practical conduct of experiments in industry.

We believe that many of the challenges described in this paper also are faced by other researchers conducting controlled software engineering experiments. To increase the knowledge of the empirical software engineering community in this area, we hope that more experiences on how to tackle these challenges will be reported in the literature.

References

[1] Basili, V.R., Selby, R.W., and Hutchens, D.H. (1986) Experimentation in Software Engineering. *IEEE Transactions on Software Engineering*, Vol. SE-12, No. 7, pp. 733–743

[2] Rombach, H.D. Basili, V.R., and Selby, R.W. (1993) *Experimental Software Engineering Issues: Critical Assessment and Future Directions, Dagstuhl Workshop, Germany*, September 1992, LNCS 706, Springer Berlin Heidelberg, NY

[3] Basili, V.R. (1996) The Role of Experimentation in Software Engineering: Past, Current, and Future. *Proceedings of the 18th International Conference on Software Engineering*, Berlin, Germany, March 25–29, pp. 442–449

[4] Tichy, W.F. (1998) Should Computer Scientists Experiment More? 16 Reasons to Avoid Experimentation, *IEEE Computer*, Vol. 31, No. 5, pp. 32–40

[5] Zelkowitz, M.V. and Wallace, D.R. (1998) Experimental Models for Validating Technology, *IEEE Computer*, Vol. 31, No. 5, pp. 23–31

[6] Wohlin, C., Runeson, P., Höst, M., Ohlsson, M.C., Regnell, B., and Wesslén, A. (1999) *Experimentation in Software Engineering – An Introduction*, Kluwer Academic Publishers, Boston, MA

[7] Juristo, N. and Moreno, A. (2001) *Basics of Software Engineering Experimentation*, Kluwer Academic Publishers, Boston MA

[8] Shadish, W.R., Cook, T.D., and Campbell, D.T. (2002) *Experimental and Quasi-Experimental Designs for Generalized Causal Inference*, Boston: Houghton Mifflin Company

[9] Montgomery, D. C. (1997) *Design and Analysis of Experiments*, 4th edition, Wiley, NY

[10] Harrison, W. (2000) *N*=1: An Alternative for Software Engineering Research?, Beg, Borrow, or Steal: Using Multidisciplinary Approaches in Empirical Software Engineering Research, Workshop, 5 June, 2000 at *22nd Int. Conf. on Softw. Eng. (ICSE)*, Limerick, Ireland, pp. 39–44

[11] Potts, C. (1993) Software-Engineering Research Revisited, *IEEE Software*, Vol. 10, No. 5, pp. 19–28

[12] Glass, R.L. (1994) The Software-Research Crisis, *IEEE Software*, Vol. 11, No. 6, pp. 42–47

[13] Sjøberg, D.I.K., Anda, B., Arisholm, E., Dybå, T., Jørgensen, M., Karahasanovic, A., Koren, E.F., and Vokac M. (2002) Conducting Realistic Experiments in Software Engineering, *ISESE'2002 (First International Symposium on Empirical Software Engineering)*, Nara, Japan, October 3–4, 2002, pp. 17–26, IEEE Computer Society

[14] Kitchenham, B.A., Pfleeger, S.L., Pickard, L.M., Jones, P.W., Hoaglin, D.C. El-Emam, K., and Rosenberg, J. (2002) Preliminary Guidelines for Empirical Research in Software Engineering. *IEEE Transactions on Software Engineering*, Vol. 28, No. 8, pp. 721–734

[15] Rogers, E.M. (1995) *Diffusion of Innovations*, 4th Edition, NY: The Free Press

[16] Arisholm, E. and Sjøberg, D.I.K. (2004) Evaluating the Effect of a Delegated versus Centralized Control Style on the Maintainability of Object- Oriented Software, *IEEE Transactions on Software Engineering*, Vol. 30, No. 8, pp. 521–534

[17] Tichy, W.F. (2000) Hints for Reviewing Empirical Work in Software Engineering, *Empirical Software Engineering*, Vol. 5, No. 4, pp. 309–312

[18] Basili, V.R., Shull, F., and Lanubile, F. (1999) Building Knowledge through Families of Experiments. *IEEE Transactions on Software Engineering*, Vol. 25, No. 4, pp. 456–473

[19] Anda, B., Sjøberg, D.I.K., and Jørgensen, M. (2001) Quality and Understandability in Use Case Models. In J. Lindskov Knudsen (Ed.): *ECOOP'2001* (Object-Oriented Programming, 15th European Conf.), Budapest, Hungary, June 18–22, 2001, LNCS 2072 Springer Berlin Heidelberg New York, pp. 402–428

[20] Jørgensen, M. A. (2004) Review of Studies on Expert Estimation of Software Development Effort, *Journal of Systems and Software* 70 (1–2), pp. 37–60

[21] Jørgensen, M. and Sjøberg, D.I.K. (2001) Impact of Software Effort Estimation on Software Work, *Journal of Information and Software Technology*, Vol. 43, pp. 939–948

[22] Anda, B. and Sjøberg, D.I.K. (2002) Towards an Inspection Technique for Use Case Models, *SEKE'2002 (Fourteenth International Conference on Software Engineering and Knowledge Engineering)*, Ischia, Italy, July 15–19, pp. 127–134

[23] Arisholm, E., Sjøberg, D.I.K., and Jørgensen, M. (2001) Assessing the Changeability of two Object-Oriented Design Alternatives – A Controlled Experiment. *Empirical Software Engineering*, Vol. 6, No. 3, pp. 231–277, September 2001

[24] Karahasanovic, A. and Sjøberg, D.I.K. (2001) Visualizing Impacts of Database Schema Changes – A Controlled Experiment, in *2001 IEEE Symposium on Visual/Multimedia Approaches to Programming and Software Engineering*, Stresa, Italy, September 5–7, 2001, pp. 358–365, IEEE Computer Society

[25] Sieber, J.E. (2001) Protecting Research Subjects, Employees and Researchers: Implications for Software Engineering. *Empirical Software Engineering*, Vol. 6, No. 4, pp. 329–341

[26] Davis, M. (2001) When is a Volunteer Not a Volunteer?, *Empirical Software Engineering*, Vol. 6, No. 4, pp. 349–352

[27] Fenton, N. (2001) Conducting and Presenting Empirical Software Engineering, *Empirical Software Engineering*, Vol. 6, No. 3, pp. 195–200

[28] Anda, B. (2002) Comparing Effort Estimates Based on Use Case Points with Expert Estimates in *Empirical Assessment in Software Engineering* (EASE 2002), Keele, UK, April 8–10

[29] Jørgensen, M. and Sjøberg D.I.K. (2003) *The Impact of Customer Expectation on Software Development Effort Estimates*. Submitted for publication

[30] Vokác, M., Tichy, W., Sjøberg, D.I.K., Arisholm, E., and Aldrin, M. A. (2003) Controlled Experiment Comparing the Maintainability of Programs Designed with and without Design Patterns – A Replication in a real Programming Environment. Submitted for Publication

[31] Deligiannis, I.S., Shepperd, M., Webster, S. and Roumeliotis, M., (2002) A Review of Experimental Investigations into Object-Oriented Technology. Empirical Software Engineering. Vol. 7, No. 3, pp. 193–232

[32] Jørgensen, M. and Bygdås, S. (1999) An Empirical Study of the Correlation between Development Efficiency and Software Development Tools. Technical Journal of Norwegian Telecom, Vol. 11, pp. 54–62

[33] Jørgensen, M. (1995) An Empirical Study of Software Maintenance Tasks. Journal of Software Maintenance, Vol. 7, pp. 27–48

[34] Arisholm, E. and Sjøberg, D.I.K. (2000) Towards a Framework for Empirical Assessment of Changeability Decay. Journal of Systems and Software, Vol. 53, pp. 3–14, September 2000

[35] Karahasanovic, A. and Sjøberg, D.I.K. Visualising Impacts of Change in Evolving Object-Oriented Systems: An Explorative Study., Proceedings of the International Workshop on Graph-Based Tools (GraBaTs'02). 2002. Barcelona, Spain, pp. 22–31

[36] Anda, B. and Sjøberg, D.I.K. (2003) Applying Use Cases to Design versus Validate Class Diagrams – A Controlled Experiment Using a Professional Modelling Tool, *Simula Research Laboratory Technical Report*, No. 2003-01

[37] Prechelt, L., Unger B., Tichy, W.F., Brössler, P., and Votta, L.G. (2001) A Controlled Experiment in Maintenance Comparing Design Patterns to Simpler Solutions, *IEEE Transactions on Software Engineering*, Vol. 27, No. 12, pp. 1134–1144

[38] Syversen, E., Anda, B. and Sjøberg, D.I.K. (2003) An Evaluation of Applying Use Cases to Construct Design versus Validate Design, *Hawaii International Conference on System Sciences* (HICSS-36), Big Island, Hawaii, January 6–9 2003

[39] Briand, L.C., Bunse, C. and Daly, J.W. (2001) A Controlled Experiment for Evaluating Quality Guidelines on the Maintainability of Object-Oriented Designs, *IEEE Transactions on Software Engineering,* Vol. 27, No. 6, pp. 513–530

[40] Karahasanovic, A., Sjøberg, D.I.K. and Jørgensen, M. (2001) Data Collection in Software Engineering Experiments, *Information Resources Management Association Conference,* Software Eng. Track. 2001. Toronto, Ontario, Canada: Idea Group Publishing, pp. 1027–1028

[41] Arisholm, E. Sjøberg, D.I.K., Carelius G.J., and Lindsjørn, Y. (2002) A Web-based Support Environment for Software Engineering Experiments, *Nordic Journal of Computing,* Vol. 9, No. 4, pp. 231–247

Section 2

Knowledge Management for SPI

Software development is a knowledge intensive endeavour requiring various forms of explicit and tacit knowledge. This knowledge is not static and verbs like "knowing" or "learning" are often used to emphasize the action oriented and dynamic properties of knowledge. A critical element of knowledge management for SPI is, therefore, the integration of knowledge creating activities with the "real work" of software development.

This section contains five articles on the experience of applying such knowledge management principles to SPI.

6. *Dingsøyr, T. (2005)* "Post Mortem Reviews: Purpose and Approaches in Software Engineering," *Information and Software Technology,* 47(5):293–303, March 2005.
This chapter shows how post mortem reviews can be used as an efficient knowledge management technique for SPI.

7. *Dingsøyr, T. (2006)* "Value-Based Knowledge Management – the Contribution of Postmortem Reviews and Process Workshops," book chapter in Stephan Biffl, Aybüke Aurum, Barry Boehm, Hakan Erdogmus, and Paul Grünbacher (Eds.): *Value-based Software Engineering,* Springer Verlag, ISBN 3-540-25993-7, pp. 309–326.
This chapter explores the value of workshop techniques for knowledge management.

8. *Dybå, T. (2003)* "A Dynamic Model of Software Engineering Knowledge Creation," book chapter in Aybüke Aurum, Ross Jeffery, Claes Wohlin, and Meliha Ha`ndzic (Eds.): *Managing Software Engineering Knowledge,* Springer Verlag, ISBN 3-540-00370-3, pp. 95–117.
This chapter proposes a dynamic model of software engineering knowledge creation that can be used as foundation for organizational SPI programmes.

9. *Dingsøyr, T. and Røyrvik, E.* (2003) "An Empirical Study of an Informal Knowledge Repository in a Medium-Sized Software Consulting Company," In Lori A. Clarke, Laurie Dillon, and Walter F. Tichy (Eds.): *Proc. 25th International Conference on Software Engineering (ICSE'2003),* Portland, Oregon, USA, 10–12 May, 2003, ACM/IEEE-CS, pp. 84–92.
This chapter provides an empirical study of knowledge management for SPI in a medium-sized company.

10. *Conradi R. and Dybå T. (2001)* "An Empirical study on the utility of formal routines to transfer knowledge and experience," In Volker Gruhn (Ed.): *Proc. 8ᵗʰ European Software Engineering Conference / 9th ACM SIGSOFT Symposium on Foundations of Software Engineering (ESEC/FSE'2001),* Vienna, 10–14 Sept. 2001, ACM, ACM Order no. 594010, ISBN 1-58113-390-1, pp. 268–276.
This chapter provides an empirical study on the tensions between managers and developers regarding the utility of formal routines for SPI.

6

Postmortem Reviews: Purpose and Approaches in Software Engineering

T. Dingsøyr

Abstract: Conducting postmortems is a simple and practical method for organizational learning. Yet, not many companies have implemented such practices, and in a survey, few expressed satisfaction with how postmortems were conducted. In this chapter, we discuss the importance of postmortem reviews as a method for knowledge sharing in software projects, and give an overview of known such processes in the field of software engineering. In particular, we present three lightweight methods for conducting postmortems found in the literature, and discuss what criteria companies should use in defining their way of conducting postmortems.

Keywords: postmortem review, knowledge management, software engineering.

6.1 Introduction

Knowledge management has received much attention in the software engineering field during the past years, partly as a promising field for software process improvement in order to increase quality and decrease costs in software development.

Software process improvement has its roots in general improvement philosophies like total quality management, which has been tailored to software engineering in the Quality Improvement Paradigm [1], and in efforts on standardization like the ISO 9001 and the Software Engineering Institute's Capability Maturity Model [2].

A common factor in knowledge management and in software process improvement is to learn from past successes and failures in order to improve future software development. Experience Factory [3] has been a central term in focusing organizational learning on improving software development processes.

Most companies that develop software organize the development in projects. In the Experience Factory, the projects are seen as the main arena for learning, and experience which appears in the projects is to be shared with other projects.

In this article, we will discuss practical methods to harvest experience from projects that are either completed or have finished a major activity or phase. We refer to these methods as "postmortem reviews" as this is a common term.

The main objective of this article is to highlight the importance of group-processes as a method for knowledge sharing in software projects, and to give an overview of known such processes in the field of software engineering.

In the rest of this article we will discuss some fundamental issues in knowledge management and learning, and then present work on postmortems from the literature. We further present three processes for conducting postmortems in detail, as well as an example of results from one postmortem review using one of the methods. We discuss what such processes should contain: What are requirements for a good postmortem process, who should be invited to a postmortem meeting, should the postmortem involve homework for participants, what should be the role for the facilitator, should the discussions be open or structured, should management participate in the meeting and should the postmortem focus on tacit or explicit knowledge? Finally, we discuss how the processes relate to fundamental issues in knowledge management and learning.

6.1.1 Knowledge Management

A recent improvement trend has been knowledge management, which is related to creating "learning organisations", in software engineering: "learning software organisations".

A learning organization is "an organisation skilled at creating, acquiring, and transferring knowledge, and at modifying its behaviour to reflect new knowledge and insight" [4]. Huber gives some advice on what managers can do to make their organisations more "learning" [5]:

- Learn from experience – systematically capture, store, interpret and distribute relevant experience gathered from projects; and also to investigate new ideas by carrying out experiments.
- Using a computer-based organisational memory – to capture knowledge obtained from experts to spread it through the organisation.

A research area that is linked to organizational learning is research on "communities of practise" as a basis for learning. Wenger writes: "learning is an issue of sustaining the interconnected communities of practise through which an organization knows what it knows" [6].

In the much-cited book on learning organizations, The Fifth Discipline [7], we find further characteristics of learning organizations: the ability of "systems thinking" – to see more than just parts of a system. This often means to involve people in an organisation to develop a "shared vision", some common grounds that make the work meaningful, and also serve to explain aspects that you yourself do not have hands-on experience in. Another way of improving communication in an organisation is to work on "mental models" that support action, "personal mastery"; that people make use of their creativity and abilities. And finally, "group learning", to enhance dialogue and openness in the organisation.

6.1.2 Learning

The process of transferring knowledge between people is usually referred to as "learning". Webster's [8] defines learning as "to acquire knowledge of or skill in by study, instruction, or experience, to become informed of or acquainted with" or "to memorize". In organisational literature, it is often defined as a "purposefully change of action".

What does it mean to say that an organisation as a whole learns? This differs from individual learning in two respects [9]: first, it occurs through shared insight, knowledge and shared models. Second, it is not only based on the memory of the participants in the organisation, but also on "institutional mechanisms" like policies, strategies, explicit models and defined processes. We can call this the "culture" of the organisation. These mechanisms may change over time, which is a form of learning.

Argyris and Schön distinguish between what they call single- and double-loop learning [10] in organisations. Single-loop learning implies a better understanding of how to change (or "tune"), say a process, to remove an error from a product. It is a single feedback-loop from observed effects to making some changes (refinements) that influence the effects. Double-loop learning, on the other hand, is when you understand the factors that influence the effects, and the nature of this influence, what they call the "governing values" [11].

In software engineering, a "learning software organisation" has been defined as an organisation that has to "create a culture that promotes continuous learning and fosters the exchange of experience" [12]. Dybå puts more emphasis on action in his definition: "A software organisation that promotes improved actions through better knowledge and understanding" [13].

In the following sections, we will present two models from the literature on how knowledge is transferred between individuals in organisations, what we can describe as "learning" on an individual level, and "organizational learning" for a community. We do not aim to cover the whole range of theories of learning, but will focus on two approaches that we consider interesting, and has been used in the knowledge management field, namely:

– Learning through participation: communities of practise
– Learning as a conversion process between tacit and explicit knowledge

Learning through Participation: Communities of Practise
The traditional view of learning has been that it best takes place in a setting where you isolate and abstract knowledge and then "teach" it to "students" in rooms free of context. Wenger describes this view of learning as an individual process where for example collaboration is considered a kind of cheating [6]. In his book about

communities of practise, he describes a completely different view: learning as a social phenomenon. A community of practise develops its own "practises, routines, rituals, artifacts, symbols, conventions, stories and histories". This is often different from what you find in work instructions, manuals and the like. In this context, Wenger defines learning as:

- For individuals: learning takes place in engaging in and contributing to a community
- For communities: learning is to refine the practise
- For organisations: learning is to sustain interconnected communities of practise

We find communities of practise everywhere: at work, at home, in volunteer work. And it can be a challenge to sustain such networks of people, for example in turbulent organisations that undergo reorganisation processes.

The work on communities of practise is closely linked to work on situated learning [14].

Learning as a Conversion Process between Tacit and Explicit Knowledge
In the much-cited book "The Knowledge-Creating Company", where Nonaka and Takeuchi explains the success of Japanese companies by their effort at "organizational knowledge creation". They also offer a model of how knowledge is transformed and converted in an organisation [15].

When we discussed the word "knowledge", we divided between tacit and explicit knowledge. Nonaka and Takeuchi claims that knowledge is constantly converted from tacit to explicit and back again as it passes through an organisation. They say that knowledge can be converted from tacit to tacit, from tacit to explicit, or from explicit to either tacit or explicit knowledge as shown in Fig. 6.1.

We now describe each of these four modes of conversion:

- Socialization means to transfer tacit knowledge to tacit through observation, imitation and practice, what has been referred to as "on the job" training. Craftsmanship has usually been learned in this way, where oral communication is either not used or just plays a minor part.

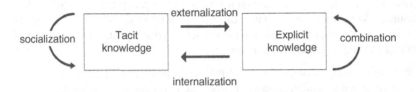

Fig. 6.1. Conversion of knowledge according to Nonaka and Takeuchi. We can imagine knowledge going through all conversion processes in a spiral form as it develops in an organisation

– Internalisation is to take externalised knowledge and convert it into individual tacit knowledge in the form of mental models or technical know-how. "Documents and manuals facilitate the transfer of explicit knowledge to other people, thereby helping them experience the experiences of others indirectly (i.e. 're-experience' them)".

– Externalisation means to go from tacit to explicit knowledge. Explicit knowledge can "take the shapes of metaphors, analogies, concepts, hypotheses or models". This conversion is usually triggered by dialogue or collective reflection, but can also be the result of individual reflection, for example in a writing process.

– Combination is to go from explicit to explicit knowledge, that is, to combine and systemize knowledge from different sources such as documents, meetings, telephone conferences and bulletin boards. Systematizing this kind of explicit knowledge is to reconfigure it by sorting, adding, combining or categorizing the knowledge.

According to Nonaka and Takeuchi, knowledge passes through different modes of conversion in a spiral which makes the knowledge more refined, and also spreads it across different layers in an organisation. Hansen et al. [16] discusses two strategies for knowledge management, one relying on codification, the other relying on sharing tacit knowledge, what they call personalization.

6.1.3 The Project as a Learning Arena

In software engineering, to reuse life cycle experience, processes and products for software development is often referred to as having an "Experience Factory" [3] – a separate organisational entity with responsibility for capturing and reusing experience. This approach has been much cited in the software engineering field. Experience is collected from software development projects, and packaged and stored in an experience base. By packaging, we mean generalising, tailoring and formalising experience so that it is easy to reuse.

The Experience Factory organisation assists software developing projects with earlier experience both in upstart and during execution, and can suggest improvements in the development processes, based on collected experience.

6.2 Postmortem Reviews

We first define what we mean by a "postmortem". Then, we describe postmortem reviews from the software engineering literature, before presenting some methods for conducting postmortem reviews.

6.2.1 What is a "Postmortem"?

By a postmortem, we mean a collective learning activity which can be organised for projects either when they end a phase or are terminated. The main motivation is to reflect on what happened in the project in order to improve future practise – for the individuals that have participated in the project and for the organisation as a whole. The physical outcome of a meeting is a postmortem report.

This type of processes has also been referred to as "project retrospectives", "post mortem analysis", "postproject review", "project analysis review", "quality improvement review", "autopsy review", "Santayana review", "after action reviews" and "touch-down meetings".

Researchers in organizational learning sometimes use the term "reflective practice", which can be defined as "the practice of periodically stepping back to ponder on the meaning to self and others in one's immediate environment about what has recently transpired. It illuminates what has been experienced by both self and others, providing a basis for future action" [17]. This involves uncovering and making explicit results of planning, observation and achieved practice. It can lead to understanding of experiences that have been overlooked in practice.

The two theories of learning that we presented in Sect.6.1.2 put different emphasis on this kind of learning. In the model of Nonaka and Takeuchi, postmortems are a combination of learning through socialization and through externalization. In listening to others you employ socialization and in reflecting and sharing your own experience you externalize your tacit knowledge. Postmortems are also a method for leveraging knowledge from the individual level to the organizational level.

In a community of practise view, postmortems are an arena for the individual to contribute with knowledge to the community, and also for the community to discuss changes of practise on key areas.

In a survey on essential practises in research and development-companies, "learning from post-project audits" are seen as one of the most promising practises that could yield competitive advantage [18].

A survey on post-project reviews in research and development companies show that only one out of five projects received a post-project review [19]. Also, the reviews tend to focus on technical output and bureaucratic measurements. Process-related factors are rarely discussed.

As a knowledge management and software process improvement tool, postmortem reviews are simple to organize. The process focuses on dialogue and discussion which is a central element in knowledge transfer. Von Krogh et al. writes that "it is quite ironic that while executives and knowledge officers persist in focusing on expensive information-technology systems, quantifiable databases, and measurement tools, one of the best means for knowledge sharing and creating knowledge already exists within their companies. We cannot emphasize enough the important part conversations play" [20].

An example of postmortem reviews are "after action reviews" conducted by the US army since after the Vietnam war, focusing on a "professional discussion of an event" to provide insight, feedback and details about the event [21].

Kransdorff [22] criticizes postmortems because people participating do not have an accurate memory, which can lead to disputes. He suggests collecting data during the project, for example through short interviews, in an effort to get more objective material.

6.2.2 Postmortem Reviews in Software Engineering

There are several ways to perform Postmortem Reviews. Apple has used a method [23] which includes designing a project survey, collecting objective project information, conducting a debriefing meeting, a "project history day" and finally publishing the results. At Microsoft they also put much effort into writing "Postmortem reports". These contain discussion on "what worked well in the last project, what did not work well, and what the group should do to improve in the next project" [24]. The size of the resulting document is quite large, "groups generally take three to six months to put a postmortem document together. The documents have ranged from under 10 to more than 100 pages, and have tended to grow in length".

In a book about team software development, Humphrey suggests a way to do postmortems to "learn what went right and wrong, and to see how to do the job better the next time" [25].

A description of another lightweight approach which seeks to elicit experience using interviews, and not a group process, is described by Schneider [26].

Kerth lists a total of 19 techniques to be used in postmortems [27], some focusing on creating an atmosphere for discussion in the project, some for reviewing the past project, some for helping a team identify and embrace change during their next project, and some for dealing with the unique effects of a failed project. Kerth recommends using three days in order to effect a lasting change in the company.

Tiedeman [28] suggests three types of postmortems, related to a waterfall model of software development, one for "planning", one for "design/verification" and one "field postmortem" to provide feedback after the developed system has been in use for some time.

The *Game Developer* magazine publishes postmortems on game development projects in most issues, see for example a postmortem on the game "Aggressive Inline" [29]. The articles contain a brief description about the game developed and the project organisation, and then usually five issues that "went right" and five issues that "went wrong".

6.2.3 Methods for Conducting Postmortem Reviews

We now present three methods for conducting postmortem reviews from the literature. We have selected three methods that can be performed in short time, and are thus suitable even for small and medium-size companies. They can also be a good start for companies wanting more in-depth methods later.

Whitten suggests the following process for conducting postproject reviews [30]:

1. *Declare intent* – the project head should state his or her intention to have a postproject review at the completion of the project, by a letter to all project participants. The letter should describe the postproject review process.
2. *Select participants* – participants from each major participating organizations should be selected: From planning, development, test, publications, performance, usability, module build group, etc. Managers should not participate in the postproject review team, as they are also evaluating the performance of people, and this might hinder topics from surfacing in the process.
3. *Prepare for workshop* – participants are asked to do homework before the workshop: To respond to a set of questions, like "What level of productivity was achieved for your tasks? How did it compare with what you expected?". Many questions can be asked from various areas like staffing, mission objectives, education and training, tools, quality to support from outside groups.
4. *Conduct workshop* – the workshop can last from half a day to two days, and include (a) 10–30 minutes presentations of feedback on the questions from each participant. (b) Construction of a things that "went right" list with the most beneficial items placed at the top. (c) Construction of a "went wrong" list in priority order. (d) Develop proposals that address the problems – either in groups or collectively.
5. *Present results* – results of the workshop are first presented to the project leadership. First and second level of the project leadership should at least be invited. Secondly, the results are presented to all participants in a meeting.
6. *Adopt recommendations* – a postproject review report is completed, which includes information from the workshop and recommendations from the project leadership. The report is either distributed to project leaders or to all personnel. The project leadership is responsible for acting on the committed recommendations.

Collison and Parcell [31] suggest the following steps for organising a retrospect meeting:

1. *Call the meeting* – hold the meeting as soon as possible after the project ends, and make the meeting a physical meeting rather than a videoconference.
2. *Invite the right people* – if a similar project is underway, invite the new project team also. The project leader needs to attend, as well as key members of the project. In the call to attendees, announce the purpose as to "make future projects run more smoothly, by identifying the learning points from this project".
3. *Appoint a facilitator* – appoint one that is not closely involved in the project, but who is outside the line-management structure, as the meeting is to be clearly separate from any personal performance assessment.
4. *Revisit the objectives and deliverables of the project* – find the original criteria for success, and ask whether the project delivered these.
5. *Revisit the project plan or process* – in complex projects, it can be useful to construct a flow chart of what happened to identify tasks, deliverables and decision points.

6. *Ask 'What went well'* – ask "what were the successful steps towards achieving your objective? What went really well in the project?". Ask "why" several times to answers.

7. *Find out why these aspects went well, and express the learning as advice for the future* – identify the success factors and base future recommendations on agreed facts. The facilitator should press for specific, repeatable advice. The facilitator can either organize a conversation through probing questions, or identify issues and then work on each as a team.

8. *Ask 'what could have gone better'?* – ask "what were the aspects that stopped you from delivering even more?". Start by asking the project leader, then go round the room.

9. *Find out what the difficulties were* – identify stumbling blocks and pitfalls to be avoided in the future. Ask "given the information and knowledge we have today, what could we have done better?"

10. *Ensure that the participants leave the meeting with their feelings acknowledged* – ask people to rate the project: "looking back, how satisfied were you with this project, marks out of ten". Follow up by asking "what could have made it a ten for you?".

11. *'What next'* – if the team is going straight into a new project, it is useful to follow the retrospect with a planning session for this.

12. *Recording the meeting* – a well-structured account of the meeting can contain (a) guidelines for the future, (b) history from the project to illustrate the guidelines, (c) names of the people involved, for future reference, and (d) any key artifacts (documents, project plans). Use direct quotes to capture the depth of feeling and to create a summary that is easily read.

Birk et al. have used Postmortem Reviews as a group process, [27, 32–35] where most of the work is done in one meeting lasting half a day. They try to get as many as possible of the persons who have been working in the project to participate, together with two process consultants, one in charge of the Postmortem process, the other acting as a secretary. The goal of this meeting is to collect information from the participants, make them discuss the way the project was carried out, and also to analyse causes for why things worked out well or did not work out. A further description of this method can be found in the "results" section.

The "requirements" for this process is that it should not take much time for the project team to participate, and it should provide a forum for discussing most important experience from the project, together with an analysis of this experience. The main findings are documented in a report.

All participants in a project are invited to a half-day postmortem meeting without any requirements for preparation. Birk et al. use two techniques to carry out the Postmortem Review. For a focused brainstorm on what happened in the project, a technique named after a Japanese ethnologist, Jiro Kawakita [36] – called "the KJ Method" is used. For each of these sessions, the participants are given a set of post-it notes, and asked to write one "issue" on each note. Five notes are handed out to each person. After some minutes, the participants are asked to attach one note to a whiteboard and say why this issue was important. Then the next person presents a note and so on until all the notes are on the whiteboard. The notes are then grouped, and each group is given a new name.

Root Cause Analysis, also called Ishikawa or fishbone-diagrams are used to analyse the causes of important issues. The process leader draws an arrow on a whiteboard indicating the issue being discussed, and attach other arrows to this one like in a fishbone with issues the participants think are causing the first issue. Sometimes, also underlying reasons for some of the main causes are attached as well.

The postmortem meeting has following steps:

1. Introduction: First, the consultants introduced the agenda of the day and the purpose of the postmortem review.
2. KJ session 1: Consultants hand out post-it notes and ask people to write down what went well in the project, hear presentations, group the issues on the whiteboard, and give them priorities.
3. KJ session 2: Consultants hand out post-it notes and asked people to write down problems that appeared in the project, hear presentations, group the issues on the whiteboard, and give them priorities.
4. Root Cause Analysis: The process consultant leading the meeting draws fishbone diagrams for the main issues, both from the things that went well and the things that were problematic.

Birk et al. use a tape recorder during the presentations, and transcribe everything that is said. The consultants write a postmortem report about the project, which contain an introduction, a short description of the project analysed, how the analysis was carried out, and the results of the analysis. The result is a prioritised list of problems and successes in the project. Statements from the meeting are used to present what was said about the issues with highest priority, together with a fishbone diagram to show their causes. In an appendix, everything that was written down on post-it notes during the KJ session is included, as well as a transcription of the presentation of the issues that were used on the post-it notes. Such reports are usually between 10 and 15 pages in length.

The day after the meeting, the consultants present the report to the people involved in the project to gather feedback and do minor corrections.

6.3 Case: Postmortem in a Medium-Sized Company

Above, we have seen different approaches to conducting postmortem reviews. In order to get at better understanding of such reviews, we now present results from one review. First, we present the company, then the project on where the review was carried out, and finally extracts from the postmortem report.

The case reported here was selected because of a wide data collection as a part of an action research [37] project on software process improvement. All written material from the postmortem meeting was photographed, and discussions were recoreded on tape and transcribed. In the project, researchers and industry participants collectively discussed problems, identified possible solutions, tried out a solution and together reflected on the results.

6.3.1 A Satellite Software Company

The company makes software and hardware for stations receiving data from meteorological and Earth observation satellites. Since the company was founded in 1984, they have delivered turnkey ground station systems, consultancy services, feasibility studies, system engineering, training and support. The company has been working with large development projects, both as a prime contractor and as a subcontractor. The company possess a stable and highly skilled staff, many with master's degrees in computer science, mathematics or physics, and have an "engineering culture". Approximately 60 people are working in the company, and the majority is working with software development. Projects are managed in accordance with the European Space Agency PSS-05 standards, and are usually fixed price projects.

The company had problems with estimating the size of new software projects. Many people in the company also felt that they did not transfer enough experience between their software development projects. Every project wrote an "experience report", but these were seldom considered interesting, and were not read very often. To improve this, the company decided to try postmortem reviews at the end of projects.

6.3.2 The Project

We organized a postmortem in one project, which had developed a software system for a satellite that was recording environmental data. The project had developed a module that was to analyze data from this satellite, from European Space Agency specifications. This was a critical project for the company, as it was the first in a line of new services. The project lasted 36 months, and employed four people in the analysis phase, 8–12 people in the design phase, and 5–9 people in testing. The project spent a total of 47, 000 work hours.

The five people in a core-team participated in the postmortem review, including the project manager. This was the first time the people in the project had participated in a postmortem meeting.

6.3.3 The Postmortem

We organised the postmortem as described by Birk et al. in Sect. 6.2.3, and will now present some of the results.

Because the participants in the postmortem meeting knew each other well, we startet with a brief introduction, followed by a KJ brainstorm session to identify issues that went well.

One result from the KJ session on problems that appeared in the project, was three post-it notes grouped together and named "changing requirements". They are

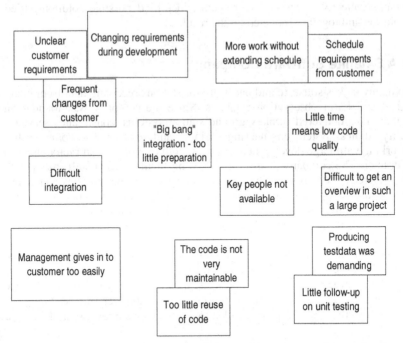

Fig. 6.2. Post-it notes showing some of the problems in a software development project, after a KJ session. The notes are grouped thematically. Each group was later given a new name, for example the three notes in the upper left corner were named "changing requirements"

shown in the upper left corner of Fig. 6.2. When presenting these notes, participants gave the following statements for two of the notes:

"Another thing was changes of requirements during the project: from my point of view – who implemented things, it was difficult to decide: when are the requirements changed so much that things have to be made from scratch? Some wrong decisions were taken that reduced the quality of the software".

"Unclear customer requirements – which made us use a lot of time in discussions and meetings with the customer to get things right, which made us spend a lot of time because the customer did not do good enough work."

When we later brought this issue up again in order to find some of the root causes for "changing requirements", we ended up with the fishbone diagram in Fig. 6.3.

The root causes for the changing requirements, as the people participating in the analysis saw it, was that the requirements were poorly specified by the customer, there were "new requirements" during the project, and the company knew little of what the customer was doing. Another reason for this problem was that documents related to requirements were managed poorly within the company. In Fig. 6.3, we have also listed some sub causes.

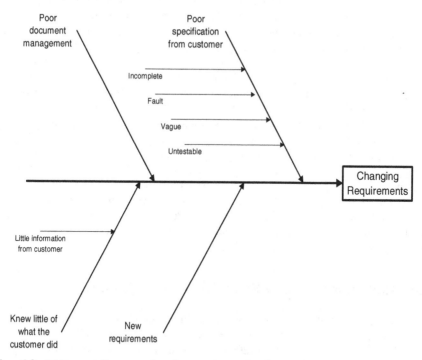

Fig. 6.3. Ishikawa diagram showing main and sub-caused for "Changing Requirements". For example, participants in the postmortem meeting thought that changing requirements was partly a problem because of a poor original specification from the cutstomer. The specification was poor because requirements were incomplete, contained faults, were vague and untestable

After the postmortem meeting was finished, we asked people to state what they thought of the process. All participants had got new insights on the project – were able to see issues from new perspectives. Also, many stated that the way of conducting postmortem was motivating in itself because it was unusual (their normal workday would be to develop software in cell offices and attend normal meetings).

Given the time restrictions to use only half a day, we did not give recommendations to management in the company, other than stating the successes and problems in the project. The report was later discussed in a meeting where all project managers in the company were invited, where they discussed changes in how projects were carried out based on what was learned in this project.

6.4 Summary and Discussion

In a study in nineteen companies across Europe in idustries such as managment consulting, engineering, construction and telecommunications on project-based learning practices, Keegan and Turner [38] found that "project team members frequently do not have the time for meetings, or for sessions to review lessons learned. Often, project team members are immediately reassigned to new projects before they have had time for lessons learned sessions or after action reviews". They did not find a single company where employees expressed satisfaction with the postmortem process. Keegan and Turner do not discuss what kind of postmortem processes existed in the companies, but the main finding was that the processes were seldom used in practice.

We think there is a need for helping software companies choosing simple and practical methods for conducting postmortems, to make it easier to perform postmortems to a higher degree. The benefit of conducting postmortem reviews are mainly that it provides a learning forum where discussions are relevant to the project and to the company. It can also be a way for management to show that they listen to what the employees say, and are willing to discuss improvement efforts.

We will now discuss the three approaches described (some of the discussion points are summarized in Table 6.1) more in depth. In the dicsussion, we use the material from the medium-sized satellite software company for examples.

6.4.1 Requirements for a Good Postmortem Process

Openness, patience, the ability to listen, experimentation with new words and concepts, politeness, the formation of a persuasive argument and courage are some ingredients for a good discussion [20]. In a postmortem this is sought by having a skilled process leader who encourages open dialogue, and should prevent critique of individuals and that dominating people get the most of the meeting time.

Kerth [27] emphasizes the importance of a good atmosphere through the "prime directive": "Regardless of what we discover, we must understand and truly believe that everyone did the best job he or she could, given what was known at the time,

Table 6.1 Summary of selected differences between three methods for conducting postmortem reviews

	Whitten	Collison and Parcell	Birk et al.
who to invite?	from each major participating organization	all project members, possibly new project	all project members
Homework?	Yes	no	no
type of discussion?	Open	open	structured
output?	recommendations	guidelines histories names of people key artifacts	structured report with issues that went well and could be better

his or her skills and abilities, the resources available, and the situation at hand". For longer postmortems, exercises such as "create safety" and "understanding differences in preferences" [27] can be used to further focus on creating a good atmosphere.

In the satellite software case, we only used a short introduction, as team members knew each other well from working closely for a long period of time. Participants spent five hours each, a total of 25 hours. Two facilitators spent ten hours each, giving a total time expense of 45 hours, which is less than 0.1% of the total time spent on the project.

It is difficult to give advice on what is the "optimal" time usage for a postmortem. More time will allow more issues to be discussed deeper, thus increasing the learning effect. The time used for a postmortem should depend on what kind of strategy a company has – codification requires more work than personalisation. It should also depend on the size of the project, as there should be more issues to discuss in a larger project than in a small.

6.4.2 Who to Invite

The three methods described all argue that one should invite a broad audience for a postmortem. Whitten mentions participants from planning, development, test, usability and module build as example roles to invite. Collison and Parcell suggests that people from similar projects that are underway should be invited as well as key members from the project. The method of Birk et al. recommends getting "as many people as possible" from the project to participate.

Looking back at the methods for knowledge sharing, it seems reasonable that all participants in a project can contribute with knowledge that is relevant for future projects through socialization. Inviting many people can also broaden existing communities of practise within an organisation, especially if people from new projects are also invited. If the postmortem is conducted as a lightweight process, the cost will not be high.

Inviting external stakeholders such as a customer will move the focus from internal events to stakeholder relations. This makes it difficult to blame stakeholders that are not present in the postmortem meeting, like the people in the satellite software company partly blame the customer for a poor requirement specification and management for giving into customer demands too easily.

6.4.3 With or Without Homework?

Should a postmortem include "homework" for the attendants? Whitten recommends that all attendees go through a set of questions to prepare themselves for the workshop. Collison and Parcell do not put emphasis on homework, neither do Birk et al. A reason for doing homework is that the learning process is taken over a longer period of time. People who prepare can also easier contribute in an open meeting session. In the method suggested by Birk et al., all participants are given time for reflection during the workshop, to identify main successes and problems. Given a high number of participants, there is a high probability that the most important issues are dealt with, even without homework. But homework can stimulate individual reflection, externalization, but will also require more time.

Another question is whether the facilitator should do homework. With the method of Birk et al., the facilitator does not need to know much about the project, as the main intention is to use techniques to get the participants to reflect. However, if the facilitator style is more intrusive, asking questions that is to stimulate reflection, preparation is necessary.

In the satellite software case, the attendants did not do any homework, and the facilitators had little information about the project – only a short discussion with the project manager before the postmortem review meeting.

6.4.4 Facilitator

All methods recommend using a facilitator for the meeting. The question is what kind of person is the right to use. The project manager can be one option, but this person is so much involved in the project that it can be difficult to allow everyone to express opinions without commenting. Also, issues that people think can be sensitive to the project manager might not appear. It is probably wise to use someone from outside of the project, whom the participants trust. It can also be someone who is external to the company. A benefit of using an external person is that participants have to explain issues to this person more thoroughly than they would to an insider. This can cause different interpretations within the project to be uncovered. The facilitator should also be properly trained in order to follow-up when statements from people are unclear.

6.4.5 Open or Structured Discussion?

Another question is whether to have an open or structured discussion of the experience from the project. An open dialogue as suggested by Whitten is seen as a central learning instrument in the works of Senge. However, this form can easily take a lot of time, and might focus on a limited number of issues. It might also be that these issues are only interesting to the most dominant people taking part in the meeting. Birk et al. are using the KJ method in order to give each participant the possibility to influence equally on the topics. The KJ method is equally strong whether the participants prefer thinking about ideas through quiet introspection or interactive brainstorming.

A drawback with the KJ method can be that it takes time to reach consensus on new names for groups of issues. In the case with the satellite software company, however, this was not timeconsuming. This might be because we did not encourage discussion about whether an issue was a problem or not, we focused on discussing "what would be a proper name for a set of issues that some participants felt were important".

6.4.6 With or Without Management?

Should the management or the project manager take part during a postmortem? We do not think the management should take part in the postmortem, as the intention is to focus on learning, and management also has a role of evaluating employees. This can be a problem as we saw in the satellite software example, where management was blamed for some of the problems in the project. But this kind of problems can be discussed with management after the postmortem meeting is over.

The project manager is very useful to include because this person has a more overall view of the project than the rest of the participants. But this person can also be quick to defend all decisions taken during the project, and make it difficult to have a free exchange of ideas on how to improve the next project. Given a strong facilitator that is aware of the possible problems with the project manager, we think a project manager should be invited to get a more complete overview in the postmortem.

6.4.7 What should be Output?

What should the output of a postmortem be? Whitten describes a list of recommendations that are given to the company management in order to ensure learning in other projects. Collison and Parcell also mention such guidelines for the future, but also mention histories to illustrate the guidelines, names of people involved and key artifacts. They also recommend using direct quotes to capture the depth of feeling and to create a summary that is easily read. Birk et al. suggests writing a report which describes the project, what went well, what went wrong, and the causes of what went well and wrong. They also transcribe much of what is said during the meeting in order to give more context for future readers. If the intention of the postmortem mainly is to come up with improvement suggestions, probably the method described by Whitten is sufficient. But if the intention is to transfer knowledge also to people who did not take part in the postmortem, the method of Birk et. al. is more appropriate.

There are many examples of postmortem reports not being used. Kerth [27] argues that the participants in the postmortem meeting should write the report,

otherwise they loose commitment to the content. The Cross-Affinity Exercise [27] produces proposals for change, which identifies people willing to work on the change.

6.4.8 Learning Focus: Tacit or Explicit Knowledge?

An area related to the previous discussion is what kind of knowledge transfer is intended from the postmortems. If we go back to the two strategies suggested by Hansen et al., we can view postmortems as supporting personalization in that it provides an arena for "reflective practice" where participants can discuss past events.

From a community of practice-view, a postmortem can be one arena to engage in and to contribute to the community. The main aim of the postmortem is to discuss changes that will lead to refined practice

We can also see postmortems as an attempt to codify knowledge from projects, where the main output is the report, which should provide insight to other project teams (as a part of systematically capturing, storing, interpreting and distributing relevant experience from projects as seen as an important learning mechanism by Huber [39]).

How postmortems are used should depend on what strategy the company has. Smaller companies should focus on sharing tacit knowledge, as a codification strategy is expensive. Larger companies are more dependent of codified knowledge, and should invest more in the documentation.

6.5 Conclusion and Future Work

We have investigated postmortem reviews from a knowledge management perspective, and presented three methods for conducting postmortems from the literature. We have also presented example results from a postmortem report.

The methods vary in several dimensions. They put different emphasis on who to invite, how to prepare, how to facilitate the postmortem meeting, how to structure discussions, and what the written output of the postmortem is to be.

Companies wanting to conduct postmortems should decide on the method to use after what general strategy they have for knowledge management. They should also decide whether they want to focus purely on internal project affairs, or also to include relations to project stakeholders. A general advice is to use people who are not directly involved in the project to facilitate the postmortem meeting.

Acknowledgement

I am grateful to many people for having discussions on postmortem reviews, particularly the research group at SINTEF ICT: Nils Brede Moe, Tore Dybå, Geir Kjetil Hanssen, Hans Westerheim and Tor Erlend Fægri. I would further like to thank Tor Stålhane at the Norwegian University of Science and Technology, Kevin Desouza from the University of Illinois, Max von Zedtwitz from Tsinghua University and especially Norman Kerth for comments on this article.

This work was conducted through the Software Process Improvement based on Knowledge and Experience (SPIKE) project, supported by the Research Council of Norway.

References

[1] Basili, V.R. (1985) "Quantitative Evaluation of Software Engineering Methodology," *Proc. of the First Pan Pacific Computer Conference*, vol. 1, pp. 379–389, Melbourne, Australia, 10–13 September 1985 (also available as Technical Report, TR-1519, Dept. of Computer Science, University of Maryland, College Park, July 1985.)

[2] Paulk, M.C., Weber, C.V., Curtis, B., and Chrissis, M.B. (1995) *The Capability Maturity Model: Guidelines for Iimproving the Software Process*, Addison-Wesley, Boston

[3] Basili, V.R., Caldiera, G., and Rombach, H.D. (1994) The Experience Factory, in Marciniak, J.J. (Ed.) *Encyclopedia of Software Engineering*, Wiley, pp. 469–476

[4] Garvin, D. (1993) Building a Learning Organization, *Harvard Business Review* pp.78–91

[5] Huber, G. (1996) Organizational Learning: A Guide for Executives in Technology-Critical Organizations, *International Journal on Technology Management*, Special Issue on Unlearning and Learning for Technological Innovation 11, pp. 821–832

[6] Wenger, E. (1998) *Communities of Practise: Learning, Meaning and Identity*, Cambridge University Press, Cambridge,

[7] Senge, P.M. (1990) *The Fifth Discipline: The Art & Practise of The Learning Organisation*, Century Business

[8] *Webster's Encyclopedic Unabridged Dictionary of the English Language*, (1989) Gramercy Books, NY

[9] Stata, R. (1996) Organizational Learning: The Key to Management Innovation, in Starkey, K., (Ed.) *How Organizations Learn*, Thomson Business Press, London, pp. 316–334

[10] Argyris, C. and Schön, D.A. (1996) *Organizational Learning II: Theory, Method and Practise*, Addison-Wesley

[11] Argyris, C. (1990) *Overcoming Organizational Defences: Facilitating Organizational Learning*, Prentice Hall

[12] Feldmann, R.L. and Althoff, K.-D. (2001) *On the Status of Learning Software Organisations in the Year 2001*, Learning Software Organizations Workshop, 2001, pp. 2-6, in K. D. Althoff, R.L. Feldmann, W. Miller (Eds.): Advances in Learning Software Organizations, Third International Workshop, LSO 2001, Kaiserslautern, Germany, September 12-13, 2001, Proceedings

[13] Dybå, T. (2001) Enabling Software Process Improvement: An Investigation on the Importance of Organizational Issues, Dr. ing thesis thesis, *Department of Computer and Information Science*, Norwegian University of Science and Technology, Trondheim, 2001, pp. 332, ISBN 82-471-5371-8

[14] Lave, J. and Wenger, E. (1991) *Situated Learning*, Cambridge University Press

[15] Nonaka, I. and Takeuchi, H. (1995) *The Knowledge-Creating Company*, Oxford University Press

[16] Hansen, M.T., Nohria, N., and Tierney, T. (1994) What's Your Strategy for

Managing Knowledge?, in: *Harvard Business Review on Organizational Learning*, Harvard Business School Press, Boston, pp. 61– 86

[17] Raelin, J.A. (2001) Public Reflection as the Basis of Learning, 32, Management Learning 11–30

[18] Menke, M.M. (1997) Managing R&D for Competitive Advantage, Research Technology Management 40, 40–42

[19] Zedtwitz, M. (2002) Organizational Learning Through Post-Project Reviews in R&D Management, 32, 255–268

[20] Krogh, G.v., Ichijo, K., and Nonaka, I. (2000) *Enabling knowledge creation*, Oxford University Press, NY

[21] Townsend, P.L. and Gebhart, J.E. (1999) *How Organizations Learn*, Crisp Publications

[22] Kransdorff, A. (1996) Using the Benefits of Hindsight – The Role of Post-Project Analysis, IEEE Software, 3, pp. 11–15

[23] Collier, B., DeMarco, T., and Fearey, P. (1996) A Defined Process for Project Post Mortem Review, 13, pp. 65–72.

[24] Cusomano, M.A. and Selby, R.W. (1995) *Microsoft Secrets – How the World's Most Powerful Software Company Creates Technology, Shapes Markets, and Manages People*, The Free Press

[25] Humphrey, W.S. (1999) The Postmortem, in *Introduction to the Team Software Process*, Addison-Wesley Longman, Reading, MA, pp. 185–196

[26] Schneider, K. (2000) LIDs: A Light-Weight Approach to Experience Elicitation and Reuse, *Second International Conference on Product Focused Software Process Improvement*, PROFES 2000, 2000, Springer LNCS 1840, pp. 407– 424

[27] Kerth, N.L. (2001) *Project Rretrospectives: A Handbook for Team Reviews*, Dorset House Publishing, NY

[28] Tiedeman, M.J. (1990) Post-Mortems – Methodology and Experiences, *IEEE Journal of on Selected Areas in Communications*, 8

[29] Condon, R. (2002) *Postmortem: Z-Axis's Aggressive Inline, Game Developer*, pp. 42–49

[30] Whitten, N. (1995) *Managing Software Development Projects: Formula for Success*, Wiley

[31] Collison,C. and Parcell, G. (2001) *Learning to Fly: Practical Lessons from One of the World's Leading Knowledge Companies*, Capstone Pub

[32] Birk, A., Dingsøyr, T., and Stålhane, T. (2002) Postmortem: Never Leave a Project Without It, *IEEE Software, Speciallissue on Knowledge Management in Software Engineering*, 19, pp. 43–45

[33] Dingsøyr, T., Moe, N.B., and Nytrø, Ø. (2001) Augmenting Experience Reports with Lightweight Postmortem Reviews, in Bomarius, F. and Komi-Sirviö, S., (Eds), *Third International Conference on Product Focused Software Process Improvement*, Springer Berlin Heidelberg New York, Kaiserslautern, Germany, pp. 167–181

[34] Stålhane, T., Dingsøyr, T., Moe, N.B., and Hanssen, G.K. (2001) *Post Mortem – An Assessment of Two Approaches*, Proc. European Software Process Improvement Conference (EuroSPI'2001), 10–12, October 2001, Limerick Institute of Technology, Limerick, Ireland, (Also available as

SU-report 15/2001, Dept. of Computer and Information Science, Norwegian University of Science and Technology, Trondheim, Norway).

[35] Dybå, T., Dingsøyr, T., and Moe, N.B. (2004) *Process Improvement in Practice – A Handbook for IT Companies*, Kluwer, Boston

[36] Scupin, R. (1997) The KJ Method: A Technique for Analyzing Data Derived from Japanese Ethnology, *Human Organization*, 56, pp. 233–237

[37] Greenwood, D.J. and Levin, M. (1998) *Introduction to Action Research*, Sage Publications

[38] Keegan, A. and Turner, J.R. (2001) Quantity versus Quality in Project-Based Learning Practises, *Management Learning*, 32, pp. 77–98

[39] Huber, G.P. (1991) Organizational Learning: The Contributing Processes and the Literatures, *Organizational Science*, 2 , pp. 88–115

7

Value-Based Knowledge Management – the Contribution of Postmortem Reviews and Process Workshops

T. Dingsøyr

Abstract: Knowledge management has been suggested as a tool to facilitate SPI Knowledge management recognizes knowledge in forms of explicit and tacit knowledge. This chapter discusses two group techniques, postmortem reviews and process workshops which can be used to elicit personal preferences and beliefs. The chapter presents the techniques and examples of results, and argue on the value of tacit knowledge in the form of personal preferences and beliefs.

Keywords: tacit knowledge, postmortem reviews, process workshop, knowledge management, group process, software engineering.

7.1 Introduction

Software development is an area with a history of cost and time overruns. Many solutions have been proposed to solving problems during the years. Knowledge management has been one area that has been discussed recently [2, 15]. To develop software is a typical example of what Drucker has called "knowledge work"; where "value is (...) created by 'productivity' and 'innovation'" [12]. Knowledge is the only scarce resource in software development – not other "means of production" like computer hardware and software, office buildings or capital.

There has been much work on knowledge management in software engineering, or learning software organizations. However, much of the work has concentrated on information technology to support knowledge-sharing, where few studies indicate impact on software development practice [10]. One reason for this might be that the knowledge represented in the tools has not had sufficient value to the users. In this chapter, we discuss two techniques that rely on group processes to share knowledge, are lightweight and focus mainly on documenting only the knowledge that the contributors see as having the greatest value.

Software development is usually performed in projects. Projects are time-limited, producing one-time outputs are "non-repetitive in nature and involve considerable application of knowledge, judgment and expertise" [6]. To better man-age knowledge in projects we will present and discuss postmortem reviews [9] as a method for analyzing past projects for the benefit of future projects.

Another important concept in software development is development processes. These are often general processes, bought in or developed in-house, and are usually tailored to suit either specific projects or types of projects. We will discuss a method for defining work processes for software companies, called process workshops [11]. The output of such workshops are usually electronic process guides [19] available on a company Intranet which provides a "how to" reference manual for people involved in projects.

The common denominator for these two techniques is that they rely on group processes using some of the same brainstorming techniques. We will later discuss the impact of brainstorming techniques on group effectiveness.

We believe good techniques for developing the knowledge required in projects through postmortems and developing the cross-project knowledge in processes can add substantial value to a software company – what some call increasing the intellectual capital of the company.

In terms of value-based software engineering, this chapter partly addresses what Boehm [5] calls "Value-based people management", which includes "stakeholder teambuilding and expectations management", but mainly focusing on the internal affairs in the project. It also presents methods that are alternatives to the Experience Factory [3], which is suggested as a tool for value-based monitoring and control of projects and organizations. Postmortem reviews and process workshops are lightweight (or "agile") methods that relies much on sharing knowledge orally, and consumes little time. A postmortem can be carried out in four hours, and running a workshop on a process such as "blastoff" can be carried out in less.

The rest of this chapter is organized as follows: In the next section we define knowledge and discuss broad issues in how knowledge can be managed. We introduce postmortem reviews and process workshops as group processes to work on project and process knowledge from software companies. We then present an action research study from a company where we used postmortem reviews and from another company where we used a process workshop. In the discussion section, we discuss how these techniques can assist in learning and eliciting knowledge. We also discuss what kind of value this knowledge can be seen as to the organization. We conclude with what we see as implications for practice for software companies.

7.2 Managing Knowledge

Davenport and Prusak [7] define knowledge as: "a fluid mix of framed experience, values, contextual information, and expert insight that provides a framework for evaluating and incorporating new experiences and information. It originates and is applied in the minds of knowers. In organizations, it often becomes embedded not only in documents or repositories but also in organizational routines, processes, practices, and norms."

We often divide knowledge into two types, tacit and explicit knowledge. By tacit knowledge [18] we mean knowledge that a human is unable to express, but is guiding the behavior of the human, like much of the organizational routines, norms, practices and inner beliefs. Webster's dictionary defines tacit as "under-stood without being openly expressed" [24]. Explicit knowledge is knowledge that we can represent, or "codify", for example in documents and repositories.

Nonaka and Takeuchi claim that tacit knowledge can be transferred between people through a process called socialization, which can involve observation and discussion [17]. Newcomers will typically need to spend time with others in an organization to get into the routines, norms and practices that exist.

When knowledge is articulated so that it can be represented in text or pictures, we say that knowledge is externalized. Brainstorming can be one technique to facilitate articulation of knowledge in order to share how "things are done".

Important assets for software companies are the employee's knowledge, and the routines that exist in the company. Often, little of this knowledge is codified, but exists in the heads of the employees and in work practices.

In order to spread knowledge in an organization from individuals to groups, we depend on what has been called "organizational learning". This differs from individual learning in two respects [22]: first, it occurs through shared insight, knowledge and shared models. Second: it is not only based on the memory of the participants in the organization, but also on "institutional mechanisms" like policies, strategies, explicit models and defined processes (we can call this the "culture" of the organization). These mechanisms may change over time, what we can say is a form of learning.

Hanssen et al. [14] define two strategies for knowledge management. "Codification" is to depend on explicit, codified knowledge, typically in databases – which require heavily investments in information technology. The competitive strategy for companies choosing codification is to "provide high-quality, reliable and fast information systems implementation by reusing codified knowledge". The other strategy is referred to as "personalization", which depends on the tacit knowledge in the company – the strategy involves developing networks to link people to share tacit knowledge. The competitive strategy for companies choosing personalization is to "provide creative, analytically rigorous advice on high-level strategic problems by channeling individual experience".

Both these strategies apply to software companies, but the research on knowledge management in software engineering has mainly been concentrated on information technology support for codification [10]. We will now present two group processes to promote sharing of knowledge, that mainly support the personalization strategy, namely postmortem reviews and process workshops.

7.2.1 Postmortem Reviews

Postmortem reviews are processes organized when projects are completed in order to discuss what can be learned from the project [9]. One way to organize postmortems [4] is to invite all project participants, and organize a postmortem meeting where a facilitator uses two techniques for first identifying issues, and then for analyzing the causes of the issues with the highest priority.

For a focused brainstorm on what happened in the project, a technique named after a Japanese ethnologist, Jiro Kawakita – can be used [20], called "the KJ Method". The technique involves giving participants a set of "post-it" notes, and ask them to write one "issue" on each. After some minutes, the first participant presents a note by attaching it to a whiteboard and saying why this issue was important. Then the next person would present a note and so on until all the notes are on the whiteboard. The notes are then grouped and renamed. This is done for "what went well" in the project, and for "what did not go well". This technique leaves a set of issues in both categories, and usually the most important ones are selected by allowing all participants to vote. The most important issues are then analyzed using the next technique. Usually, it is the whole team who participates in deciding what is most important. One way of organizing this is to give each participant two votes, which can be placed on the categories the voter thinks were most important in this project, or the categories the voter thinks they are most likely to influence in the next project.

Root Cause Analysis (also called Ishikawa or fishbone-diagrams) [23] can be used to analyze the causes of important issues. We draw an arrow on a whiteboard indicating the issue being discussed, and attach other arrows to this one like in a fishbone with issues the participants think caused the first issue. Sometimes, we also think about what was the subcauses for some of the causes and attached those as well.

As a group process, the postmortem allows everyone participating in a project to know what other participants thought were important issues. It also allows for both positive and negative criticism of actions taken, processes followed, and products delivered from the project.

7.2.2 Process Workshops

Process workshops [1, 11] are made in order to discuss how work is to be carried out in the organization. The output is descriptions of "best practice" in an area, for example in software development. A typical process workshop consists of the following steps:

1. Identify activities. Find the main activities of the process using a group brainstorm (KJ process).
2. Define the sequence of activities: Take the activities from the previous phase and make a sticker for each. Place them on the activities-field of the process work-sheet, where time goes from left to the right. Find a suitable workflow between the activities.

3. Define input and output: Find the documents or artifacts that must be available (and possible preconditions that exist) to start the process, and the documents (and possible post conditions) that mark the end of the process. Use stickers with other colors than for the activities to mark input and output, and attach them to process worksheet on the wall alongside the activities. Conditions that must be satisfied to begin or exit the process can be described in checklists.
4. Define roles: Find the roles (developer, project leader, manager, etc.) that should contribute to each activity – and define responsibilities.
5. Find related documents: Identify documents that already exist in the company, and new documents that could be helpful in carrying out the activities. Such documents can be templates, checklists and good examples of input or output documents.

The result of a process workshop is a draft process guide based on a minute of the workshop. The next step would be to assign someone the task of preparing a more readable process guide based on the first draft. In the end, the process guide is a workflow-oriented document available on the company Intranet. This is usually a tool which can be used voluntarily, and is intended to assist people in developing software effectively.

7.3 Case: Knowledge Products from a Postmortem Review and a Process Workshop

We present an example postmortem review from a company we will refer to as "Delta", and a process workshop in another company "Gamma". Both techniques were used in an action research project where researchers and company representatives tried out techniques, and together reflected on the results.

7.3.1 An Example Postmortem

This postmortem was done on a project to develop a web-based ticket ordering system for a major transport company in Norway. The project was critical for the transport company, as it introduced fundamental changes to their revenue management process. The project team from Delta at the end of the project consisted of eight people, who all took part in the postmortem meeting (the project had involved three more people earlier, but they were removed from the project because of costs). The company that was running the software project is a large software house with approximately 500 employees.

The postmortem analysis followed the approach described above [5] except for starting with a timeline-exercise [16], as the project had lasted for almost two years. This exercise was done by asking all participants to remember key events, and write down the names of the events on stickers and attach them to grey paper on a wall, rectangular stickers for events and round stickers for dates. Important

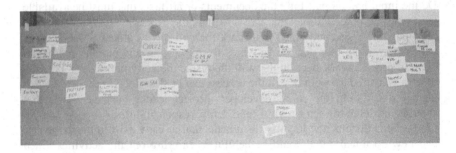

Fig. 7.1. Timeline for the project. Important events are written on the rectangular stickers, and dates on the round stickers

events in this project were tasks like: choosing platform, deciding on coding standard, choosing the database, intense work period, etc. The timeline produced is shown in Fig. 7.1. Participants were asked to write down up to four positive and negative experiences they faced during the project. These notes were then put on a whiteboard and grouped into categories or themes. Issues that went well were: team-spirit, competence development, human competence, will and ability to solve problems, customer responsibility, good products and improved customer relation. Issues that were problematic were: testing, technical investments, lack of knowledge, and immature technology.

We will now analyze two of the issues that went well and two that did not work out well more in detail. We will show excerpts of what people said about the issues, and what we found to be possible causes in this project.

Team-spirit: "If you look at the people involved in this project, you see that we are very different, but are anyway able to work well together. I think that has been unbelievable, I see so many other places that this does not work", "I would also like to emphasize that it has been very nice socially in the project, although there have not been much [activities] after working hours ...professionally there has been people whom you could ask all the way, people have not had enough with their own problems".

Testing: "The greatest mistake we did is that we said 'no' to more load testing before we went to production", "I think we ought to have done more automatic testing earlier, and should have done load testing earlier. We also should have had a better understanding of what load testing means – we have at least two different views of it".

To determine the contributing factors for critical issues, we did root cause analysis, using fishbone diagrams [23]. In the root-cause analysis, main causes for team-spirit were found to be good mix of people, solution-oriented people, co-location of the project team, ownership to solutions and that it was easy to have a good overview of the group. Similarly, we found the following reasons for problems with testing: lack of automated tests, difference in development and production environment, test process was not followed, and testing did not measure the right features. Upon completion of the postmortem analysis, two facilitators wrote

Fig. 7.2. Mind map showing reasons for issue "competence development"

an eighteen-page report, which was organized with an introduction giving background on the project and the purpose of the postmortem, which was to share experience from the project in a structured manner. Then, the report explains how the work was done, which activities were performed during the postmortem meeting. The results are presented as seven issues that went well, and then the most important (after voting) were described in more detail with quotes from transcripts of the postmortem meeting. In this report we used mind maps to document root causes for the main issues as in Fig. 7.2 (fishbone diagrams were used during the postmortem meeting).

The seven issues that did not work out well are described in the same manner as the issues that went well. A further discussion of this postmortem can be found in [8].

7.3.2 An Example Process Workshop

The satellite software company Gamma, where a series of process workshops were performed [11] delivers turnkey ground station systems, consultancy, feasibility studies, system engineering, training, and support. The company has been working with large development projects, both as a prime contractor and as a subcontractor.

Customers range from universities to companies like Lockheed Martin and Alcatel to governmental institutions like the European Space Agency and the Norwegian Meteorological institute.

Most of the software systems that are developed are running on Unix, many on the Linux operating system.

The company possesses a stable and highly skilled staff, many with master's degrees in computer science, mathematics or physics, and have what we can describe as an "engineering culture". Approximately 60 people are working in the company, and the majority is working with software development. Projects are managed in accordance with quality routines fulfilling the European Space Agency PSS-05 standards and ISO 9001–2000.

The company had an extensive quality system, but the system was cumbersome to use because of the size – and because it existed partly on file and partly on paper. As a part of being certified according to ISO 9001–2000, the company decided to document all main processes in the company.

In a process workshop on the initiation phase of projects, we identified three sub-processes: "offer", "follow-up" and "blast off".

As the initiation of projects is an interface between different parts of the organization, it was important to bring together people from marketing, quality assurance and the development department. We started the workshop by giving a 15-min presentation of what we were going to do, and put a large sheet with a figure of the process worksheet (as in Fig. 7.3) on the wall – one for each process that would be discussed in the meeting.

For each sub-process we wanted to define, "offer", "follow-up" and "blast-off", we went through the steps mentioned earlier, to identify activities, define the sequence, and define input/output, roles and related documents. The main activities identified in this step for the "blast-off" sub-process were:

– appoint project manager
– organize "Handover meeting"
– first project analysis

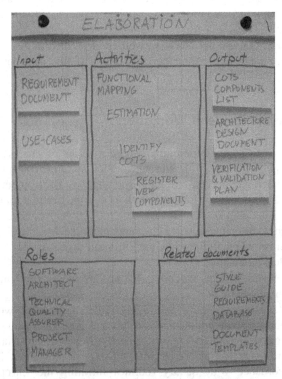

Fig. 7.3. A process worksheet with input, activities, output, roles and related documents defined

- Allocate resources
- Prepare for kick-off meeting
- Internal kick-off

We brainstormed on which roles should contribute in each activity and found the following roles for the "blast off" phase: project manager, quality assurance, development responsible, technical responsible, product committee, bid manager, purchasing manager and logistics expert.

Related documents: We identified documents that either already existed in the company, or new documents that would be helpful in carrying out the activities. Such documents were templates, checklists and good examples of input or output documents

We found it helpful to ask the people who participated in the process workshop to read the result and comment on it (see [21] for an example of such a technique in requirements inspection). We assigned the most typical roles that were involved in the processes to people – and asked them to find if there was information that was lacking or irrelevant for this role in the description. This reading resulted in a number of modifications and clarifications on the process description.

Finally, two people in the company were responsible for making a draft process guide, based on the overall description of the processes which are developed in the workshop. Each activity was then described in much more detail than what appeared in the workshop minutes – the participants gave feedback on these before the processes were implemented in the process guide, as shown in Fig. 7.4

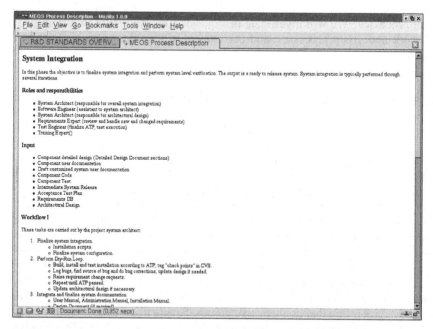

Fig. 7.4. A screenshot of a part of the resulting electronic process guide on the company company Intranet

The main part of the final process guide is the description of the activities (called "workflow" in Fig. 7.4). For the example shown in the figure, the subprocess for system integration lists the following initial activities: "1. Finalize system integration (installation scripts, finalize system configuration), 2. Perform dry-run loop (build and test installation, log and correct bugs, raise requirement changes, update architecture design if necessary)…"

7.4 Discussion

We have described two methods for conducting postmortem reviews and process workshops, both relying on group processes as a central element. The methods produce discussions which should lead to reflections amongst participants, and some of the main discussion points are documented in minutes. It is the participants who decide what are the most important issues to concentrate on in analysis and in documentation.

In software engineering, the critical elements are how many hours it takes to develop the software, that the customer gets the right functionality, and that the software system has the desired quality. Deciding to invest in knowledge management should be because of a belief that the investment will lead to better efficiency and effectiveness in software development; better understanding of customer requirements, greater insight in factors that lead to high or low quality of software.

In this context we ask, what is the effect of managing knowledge through group processes? We will investigate this question by examining studies of project work and group processes, and use examples from the cases of Delta and Gamma.

7.4.1 Group Processes and Group Effectiveness

To what extent can management of knowledge influence the effectiveness of software development? From studies of team effectiveness we find that team members rate the performance of the team high if the team has "healthy internal processes, such as collaboration and resolution conflict" [6]. We also find that group cohesiveness – how united the team is, is related to performance [6]. A survey article on brainstorming research [13] cite several brainstorming studies that report satisfaction with the group (increased cohesiveness) as an outcome of a brainstorming session. Also, the survey reports that there is "abundant evidence that nominal groups (i.e., groups of individuals working together independently, but in the presence of another) outperform interactive groups (i.e. groups where ideas are generated through face to face discussions) in both the quality and the quantity of ideas generated in brainstorming sessions". Reasons why nominal groups outperform interactive groups are that in interactive groups, having to state ideas orally makes it possible for only one person to present an idea at the time. Also, fear of negative evaluation from group members and "free riding" – reducing effort when individual contribution is not identifiable has been suggested.

In the example from Delta, the group agreed on seven categories of issues that went well, and four categories of issues that did not work out well.

The results from the fields of research above indicates that group processes using brainstorming techniques such as the KJ process used in postmortems and process workshops has a positive effect on the performance of the participants. Also, we think that techniques for postmortem reviews can be seen as a "healthy internal process" – that can lead to conflict resolution and better collaboration because team members get better insight into other team member's views. Having a post-mortem process can then lead to a perception of better effectiveness in the team.

The postmortem at Delta led to praise of the project team in the session on issues that went well. Also, agreeing on the four issues that did not work out well, and their importance is something we can see as a "healthy" internal process where criticism is allowed, and critical opinions discussed.

In the process workshop at Gamma, the discussion on the blast-off phase involved people from different parts of the company: from the marked and software development departments. Sharing views on the interface between the departments are likely to lead to better understanding of others work, and a lower risk of cooperation problems later.

Studies of group performance, does however, state that this is perceived differently by internal project members and external stakeholders such as managers: "Team members tend to rate the team's performance high if the team has engaged in healthy internal processes, such as collaboration and resolution conflict. Managers ... rate a team highly according to more external factors like the amount of communication the group has with external agents" [6]. However, a high perception of effectiveness is likely to lead to better motivation within the team.

Another argument for the suggested group processes are findings on the importance of conducting work in the project according to tailored processes. The survey on team effectiveness report that "projects where the coordination mechanism fit the newness of the project resulted in products that were higher in quality, were more likely to achieve sales objectives, and reached their break-even point sooner than those projects whose coordination mechanisms were too bureaucratic or too informal given the newness of the product". Also, the survey report that "when team design and processes are properly fit to product characteristics, performance can be high, but when they are not so, performance will suffer". Organizing process workshops in a company is a way to make the work processes more adapted to the real problems in the company than using a more general available model.

In addition to the implications on effectiveness we have discussed, we have a possible effect of sharing the knowledge with other projects in the company who might be in similar situations and could benefit from avoiding mistakes or reusing work products. The example postmortem from Delta reports on problems with testing: "I think we ought to have done more automatic testing earlier, and should have done load testing earlier" was a statement from one participant. This was probably not something that was new to the project team. But that it was stated and generally agreed on that this should have been handled differently in this project will probably lead to that the people who participated in the postmortem are more likely to do something about it in their next project than if the belief was not discussed.

7.4.2 Group Processes to Improve Product Quality

In order to improve product quality, there are two possible effects from postmortems and process workshops. There have been many claims in software engineering about the relationship between development process and product quality. In order to ensure that the process influences quality, the development process of course needs to take place in action – not only be described. Process workshops are a method to discuss the work processes, which could then influence how the processes are used in practice. We have not found evidence for this claim in the software engineering literature, but we are currently working with research on the hypothesis that process workshops – which means user involvement, leads to a higher degree of process conformance.

Another possibility to improve quality comes from the postmortem – to ensure that problems that happened in producing one product does not happen again when producing something similar. In the example from Delta, testing is one issue which is likely to be dealt with otherwise after the project postmortem.

An experiment on group processes for software effort estimation reports that groups outperform individuals in making less optimistic and more realistic estimations of required effort [16].

7.5 Conclusion and Further Work

We have discussed two techniques to work with software process improvement, namely postmortem reviews and process workshops, and argued that these methods focus both on sharing tacit knowledge between participants as well as documenting knowledge that can be shared in a broader context in the company. We have argued on the value of the knowledge by examining work on project team effectiveness, brainstorming research and studies of the integration of domain and technical knowledge, and have used these findings to argue that the group processes involved in postmortems and process workshops can lead to more efficient project work, more satisfied project team and a higher probability of keeping the project schedule and budget.

Acknowledgement

I am very grateful to colleagues at SINTEF ICT, software engineering group for discussions about postmortem reviews and process workshops: Tore Dybå, Tor Erlend Fægri, Geir Kjetil Hanssen, Nils Brede Moe and Hans Westerheim. This work was supported by the SPIKE project, partially funded by the Research Council of Norway.

References

[1] Ahonen, J.J., Forsell, M., and Taskinen, S.-K. (2002) A Modest but Practical Software Process Modeling Technique for Software Process Improvement, *Software Process Improvement and Practice*, No. 1, Vol. 7, pp. 33–44

[2] Aurum, A., Jeffery, R., Wohlin, C., and Handzic, M. (2003) *Managing Software Engineering Knowledge.*Springer Berlin Heidelberg New York

[3] Basili, V.R., Caldiera, G., and Rombach, H.D. (1994) The Experience Factory, in *Encyclopedia of Software Engineering*, Vol. 1, J. J. Marciniak, Ed.: John Wiley, 1994, pp. 469–476.

[4] Birk, A, Dingsøyr,T, and Stålhane,T, (2002) Postmortem: Never Leave a Project Without It, *IEEE Software, Special Issue on Knowledge Management in Software Engineering*, No. 3, Vol. 19, pp. 43–45

[5] Boehm, B. (2003) Value-Based Software Engineering, *ACM SIGSOFT Software Engineering Notes*, No. 2, Vol. 28

[6] Cohen, S.G. and Bailey, D.E. (1997) What Makes Teams Work: Group Effectiveness Research from the Shop Floor to the Executive Suite, *Journal of Management*, No. 3, Vol. 23, pp. 239–290, 1997

[7] Davenport, T.H. and Prusak, L. (1998) *Working Knowledge: How Organizations Manage What They Know*, Harvard Business School Press, ISBN 0-87584-655-6

[8] Desouza, K., Dingsøyr, T., and Awazu, Y. (2005) Experiences with Conducting Project Postmortems: Reports vs. Stories and Practitioner Perspectives, *Hawaii International Conference on System Sciences (HICSS 38)*

[9] Dingsøyr, T. Post Mortem: Purpose and Approaches in Software Engineering, *Information and Software Technology*, Accepted for publication.

[10] Dingsøyr, T. and Conradi, R. (2002) A Survey of Case Studies of the Use of Knowledge Management in Software Engineering, *International Journal of Software Engineering and Knowledge Engineering*, No. 4, Vol. 12, pp. 391–414

[11] Dingsøyr, T., Moe, N.B., Dybå, T., and Conradi, R. (2005) A Workshop-Oriented Approach for Defining Electronic Process Guides – A Case Study, in *Software Process Modelling, Kluwer International Series on Software Engieering*, Acuña, S.T. and Juristo, N. (Eds.) Boston: Kluwer Academic Publishers, pp. 187–205

[12] Drucker, P.F. (1999) The coming of the New Organization, in *Harvard Business Review on Knowledge Management*, Harvard Business School Press

[13] Faure, C. (2004) Beyond Brainstorming: Effects of Different Group Procedures on Selection of Ideas and Satisfaction with the Process, *Journal of Creative Behaviour*, No. 1, Vol. 38, pp. 13–34

[14] Hansen, M.T., Nohria, N., and Tierney, T. (1999) What is Your Strategy for Managing Knowledge?, *Harvard Business Review*, No. 2, Vol. 77, pp. 106–116

[15] Lindvall, M. and Rus, I. (2002) Knowledge Management in Software Engineering, *IEEE Software*, No. 3, Vol. 19, pp. 26–38

[16] Moløkken-Østvold, K.J. and Jørgensen, M. (2004) Group Processes in Software Effort Estimation, *Journal of Empirical Software Engineering*, No. 4, Vol. 9, pp. 315–334

[17] Nonaka, I. and Takeuchi, H. (1995) *The Knowledge-Creating Company*, Oxford University Press, ISBN 0-18.509269-4

[18] Polanyi, M. (1967) *The Tacit Dimension*, Vol. 540, Garden City, NY: Doubleday, ISBN 0-385-06988-x

[19] Scott, L., Carvalho, L., Jeffery, R., D'Ambra, J., and Becker-Koernstaedt, U. (2002) Understanding the Use of an Electronic Process Guide, *Information and Software Technology*, Vol. 44, pp. 601–616

[20] Scupin, R. (1997) The KJ Method: A Technique for Analyzing Data Derived from Japanese Ethnology, *Human Organization*, No. 2, Vol. 56, pp. 233–237

[21] Shull, F., Rus, I., and Basili, V.R. (2000) How Perspective-Based Reading Can Improve Requirements Inspections, *IEEE Computer*, No. 7, Vol. 33, pp. 73–79

[22] Stata, R. (1996) Organizational Learning: The Key to Management Innovation," in *How organizations learn*, Starkey, K., Ed. London: Thomson Business Press, pp. 316–334

[23] Straker, D. (1995) *A Toolbook for Quality Improvement and Problem Solving*: Prentice hall International (UK) Limited

[24] Webster's Encyclopedic Unabridged Dictionary of the English Language. (1989) NY: Gramercy Books

8

A Dynamic Model of Software Engineering Knowledge Creation

T. Dybå

Abstract: Software-intensive organizations that intend to excel in the twenty-first century must learn to manage change in dynamic situations. Rather than seeking stability, they should focus on creating software engineering knowledge and mind-sets that embrace environmental change. The model developed in this chapter supports this shift by directing attention to the need for *communication, coordination,* and *collaboration*. The key to successful knowledge creation is continuous and simultaneous dialectic interplay between the knowledge that the organization has established over time, and the knowing of the organization's members in their respective contexts.

Keywords: software engineering, knowledge management, knowledge creation, organizational learning, software process improvement.

8.1 Introduction

Current models of change, which are founded on the old "unfreeze-move-refreeze" paradigm [35], provide insufficient guidance in a constantly changing and increasingly unpredictable environment. Rather than seeking an unachievable stability, software organizations should focus on creating software engineering (SE) knowledge and mind-sets that embrace environmental change.

The model developed in this chapter supports this shift by directing attention to the needs for *communication, coordination,* and *collaboration* within and between software teams. The model is about how software teams acquire and use knowledge in an organizational setting in order to improve their software processes. Verbs like "knowing" or "learning" are used to emphasize action oriented and dynamic properties, while the noun "knowledge" is used to describe static properties.

In developing the model, we have emphasized *the fundamental principle of the hermeneutic circle* [29] in which knowledge is gained dialectically by proceeding from the whole to its parts and then back again. This is also what happens in practice; each time incongruence occurs between part and whole, a reconceptualization takes place. The frequency of such reconceptualizations decreases as the match improves between the conceptualization of the organization and that held by the organization's members.

Another important principle behind the model is the focus on *context-specific needs*. The knowledge that the software organization creates, its methods for creating it, and the criteria by which these methods are considered valid are all based on the organization's prior experience for dealing with "problematic situations" [16]. As situations, which the organization considers problematic, change, so may its methods for dealing with them and the criteria for judging them as valid. The uncertainty about situations or what actions to take in them is what makes them problematic. This is the point from which SE knowledge creation begins and is very different from current models in which improvement is seen as starting with the implementation of "best practices" according to a predetermined scheme, independent of the organization's experience of problematic situations.

A critical element in our model, therefore, is the integration of knowledge creating activities with the "real work" of software development. This way, we consider software teams and their projects as the baseline for knowledge creation and software process improvement (SPI) and as foremost responsible for keeping the organization's processes on the leading edge of technology.

Figure 8.1 presents an overview of the dynamic model of software engineering knowledge creation. The model contains the following four major elements:

– *Organizational conext.* This is the general environment that imposes constraints and opportunities about what the organization can and cannot do. Furthermore, since we perceive the organization as an open system, the reality experienced by the various software teams contains elements from outside the organization as well as from the organization itself.

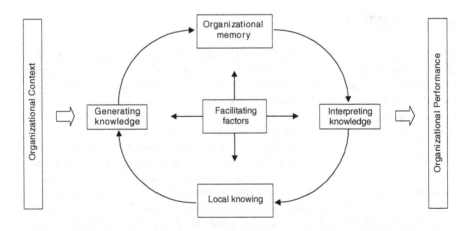

Fig. 8.1. A dynamic model of software engineering knowledge creation

- *Learning cycle.* The organization's learning cycle is a dialectical process that integrates local experience and organizational concepts. All members and groups of members in the organization contribute in the social construction of the software organization's knowledge. At the same time, the organization's memory limits the range of the possible actions for its members.

- *Organizational performance.* This is the performance or results of the organization's improvement activities. It is the dependent variable that is used to measure whether gains have in fact been made with respect to organizational behavior and performance, and not merely at the cognitive level.

- *Facilitating factors.* These are the conditions that facilitate or enable knowledge creation and SPI. They are the key factors for success that the software organization must put in place in order to facilitate the organization's learning cycle and improve its development process.

According to this model, SE knowledge creation is defined as a dynamic interplay between two primary dialectics. The first is that between the local and organizational level. The other is that between generating and interpreting organizational knowledge. These dialectics represent the interplay between the knowing of the organization's members in their respective contexts and the knowledge that the organization has established over time. This interplay is a dynamic and simultaneous two-way relationship between the organization and its members, which combines local transformation with the evolution of the organization. This is similar to Piaget's [43] description of the learning process as a dialectic between *assimilating* experience into concepts and *accommodating* concepts to experience. In our model, knowledge is created from the balanced tension between these two processes. Our emphasis is thus on knowledge creation as a dialectic process that integrates local experience and organizational concepts.

The model presented in this chapter has several advantages compared with current "best practice" models. First, it should be clear that organizational knowledge is not being created to mirror a reality that is independent of human action, but to deal with it. Second, starting SPI from problematic situations in software teams reduces the risk that SE knowledge creation will be detached from action, and undertaken to build knowledge for its own sake. Third, it increases the likelihood that knowledge intended for application to practical problems will ultimately serve its purpose given that knowledge gained from concrete situations is more likely to remain applicable to future concrete situations.

8.2 Organizational Context

Generally, quality management literature supports the proposition that ideal quality management should not be affected by contextual variables. Juran and Godfrey [27], for example, stated that ideal quality management is "universal" and suggested that the expectations regarding quality management should be the same regardless of the context "no matter what is the industry, function, culture, or whatever" ([27, p.25] p. 2.5). Crosby [10, 11], Deming [15], and Feigenbaum [22] also support this context-free view of quality management. However, empirical studies have indicated that nevertheless, organizational context influence manager's perceptions of both ideal and actual quality management, and that contextual variables are useful for explaining and predicting quality management practices [5].

Like most of the quality management approaches, a context free view of process improvement is at the heart of the "best practice" paradigm and models like CMM, ISO/IEC 15504, Trillium, and Bootstrap. In contrast to the "best practice" or model-based approach to SPI, the analytic approach [9] is more concerned with the contingent characteristics of individual organizations. For example, the importance of context is made explicit in the different steps of QIP [2] and also in the various templates and guidelines for the use of GQM [3, 55].

However, despite important differences, both the model-based and analytical approach to SPI seem to be most concerned with solving the needs of *large organizations* operating in highly *stable environments* with long-term contracts (e.g. the US Department of Defense and NASA). This is further confirmed by famous cases of successful SPI such as Alcatel [14], Hewlett-Packard [24], Hughes [26], Motorola [13], Philips [44], Raytheon [18], and Siemens [39], which are veritable giants compared to small and medium-sized enterprises (SMEs).

Most SMEs face two challenges: (1) an ever-changing environment and (2) few projects running at any given point in time. As a result of this, they have few data, which they can analyze and use to build up an experience base. In addition, collected data soon becomes outdated and left irrelevant or – in the best case – uncertain. Taken together, this implies that SMEs cannot base their improvement actions on collecting long time series or amass large amounts of data needed for a tradition statistical improvement approach.

Thus, two contextual variables are included in the model to capture the most influential sources of variation in software organizations: *environmental turbulence* and *organizational size*.

8.2.1 Environmental Turbulence

The software organization's environment refers to various characteristics outside the control of the organization that are important to its performance. These characteristics include the nature of the market, political climate, economic conditions, and the kind of technologies on which the organization depends.

The environment of a particular software organization may range from stable to dynamic – from predictable to unpredictable. In a stable environment the software organization can predict its future conditions and rely on standardization for coordination [40]. Certainly, a stable environment may change over time, but the variations are still predictable. But when the conditions become dynamic, i.e. when the market is unstable, the need for product change is frequent and turnover is high. Such change is highly unpredictable and the software organization cannot rely on standardization. Instead, it must remain flexible through the use of direct supervision or mutual adjustment for coordination, calling for the use of a more *organic* structure. Therefore, the effectiveness of a software organization's structure will depend on the environment of the organization.

8.2.2 Organizational Size

Organizational literature suggests that large organizations are less likely to change in response to environmental changes than small organizations. Tushman and Romanelli [51], for example, argued that increased size leads to increased complexity, increased convergence, and thus, increased inertia. Likewise, Mintzberg [40] postulated that the larger an organization, the more formalized its behavior. So, while small organizations can remain organic, large organizations develop bureaucracies with job specialization and sharp divisions of labor, emphasizing stability, order, and control. As a consequence, they often have great difficulties in adapting to changing circumstances because they are designed to achieve predetermined goals – they are not designed for innovation.

From a learning perspective, however, inertia develops as a result of the organization's performance history [33]. Large organizations tend to be successful since an organization will grow larger with repeated success. However, since success reduces the probability of change in a target-oriented organization [12], large software organizations will be less likely to change when the environment changes.

8.3 Learning Cycle

As we have already argued, SE knowledge creation is defined as a dynamic interplay between two primary dialectics. The first is that between the local and organizational level. The other is that between generating and interpreting organizational knowledge. In this section, we make a detailed description of each of these four elements of the learning cycle.

8.3.1 Local Knowing

The primary context, within which meaning is constructed, new knowledge created, and improved courses of action are taken, is the shared practice within local software development teams. Software developers do not work in isolation – they work together to develop products that they could not develop by working as individuals. This focus on teams and their collaborative processes is important because no single developer embodies the breadth and depth of knowledge necessary to comprehend large and complex software systems. Also, it is important because codified or explicit organizational knowledge is seldom sufficient to solve a particular problem. Thus, just as a single soccer player cannot play a game of soccer by himself or herself, only a group of software developers, working as a team, can develop software of a certain size and complexity.

The software teams' way of grasping the world and forming local realities is by apprehension – in the present movement of "here-and-now" [30]. They are concerned with concrete situations as experienced in all their complexity during software development. They act in a specific context in which reality is constantly being created and recreated. Local knowledge is therefore not an explicated and static model of causal relationships for software development. Rather, it shows up in the local actions taken by the developers in the team and can, thus, better be characterized as "knowing".

Therefore, by *local knowing* we refer to the knowledge-in-action associated with participating in the collective practice of software development in a specific context. It is important to stress this, since a software organization's primary concern is the actual *practice* of developing software, and not merely the creation of knowledge on how to do it. Local knowing is, therefore, about how the software organization works, or its theories-in-use, as seen from the local teams or work groups in the organization. Participating in software teams is consequently not only a matter of developing software, but also of changing the organization's knowledge about software development and to generate improvement.

The context in which software developers interact contributes to the knowledge creating process in several ways. First, each software team or work group operates in a particular setting with a particular mix of people, tools, and techniques to define and solve a particular software development problem. Also, the way in which software developers use prior experience and available tools and techniques varies with the particular, concrete circumstances. That is, software developers will approach a certain problem depending on the actual setting because each setting tends to evoke certain kinds of "appropriate" modes of thought and action [52]. Moreover, software developers often take advantage of the setting itself to help them define a problem or to discover solutions.

Also, software developers incorporate codified organizational routines into local, informal practices, freely adapting the routines as they work on solving actual problems in their particular circumstances. Local knowing draws on both the organizational members' individual understandings of the situation and their ability to use the relevant parts of organizational memory that is available in a given context. Therefore, the context in which software development takes place partly determines what the organization's members can do, what they know, and what they can learn. Moreover, since different local settings provide different opportunities for learning, any SE knowledge creation activity will also be a *situated* process.

Therefore, all software development and SE knowledge creation have an ad hoc adroitness akin to *improvization* because they mix together the contingency of the present situation with lessons learned from prior experience [20]. Ryle described this mixture as "paying heed" [45], to be thinking at what one is up against here and now by adjusting oneself to the present situation while at the same time applying the lessons already learned. In other words, local knowing is affected by the current setting as well as by the organization's memory of its past experience.

Such an improvizational theory of local knowing has its roots in pragmatists' notion that knowledge is not absolute, but rather can only be defined in relation to a specific situation or context [17]. Questions about what is "true" are answered in relation to what works in a given setting. Consequently, local knowing is *pragmatic* and produces actions that are oriented toward established goals, directed at doing whatever is necessary to reach the objective.

Thus, *SE knowledge creation occurs through people interacting in context* – or, more precisely, in multiple contexts. This situated and pragmatic characteristic of knowledge creation has important implications for how problem framing, problem solving, and SPI take place in software organizations. Most importantly, this perspective suggests that traditional, decontextualized theories of SPI cannot completely account for learning in software organizations. Rather, since learning is an interactive, social process, contextual factors will affect both how and what orgaizational members learn.

There are several social groups within a software organization that share knowledge and that may be identified as having a distinct local reality. Examples of such groups are formal project teams and informal groups of software developers and managers. A group's local reality can be seen as a way of acting in relationship to the rest of the organization. However, *shared practice by its very nature creates boundaries* [61].

There are two basic conditions for establishing connections across such boundaries and making communications between the groups effective. First, each group must respect the expertise of the other, and must acknowledge the relevance of that expertise to their own problems. Second, each group must have sufficient knowledge and understanding of the other groups' problems to be able to communicate effectively with them. However, experience shows that these conditions are unlikely to be satisfied unless a sufficient number of members of each group have had actual experience with the activities and responsibilities of the other groups [50].

Mutual adjustment [40], which largely depends, on face-to-face contact, is the richest communication channel we have and by far the most effective form of transferring and exchanging knowledge and experience in local teams. Also, face-to-face experience and interaction are the keys to creating and diffusing tacit knowledge. Therefore, people working together with frequent, easy contact will more easily exchange knowledge and experience with each other than people that are separated by time and space. This has important implications for SE knowledge creation, since local software development teams can utilize the flexibility of face-to-face communication and shed bureaucracy.

However, communication capacity rapidly becomes saturated as the group grows. Without compromises, it is impossible to extend mutual adjustment in its pure form to organizations larger than the small group. Nevertheless, with the support of proper technology, considerable extension of the coordination of work by mutual adjustment is possible if the adjustment is mediated by indirect communication through a repository of externalized organizational memory. Such *implicit coordination* [25] of software developers working from a common experience base greatly reduces the need for extra communication and direct supervising efforts in the organizational learning process. Contrary to efforts to provide better tools for handling the increased communication, such as groupware solutions or efforts at standardizing the work process, the attack point in our model is to *reduce the volume of communication needed for coordination.*

In the next section, we describe the process of generating new explicit knowledge based on local knowing so that lessons learned can be incorporated in organizational memory and shared outside the team.

8.3.2 Generating Knowledge

Generating new explicit knowledge is a *collective* process where a group of software developers attempts to externalize their local knowing. This means, for example, that a software team must take time to express its shared practice in a form that can meaningfully be understood and exploited by other organizational members. This process involves the articulation of tacit knowledge into such explicit knowledge as concepts, models, and routines through the use of words, metaphors, analogies, narratives, or visuals. The result of this process is new organizational knowledge and an extended range of explicit organizational memory.

In practice, dialogue [7] and collective reflection [47], or reflective observation to use Kolb's terminology [30], triggers the articulation of explicit knowledge. This process of generating new explicit knowledge brings some of what the software team apprehends into what the team comprehends.

Dialogue is an important way of collectively grasping experience through comprehension such that the software team is able to articulate and build models of their experience and thereby communicate it to others. The team allows others to predict and recreate knowledge to the extent that such experience models are accurately constructed from the team's local knowing.

Collective reflection and dialogue facilitate a greater coverage of past experience, since individual developers can prompt each other to help remember the past. In this sense, multiple and even conflicting individual experience enables a more comprehensive recollection of past events. Such diversity in local knowing between software teams should not be seen as a problem, but rather as a valuable source for SE knowledge creation. It is the differences, not the agreements that are the possibilities for learning and change.

One of the most effective ways of externalizing local knowledge in software organizations is through the use of models, tools, and techniques. When constructing models or systems, however, only parts of the local reality will be externalized since "The program is forever limited to working within the world determined by the programmer's explicit articulation of possible objects, properties, and relations among them." [62, p. 97]. Such modeling creates a blindness that limits to what can be expressed in the terms that the organization has adopted. Although this is an unavoidable property of models and technology, the software organization should, nevertheless, be aware of the limitations that are imposed.

We have used several knowledge-creation techniques to externalize, evaluate, and organize new knowledge. Among the most widely used have been the *GQM approach* [3, 55], the *KJ Method* [48], and *Mind Maps* [8]. Common to these techniques is that they help a group of developers to create ideas and articulate their knowledge through two phases. During the *divergent thinking phase*, the participants articulate key words, phrases, goals, questions, or metrics which they think are relevant for the dialogue. In GQM, these concepts are documented in GQM abstraction sheets, while the KJ method uses less structured Post-it Notes, and Mind Maps uses a picture of words.

During the *convergent thinking phase*, groups using GQM combine their abstraction sheets into one sheet per goal, and jointly try to resolve any conflicts and inconsistencies. With the KJ method, the participants organize their Post-it Notes into logical groups, which are then related into a diagram of concepts and ideas as the conclusion. In a similar way, Mind Maps are used to organize concepts by placing each idea next to what it is related to.

This dialectic of divergent and convergent inquiry facilitates the surfacing of hidden assumptions. The collaborative nature of these processes and the utilization of figurative language for concept creation are what, in our experience, make these techniques so powerful tools for collectively externalizing the tacit knowledge of a group of software developers and, thus, generating new organizational knowledge.

Articulating tacit knowledge and creating new, explicit concepts is not enough. For new knowledge to be useful for others outside the team, it must also be packaged. Knowledge gained locally should be consolidated and globalized in the form of *experience packages* and stored in an Organizational Memory Information System, or Experience Base [4], so it is available for future projects. In principle, most kinds of experience can be externalized, packaged, and made available in the organization's experience base.

Still, each organization must decide for itself what knowledge needs to be packaged based on its business values and needs. Furthermore, since face-to-face interactions need to be high when transferring new concepts to a different location, each experience package should be indexed with local areas of expertise and references to groups or individuals who can help the receiving unit. Moreover, the organization should decide on how its experience packages should be stored in organizational memory.

However useful techniques a software organization might use for the articulation of explicit knowledge and experience packaging, the local knowing can never be fully represented in organizational memory. Contextual information is inevitably lost in this process and what is stored in organizational memory will be a decontextualized subset of local knowledge. Therefore, proper consideration of how memory objects will be decontextualized and then recontextualized in future use is necessary. In other words, we must be able to consider the present through the lens of future activity [1].

In Sect. 8.3.3, we describe the process of incorporating experience packages into organizational memory together with examples of typical memory categories.

8.3.3 Organizational Memory

Organizational memory is a generic concept used to describe an organization's capability for adoption, representation, and sharing of new beliefs, knowledge, or patterns for action. It is essential for SE knowledge creation to occur by embedding organizational members' discoveries, inventions, and evaluations. Sometimes this may require official action and issuing revised regulations or operating guidelines. However, since each local group within an organization has its own culture, it also requires informal acceptance by enough opinion leaders and rank and file members for it to be disseminated as valid and valued knowledge.

In other words, that which is accepted in one part of an organization may or may not be passed on to other units or parts of the organization – one unit's knowing could be another unit's rubbish or heresy. Thus, lessons-learned cannot easily be transferred from one setting to another. Also, higher levels of the power structure can destroy the learning of lower levels as a matter of policy, or even as a matter of neglect or indifference – except sometimes in the case of a strong counter-culture arising out of long conflict and shared grievance. Thus, memories are cooperatively created and used throughout the organization. In turn, they influence the learning and subsequent actions that are taken by the local groups in the organization.

Each time a software organization restructures itself, the contents of its memory are affected. Since much of the organization's memory is stored in human heads, and little is put down on paper or held in computer memories, *turnover of personnel is a great threat to long-term organizational memory*. When experts leave, the costs to the organization are even greater because it takes years of education, training, and experience to become one [50]. Loss of such knowledge can undermine the competence and competitiveness of the organization, and can also have a serious impact on cultural norms and values. However, we should be careful not to assume that the availability of organizational memory necessarily leads to organizations that are effective; it can also lead to lower levels of effectiveness and inflexibility [59].

Based on Walsh and Ungson's definition [58], we focus on organizational memory as *the means by which a software organization's knowledge from the past is brought to bear on present activities*. This definition makes no assumptions regarding the impact of organizational memory on organizational effectiveness since this depends on the ways in which the memory is brought to use. For example, when organizational knowledge is consistent with the goals of the organization, organizational memory can be said to contribute to organizational effectiveness. At the other extreme, organizational memory can be seen as a structure that objectivates a fixed response to standard problems that constrains and threatens the viability of organizations operating in turbulent environments.

Therefore, the members of the software organization must themselves determine what to do with the knowledge they acquire in order to meet the incompatible demands of change and stability. Organizational memory can be viewed as a structure that both enables action within the software organization by providing a framework for common orientation and, at the same time, limits the range of action by constraining the possible ways of developing software. Thus, just as organizational memory provides stability; it can also serve to block change.

To be useful for the software organization as a whole, newly created concepts have to be communicated and explained to others who have not shared the concrete experience. This makes *justification* an essential process since the organization must decide whether new concepts and beliefs are worthy of further attention and investment [56]. There is an inherent dialectic here that the justification process tries to balance. On the one hand, newly generated knowledge has to be related to existing organizational knowledge in order to be acceptable and understandable. On the other hand, new knowledge challenges the organization's existing understanding of the world through its novelty, provoking complex processes of argumentation and justification, to be decided in favor of the existing or the newly emerging views.

Justification processes are therefore important for the software organization's memory since they decide whether new knowledge is *rejected* as irrelevant or uninteresting, *returned* to the local team for further elaboration, or *appropriated* as justified true belief and therefore integrated into organizational memory.

However, for a software development team to be able to reuse a memory object like an experience package (see Table 8.1 for typical examples), it must be recontextualized and made relevant for the new situation. That is, the memory object must be reunderstood for the developers' current purpose. A proper understanding of how local knowing is first decontextualized and adopted as organizational memory and then recontextualized into new local knowing is of critical importance for the utilization of organizational memory. This problem has largely been unnoticed in contemporary debates on experience bases within SPI, which is often limited to the technical challenges of implementing a database. However, if we do not address the problems of recontextualization, the whole concept of organizational memory and experience bases will be more or less useless.

Section 8.3.4 describes how the organization's memory can be put back into use and become part of local knowing through a process of collective interpretation.

Table 8.1. Memory categories and examples of typical elements

memory category	typical elements
worldview	culture, beliefs, assumptions, values, norms, strategies, power relations, symbols, habits, expectations
structure	task structure, roles, behavior formalization, coordinating mechanisms, unit grouping, workplace ecology
plans and models	life cycle models, assessment models, project plans, milestone plans, quality plans, improvement plans, measurement plans, action plans
systems	information systems, tools and techniques, quality control systems, training systems, social systems
routines	rules, standard operating procedures, development processes
lessons learned	experience reports, articles, memos, newsletters, stories, feedback sessions, peer reviews, post mortem reviews

8.3.4 Interpreting Knowledge

The collective interpretation of knowledge is the process of making organizational memory an integral part of local knowing by making sense out of the actions, systems, structures, plans, models, and routines in the organization. Through this process, the organization's memory is recontextualized and taken up into the practice of local software development teams. It is a process of "re-experiencing" [42] other team's experiences.

A major confusion in much of the thinking in contemporary knowledge management and SPI is equating easy access of information with learning. However, there is an important difference between passively receiving information and actively interpreting and making sense of it. When an individual software developer receives information, he or she relates that information to past moments of experience in order to make sense of it. It is the differences from what is expected, and not the agreements, which provide the possibilities for SE knowledge creation. Therefore, we attend to that which is different from our current understandings and from our expectations in order to compare it with already extracted cues. Learning can only be said to have taken place when the individual has formed new networks of meaning and new reference points for future sensemaking processes from the information encountered.

Collective interpretation processes are still more complex. Not only must each software developer engage in an individual process of sensemaking, he or she must do so while simultaneously interacting with other developers. By engaging in *collective interpretation*, each developer is influenced by the meanings held by others and in turn influences the meanings of others. This way, each developer can better understand the experiences and reasoning the other developers are using in their interpretations and by comparison, understand each other's meanings more fully. Based on these interactions, the developers are in a position to form a collective interpretation of the organizational knowledge that is available to them.

Therefore, collectively interpreting organizational knowledge involves *active construction of knowledge* in the form of active formulation and solution to problems with the help of explicit models, guiding routines, and feedback. This highlights an important aspect of SE knowledge creation: collective interpretation is effective not necessarily as a function of simple internalization, with modeled information being transferred across a barrier from the organization to the inside of a team, or with information being transmitted. Rather, these interpretations are effective through peripheral and active participation [34], whereby the members of a team collectively transform their understandings and skills in framing and solving a problem. According to this view, it is the active construction through firsthand experience that is so crucial to SE knowledge creation, not some distant guidance or universal rule.

Rather than being transmitted or internalized, *knowledge becomes jointly constructed in the sense that it is neither handed down ready-made from the organization, nor something a team constructs purely on its own.* Knowledge, understandings and meanings gradually emerge through interaction and become distributed among those interacting rather than individually constructed or possessed.

Furthermore, since knowledge is distributed among participants in a specific activity context it is necessarily situated as well. That is, intimately welded to the context and the activity in which and by means of which it is constructed. Importantly therefore, *participation* becomes the key concept here, as contrasted with acquisition, conceptual change serving as both the process and the goal of learning.

In the process of forming collective interpretations, it is important that we distinguish between reducing *ambiguity* and reducing *uncertainty*. Ambiguity is the lack of clarity about the technologies and processes of software development when the environment is difficult to interpret, and when cause and effect are disconnected so that the organization is unable to link its actions to their consequences. It has more to do with the confusion of multiple meanings than with the absence of sufficient quantities of information. The lack of meaning drives sensemaking, while the lack of certainty drives data collection and information gathering: "In the case of ambiguity, people engage in sensemaking because they are confused by too many interpretations, whereas in the case of uncertainty, they do so because they are ignorant of any interpretations." [60, p. 91]. Thus, approaches to measurement-driven SPI can support the reduction of uncertainty, but they don't necessarily assist the software organization in reducing the ambiguity that is essential for SE knowledge creation.

The process of "re-experiencing" other teams' experiences involves experimenting with organizational knowledge in local contexts by "giving it a try". Based on the concepts of ambiguity and uncertainty, we can distinguish between two types of such experiments that are crucial for SE knowledge creation: hypothesis-testing experiments and exploratory experiments. *Hypothesis-testing experiments* are field experiments designed to reduce the organization's uncertainty by discriminating among alternative explanations or solutions from many possibilities. This is the usual way of conducting process improvement experiments according to the experimental approach. Of special concern to us here, therefore, is the conduct of exploratory experiments to reduce ambiguity.

Exploratory experiments involve learning through discovery, encouraging the flexibility and resilience needed to cope with the situation at hand. When ambiguity is high, the knowledge represented by the organization's memory provides little support. So, during this phase of the learning cycle the focus shifts from justification and exploitation of existing knowledge, to skepticism and exploration of new opportunities.

Such exploration or "learning by doing" is of utmost importance in unfamiliar and ambiguous situations and only works when a team receives rapid and unambiguous feedback on its actions. However, in the complex reality experienced by most software teams, the consequences of their actions are neither immediate nor unambiguous. Nevertheless, in these situations, effective learning can be achieved by the use of simulated environments, what Nonaka and Konno termed "exercising *ba*" [41], or "microworlds" to use Senge's terminology [49]. In such microworlds, it becomes possible for software teams to learn about future and distant consequences of their actions by experimenting in environments that "compress time and space" [49].

Prototypes are examples of microworlds that enable the collective interpretation of knowledge. Developing a prototype is an experimental activity mainly concerned with reducing the inherent uncertainty and ambiguity of specifications [38], thus facilitating a shared understanding of the system to be developed.

There are two main approaches to exploration in which prototypes serve an important role: probing and learning; and pilot projects. In *probing and learning* the software organization constructs "quick-and-dirty" mock-ups. To be useful for the learning process, these prototypes still have to be close enough approximations of the final product or development process. Otherwise, such experimentation will be of little value since generalizations will be virtually impossible. Furthermore, the probing and learning process should be designed as an *iterative* process, since it is hardly possible to "get it right the first time" in an ambiguous environment.

Pilot projects are projects aimed at on-line experimentation in real software projects or large-scale simulations in separate demonstration projects (see [21]). Typically, they are the first projects to embody principles and approaches that the organization hopes to adopt later on a larger scale. They implicitly establish policy guidelines and decision rules for later projects. They often encounter severe tests of commitment from employees who wish to see whether the rules and practices have, in fact, changed. They are normally developed by strong multifunctional teams reporting directly to senior management. Finally, they tend to have only limited impact on the rest of the organization if they are not accompanied by explicit strategies for the diffusion of knowledge gained from the pilot projects [23].

The context dependent inferences of prior experience and memory objects can only be carried over from one organizational situation to another through "seeing-as" [47]. When a software team makes sense of a situation it perceives to be unique, it *sees* it *as* something already present in the repertoire represented by organizational memory. Therefore, "Seeing *this* situation as *that* one, one may also *do* in this situation *as* in that one." [47, p. 139, italics in original].

Consequently, in order to learn and improve their software processes, software teams can sometimes figure out how to solve unique problems or make sense of puzzling phenomena by modeling the unfamiliar on the familiar. Depending on the initial proximity or distance of the two things perceived as similar, the familiar may serve as an "exemplar" or as a "generative metaphor" for the unfamiliar [47]. In both cases, the software team arrives at a new interpretation of the phenomena before it by "reflecting-in-action" on an earlier perception of similarity.

The utility of an experience package lies in its ability to generate explanation and experimentation in a new situation. When the experience package is carried over to the new situation, its validity must be established there by a new round of experimentation through which it is very likely to be modified. The modified experience package that results from this new round of experimentation may, in turn, serve as a basis for transfer and re-creation to a new situation.

So, for SE knowledge creation to happen, organizational members must act on the collective interpretations they have made – starting a new cycle of organizational learning. Thus, purposeful action at the local level is a means for the interpretation of organizational knowledge as well as for the generation of new knowledge. Consequently, it is essential for organizational learning and SPI.

8.4 Organizational Performance

Organizational performance is the ultimate criterion for SE knowledge creation. Performance is a complex construct, however, reflecting the criteria and standards used by decision-makers to assess the functioning of a software organization. That is, performance is a value judgment on the results desired from an organization [53].

Traditionally, the assessment of organizational performance has focused on long term profitability and financial measures. However, in today's technologically and customer-driven global competition, financial measures often provide incomplete guides to performance, i.e. they are insufficient to predict future competitiveness in the software business.

As a fundamental part of our model, therefore, we need a dynamic concept of success that represents a software organization's competitiveness. Performance, which is something an organization does (process) or achieves (outcome), is a concept that better can serve as an operational tool for improvement of competitiveness than pure financial measures.

Furthermore, satisfied customers is an important asset for a software organization, it is the cornerstone of any TQM program, and it is the most important principle in the recent revision of ISO 9000:2000. Therefore, the customer perspective should be a central part in any model of a software organization's performance.

Lynch and Cross [36] defined customer satisfaction as the difference between the customers' perceived performance and their needs and expectations:

Customer satisfaction = Perceived performance – Expectations

A classic problem, however, is that both performance and expectations are subjective terms and that performance as seen from the software organization, can be viewed differently than performance as seen from the customer. Typically, the customer will focus on *external performance measures* such as price and delivery time, while the software organization focuses on *internal performance measures* such as cost and lead-time. Therefore, the relationships between such external and internal performance measures are critical for the integration of customer satisfaction in any model that purports to measure success. However, improved profitability is not an automatic outcome of organizational programs to improve customer satisfaction.

All software processes are expected to deliver a quality product on schedule and on budget in order to achieve customer satisfaction and thereby to ensure long-term profitability for the software organization. Moreover, these fundamental characteristics have importance to both customers and the software organization. Therefore, they are important for the understanding and definition of organizational performance. In other words, SE knowledge creation should lead to "better, faster, [and] cheaper software development" [46]. This is also clear in Krasner's [32] model of the challenges in software development projects, which focuses on the dynamic relationships between software processes and the three outcome factors: cost, schedule, and quality.

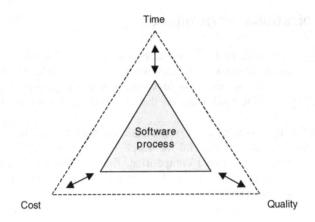

Fig. 8.2. The organizational performance dimension of SPI success [32]

From the preceding discussion we have identified organizational performance as an important dimension in the measurement of successful SE knowledge creation. Furthermore, we have identified the following three elements as central constituents of organizational performance as seen from a customer satisfaction perspective (see Fig. 8.2):

- *Time.* Time to market has become a critical measure for software organizations in today's turbulent markets. Being able to respond rapidly and reliably to customer requests and changing market conditions is often critical for a software organization's competitiveness. Including time-based metrics as part of the organizational performance measure, therefore, signals the importance of achieving and continually reducing lead-times for meeting targeted customers' expectations. Yet, other customers may be more concerned with the reliability of lead times than with just obtaining the shortest possible lead-time. In addition to lead-time or cycle-time reductions, therefore, measures of on-time delivery rate improvement and schedule slippage rate reductions can also be useful time-based indicators of customer satisfaction and retention.
- *Cost.* Customers will always be concerned with the price they pay for products and services. Long-term profitability, therefore, requires that there is a healthy relationship between price and cost and, consequently, that we include process cost metrics as part of the organizational performance measure. Process cost includes the cost of primary activities (marketing and sales, inbound logistics, operations, outbound logistics, and service) and support activities (infrastructure, human resource management, technology development, and procurement) in the software development value chain [6]. Although the major source of software costs is the "operations" component, virtually all components are still highly labor-intensive. Thus, effort is frequently the predominant cost driver for most software processes. Examples of potentially useful cost metrics are:

ratio of actual versus planned cost of work effort, development hours saved, productivity increases, rework cost reduction, and reuse increases.

– *Quality.* Using the Kano model as the frame of reference [28], we have witnesses a tendency among large customer groups that quality is not always expressed as an explicit requirement – it is so obvious that it is often not even mentioned. Nevertheless, the customers' expectations consist of both the explicitly stated, *functional* and *non-functional*, requirements and the obvious implicit, or tacit, requirements. However, in certain parts of the software industry, the situation is such that excellent quality may still offer opportunities for companies to distinguish themselves from their competitors. In any case, customer perceived quality is always relevant to include as an organizational performance measure. Examples of such quality metrics are defect density reductions, and customer satisfaction increases. An important part of this picture, however, is that the software organization may not even be aware of the unsatisfied customers – they simply cease to use the organization's products or services. Interestingly, an American study revealed that 96 % of unhappy customers never tell the company [31].

To summarize, if our goal is to assess the improvement of software development processes, the ability to answers the following three questions should be regarded as a central concern for the measurement of organizational performance:

1. Are software projects delivered on time?
2. Are software projects delivered on budget?
3. Are customers satisfied with the delivered software?

Using organizational performance as the only dimension of success can entail some adverse complications. These complications include the instabilities of performance advantages, the causal complexity surrounding performance, and the limitations of using data based on retrospective recall of informants [37]. Furthermore, the extent to which organizational members' perceptions of SPI success reflect organizational performance is unclear, as is the extent to which perceptions are influenced by the software organizations' standards. Besides, research on both individual and organizational learning indicates that items that are perceived to be important by the persons concerned will be paid more attention to than items perceived as tangential to these persons [54].

If organizational members' perceptions do not reflect organizational performance, then increases (or decreases) in performance will not necessarily be translated into increased (or decreased) levels of perceived success. A decrease in the perceived level of success, for example, may occur either because the software organization's performance has decreased, or because the organization has not adequately managed the perceptions of its members. Assessment of success is a question of both organizational performance and the perceptions of the organization's members in the absence of data about the relationships between actual performance, perceived performance, and customer satisfaction.

8.5 Facilitating Factors

SE knowledge creation cannot simply be managed like any other project. This is due to the simple fact that the term "manage" typically implies control, while the nature of the learning process is typically uncontrollable or, at the least, stifled by heavy-handed direction [57]. From our perspective, therefore, software organizations need to acknowledge that *SE knowledge creation needs to be enabled rather than controlled.*

We have identified six facilitating factors during our investigations (see [19]):

- *Business orientation*: the extent to which SE knowledge creation goals and actions are aligned with explicit and implicit business goals and strategies.
- *Involved leadership*: the extent to which leaders at all levels in the organization are genuinely committed to and actively participate in SE knowledge creation.
- *Employee participation*: the extent to which employees use their knowledge and experience to decide, act, and take responsibility for SE knowledge creation.
- *Concern for measurement*: the extent to which the software organization collects and utilizes quality data to guide and assess the effects of SE knowledge creation.
- *Exploitation*: the extent to which the software organization is engaged in the exploitation of existing knowledge.
- *Exploration*: the extent to which the software organization is engaged in the exploration of new knowledge.

The links between the knowledge creating processes and the facilitating factors that, according to our experience, are the most important are revealed by the 6x4 grid in Table 8.2.

Table 8.2. Links between knowledge creating processes and facilitating factors[a]

facilitating factors	local knowing	generating knowledge	organizational memory	interpreting knowledge
business orientation		✓	✓✓	✓
involved leadership	✓	✓✓	✓	
employee participation	✓✓	✓✓		✓✓
concern for measurement	✓✓	✓		
exploitation of existing knowledge	✓	✓✓	✓	✓
exploration of new knowledge	✓✓			✓✓

[a]✓ denotes an important link; ✓✓ denotes a very important link.

A clear *business orientation* legitimizes the knowledge creating initiative throughout the software organization. It has a relatively low impact on local knowing but may, nevertheless, help software teams articulate the knowledge created in local groups. Business orientation is especially important in justifying concepts for inclusion in the organization's memory, since concepts must be selected that help the organization achieve its business goals. Therefore, a clear business orientation will also encourage better utilization of organizational knowledge and facilitate the collective interpretation of knowledge.

Involved leadership is important for any organizational learning initiative. By involving themselves in the challenges of software development and allowing software teams to act autonomously, the organization's leadership facilitates local knowing. Furthermore, they have an important role in facilitating the generation of new knowledge by creating a context that prioritizes and encourages dialogue and collective reflection. Also, the degree of leadership involvement influences what is considered important for inclusion in organizational memory.

Employee participation is the cornerstone of our model. It is important for all the knowledge creating activities in the learning cycle. It is the basis for local knowing, since it is only through participation that collective action can be taken and tacit knowledge can be shared. Dialogue and collective reflection are meaningless concepts without participation and it is, therefore, an important facilitator for the generation of valid organizational knowledge. Likewise, it is through collective processes of sensemaking and active participation through e.g. personnel rotation programs that organizational knowledge is diffused and brought to use in new situations.

In addition to personal and collective experience, a *concern for measurement* is important in order to validate the newly created knowledge and to ensure that gains have in fact been made. Most importantly, a concern for measurement facilitates local knowing by acting as a foundation for the collection, analysis, and feedback of data. Ongoing feedback as a group process is particularly important since it can be an effective tool for bringing about changes in the way work is done as well as in establishing causal relationships and generating new knowledge.

Exploitation of existing knowledge is closely tied to all the knowledge creating activities in the learning cycle. It facilitates local knowing by presenting a set of previously learned lessons that can be used in exploring the contingencies of the current setting. It is particularly important in facilitating the generation of new organizational knowledge since this involves the articulation and packaging of local knowledge and experience. Furthermore, before locally created knowledge is appropriated as part of the organization's memory it must be related to the existing knowledge. Also, as we have seen in the previous section, the interpretation of knowledge necessarily involves a relation between new and existing knowledge.

Exploration of new knowledge is particularly important in facilitating the collective interpretation of knowledge through exploratory experiments and prototyping. It is also the basis for local knowing by mixing together the contingency of the present situation with the lessons learned from prior experience [20].

8.6 Chapter Summary

In this chapter, we have developed a dynamic model of SE knowledge creation. A critical element for developing the model was the integration of SPI activities with the real, situated nature of software development, and to focus on the role of certain facilitating factors in the diffusion of knowledge and experience within and between groups of software developers.

First, organizational context was described as an important element that imposes constraints and opportunities about what and how the organization can learn. Two contextual variables were included in the model to capture the most influential sources of variation: environmental turbulence and organizational size. Then, we emphasized the importance of acknowledging that the learning process is a dynamic interplay between two primary dialectics: one between the local and organizational level, the other between generating and interpreting knowledge. Next, the success of an organization's knowledge creation was described in terms of organizational performance and the software organization's perceived level of success. Finally, we described the key factors of success in SE knowledge creation and their links with the learning processes in the model.

References

[1] Ackerman, M.S. and Halverson, C.A. (2000) Reexamining Organizational Memory, *Communications of the ACM*, 43(1), pp. 58–64

[2] Basili, V.R. and Caldiera, G. (1995) Improve Software Quality by Reusing Knowledge and Experience, *Sloan Management Review*, 37(1), pp. 55–64

[3] Basili, V.R. and Weiss, D. (1984) A Methodology for Collecting Valid Software Engineering Data, *IEEE Transactions on Software Engineering*, 10(6), pp. 728–738

[4] Basili, V.R., Caldiera, G., and Rombach, H.D. (1994) Experience Factory, in J.J. Marciniak (Ed.), *Encyclopedia of Software Engineering*, Wiley, Vol. 1, pp. 469–476

[5] Benson, P.G., Saraph, J.V., and Schroeder, R.G. (1991) *The Effects of Organizational Context on Quality Management: An Empirical Investigation*, Management Science, 37(9), pp. 110–1124

[6] Boehm, B.W. and Papaccio, P.N. (1988) Understanding and Controlling Software Costs, *IEEE Transactions on Software Engineering*, 4(10), pp. 1462–1477

[7] Bohm, D. and Peat, F.D. (2000) *Science, Order, and Creativity*, Second Edition, London: Routledge

[8] Buzan, T and Buzan, B. (2000) *The Mind Map Book*, Millenium Edition, London: BBC Books

[9] Card, D. (1991) Understanding Process Improvement, *IEEE Software*, 8(4), pp. 102–103

[10] Crosby, P.B. (1979) *Quality is Free: The Art Making Quality Certain,* NY: McGraw-Hill

[11] Crosby, P.B. (1996) *Quality Is Still Free: Making Quality Certain in Uncertain Times,* NY : McGraw-Hill

[12] Cyert, R.M. and March, J.G. (1992) *A Behavioral Theory of the Firm,* Second Edition, Oxford, UK: Blackwell

[13] Daskalantonakis, M.K. (1992) A Practical View of Software Measurement and Implementation Experiences within Motorola, *IEEE Transactions on Software Engineering,* 18(11), pp. 998–1010

[14] Debou, C., Courtel, D., Lambert, H.-B., Fuchs, N., and Haux, M. (1999) Alcatel's Experience with Process Improvement, in R. Messnarz and C. Tully (Eds.), *Better Software Practice for Business Benefit: Principles and Experience,* Los Alamitos, CA: IEEE Computer Society Press, pp. 281–301

[15] Deming, W.E. (1986) *Out of the Crisis.* Cambridge, MA: MIT Center for Advanced Engineering Study

[16] Dewey, J. (1929) *The Quest for Certainty,* NY: Minton, Balch

[17] Dewey, J. (1938) *Logic: The Theory of Inquiry,* NY: Holt and Company

[18] Dion, R. (1993) Process Improvement and the Corporate Balance Sheet, *IEEE Software,* 10(4), pp. 28–35

[19] Dybå, T. (2000a) An Instrument for Measuring the Key Factors of Success in Software Process Improvement, *Empirical Software Engineering,* 5(4), pp. 357–390

[20] Dybå, T. (2000b) Improvisation in Small Software Organizations, *IEEE Software,* 17(5), pp. 82–87

[21] Dybå, T. (Ed.) (2000c) *SPIQ – Software Process Improvement for better Quality: Methodology Handbook* (in Norwegian), IDI Report 2/2000, Trondheim, Norway: Norwegian University of Science and Technology

[22] Feigenbaum, A.V. (1991) *Total Quality Control, Fortieth Anniversary Edition,* NY: McGraw–Hill

[23] Garvin, D.A. (2000) *Learning in Action: A Guide to Putting the Learning Organization to Work,* Boston, MA: Harvard Business School Press

[24] Grady, R.B. (1997) *Successful Software Process Improvement, Upper Saddle River,* N J: Prentice-Hall

[25] Groth, L. (1999) *Future Organizational Design: The Scope for the IT-Based Enterprise,* Chichester: Wiley

[26] Humphrey, W.S., Snyder, T. and Willis, R. (1991) Software Process Improvement at Hughes Aircraft, *IEEE Software,* 8(4), pp. 11–23

[27] Juran, J.M. and Godfrey, A.B. (Eds.) (1999) *Juran's Quality Handbook, Fifth Edition,* NY: McGraw-Hill

[28] Kano, N., Nobuhiro, S., Takahashi, F., and Tsuji, S. (1984) Attractive Quality and Must Be Quality, *Quality Magazine,* 14(2), pp. 39–48

[29] Klein, H.K. and Myers, M.D. (1999) A Set of Principles for Conducting and Evaluating Interpretive Field Studies in Information Systems, *MIS Quarterly,* 23(1), 67–93

[30] Kolb, D.A. (1984) *Experiential Learning: Experience as the Source of Learning and Development,* Englewood Cliffs, NJ: Prentice-Hall

[31] Kotler, P. (1988) *Marketing Management: Analysis, Planning, Implementation, and Control,* Englewood Cliffs, NJ: Prentice-Hall

[32] Krasner, H. (1999) The Payoff for Software Process Improvement: What it is and How to Get it, in K. El Emam and N.H. Madhavji (Eds.), *Elements of Software Process Assessment and Improvement,* Los Alamitos, CA: IEEE Computer Society Press, pp. 151–176

[33] Lant, T.K. and Mezias, S.J. (1992) An Organizational Learning Model of Convergence and Reorientation, *Organization Science,* 3(1), pp. 47–71

[34] Lave, J. and Wenger, E. (1991) *Situated Learning: Legitimate Peripheral Participation,* Cambridge: Cambridge University Press

[35] Lewin, K. (1951) *Field Theory in Social Sciences,* NY: Harper and Row

[36] Lynch, R.L. and Cross, K.C. (1991) *Measure Up! Yardstick for Continuous Improvement,* Cambridge, MA: Blackwell Business

[37] March, J.G. and Sutton, R.I. (1997) Organizational Performance as a Dependent Variable, *Organization Science,* 8(6), pp. 698–706

[38] Mathiassen, L. and Stage, J. (1992) *The Principle of Limited Reduction in Software Design,* Information Technology & People, 6(2-3), pp. 171–185

[39] Mehner, T. (1999) Siemens Process Assessment Approach, in R. Messnarz and C. Tully (Eds.), *Better Software Practice for Business Benefit: Principles and Experience,* Los Alamitos, CA: IEEE Computer Society Press, pp. 199–212

[40] Mintzberg, H. (1989) *Mintzberg on Management: Inside Our Strange World of Organizations,* NY: The Free Press

[41] Nonaka, I. and Konno, N. (1998) The Concept of "Ba": Building a Foundation for Knowledge Creation, *California Management Review,* 40(3), pp. 40–54

[42] Nonaka, I. and Takeuchi, H. (1995) *The Knowledge-Creating Company: How Japanese Companies Create the Dynamics of Innovation,* NY: Oxford University Press

[43] Piaget, J. (1970) *Genetic Epistemology,* NY: Columbia University Press

[44] Rooijmans, J., Aerts, H., and van Genuchten, M. (1996) Software Quality in Consumer Electronics Products, *IEEE Software,* 13(1), pp. 55–64

[45] Ryle, G. (1979) Improvisation, in G. Ryle (Ed.), *On Thinking,* London: Blackwell, pp. 121–130

[46] Sanders, M. (Ed.) (1998) *The SPIRE Handbook: Better, Faster, Cheaper Software Development in Small Organisations,* Dublin: Centre for Software Engineering Ltd

[47] Schön, D.A. (1983) *The Reflective Practitioner: How Professionals Think in Action,* NY: Basic Books

[48] Scupin, R. (1997) The KJ Method: A Technique for Analyzing Data Derived from Japanese Ethnology, *Human Organization,* 56(2), pp. 233–237

[49] Senge, P.M. (1990) *The Fifth Discipline: The Art and Practice of the Learning Organization,* NY: Doubleday

[50] Simon, H.A. (1991) Bounded Rationality and Organizational Learning, *Organization Science,* 2(1), pp. 125–134

[51] Tushman, M.L. and Romanelli, E. (1985) Organizational Evolution: A Metamorphosis Model of Convergence and Reorientation, in L.L. Cummings and B.M Staw (Eds.), *Research in Organizational Behavior,* Vol. 7, Greenwich, Connecticut: JAI Press, pp. 171–222

[52] Tyre, M.J. and von Hippel, E. (1997) The Situated Nature of Adaptive Learning in Organizations, *Organization Science,* 8(1), pp. 71–83

[53] van de Ven, A.H. and Ferry, D.L. (1980) *Measuring and Assessing Organization,* NY: John Wiley & Sons

[54] van der Bent, J., Paauwe, J., and Williams, R. (1999) Organizational Learning: An Exploration of Organizational Memory and its Role in Organizational Change Processes, *Journal of Organizational Change Management,* 12(5), pp. 377–404

[55] van Solingen, R. and Berghout, E. (1999) *The Goal/Question/Metric Method: A Practical Guide for Quality Improvement of Software Development,* London: McGraw-Hill

[56] von Krogh, G. and Grand, S. (2000) Justification in Knowledge Creation: Dominant Logic in Management Discourses, in G. von Krogh, I. Nonaka, and T. Nishiguchi (Eds.), *Knowledge Creation: A Source of Value,* London: MacMillan, pp. 13–35

[57] von Krogh, G., Ichijo, K., and Nonaka, I. (2000) *Enabling Knowledge Creation: How to Unlock the Mystery of Tacit Knowledge and Release the Power of Innovation,* NY: Oxford University Press

[58] Walsh, J.P. and Ungson, G.D. (1991) *Organizational Memory,* Academy of Management Review, 16(1), 57–91

[59] Weick, K.E. (1979) *The Social Psychology of Organizing,* Second Edition, Reading, MA: Addison-Wesley

[60] Weick, K.E. (1995) *Sensemaking in Organizations,* Thousand Oaks, CA: Sage Publications

[61] Wenger, E. (1998) *Communities of Practice: Learning, Meaning, and Identity,* Cambridge: Cambridge University Press

[62] Winograd, T.A. and Flores, F. (1986) *Understanding Computers and Cognition: A New Foundation for Design,* Reading, MA: Addison-Wesley

9

An Empirical Study of an Informal Knowledge Repository in a Medium-Sized Software Consulting Company

T. Dingsøyr and E.A. Røyrvik

Abstract: Numerous studies have been conducted on design and architecture of knowledge repositories. This chapter addresses the need for looking at practices where knowledge repositories are actually used in concrete work situations. This insight should be used when developing knowledge repositories in the future.

Through methods inspired by ethnography this chapter investigates how an unstructured knowledge repository is used for different purposes by software developers and managers in a medium-sized software consulting company. The repository is a part of the company's knowledge management tool suite on the Intranet. We found five distinct ways of using the tool, from solving specific technical problems to getting an overview of competence in the company. We highlight the importance of informal organization and the social integration of the tool in the daily work practices of the company.

Keywords: knowledge repository, knowledge management, software process improvement, software engineering, empirical study.

© 2003 IEEE. Reprinted, with permission, from Clarke, Dillon, and Tichy (Eds.): Proc. 25th International Conference on Software Engineering (ICSE'2003), Portland, Oregon, USA, 10–12 May, 2003, IEEE-CS Press, pp. 84–92.

9.1 Introduction

Knowledge management has attracted a lot of attention in various business domains in the past years, including software engineering [1]. Reasons for the interest in knowledge management are that:

- Software Engineering is knowledge-intensive work; the main asset in software companies is what has been called the "intellectual capital".
- In order to improve software development, the management of knowledge has to be improved as well.

Hanssen et al. [2] divide between two main strategies for knowledge management:

- *Codification.* To systematize and store information that represents the knowledge of the company, and make this available for the people in the company.
- *Personalization.* To support the flow of information in a company by storing information about knowledge sources, like a "yellow pages" of in-house expertise.

Most of the work that has been reported on knowledge management in the software engineering literature (often referred to as work on "experience factory") are from large organizations, such as Chrysler [3, 4], The NASA Software Engineering Laboratory [5] and Ericsson [6]. See [7] for an overview.

Such organizations can devote a lot of resources on organizational issues such as knowledge management. Many of the software engineering companies have opted for a strategy involving both codification and personalization.

Codification is the strategy that requires the heaviest investment – both in codifying knowledge that exist tacit in people or teams, and also in having an infrastructure for distributing it in the organization.

It is interesting to see how smaller (in this case: medium-size) organizations cope with a codification strategy on scarce resources. In particular, we will examine how a medium-sized software consulting company is using a knowledge repository. But first, we will describe knowledge management tools more in general in Sect. 9.2.

9.2 Knowledge Management Tools

When we talk of tools for knowledge management, we will mean tools that have several users, and are widely available for employees in an organization. This is usually what we can call Intranet tools, that support knowledge management [8] in "at least three ways (1) Providing compression of time and space among the users. (2) Offering the flexibility to exchange information, and (3) Supporting information transfer and organizational networking independent of direct contacts between the users".

There are many dimensions for describing knowledge management tools. Ruggles [9] mentions tools that "generate knowledge", where tools for data mining (to discover new patterns in data) can be an example. Further, we have "knowledge codification tools" to make knowledge available for others, and "knowledge transfer tools" to decrease problems with time and space when communicating in an organization.

Another dimension is whether the tools are "active" [10] or "passive". By active tools, we mean tools that notify users when it is likely that users require some kind of knowledge. Passive tools require a user to actively seek knowledge without any system support.

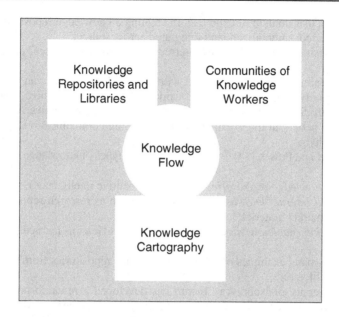

Fig. 9.1. Types of Knowledge Management Tools or Architecture (Borghoff and Pareschi)

We also find another way of categorizing the tools other than the ones mentioned so far, from the book Information Technology for Knowledge Management [11]. The authors divide technology for a "corporate memory" into four parts, shown in Fig. 9.1.

- *Knowledge repositories and libraries.* Tools for handling repositories of knowledge in the form of documents.
- *Communities of knowledge workers.* Tools to support communities of practice in work; like organizing workspaces for communities for online discussions and distributed work.
- *Knowledge cartography.* Tools for mapping and categorizing knowledge, from core competence in a company to individual expertise; what we can refer to as "metaknowledge".
- *The flow of knowledge.* Here we find tools for supporting the interaction between tacit knowledge, explicit knowledge and metaknowledge; that is, that combines the three parts above.

Now, we describe knowledge repositories and libraries in more detail.

9.2.1 Knowledge repositories

Liebowitz and Beckman [12] define knowledge repositories as an "on-line computer-based storehouse of expertise, knowledge, experiences, and documentation about a particular domain of expertise. In creating a knowledge repository, knowledge is collected, summarized, and integrated across sources".

Such repositories are sometimes referred to as "experience bases" or "corporate memories".

The repository can either be filled with knowledge by what van Heijst et. al [13] call "passive collection" – where workers themselves recognize what knowledge has sufficient value to be stored in the repository, or "active collection" – where some people in the organization are scanning communication processes to detect knowledge.

Davenport and Prusak [14] divide between three types of knowledge repositories:

1. *Eternal knowledge repositories* (such as competitive intelligence)
2. *Structured internal knowledge repositories* (such as research reports, product-oriented market material).
3. *Informal internal knowledge repositories* (such as "lessons learned").

There are many examples of informal knowledge repositories from the software engineering literature.

The University of Nebraska-Lincoln has developed a research prototype tool for knowledge management support in software development called BORE [15]: This is a tool which contains information in cases about problem solving experience, and descriptions of resources like tools, projects, people and development methods. These descriptions are used to find relevant solutions when software developers are faced with a new problem.

Another prototype system, is CODE – a general-purpose knowledge management tool which serves as a medium for knowledge capture, transfer and iteration, as well as editing or "packaging" knowledge to make it easily available [16].

The Fraunhofer Institute for Experimental Software Engineering has developed "COIN Experience Factory" – a tool for capturing experience from research projects in software engineering [17].

ICL Finland has developed a knowledge management system, which includes a repository divided in two parts [18]:

– Structured internal knowledge: includes databases for sales and marketing information and employee competence, as well as examples of frequently used documents, templates, software components, best practice information, and research reports.
– Informal internal knowledge: includes electronic discussion forums, news and "project folders". The project folders contain overviews of the projects, news and important announcements, technical documents and reusable components (for a complete list, refer to the paper cited earlier).

What kind of knowledge can we expect to find in these repositories? Taylor [19] who has been working in the "information use" field, divides information into seven groups: *Enlightenment* – to use information for ones own amusement, an example can be company-internal news that are not fully relevant to normal work. *Problem understanding* – using information to increase the comprehension of a problem.

Instrumental – follow guidelines or procedures. *Factual* – use information to determine facts. *Confirmational* – use information to verify other information. *Projective* – make forecasts or scenarios. *Personal or political* – use information to develop relationships.

There has been little work describing how knowledge repositories are used in practice. That is what we aim to do in this paper, and we will be using the classification developed by Taylor in examining the types of usage later.

9.3 Research Method

To obtain the data for the research reported in this Chapter, we used a method inspired by ethnography [20]. For the analysis, we used grounded theory [21]. We observed for four weeks at the software consulting company Computas during the autumn 2000. This company was selected because we knew they had been working with knowledge management for a long time and had some interesting tools. We got access to their Intranet systems, and attended all meetings where all the employees were invited as well as meetings in one project. The project was chosen by Computas: a software development project for a public customer. We interviewed eight developers and six managers. Three developers worked in the project we followed, the others had got awards as "knowledge sharers of the month". We interviewed the project leader in the project we followed, as well as two process owners for knowledge-management related processes. We also interviewed two general managers, and three managers who had got a "knowledge sharer of the month" award.

In addition we conducted a so-called Learning History [22] from the development and implementation process of an informal knowledge repository. This entailed interviews and process-meetings with six central contributors.

9.3.1 Data Collection

We used the following data sources:

- *Interviews* – we used semi-structured interviews with open-ended questions. The interviews were transcribed in full, and in total, we got around 120 pages of transcripts for analysis (also on other knowledge management tools than the knowledge repository). We asked questions like "how do you assess the tools for knowledge management that you have available?", "what knowledge have you found useful from these tools?" and "when do you use the tools?".
- *Screenshots* – we gathered screenshots from different areas of the knowledge management system.
- *Pictures* – we took pictures of people in normal work-situations to get a better understanding of the workplace and work processes.
- *Logbook* – we wrote down observations from everyday life in the company in a logbook, together with memorandums from conversations we had, meetings and presentations we attended.

9.3.2 Data Analysis

How did we organize the analysis of the data that was collected? First, we constructed a database with information from the interviews, documents, and our own logbook observations (using N5, a tool for analysis of qualitative research data). We tagged the information to show what kind of source it came from, and applied a simple categorization of the people that were interviewed: managers, project managers, developers, and people responsible for knowledge management.

We searched in this database for areas of interest, and got the information from the different sources. For example, searching this database for the keyword "skill" would result in 43 occurrences in 10 documents.

After that, we analyzed (and "coded") these chunks of information to find interesting categories that would be usable to build theory later. Would there be any special patterns in what the people were saying? We applied triangulation to see if there were differences between groups of people.

9.4 The Computas Software Consulting Company

We investigated the usage of a knowledge repository at Computas. Computas is a medium-sized consulting company based in Norway, developing knowledge-based systems for a variety of customers. When it was founded in 1985, it was a spin-off of a larger, more general consulting company, and according to a Norwegian newspaper, "an international staff of specialists will develop expert systems that above all will cover the needs of the demanding oil industry". The newspaper continues: the company shall "offer services in industrial use of knowledge-based expert systems, and software in the field of artificial intelligence".

Since then, the company has grown organically, from just a few employees in the beginning, to around 150 in year 2000. The company has also extended their services and market.

The company's core competence is knowledge management, process-support and implementation of intelligent systems for knowledge-based behavior and knowledge processes.

Important technology for delivering these solutions, are "network and database technology, document management and search, web technology, work process support, coordination technology, artificial intelligence and data mining". The underlying technology for this is Java, Microsoft and SmallTalk technology.

Customers come from three main groups, the public sector, the marine sector and industry. Projects for these customers typically include 3–10 people working for at least half a year, and in some cases for several years. In projects, the participants take on different roles, as "project manager", "technical manager", and "customer contact".

The company is organized around "processes" and "projects". The "process organization" means that they have defined important areas for the company, which has one "process manager", usually with support from a small team. Examples of processes are "Management", "Delivery" and "Support", and also "Knowledge

Management". Many employees in the company are responsible for some process issue while working on a project. Most employees have a university degree in Computer Science, and some have a Ph.D. degree, especially in Artificial Intelligence.

The Knowledge Management Process at Computas includes handing out a prize to the "knowledge sharer of the month" in order to promote knowledge management. This prize has been given to people who share their knowledge through Computas's knowledge management tools, or through oral communication.

On first sight, the organization seems very "flat" – with people rotating between different "process manager" positions. But as one employee told us, "of course, there is a hierarchy here as well, it is just not written down any place".

When working in projects, most of the development has traditionally been done "in-house", and not at the customer's site. But it is now getting more frequent that employees work in the customer companies. When we were visiting the company, around 20% of the staff were working somewhere else than in the main company building.

9.5 The Knowledge Repository: Well of Experience

Computas has a variety of knowledge management tools available on their Intranet, see [23] for an overview. One of the tools is the unstructured knowledge repository "Well of experience", or WoX. According to Davenport and Prusak's classification it would be an informal internal knowledge repository. It is a small tool for capturing knowledge that would normally be written on yellow stickers, what the company calls "collective yellow stickers". The yellow sticker analogy was in fact a major midwife aid in the initial understanding and practice for getting the system to be used. "Rather than using the post-it note, write your private yellow sticker in the WoX system so others can make use of them". That way the employees always know that there will be some information of use in the system. This way of contributing to the repository is what Heijst et al. describes as a passive collection process.

WoX contains everything from the phone-number to the pizza restaurant on the corner to "how you set up SmallTalk on a special platform". You find information by searching an unstructured database, and can give "credits" to notes that you find useful. Notes with more accumulated credits about an issue show up before notes with less. The tool contains a mechanism to give feedback to the person who wrote the note, and there has been a kind of competition in the company to get the most credits. One developer described this repository as "quite useful - it is simple enough to be used in practice". Another said "you can use WoX as a personal notice board where you can put the same information as you would on a yellow sticker. It's fast to insert notes, and you do not have to worry about where to put it".

When we visited the company, it contained around 600 "experience notes". In 2003, WoX contained around 990 notes and have had about 15,000 searches by 260 users (some customers are also allowed to use the tool in addition to Computas employees). There are 2,300 keywords in the repository.

Employees can search the knowledge repository using a simple search interface available on the company Intranet, see Fig. 9.2. The functionality is simple keyword search, and you can browse the notes and comments on other people's notes that you have contributed, the credits your notes have gotten from others, the latest 10 notes that have been added to the repository, popular keywords as well as the notes with the most credits. In the simple search, you can select if you want to search in the text and subject information of the notes or also in the comments on notes.

Examples of such notes are "how to reduce the size of your profile in Windows NT", "How to remove garbage from an image in SmallTalk", "Technical problems with cookies" and "An implementation of the soundex algorithm in Java". See Fig. 9.3 for a complete example of a note.

Each note contains a subject, a descriptive text, as well as keywords (the one submitting the note defines the keyword, there is no predefined list of keywords), author information and the date it was submitted. When viewing a note, everyone can add a comment to the note, give the note a credit or mail the note as a tip to someone else.

According to one developer "people are very good at submitting notes when they think that something can be useful for others". A manager described it as "a behavioral arena that people use in different ways, that is creating a culture of knowledge sharing, and even creates expectations and lets people experience that others make use of their knowledge". The tool is promoted by posters which can be found on places that people visit a lot, like the one in Fig. 9.4 which was located just outside the staff restaurant.

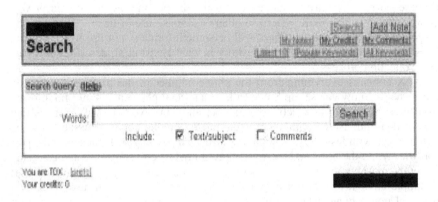

Fig. 9.2. The "Well of experience" (WoX) search interface for the knowledge repository of "experience notes"

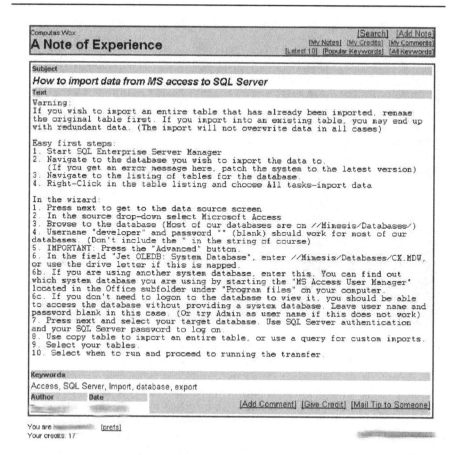

Fig. 9.3. An example experience note

When we asked people to describe what kind of tools they were using in their work, almost all of the developers mentioned that they were using WoX. All developers but one (seven out of eight) say that they have written experience notes, and all of them have tried to search for experience notes. Among the managers, much fewer were using it actively. Three out of six did not mention WoX when we asked about knowledge management tools in the company.

Are there areas where the tool has been found not to be effective? At least it is not a space devoted to routines and reflection: "WoX is not suitable as an arena for rutinized knowledge and long strings of reasoning." Another critical factor is that "if a tool like WoX shall be useful, the total amount of available information must reach above a critical mass." Hence, the analogy with the yellow stickers. It was vital to get the consultants themselves to put information into the system.

Fig. 9.4. "I've been WoX'ing today, have you?". One of several posters promoting the use of the WoX knowledge repository at Computas

Summarizing some of the potentials in WoX, one employee said: "New functionality and technical tips are suitable to be mediated by WoX. Also, it is usable for putting bits of programs and reusable components. Put another way, WoX-notes should be little patterns of applied knowledge engineering".

Based on the material from Computas we found five different types of usage of the knowledge repository:

- solve a specific technical problem
- getting an overview of problem areas
- avoiding redundancy in having to explain the same solution to several people
- improve individual work situation by adjusting technical tools
- finding who has a specific competence in the company

We describe each of these types of usage in more depth:

9.5.1 Solve a Specific Technical Problem

The most prominent use of this tool seemed to be in "problem solving". As one developer put it "if you run into a problem, then you can use WoX to see if anyone else in the company has had a similar problem", or "when you sit with a problem that you can't solve, or a strange bug, or if you do not understand why the computer does not behave the way it should".

Another developer says: "It happens that I have been searching and have found things in WoX. Then you do not have to search in other places, and maybe spend two or three days".

It is also a good tool for sharing pieces of code, patterns, and reusable components with others.

A problem with the notes that one developer mentioned, is that "the person that writes something has a certain background, and with that background they presume that when they write 'first you do this, then that...' – that the others also know what to do". Which is not always the case for complicated matters.

9.5.2 Getting an Overview of Problem Areas

One said: "if I am stuck and wonder about something, usually I remember that it was written somewhere in WoX in fact, and then I go back and find it". An example is some notes about project-startup that this developer will usually go back to when being in that phase, which happens every six months or so. Another developer and another manager also said that they would see almost every day what was new "so I know what is in there, and do not have to search for things".

But people do not write about all types of problems as experience notes. Issues that are more "unofficial knowledge" - as one developer put it: "not things that are unethical, but things that you do that could easily be interpreted wrongly by customers, even though I mean we can stand for it" – that kind of issues you do not find any notes about, and that knowledge is transferred through informal oral communication.

9.5.3 Avoiding Redundancy

Some would use the WoX system to avoid redundancy in the sense of having to explain the same solution to several people. One developer said: "when the third person comes and asks about the same thing – then you realize that it is about time to document it". He would then later tell people who were asking about the new topic to look it up in WoX. WoX notes can be mailed easily by clicking on "Mail Tip to Someone" when looking at the note.

9.5.4 Improve Individual Work Situation

Others would improve their individual work situation by adjusting technical tools based on information found in WoX. They would find information on how to improve the tools that they use in their daily work, like Outlook, to make them more easy to use. Another example would be to get to know "how to reduce your profile in Windows NT" – which reduces the booting-time of your operating system quite a bit. A third example of a small improvement is a note on how to burn CDs for customers; which explained how to design covers for the CDs so that they look more professional when delivering a final software product.

9.5.5 Finding Competence

The last major category of types of WoX usage we found in Computas was finding who has a specific competence in the company: "Newbies get a shortcut to
discover things that I have spent some time to build up. If they browse WoX a bit,
they can find that 'this person knows a lot about low-level Windows-patching' and
that 'this person is good at Apache webserver set up'", one developer said. This
function of finding and linking "who knows what" is often an underestimated
function of knowledge management systems, and in the case of Computas it over-
laps with their "Skills-management" system [24]. The WoX notes gives clues to
where to search for further knowledge, and may in this way be said to broaden the
opportunity structures for knowledge sharing in Computas [25].

9.6 Discussion

From our interviews with developers and managers at Computas, it seems that the
WoX is a tool that is actively used, and is helpful for several purposes, although
the knowledge that it contains is unstructured, and the tool was easy to develop.

We note that managers contribute less frequently to the repository than developers. This might be because the kind of knowledge that is useful for developers is
easier to codify than knowledge, say on estimation of software projects, or project
management.

If we compare the types of usage we found in our interviews with the categories
developed by Taylor, we see that "solving a technical problem" and "improving
individual work situation" are types of knowledge that we can classify as "instrumental" – something you would look up and follow. "Avoiding redundancy" is
also in this category. "Getting an overview of problem areas" is similar to Taylor's
"problem understanding". "Finding competence" can be seen as using knowledge
as "personal or political".

Why is it that WoX is a popular tool to use at Computas? There were many
other tools in the company that were not used as much. WoX had many users and
many different types of usage. One reason can be that this tool serves a purpose
that other tools in the company do not. It is like a newsgroup on the Internet in one
sense, but contains mostly knowledge that is local to the company. Employees
have also been encouraged to contribute with experience notes in the tool –
through advertisements in the company as in Fig. 9.4, and also through "commercial banners" at the company Intranet. The tool is also easily accessible from the
Intranet that most people at Computas use daily. Another reason can be the use of
"credits" – that people get feedback on what they have contributed – and are thus
motivated to contribute more. A final reason can be the company emphasis on
sharing knowledge, that employees who have written many experience notes get a
small prize as the "knowledge sharer of the month".

One of the topics discussed in Computas is the organization of the WoX system.
Should it be structured or not? For example we found the opinion that too much
structure hinders the growth of notes: "We must not construct too many links in

WoX. It must not be too formalized. The strength of WoX is that it is organically growing. We have a hierarchy several other places, for example on the [internal] web." On the other hand, utility of the system to some degree means fast access: "WoX is a bit slow, and I miss the opportunity to browse".

"When WoX is so unstructured it is difficult to reuse information. I can see a danger that WoX becomes a kind of Internet (in the negative sense). A huge archive where it is difficult to maneuver and find useful information".

Another discussion in Computas was the explicit integration of WoX with other knowledge management tools, as for instance the Skills Manager. "We have competing mechanisms for knowledge sharing. We have to work more on developing distinct roles for the different electronical mediums we use for sharing knowledge". As an integrated part of dialogues with customers, for example concerning change requests, WoX could also play a part: "WoX could be used as a channel for change request from customers. WoX should be an integral part of development projects with customers and a central part of communication with them. In this way we could have built a pool of experience concerning the establishment of a system for the customer, a pool that both of us could have utilized". WoX would then have stored tips for other users and tips for revisions of the system.

9.7 Conclusion and Further Work

We have examined how an informal knowledge repository is used in a medium-sized software consulting company. We found that the well of experience, WoX, is especially appreciated amongst developers and used to a wide degree compared to other similar tools in other companies, even though the company is quite small for a codification strategy. We also found that:

- The Knowledge repository is used for different types of instrumental knowledge, as well as knowledge to increase problem understanding, and to strengthen personal and political ties.
- The company plans to develop the tool further.

What can we learn from the usage of the knowledge repository at Computas when developing similar tools in other companies? First of all, we think the emphasis on combining an easy to use technical tool, which does not require rigor in contributing with knowledge (the unstructured nature) and the social incentives for use in the company were fruitful.

We think the emphasis on formal structures, techniques and procedures are generally overrated in the software engineering field, while the power of social aspects are underestimated.

Some main discussion points in the company on how to develop the repository further are:

- There has been a discussion in the company on whether to make the knowledge in the tool more structured. Many have opposed as structure can be found in other tools, and would make the tool harder to use.

– The company has raised a discussion on if it should combine the tool with other tools.

Acknowledgement

We are deeply grateful to all employees we have talked to at Computas for sharing their opinions on experience sharing, and especially Hans Karim Djarraya who has been our main contact person. We would further like to thank Gavin Gaudet and the anonymous reviewers for helpful comments.

We are further grateful to the Research Council of Norway for supporting this work through the projects PROFIT and KUNNE.

References

[1] Rus, I. and Lindvall, M. (2002) Knowledge Management in Software Engineering, *IEEE Software,* No. May/June, pp. 26–38

[2] Hansen, M.T., Nohria, N., and Tierney, T. (1999) What is your strategy for managing knowledge?, *Harvard Business Review,* No. 2, Vol. 77, pp. 106–116

[3] Schneider, K., Von Hunnius, J.P., and Basili, V.R. (2002) Experience in Implementing a Learning Software Organization, IEEE Software, No. May/June, pp. 46–49

[4] Houdek, F., Schneider, K., and Wieser, E. (1998) Establishing Experience Factories at Daimler-Benz. An Experience Report, *Proceedings of the 20th International Conference on Software Engineering,* ICSE 20, Kyoto, Japan

[5] Basili, V.R., Caldiera, G., Mcgarry, F., Pajerski, R., Page, G., and Waligora, S. (1992) The Software Engineering Laboratory - An operational software experience factory, *Proceedings of the 14th International Conference on Software Engineering,* ICSE 14

[6] Johansson, C., Hall, P., and Coquard, M. (1999) "Talk to Paula and Peter - They Are Experienced" – The Experience Engine in a Nutshell, in Learning Software Organizations: Methodology and Applications; Proceedings from the 11th International Conference on Software Engineering and Knowledge Engineering, SEKE 1999, Kaiserslautern, Germany, June 16–19, 1999., Lecture Notes in Computer Science, Vol. 1756, G. Ruhe and F. Bomarius, Eds. Springer Berlin Heidelberg New York, 1999, pp. 171–186

[7] Dingsøyr, T. and Conradi, R. (2002) A Survey of Case Studies of the Use of Knowledge Management in Software Engineering, *International Journal of Software Engineering and Knowledge Engineering,* No. 4, Vol. 12, pp. 391–414

[8] Ruppel, C.P. and Harrington, S.J. (2001) Sharing Knowledge Through Intranets: A Study of Organizational Culture and Intranet Implementation, *IEEE Transactions on Professional Communication,* No. 1, Vol. 44, pp. 37–52

[9] Ruggles, R.L. (1997) Knowledge Management Tools, in *Resources for the Knowledge-Based Economy,* Boston: Butterworth-Heinemann

[10] Sørlie, A., Coll, G.J., Dehli, E., and Tangen, K. (1999) Knowledge Sharing in Distributed Organizations, *IJCAI Workshop on Knowledge Management and Organizational Memories,* Stockholm, Sweden

[11] Borghoff, U.M. and Pareschi, R. (1998) *Information Technology for Knowledge Management.* Springer Berlin Heidelberg New York, ISBN 3-540-63764-8

[12] Liebowitz, J. and Beckman, T. (1998) *Knowledge Organizations: What Every Manager Should Know,* Boca Raion, FL: CRC Press

[13] Van Heijst, G., Van Der Spek, R., and Kruizinga, E. (1997) Corporate Memories as a Tool for Knowledge Management, *Expert Systems with Applications,* No. 1, Vol. 13, pp. 41–54

[14] Davenport, T.H. and Prusak, L. (1998) *Working Knowledge: How Organizations Manage What They Know,* Harvard Business School Press, ISBN 0-87584-655-6

[15] Henniger, S. (1997) Case-Based Knowledge Management Tools in Software Development, *Automated Software Engineering,* No. 3, Vol. 4, pp. 319–339

[16] Skuce, D. (1995) Knowledge management in software design : a tool and a trial, *Software Engineering Journal,* No. 5, Vol. 10, pp. 183–193

[17] Decker, B. and Jedlitschka, A. (2001) The Integrated Corporate Information Network: iCoIN: A Comprehensive, Web-Based Experience Factory, *Proceedings of the Learning Software Organizations Workshop,* Kaiserslautern, Germany

[18] Markkula, M. (1999) Knowledge Management in Software Engineering Projects, *Proceedings of the International conference on Software Engineering and Knowledge Engineering,* SEKE'99, Kaiserslautern, Germany

[19] Taylor, R.S. (1991) Information Use Environments, *Progress in Communcation* Science

[20] Fetterman, D.M. (1998) *Ethnography: Step by Step,* Vol. 17: Sage Publications, ISBN 0-7619-1384-X

[21] Strauss, A. and Corbin, J. (1998) *Basics of Qualitative Research,* Second edition: Sage Publications, ISBN 0-8039-5939-7

[22] Roth, G. and Kleiner, A. (1999) *Car Launch: The human side of managing change,* NY: Oxford University press

[23] Dingsøyr, T. (2002) *Knowledge Management in Medium-Sized Software Consulting Companies,* doctoral thesis, Department of Computer and Information Science, Norwegian University of Science and Technology, Trondheim, p. 206, ISBN 82-7477-107-9

[24] Dingsøyr, T. and Røyrvik, E. (2001) Skills Management as Knowledge Technology in a Software Consultancy Company, in *Proceedings of the Learning Software Organizations Workshop, Lecture Notes in Computer Science,* Vol. 2176, K.-D. Althoff, R.L. Feldmann, and W. Müller, Eds. Kaiserslautern, Germany: Springer Verlag, pp. 96–107

[25] Røyrvik, E. and Wulff, E. (2002) Mythmaking and Knowledge Sharing. Living Organizational Myths and the Broadening of Opportunity Structures for Knowledge Sharing in a Scandinavian Engineering Consultant company, *Journal of Innovation and Creativity Management,* No. 3, Vol. 11

10

An Empirical Study on the Utility of Formal Routines to Transfer Knowledge and Experience

R. Conradi and T. Dybå

Abstract: Most quality and software process improvement frameworks emphasize written (i.e. formal) documentation to convey recommended work practices. However, there is considerable skepticism aomong developers to learn from and adhere to prescribed process models. The latter are often perceived as overly "structured" or implying too much "control". Further, what is relevant knowledge has often been decided by "others" – often the quality manager.

The study was carried out in the context of a national software process improvement program in Norway for small and medium-sized companies to assess the attitude to formalized knowledge and experience sources. The results show that developers are rather skeptical at using written routines, while quality and technical managers are taking this for granted. This is an explosive combination.

The conclusion is that formal routines must be supplemented by collaborative, social processes to promote effective dissemination and organizational learning. Trying to force a (well-intended) quality system down the developers' throats is both futile and demoralizing. The wider implications for quality and improvement work is that we must strike a balance between the "disciplined" or "rational" and the "creative" way of working.

Keywords: software process improvement, knowledge transfer, knowledge management, formal routines, developer attitudes.

10.1 Introduction

To regulate and improve the work in software development, many organizations and projects have documented their "best work practices" as *formal routines*. These may be prescribed process models, guidelines, rules, check-lists etc.

On the other hand, we cannot expect adherence to formal routines ("process conformance") unless the routines are understood, respected and demonstrated to be useful in daily practice. We can mention two extremes: young programmers are famous for their improvisation and disregard for written laws and regulations (the "creative" work mode). On the other hand, we have the military commando system where rules and commands should be obeyed to the letter (the "disciplined" work mode).

The described study was carried out in the context of a Norwegian software process improvement program, SPIQ, involving a dozen small and medium-sized software-intensive companies. Many of these companies have installed their own quality systems and/or experience bases, but not all these were fully exploited by the developers.

Thus, it was natural to investigate how different user groups, such as developers and managers, perceived formal routines as a medium to express and disseminate knowledge and experience.

The structure of the rest of the paper is as follows: Section 10.2 gives a summary of related work. Section 10.3 explains the issues and hypotheses raised and the research method to explore these. Section 10.4 reports the results, Sect. 10.5 discusses these, and Sect. 10.6 contains a conclusion.

10.2 Related Work

This section summarizes related work on a more general level. The discussion in Sect. 10.5 contains some more specific references to related work.

The emphasis on formal routines reflects a common assumption in software process improvement (SPI) and quality assurance (QA), that "*the quality of a software product is largely governed by the quality of the process used to develop and maintain it*" [30], p. 8. This often means that relevant work practices (processes) must be systematically documented as formal routines, often as standard process models. These routines must then be communicated to the developers, customized and adopted by them and later revised based on experience and overall strategies. Many companies have established sophisticated *quality systems,* encoding such routines. Such a quality system may be coupled to a *software experience base (SEB)*, containing both experimental data and aggregated models (i.e. "knowledge") based on such data.

With the advent of Internet and Web technologies, many quality systems and experience bases are now using such electronic media. We should, however, emphasize that such technological remedies are only a means to reach a goal. In all quality and improvement work, the ultimate success criterion is *satisfied customers* in the spirit of Total Quality Management (TQM) [15] or ISO-9001 [28].

---

[6] SINTEF is The Foundation for Scientific and Industrial Research at the Norwegian Institute of Technology.

Some definitions Within the context of this study, we define *formalization* as written rules, procedures, and instructions. *Explicit* knowledge is formalized knowledge, e.g. as process models or guidelines. *Tacit* knowledge is the operational skills that practitioners possess, including practical judgement capabilities (e.g. intuition) [27]. Tacit knowledge cannot always be made explicit. *Learning* is lasting modification in behavior, based on experience and understanding, and requires *both* formal training and informal information exchange. Many theories of learning exist, see e.g. [5, 35]. For transfer of experience, a useful model is developed by Nonaka and Takeuchi [27]:

Figure 10.1 expresses that practitioners first *internalize* new knowledge (i.e. individual learning). The new knowledge is then *socialized* into revised work processes and changed behavior (group learning). The new work processes and the changed behavior are then observed and abstracted, i.e. *externalized*. This new knowledge is then *combined* to refine and extend the existing knowledge (organizational learning). This process continues in new cycles etc.

To enable *learning* is the crucial issue, both at the individual, group, and organizational level. The latter means creating and sustaining a *learning organization* that constantly improves its work, by letting employees share experience with each other. Around the underlying experience bases, there may be special (sub) organizations to manage and disseminate the stored experience and knowledge, as exemplified by the *Experience Factory* [7]. We also refer to the workshop series of *Learning Software Organizations* [4, 9].

Other fields have introduced the term *organizational* or *corporate memory* to characterize an organization's strategic assets, although not only from a learning point of view [1].

The *knowledge engineering* community has also worked on experience bases, often with emphasis on effective knowledge representations, deduction techniques

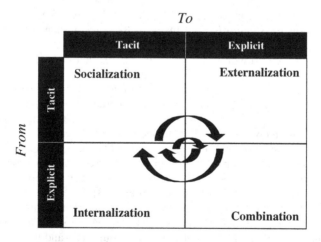

Fig. 10.1. A model of knowledge conversion between tacit and explicit knowledge [27]

etc., and towards a wide range of applications. The subfield of *Case-Based Reasoning* [3] has sprung up from this work, enabling reuse of similar, past information ("cases") to better master new situations. We will also mention the subfield of *Data Mining* [20].

Social anthropologists and *psychologists* have studied how organizations "learn", and how their employees make use of information sources in their daily work. Much R&D effort has been spent on the "externalizing" flow, looking for valid experience that can be analyzed, generalized, synthesized, packaged and disseminated in the form of improved models or concepts. For instance, to make, calibrate and improve an estimation model based on the performance of previous software projects. Explicit knowledge may nevertheless be misunderstood due to lack of context and nuances, e.g. how to understand the context of post-mortems?

However, the hard part is the "internalizing" flow. That is, how to make an impact on current practice, even if updated knowledge may be convincingly available? See for instance the ethnographic study on the use of quality systems in [40]. Typical inhibitors are "not-invented-here", mistrust ("been-burned-before"), lack of extra time/resources ("not-getting started"), or plain unwillingness to try something new or different (like adhering to formal procedures in a quality system). A study of maintenance technicians for copy machines indicated that such experts were most likely to ask their colleagues for advice, rather than to look it up in or even to follow the "book" [10]. Indeed, how many times have not computer scientists asked their office mates about commands in Word or NT-Windows, instead of directly consulting relevant documentation – although a "query" into the latter can be hard to formulate.

Furthermore, the existence of *software quality manuals,* either on paper in thick binders (sometimes 1-2 m in the shelves) or in web documents on an Intranet, is no guarantee for their use. In fact, since manuals may dictate people on how to perform their job, traditional quality departments in many software organizations are not looked upon with high esteem by developers. For instance, there are over 250 proposed *software standards* [32], many of them recommending "standard" process models, but how many of these are in practical use?

So, if we are to succeed with formal routines and explicit knowledge in a quality system or a SEB to achieve *learning*, we must *not* carry the traditional "QA hat" of *control*. This does *not* mean that all, formal knowledge in the form of books, reports etc. (like this chapter) has to be discarded. The lesson is just that formal routines must be formulated and introduced with proper participation from the people involved, in order to have the intended effect on practice.

Lastly, many of the ideas and techniques on quality improvement (TQM and similar) come from manufacturing, with rather stable products, processes and organizations. Information technology, on the other hand, is characterized by rapid *product innovation*, not gradual process refinement [33]. One "IT" year is like a "dog" year (7 years) in other disciplines, and time-to-market seems sacred (i.e. schedule pressure). The strength of many software SMEs (Small and Medium-sized Enterprises) lies in their very ability to turn around fast and to convert next week's technologies into radically new products and services. Barrett [6] has used the term *improvisation*, a jazz metaphor, to characterize performers that execute evolving activities while employing a large competence base. With reference to our software development context, we must carefully adopt a set of quality and improvement technologies that can function in a very dynamic environment – so how to *manage constant change* [17]? Since SPI assumes that there is "something" stable that can be "improved", we must pick our learning focus accordingly. For instance, the Norwegian Computer Society (www.dnd.no) is now offering a course in "chaos and complexity theory" as an alternative to manage highly evolving projects.

However, it is fair to say that especially TQM *is* aware of the cultural and social dimensions of quality work. TQM has a strong emphasis on creating a learning organization, and having all employees participate and involve themselves in order to satisfy their customers.

So, how can software organizations best systematize, organize and exploit previous experience in order to improve their work?

10.3 Context, Questions, and Method

10.3.1 The SPIQ Project

The **SPIQ** project [12] was run for three years in 1997–1999, after a half-year pre-study in 1996. SPIQ stands for *SPI for better Quality*. The project, which was funded in part by the Research Council of Norway, involved three research institutions and 12 IT companies, mostly SMEs. More than 20 SPI pilot projects were run in these companies. A follow-up project called **PROFIT** is now carried out in 2000–2002.

The main result of the SPIQ project was a pragmatic *method handbook* [16], with the following components:

– A *dual,* top-down/bottom-up approach, using *TQM* [15] and *Quality Improvement Paradigm* [7] ideas.
– An adapted process for *ESSI-type* [19] *Process Improvement Experiments (PIEs).*
– The *Goal-Question-Metric* (GQM) method [8], and e.g. GQM feedback sessions.
– The *Experience Factory* concept [7], to refine and disseminate project experiences.
– An *incremental* approach, relying on action research [22].
– Reported *empirical studies* from five "SPIQ" companies.

Typical work in the 12 SPIQ companies included pilot projects to test out a certain improvement technology, like novel inspection techniques, incremental development, or use of measurement and software experience bases.

For further results from comparative studies of SPI success in the SPIQ companies and in several other Scandinavian PIEs, all emphasizing organizational and cultural factors see e.g. [13, 14, 18, 37].

10.3.2 How the Study Was Performed

Overall Organization. The actual study was carried out between NTNU/SINTEF and five companies participating in the SPIQ project. Data collection was carried out by two NTNU students in the last year of their M.Sc. study, as part of a "pre-thesis" project [11]. The two students were advised by the two authors of this paper, the former being their teacher and also a SPIQ researcher, the latter being a researcher and Ph.D. student attached to the SPIQ project.

Preparation. First, the student read and learnt about the project and relevant literature. Then we tried an initial formulation of some important issues in the form of research questions, and discussed these. At the same time, we contacted potential companies and checked their willingness to participate and their availability. Then a more detailed interview guide (see Sect. 10.3.3) was designed, in dialogue between the students and their advisors. The companies had been briefed about the questions, and when and how the interviews were going to be run.

Research Questions – important issues to address are:

Q1: What is the knowledge of the routines being used?
Q2: How are these routines being used?
Q3: How are they updated?
Q4: How effective are they as a medium for transfer of knowledge and experience?

And, furthermore, are there important differences between developers and managers, and how much cooperation is involved in making and updating the routines?

Subjects. Initially, we tried to have a dozen companies involved, but the time frame of the students' availability (three months in spring of 1999) only allowed five companies. One of these was in Trondheim, the rest in Oslo. Three of the companies were ISO-9001 certified. Two of the companies were IT/telecom companies, the rest were software houses. A convenience sample (i.e. available volunteers) of 23 persons were interviewed based on their experience with SPI, whereof 13 developers and 10 managers. The latter group included one quality manager and one software manager (e.g., division or project manager) from each of the five companies.

Data collection. After finishing the interview guide, this was sent by email to the respondents. A few days later, the two students visited the companies, and spent a full day at each company. At each place they spent up to one hour with each respondent in semi-structured interviews. In each interview, the four questions were treated one after another. One of the students was asking the questions, and both students made notes (interview records) during the interview. The other student served as a scribe, and wrote down a structured summary immediately after the interview. The first student then checked this against his own notes.

Data analysis. The ensuing categorization and data analysis was done by the two students, in cooperation with the authors, and reported in the students' pre-diploma thesis.

10.3.3 The Interview Guide

As mentioned, we formulated four main research questions, with a total of 14 sub-questions:

Q1. Knowledge of the routines.
    1.1 Describe the (possible) contents in routines being used for software development.
    1.2 How were these routines introduced in the company?
    1.3 What was the purpose of these routines?
    1.4 What is you personal impression of the routines?

Q2. Use of routines.
    2.1 What status does a given routine have among developers?
    2.2 To what degree are the routines actually being used?
    2.3 Who are the most active/passive users?
    2.4 What is the availability of the routines?
    2.5 How is follow-up and control of usage done?

Q3. Updating of routines.
    3.1 What procedures are used to update the routines?
    3.2 Who participates in the update activities?

Q4. Routines as a medium for transfer of Knowledge and Experience.
    4.1 Do you regard written routines as an efficient medium for transfer of knowledge and experience?
    4.2 What alternatives to written routines do you think are useful or in use in the company?
    4.3 What barriers against transfer of experiences do you think are most important?

The interview guide contained advice on how to deal with structured questions, usually with three answer categories such as "yes-maybe-no" or "little-some-much". We allowed more unstructured commentaries in the form of prose answers to solicit more direct and commentary opinions.

10.4 Results

In this section, we present the results of our study regarding the utility of formal routines as a medium for transfer of knowledge and experience. The focus is on participation and potential differences in opinion between developers and managers regarding the utility of the routines.

10.4.1 Knowledge of the Routines

All respondents had a fairly good knowledge of the routines that were in place in their respective companies. In fact, two thirds of the respondents showed good knowledge about the content of the routines. Table 10.1 illustrates this, and shows how well developers and managers were able to describe the specific contents of the routines in their company.

However, when it came to knowledge about how the routines were introduced, 50% of the developers did not know anything about this process. On the other hand, only one manager did not know about the introduction process. All in all, it turned out that about 30% of the developers and 70% of the managers had actively *participated* in the introduction of routines (Table 10.2).

Furthermore, it seemed to be a common understanding regarding the *objective* of having formal routines. Most respondents said that such routines were useful with respect to quality assurance. Other respondents said that they would enable a more unified way of working. However they emphasized that:

"Routines should not be formalistic, but rather useful and necessary".

Respondents in the three ISO-9001 certified companies claimed that their routines were first and foremost established to "get the certificate on the wall", and that the quality of their software processes had gained little or nothing from the ISO certification. One of the respondents expressed his views on this by the following example:

"You might be ISO certified to produce lifebelts in concrete, as long as you put the exact same amount of concrete in each lifebelt."

Table 10.1. Knowledge of company routines

	software developers (n = 13)		managers (n = 10)	
	frequency	percent	frequency	percent
little	-	-	-	-
some	6	46	2	20
much	7	54	8	80

Table 10.2. Degree of involvement during introduction of routines

	Degree of involvement			
	Low		High	
	frequency	percent	freqency	percent
Developers	9	69	4	31
Managers	3	30	7	70

Although some of the respondents were critical to the routines, stating that:

"10% of the routines are useful, while the remaining 90% is nonsense"

Most respondents, nevertheless, had a good impression of the routines, typically stating that:

"Routines are a prerequisite for internal collaboration."
"Routines are a reassurance and of great help."

10.4.2 Use of Routines

Software developers and managers agreed on the degree to which the routines were used. In general, they answered that about 50% of the routines were in use, and that the more experienced developers used the routines to a lesser extent than the more inexperienced developers do. Furthermore, it was a common agreement that:

"There is no point in having routines that are not considered useful".

However, the status of the routines among the software developers was highly divergent, as seen from the following statements:

"The routines are generally good and useful, but some developers are frustrated regarding their use."
"The system is bureaucratic – it was better before, when we had more freedom to decide for ourselves what should best be done."
"The routines are easy to use."
"Routines are uninteresting and revision meetings are boring."

10.4.3 Updating of Routines

None of the companies had scheduled revisions as part of the process for updating their routines. Most answers to this issue were rather vague. Some respondents explained that such revisions were informally triggered, while other respondents did not know how to propose and implement changes to existing routines.

However, respondents from all of the companies, both managers and software developers, said that all employees in their respective companies could participate in the revision activities if they wanted to.

10.4.4 Routines as a Medium for Transfer of Knowledge and Experience

The answers to this issue varied a lot, and indicated highly different attitudes regarding the effectiveness of formal routines for knowledge and experience transfer. Particularly, it seemed to be a clear difference in judgment between software developers and managers. While seven of the ten managers regarded written routines as an efficient medium for knowledge transfer, none of the developers did! Furthermore, half of the developers considered such routines to be inefficient for knowledge transfer, while only one of the managers shared this view.

Typically, managers said that written routines were important as means for replacing the knowledge of the people that had left the company. Software developers, on the other hand, did not make such a clear connection between experience, knowledge transfer and formal routines. One software developer said that different groups within the company never read each other's reports, while another developer maintained that it would take too much time to learn about the experience of the other groups. Several of the developers explained their views by stating that the documentation was not good enough, it was hard to find, boring to use and that it takes too much time.

When asked about useful alternatives to written routines, the respondents answered that they regarded some kind of "Experience base" or "Newsgroup" as the highest ranked alternative. Other high-ranked alternatives were "Socialization", "Discussion groups", "Experience reports", "Group meetings", and "On-the-job training". Table 10.3 shows these alternatives in rank order (1 is best) for software developers and managers respectively.

We also asked the respondents about what they regarded as the most important barriers against transfer of knowledge and experience. Nearly all of them said that such transfer, first and foremost, is a personal matter depending on how much each individual whishes to teach their lessons-learned to others. Furthermore, the willingness to share depends on available time, personality, self-interest, and company culture.

Due to the rather small sample size in this study, and the low expected frequency in several of the cells in Table 10.4, we compared the respondents' assessments of the routines and their job function using Fisher's exact probability test. With this test, the exact probability (or significance level) that the obtained result is purely a product of chance is calculated [23]. The test statistic of 13.02 was highly significant ($p = 0.002$, two-tailed). Thus, we rejected the hypothesis of independence and concluded that there is a difference in the distribution of assessment of the usefulness of formal routines as an efficient medium for transfer of knowledge and experience between software developers and managers.

Table 10.3. Alternative media for knowledge transfer

	rank	
medium	developers	managers
experience bases/newsgroups	1	1
socialization	2	3
discussion groups	3	2
experience reports	4	3
on-the-job-training	5	6
work with ext. consultants	6	-
group meetings	7	5

Table 10.4. Do you regard written routines as an efficient medium for transfer of knowledge and experience?

	software developers (n = 13)		managers (n = 10)	
	frequency	percent	frequency	percent
yes	-	-	7	70
both	7	54	2	20
no	6	46	1	10

Table 10.5. Degree of involvement vs. assessment of formal routines as an efficient medium for transfer of knowledge and experience

	degree of involvement	
efficient medium?	low	high
yes	-	7
both	5	4
no	7	-

Since software developers had been involved in the process of introducing the routines to a much lesser extent than the managers, we compared the respondent's assessment of the routines with the level of involvement using Fisher's exact test (Table 10.5). The test statistic of 14.71 was highly significant ($p < 0.0005$, two-tailed). Thus, we concluded that there is a difference in the assessment of the usefulness of formal routines as an efficient medium for transfer of knowledge and experience with respect to the degree of involvement in the introduction process.

10.5 Discussion

In this section, we restrict the discussion to possible explanations of why none of the software developers in our study regarded formal routines as an efficient medium for transfer of knowledge and experience. The reason for this is that we regard formalization and participation as important issues for the relevance of much of the SPI work done today by both researchers and practitioners.

The respondents in the study were software engineers and managers with an engineering background. Furthermore, software and quality managers with an engineering background wrote most of the routines. Thus, the routines were for a large part written by engineers – for engineers. Still, there was a highly significant difference in attitudes regarding the usefulness of the routines for transferring knowledge and experience between software engineers and managers.

As seen from our point of view, there are three main reasons for the observed diversity regarding the assessment of the efficiency of routines. One is the potential conflict between the *occupational cultures* of software developers and managers. The second reason has to do with the degree of *developer participation* in developing and introducing the routines. The third explanation has to do with the *views of working and learning* and thus, the ability of written routines in general to transfer human knowledge and experience. These reasons are discussed in Sect. 10.5.1–10.5.3.

10.5.1 Occupational Culture

There was a general agreement among all respondents that the intention of introducing formal routines was to contribute to an efficient process of developing quality software. In other words, the intention behind the formal routines was to provide appropriate methods and techniques, and standardize work processes needed to solve the problems at hand.

The differences we observed in attitude to the efficiency of formal routines between software developers and managers has close resemblance to the lack of alignment among executives, engineers, and operators described by Schein [34]. He explained these differences from a cultural perspective, defining culture as "a set of basic tacit assumptions about how the world is and ought to be, that a group of people share and that determines their perceptions, thoughts, feelings, and, to some degree, their overt behavior" [3.4., p. 11). Schein claimed that major occupational communities do not really understand each other, and that this leads to failures in organizational learning. According to Schein, the engineering culture and the executive culture has a common preference to see people as impersonal resources that generate problems rather than solutions. Furthermore, the engineers' need to do "real engineering" will drive them toward simplicity and routinized solutions that often ignore the social realities of the workplace, see work by Kunda [24] and Thomas [38].

Against this background, we can more easily understand the preference of formal routines within the SPI community as espoused by quality managers or members of Software Engineering Process Groups (SEPGs). Likewise, managers will rather put emphasis on rules, procedures, and instructions than on dialog, discussion and employee participation.

Further, software development is radically different from manufacturing. The former is not a mechanical process with strong causal models, where we just need to establish the "right" formal routines. Rather, the developers view software development largely as an intellectual and social activity. Therefore, we cannot apply a rationalistic, linear model to software engineering. We should admit that reality for most software organizations is a non-deterministic, multi-directional flux that involves constant negotiation and renegotiation among and between the social groups shaping the software [17].

This does not mean that we should discard discipline and formalization altogether. What is needed, is to *balance* the "odd couple" of discipline and creativity in software development [21]. This balance can be challenging, since losing sight of the creative, design-intense nature of software work leads to stifling rigidity, while losing sight of the need for discipline leads to chaos.

This leads us to the second possible reason for the divergent attitudes between developer and managers; that of employee participation around formal routines.

10.5.2 Participation

Employee participation, and the way people are treated, has been noted as a crucial factor in organizational management and development ever since the famous productivity studies at Western Electric's Hawthorne plant in the 1920s. The results of these studies started a revolution in management thinking, showing that even routine jobs can be improved if the workers are treated with respect.

Interestingly our study shows, that not only did managers participate significantly more during the introduction of routines, but also during the actual development of the routines. However, no one is more expert in the realities of a software company's business than the software developers themselves. They are not only experts on how to do the work – they are also the experts on how to improve it. Thus, the developers are a software organization's most important source of productivity and profits – the "human capital" view. It is therefore important to involve all the people that take part in a problem or its solution, and have decisions made by these. In this respect, all of the companies violated one of the most important aspects of employee involvement on their own work environment. They may even have "violated" the Norwegian work environment legislation!

Formalization is a central feature of Weber's [39] *bureaucratic* ideal type. Viewed in the light of our results, it is not surprising that research on formalization often presents conflicting empirical findings regarding its efficiency. Adler and Borys [2] explained this divergence by saying that prior research has focused on different *degrees* of formalization, and has paid insufficient attention to different *types* of formalization. They emphasize an *enabling* type of formalization, where procedures provide organizational memory as a resource to capture lessons-learned or best practice. The opposite is the *coercive* type of formalization, where procedures are presented without a motivating rationale and thus tend to be disobeyed, resulting in a non-compliant process.

Our results regarding the developers' assessment of the routines closely resemble the coercive type of formalization. The developers are clearly not against formal routines. In fact, they expressed views in favor of such routines, especially those that captured prior project experience. Contrary to the existing routines, which they deemed coercive, they wanted routines of the enabling type of formalization. Thus, the highest ranked alternative to formal routines was some sort of "experience base" or "newsgroup".

10.5.3 Working and Learning

Another aspect of our results is that they support Brown and Duguid's [10] perspective on learning-in-working. That is, we should emphasize informal, as opposed to formal learning. The same authors referred to these learning modes, respectively, as "non-canonical" and "canonical" practices. They suggested that training and socialization processes are likely to be ineffective if based on canonical practice, instead of the more realistic non-canonical practice:

"People are typically viewed as performing their jobs according to formal
job descriptions, despite the fact that daily evidence points to the contrary.
They are held accountable to the map, not to road conditions." (10., p. 42)

Thus, formal routines alone are inadequate, and might very well demand more
improvisational skills among developers. This is because of the rigidities of the
routines, and the fact that they do not reflect actual experience [17]. Although
many routines are prescriptive and simple, they are still hard to change, and they
cannot help in all the complex situations of actual practice from which they are
abstracted.

It is not surprising, therefore, that "socialization" and "discussion groups" were
among the highest ranked alternatives to formal routines. This is also in agreement
with Brown and Duguid's finding that "story-telling" is of utmost importance for
dealing with the complexities of day-to-day practice. Furthermore these authors
highlighted story telling as a means of diagnosing problems and as shared repositories of accumulated wisdom. This is similar to Zuboff's [40] emphasis on story-
telling to deal with "smart" machines, and to Greenwood and Levin's [22] use of
narratives in action research. Thus, contrary to the rigidities of formal routines,
stories and the tacit social activities are seen as more flexible, adaptable and relevant by the software developers in our study.

Furthermore, our results support the assertion that significant learning should
not be divorced from its specific context – so-called situated learning. Therefore,
any routines, generalizations or other means that strip away context should be
examined with caution. Indeed, it seems that learning could be regarded as a product
of a community i.e. organizational learning, rather than of the individual in it.
Thus lessons-learned cannot easily be transferred from one setting to another, see
Lave and Wenger [25].

10.5.4 Implications

Although the study is limited, the discussion earlier suggests several implications.
First, studies of the effects of formalization, whether they are enabling or coercive,
should focus on the features of the actual routines as well as their implementation.
In addition, we should pay attention to the process of designing the features and
the goals that govern this process.

Second, we must recognize and confront the implications of the deeply embedded and tacit assumptions of the different occupational cultures. And, furthermore, learn how to establish better cross-cultural dialogues in order to enable
organizational learning and SPI.

Third, a major practical implication is that managers should recognize the
needs of balancing discipline and creativity, in order to supplement formal routines with collaborative, social processes. Only by a deep and honest appreciation
of this, can managers expect effective dissemination of knowledge and experience
within their organization.

Based on the findings of this study, we conclude that both software managers
and developers must maintain an open dialogue regarding the utility of formal

routines. Such a dialogue will open the way for empirically based learning and SPI, and thus attain the rewards of an enabling type of formalization.

10.5.5 Limitations and Recommendations for Future Research

This study focused on the utility of formal routines to transfer knowledge and experience. Although it can provide valuable insights for introduction of formal routines in the software industry, our study is not without limitations.

First, the small sample and lack of randomness in the choice of respondents may be a threat to *external validity*. In general, most work on SPI suffers from non-representative participation, since companies that voluntarily engage in systematic improvement activities must be assumed to be better-than-average.

Second, a major threat to *internal validity* is that we have not assessed the reliability of our measures. Variables such as degree of involvement and efficiency of routines are measured on a subjective ordinal scale. An important issue for future studies is therefore to ensure reliability and validity of all measures used, see [18]. We may also ask if the respondents were truthful in their answers. For instance, they may have sensed we were "looking for trouble", and thus "giving us what we wanted" – i.e. exaggerating possible problems. However, their answers to the four main questions and their added qualitative comments show a consistent picture of skepticism and lack of participation concerning formal routines. We therefore choose to generally believe their answers.

Despite the mentioned limitations and lack of cross-checks, we feel that this study makes an important contribution to the understanding of formal routines and their role in organizational learning and SPI.

Future studies should examine the enabling features of formal routines in much more detail. The features could be refined and operationalized and used for cross-sectional and longitudinal studies of a much larger number of companies. Furthermore, such studies should include a multiple respondent approach to cover all major occupational cultures. They should also perform supplementary, ethnographic studies on how developers *really work* and how their work relate to formal routines – see [31] on observational studies of developers at ATT.

10.6 Conclusion

Results from the survey reported in this paper show that software developers do not perceive formal routines alone as an efficient way to transfer knowledge and experience. Furthermore, the study confirms our suspicions about large differences in perception of the utility of formal routines to transfer experiences and knowledge. That is, developers are skeptical to adopt formal routines found in traditional quality systems. They also want that such routines are introduced and updated in a more cooperative manner.

These results are not revolutionary and in line with many other investigations on similar themes [2, 24, 34]. See also Parnas and Clements' article [29] on how to fake a rational design process. So in spite of a small sample, we think that the results are *representative* for a large class of software companies.

The remedy seems to create a more *cooperative* and open work atmosphere, with strong developer participation in designing and promoting future quality systems. The developers also seem open to start exploiting new electronic media as a means for collaboration and linking to newer SEB technologies – see also our previous studies [13] on this. However, the major and most difficult work remains non-technical, that is, to build a *learning organization.*

Lastly, we were not able to make precise hypotheses on our four issues beforehand, so the study has a character of a preliminary investigation. Later studies may be undertaken with more precise hypotheses and on a larger sample.

Acknowledgments

Thanks to colleagues in the SPIQ project, to colleagues at NTNU and SINTEF, and not at least to the students Jon E. Carlsen and Marius Fornæss that did the fieldwork.

References

[1] Ackerman, M.S. and Halverson, C.A. (2000) Reexamining Organizational Memory, *CACM*, Vol. 43, No.1, pp. 59–64

[2] Adler, P.S. and Borys, B. (1996) Two Types of Bureaucracy: Enabling and Coercive, *Administrative Science Quarterly*, Vol. 41, pp. 61–89

[3] Althoff, K.-D., Birk, A., Hartkopf, S., Müller, W., Nick, M., Surmann, D., and Tautz, C. (1999) Managing Software Engineering Experience for Comprehensive Reuse, in *Proc. 11th Conf. on Software Engineering and Knowledge Engineering (SEKE'99)*, 16–19 June 1999, Kaiserslautern, Knowledge Systems Institute, Skokie, IL, pp. 10–19

[4] Althoff, K.-D.(Ed.) (2000) *Proc. 2nd Workshop on Learning Software Organizations* (associated to PROFES'2000), Oulu, 20 June 2000, Fraunhofer IESE, Kaiserslautern, 130 p

[5] Argyris, C. and Schön, D.A. (1996) *Organizational Learning II: Theory, Method, and Practice*, Reading, MA: Addison-Wesley, 1996

[6] Barrett, F.J. (1998) Creativity and Improvisation in Jazz and Organization: Implications for Organizational Learning, *Organization Science*, Vol. 9, No. 5, pp. 605–622

[7] Basili, V.R., Caldiera, G., and Rombach, H.-D. (1994)"The Experience Factory, In [26], pp. 469–476

[8] Basili, V.R., Caldiera, G., and Rombach, H.-D. (1994) The Goal Question Metric Paradigm, In [26], pp. 528–532

[9]   Bomarius, F. (Ed.) (1999) *Proc. 1st Workshop on Learning Software Organizations* (associated to SEKE'99), Kaiserslautern, 16 June 1999, Fraunhofer IESE, Kaiserslautern 126 p

[10] Brown,J.S. and Duguid, P. (1991) Organizational Learning and Communities of Practice: Toward a Unified View of Working, Learning, and Innovation, *Organization Science*, Vol. 2, No. 1, pp. 40–57

[11] Carlsen, J.E. and Fornæss, M. (1999) Undersøkelse om Prosessforbedring (in Norwegian – On How Quality Systems are Perceived), IDI, NTNU, Trondheim, 30 April 1999, 72 p., EPOS TR 357 (pre-diploma project thesis)

[12] Conradi,R. (1996) SPIQ: A Revised Agenda for Software Process Support, in Carlo Montangero, Ed., *Proc. 4th European Workshop on Software Process Technology (EWSPT'96)*, Nancy, France, 9–11 October 1996 Springer Berlin Heidelberg New York LNCS 1149, pp. 36–41

[13] Conradi, R., Lindvall, M., and Seaman, C. (2000) Success Factors for Software Experience Bases: What We Need to Learn from Other Disciplines, in J. Singer et al., (Ed.), *Proc. ICSE'2000 Workshop on Beg, Borrow or Steal: Using Multidisciplinary Approaches in Empirical Software Engineering Research*, Limerick, Ireland, 5 June 2000, 6 p

[14] Conradi, R. and Dingsøyr, T. (2000) Software Experience Bases: A Consolidated Evaluation and Status Report, in F. Bomarius and M. Oivo, (Ed.), *Proc. 2nd International Conference on Product Focused Software Process Improvement (PROFES'2000)*, 20–22 June 2000, Oulu, Springer Berlin Heidelberg New York LNCS 1840, pp. 391–406

[15] Deming, W.E. (1986) *Out of the Crisis*, MIT Center for Advanced Engineering Study, MIT Press, Cambridge, MA

[16] Dybå, T. (Ed.) (2000) *SPIQ metodebok for prosessforbedring i programvareutvikling – v3.0* (in Norwegian), SINTEF/ NTNU/UiO, Trondheim and Oslo, Norway, January 2000, ca. 200 p

[17] Dybå, T. (2000) Improvisation in Small Software Organizations, *IEEE Software*, Vol. 17, No 5, September-October 2000, pp. 82–87

[18] Dybå, T. (2000) An Instrument for Measuring the Key Factors of Success in Software Process Improvement, *Empirical Software Engineering*, Vol. 5, No. 4, December 2000, pp. 357–390

[19] ESSI Project Office (1995) Template for Running Software Process Improvement Experiments (PIEs), ESPRIT office, CEC, Brussels

[20] Fayyad, U., Piatetsky-Shapiro, G., and Smyth, P. (1996) Chapter on "From Data Mining to Knowledge Discovery: An Overview", in *Advances in Knowledge Discovery and Data Mining*, AAAI/MIT Press

[21] Glass, R.L. (1995) *Software Creativity*, Prentice Hall, Englewood Cliffs, NJ

[22] Greenwood, D.J. and Levin, M. (1998) *Introduction to Action Research: Social Research for Social Change*, Thousand Oaks, CA, Sage

[23] Hays, W.L. (1994) *Statistics*, Fifth edition, Harcourt Brace, NY

[24] Kunda, G. (1992) *Engineering Culture: Control and Commitment in a High-Tech Corporation*, Temple University Press, Philadelphia

[25] Lave, J. and Wenger, E. (1991) *Situated Learning: Legitimate Peripheral Participation*, Cambridge University Press

[26] Marciniak, J.J. (1994) (Ed.), *Encyclopedia of Software Engineering*, John Wiley & Sons, ISBN 0-471-54004-8

[27] Nonaka, I. and Takeuchi, H. (1995) *The Knowledge-Creating Company*, Oxford University Press

[28] Oskarsson, O. and Glass, R.L. (1996) *An ISO 9000 Approach to Building Quality Software*, Prentice Hall

[29] Parnas, D.L. and Clements, P.C. (1986) A Rational Design Process – How and Why to Fake it, *IEEE Trans. on Software Engineering*, Vol. 12, No. 2, pp. 251–257

[30] Paulk, m.C., Weber, C.V., Curtis, B., and Chrissis, M.B. (1995) *The Capability Maturity Model for Software: Guidelines for Improving the Software Process*, SEI Series in Software Engineering, Addison-Wesley, 640 p

[31] Perry, D.E., Staudenmayer, N., and Votta, L.G. (1994) People, Organizations, and Process Improvement, *IEEE Software*, Vol. 11, No. 4, July 1994, pp. 36–45

[32] Pfleeger, S.L., Fenton, N., and Page, S. (1994) Evaluating Software Engineering Standards, *IEEE Computer*, pp. 71–79

[33] Rifkin, S. (1999) Discipline of Market Leaders and Other Accelerators to Measurement, *Proc. 24th Annual NASA-SEL Software Engineering Workshop* (on CD-ROM), NASA Goddard Space Flight Center, Greenbelt, MD 20771, 1–2 December 1999, 6 p

[34] Schein, E.H. (1996) Three Cultures of Management: The Key to Organizational Learning, *Sloan Management Review*, Vol. 38, No. 1, Fall, pp. 9–20

[35] Senge, P.M. (1990) *The Fifth Discipline: The Art and Practice of the Learning Organization*, Currency/Doubleday

[36] Sharp, H., Woodman, M., and Robinson, H. (2000) Using Ethnography and Discourse Analysis to Study Software Engineering Practices, in Janice Singer et al., (Ed.), *Proc. ICSE'2000 Workshop on Beg, Borrow or Steal: Using Multidisciplinary Approaches in Empirical Software Engineering Research'*, Limerick, Ireland, 5 June 2000, pp. 81–87

[37] Stålhane, T. and Wedde, K.J. (1999) SPI – Why isn't it more used?, *Proc. EuroSPI'99*, Pori, Finland, pp. 26–27

[38] Thomas, R.J. (1994) *What Machines Can't Do*, Berkeley, California, University of California Press

[39] Weber, M. *Makt og byråkrati: Essays om politikk og klasse, samfunnsforskning og verdier* (Power and Bureaucracy: Essays about politics, class, social science and values), Third Edition, from *Wirtschaft und Gesellschaft* (1922), *Gesammelte Aufsätze zur Wissenschaftslehre* (1922) and *Gesammelte politische Schriften* (1921), Gyldendal, Oslo, Norway (in Norwegian), 2000

[40] Zuboff, S. (1988) *In the Age of the Smart Machine*, Basic Books, NY

Section 3

Process Modelling and Electronic Process Guides

Effectively disseminating process knowledge to process participants is crucial in any SPI effort. For process models to be useful, increasingly more software companies not only tailor their process models to the specific needs of the company, but also make them available on the company's intranet as a flexible on-line structure by means of an electronic process guide.

This section contains four chapter on the experience of using such process models and their electronic representations for SPI.

11. *Hanssen, G.K., Westerheim, H., and Bjørnson, F.O. (2005)* "Tailoring RUP to a defined project type: A case study," In Frank Bomarius and Seija Komi-Sirviö (Eds.): *Proc. 6th International Conference on Product Focused Software Process Improvement (PROFES'2005)*, 13–16 June, 2005, Oulu, Finland, Springer LNCS 3547, pp. 314–327.
This chapter reports on the experience of tailoring RUP to specific project types in a medium-sized consultancy company.

12. *Dingsøyr, T., Moe, N.B., Dybå, T., and Conradi. R. (2004)* "A workshop-oriented approach for defining electronic process guides – A case study," book chapter in *Software Process Modelling, Kluwer International Series on Software Engieering*, Silvia T. Acuña and Natalia Juristo (Eds.). Boston: Kluwer Academic Publishers, pp. 187–205.
This chapter reports from an empirical study on the use of workshop techniques for defining process models and their electronic counterparts.

13. *Dybå, T., Moe, N.B., and Mikkelsen. E.M. (2004)* "An Empirical Investigation on Factors Affecting Software Developer Acceptance and Utilization of Electronic Process Guides," In Martin Shepperd and Audris Mockus (Eds.): *Proc. 10th IEEE International Software Metrics Symposium (METRICS'04)*, Chicago, Illinois, USA, 14–16 September, 2004, IEEE-CS Press, pp. 220–231.
This chapter discusses the results of an empirical study on the factors affecting software developer acceptance and utilization of electronic process guides.

14. *Conradi, R., Fuggetta, A., and Jaccheri. M.L. (1998)* "Six theses on Software Process Research," In Volker Gruhn (Ed.): *Software Process Technology, Proc. 6th European Workshop (EWSPT'98)*, Weybridge, UK, 16–18. Sept. 1998, Springer Verlag LNCS 1487, pp. 100–104.
This chapter proposes some theses that synthesizes the research on software process technologies.

11

Tailoring RUP to a Defined Project Type: A Case Study

G. K. Hanssen, H. Westerheim, and F.O. Bjørnson

Abstract: The Unified Process is a widely used process framework for software development. The framework is covering many of the roles, activities and artifacts needed in a software development project. However, a tailoring of the framework is necessary to fit specific needs. This tailoring may be accomplished in various ways. In this chapter we describe a concrete attempt to tailor the Rational Unified Process to a defined project type; a Mainstream Software Development Project Type. The chapter has focus on the process of creating the tailored Rational Unified Process as well as the resulting Rational Unified Process. The chapter makes some conclusions and has a proposition for further research.

11.1 Introduction

The Unified Process [1] and the commercial variant, the Rational Unified Process, RUP [2] are comprehensive process frameworks for software development projects. RUP defines a software development project as a set of disciplines, e.g. requirements handling, implementation etc., running from start to end trough a set of project phases. A project is performed by a group of actors, each having one or more well defined roles. Each role participates in one or more activities producing one or more artifacts. A discipline can run in iterations, that is, repetitions within a phase. Activities, roles and artifacts are the basic process elements of RUP.

However, RUP is a comprehensive framework, meaning that it is a more or less complete set of process elements that has to be tailored to each case as no project needs the complete set of elements.

Jacobson, Booch and Rumbaugh says in [1] p.416:

"It [RUP] is a framework. It has to be tailored to a number of variables: the size of the system in work, the domain in which that system is to function, the complexity of the system and the experience, skill or process level of the project organization and its people." Further on they say: *"Actually, to apply it, you need considerable further information."*

So, it is clear that RUP needs to be tailored, downscaled and specialized to the context of use. Looking at literature there are not many guidelines on doing this

[3, 4, 5] although the need for good practical guidelines and advice definitively is present.

While discussing adaptation of RUP, it is important to have in mind that RUP is a methodology suited for some software development projects, not all. Before you consider using RUP as a basis for your processes you should think of what you really need and what you really do not need. RUP is designed to support four basic properties of software projects: use-case based customer dialogue and documentation, an architecture focus, iterative processes and incremental product development. The idea of adapting RUP is to make it fit each specific project not loosing these properties. It is important to keep the integrity of RUP as a framework. So, an adapted or downscaled variant still defines a project in terms of phases and still describes the work as a complimentary set of disciplines. However, some disciplines may be omitted or even added.

The goal of this chapter is to provide others considering remodeling and adapting a process framework in general, and RUP particularly, an insight in how this has been done in a small software company. Some aspects of the specialization process seems to have been working well, others not. This chapter presents the adaptation process and also gives an analysis of this process and its result.

The work detailed in this article was carried out as part of a national research project in process improvement and software quality called SPIKE. SPIKE is short for Software Process Improvement through Knowledge and Experience. The participants are SINTEF, NTNU, the University of Oslo and several partners (companies) in the Norwegian ICT-industry. The industrial partners are interested in improving their development process, and are seeking concrete processes and methods to help them deliver high quality software with shorter time to market.

The chapter starts with a **Theoretical context**, giving a brief introduction to methodologies and frameworks and various strategies of making these fit specific project needs of process support. It then describes the action research as the **Research method** of choice. The rest of the paper is arranged according to the research method phases; **Diagnosing**, **Action planning**, **Action taking**, **Evaluating** and **Learning**. Finally a **Conclusion** is given and **Further research** suggested.

11.2 Theoretical Context

11.2.1 Software Development Methodology and Frameworks

The term methodology is defined as "A body of methods, rules, and postulates employed by a discipline: a particular procedure or set of procedures" by the Merriam-Webster dictionary [6]. Basically, a methodology describes how someone, e.g. an organization performs a task, e.g. software development. In a broad sense, a software development methodology describes aspects such as how to communicate with customers, sales strategy, how to describe requirements, use of tools, test practices, documentation, planning, reporting and so on. In our context we talk about methodologies for running projects with a defined customer having more or less defined goals initially. Besides describing techniques, roles etc. most methodologies are based on a set of basic values. Examples are *User centric, Architecture centric, Agile, Risk driven* and many more. RUP has four basic values: *Use-Case Driven, Architecture-Centric, Iterative* and *Incremental*. These values should be retained regardless of how RUP as a framework is adapted. A methodology framework is a comprehensive description of a methodology describing approximately all possible details of almost all possible processes within the scope of the framework. This means that a framework is not a description of a specific case; it is a foundation for adaptation. The challenge is how to adapt it to each case (project) and keep the basic values and features of the framework.

11.2.2 Adaptation of RUP

The process of adapting RUP can possibly take many forms. IBM Rational, the provider of RUP has defined the *Process Engineering Process (PEP)* [5]. This is a comprehensive adaptation process requiring a fairly big amount of resources (people and time). This may very well be appropriate for larger companies, but for the small ones this process may be too expensive.

Adaptation of a framework, such as RUP, can take one of (at least) three approaches; see Fig. 11.1. The starting point is a process framework that is general and complete with respect to tasks, roles and products. In approach A, the framework is adapted, in one step, for each project, thus representing a heavy job in each case. This can be justified for large projects where the initial adaptation process itself becomes only a small part of the total amount of work being done in the project. In approach B, the organization does an up-front adaptation producing a subset of the framework, still being a framework, but now tuned to the organizations general characteristics. This is the intentional process of PEP. In approach

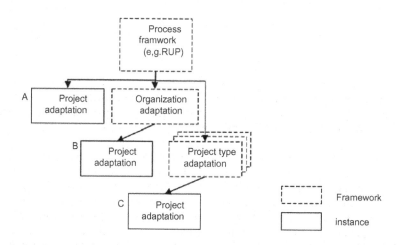

Fig. 11.1. Three possible approaches for adaptation

C, the organization first identifies and describes a set of recurring project *types*. Having knowledge of characteristics and differences of these types, an adaptation is done for each type.

No matter which approach being used; in the last step, a final adaptation is done to each case (project). The agility of this final fine tuning increases with respect to the extent of the up-front adaptation.

This is a general view of methodological adaptation or down-scaling. It applies to many types of process frameworks, including RUP. Further on, adapting RUP in practice means to decide on which process elements to keep, remove, alter or add. These decisions can be based on assumptions, experience, goals and visions. It is the quality of this underlying knowledge and experience that determines how good these decisions are.

Running an adaptation process, in general, can be seen as a knowledge management activity as experience and knowledge, both tacit and explicit, is being structured, documented and communicated trough the resulting software process description [7].

11.3 Research Method

Due to the cooperative nature of this research project with company external researchers acting partly as consultants and partly as researchers, we decided to adopt action research as our approach. Avison et al. [8] describes action research as: "unique in the way it associates research and practice. ... Action research combines theory and practice through change and reflection in an immediate problematic situation within a mutually acceptable ethical framework."

Susman and Evered [9] described an approach to action research that is widely used today. We have adopted elements from this approach in our research project. The approach requires the establishment of a client-system infrastructure or research environment. In our case this was already taken care of through the researchers and company's involvement in the SPIKE research program. The approach further specifies five identifiable phases, which are iterated: *diagnosing*, *action planning*, *action taking*, *evaluating* and *specifying learning*. This report details some of our findings and experiences from the initial phases. Our coverage of the evaluating and learning phases are based on our own observations of the process so far. A more thorough evaluation will be carried out as the company takes the resulting process description into use in real projects.

In the diagnosing phase, we used semi structured interviews and workshops with key employees. We interviewed five employees concerning their general experience with projects in the company. This gave us the material to do a more focused interview with five other employees concerning their specific experience with RUP in the company. In addition to this, several work-meetings were held with the management of the company where the SPI approach was discussed.

In the action planning phase, the researchers made a literature survey of the field of adapting RUP. It was decided to identify possible project types run by the company. This was done during two iterations, the first one a bottom-up approach, the second one a top-down approach. The top-down approach led to definition of three project types. In order to adapt the first project type, it was decided that the researchers should facilitate a workshop where key employees were invited to define the adapted process.

The workshop was carried out as part of the action taking phase. It was carried out over two days, since it was discovered that we needed more time than originally planned. At the first day we noted that the lack of a RUP mentor slowed the process considerably due to a lot of discussion on what was actually meant by the different concepts. At the second day, one such mentor was present, and the process was much more fluent. The result from the workshop was a coarse RUP skeleton, which was given to the company for more refinement. The company has conducted two internal workshops with its employees to refine the process. In addition they have initiated a project to put this information on a Wiki web, in order to make the adapted process available to all employees.

As the project moves into the evaluation phase, the role of the scientists switches to a more observational role. We plan on following the use of the adapted process for several development projects. By taking measures along the way we hope to be able to ascertain how successful the initiative has been for the company in its current context.

11.4 Research Context

The company described in this case is today a Norwegian software consultancy company with 50 employees, located in two different geographic offices. During the work described in this chapter the company was declared bankrupt, and then restarted with new owners. The first part of the action planning and action taking described in this chapter took place before the bankruptcy. The first attempt to identify project types was done, using a bottom-up approach. Just before the bankruptcy this approach was evaluated and the company and the researchers decided that this approach did not work. The company then had about 70 employees.

When the company was restarted, the researchers continued to the work mainly together with the other office, but the focus was still the same, and the most actual people from the company did not change. The company is mainly developing software systems with heavy back-end logic and often with a web front-end, typically portals. However, they also develop lighter solutions with most emphasis on the front-end.

The company acts as an independent software supplier, though there are close relationships to the biggest customers. Of the 50 employees today, 35 are working as software developers. Java and J2EE are used as development platform. The domain of which the company develops software is mainly for the banking and finance sector, as well as for public sector. The company has run 50 development projects within the bank and finance sector the last twelve years, and about 30-40 projects within the public sector the last 15 years.

Four employees are certified RUP-mentors acting as advisors in other SW-organizations, in addition to this they run training courses in RUP and related subjects. The company utilizes their high competence in RUP and most projects are more or less inspired by RUP, however, the company's management has seen a need and a possibility to improve their use of RUP.

11.5 Diagnosing

The decision to initiate a project-type specific adaptation process was made by the company when SPIKE started.

The diagnosing phase was initiated by a few workshops where an internal software development process group defined the strategy in cooperation with the authors. With the past experience in mind they decided to go for a top-down approach, starting out with the complete RUP set of process elements and then customize this set to a set of defined project types. This decision was supported by the findings in two rounds of interviews in the company.

This phase of the work was conducted mainly by three different motivations:

1. The researchers needed more insight into the company, the development organization of the company, as well as the most recent software development projects conducted by the company.
2. The company needed to be more conscious about its own use of RUP; these interviews were means in that respect.
3. The use of RUP in the company needed to be documented as a basis for further work; this includes the overall use, but also strengths and weaknesses by the use, in the view of people working in projects in the company.

Interview 1: General experiences from project work

Five employees having various project experiences were interviewed. The roles of these persons were developer/systems architect, project leader/manager, project leader, senior developer and developer/architect/DBA.

The intention of this group of interviews was to get a perception of common problems and challenges in development projects to establish a basis for process improvement initiatives in the company.

The interviews revealed that the customer dialogue could be better (requirements handling and project planning). The reuse of templates could be better. It is too much documentation formalism. Estimates often fail and there is a need of better change management

Interview 2: Special experiences with RUP

Another group of 5 employees was interviewed to get a view of their experience using RUP. The role of these persons was developer, developer/project leader, developer/project leader/test leader, project leader/requirements responsible, and customer contact.

All of the five had some knowledge and experience with RUP, some had participated on internal courses, and some had read literature. However, none had thorough knowledge and experience. About the practical use, it seemed that RUP was used just to a small extent, it depended on the type of project. The reason for this may be superficial knowledge of RUP and that some felt that RUP does not fit their needs.

These two iterations of interviews gave no clear answer, however they indicate that RUP and the use of it can be improved. The summary from the interviews was used to decide to initiate an adaptation process as described in this chapter.

11.6 Action Planning

Projects conducted by the company varied with respect to domain, degree of experimentation, technology, contract form etc. In addition, most projects were too small to initiate a project-specific specialization (Fig. 11.1, approach A). However, it seemed that this company usually ran a few similar types of projects. This lead to the idea to define a set of processes fitting each type of project. The idea is that this will reduce the need of a costly up-front specialization per project and also avoid an expensive per-project adaptation. Based on this realization the company decided to try out approach C in Fig. 11.1 in co-operation with the authors. The company would define a set of project types which covered most of their projects and define a downscaled RUP to each project type.

To define a set of project types we decided to hold a workshop to identify the company's three main project types based on a top down approach. The reason for selecting the top down approach was the company's previous failure to define project types based on a bottom up approach. The participants of the workshop consisted of people from the company with a complimentary and thorough knowledge of the company's software development projects, some of them were also RUP mentors. It was also decided that the participants should come up with a classification system to describe and distinguish the three project types.

Given the three distinct project types, the challenge was how to adapt RUP to each project type. There seemed to be wide agreement that adapting RUP was necessary, yet little information was available on how to actually carry out this adaptation process. What little information was available consisted of rather complex and expensive methods. Instead of using any of these methods we decided to go for a simpler and pragmatic approach. It was decided that the researchers should facilitate a workshop where key employees were invited to define the adapted process. The structure of the workshop was planned by the researchers based on their experience and input from the literature, and the participants were selected by the company based on their experience with different disciplines.

After this workshop the material was left to the company to refine and document with little input from the researchers.

11.7 Action Taking

The RUP adaptation itself was separated in four main phases:

A. Defining the project types
B. The definition of the mainstream project type
C. Maturing the downsized RUP
D. The initial documentation of the mainstream project activities

A: Defining the project types

We conducted a workshop where five participants from the company, representing a group with a complimentary and thorough knowledge of software development projects in general and RUP in special (some of them RUP mentors), were allowed to define three to four common types of projects. To be able to distinguish and describe the project types we defined a simple classification system. During a series of workshops a group representing all project roles identified a set of project capabilities to be used to describe the project types. A project capability, in this context, is a feature or a characteristic that is general to all projects but where the size or weight does vary. We identified 13 characteristics; business critically for the customer, technology knowledge, access to resources, risk, test environment, size, degree of reuse, contract form, project team, exposure, customer orientation, system integration and scope.

The three selected types of projects were Mainstream Projects, Push-button Projects and Greenfield Projects. Here presented with a few characteristics:

B: The definition of the mainstream project type

We selected the mainstream project type since this was the most important type for the company with respect to earning. The two other project types will be handled later.

Originally we envisaged a workshop to define a list of RUP elements necessary for the different disciplines and phases. The result from this would be a list that needed some refinement and quality assurance before it could be documented and put into use in a project. The method we ended up with was not far from this. It consisted of two days where the focus was defined by RUP elements viewed from the point of view of either the RUP phases or the RUP disciplines.

mainstream projects	push-button projects	greenfield projects
- integration with other systems are important - the technology are well known - the size are initially unclear - the risk is moderate	- the technology is well known - low-risk project - well defined project size - often a fixed price project	- need of extensive research and innovation - the size are initially unclear - high risk project - newer fixed price

On the first day we gathered a group of employees with relevant experience from mainstream projects, meaning people that have both the theoretical and practical knowledge of RUP from projects as well as experience relevant to the defined project type. We tried to ensure that all the disciplines of RUP should be covered by the experience of the workshop participants. The process of the initial workshop was as follow:

1. The workshop facilitators (the researchers) explained the defined project type for the group and this was discussed. This was done to establish a common mindset for the rest of the work.
2. We used a whiteboard with a vertical lane for each RUP-phase (inception – elaboration – implementation – transition) to document opinions of what was especially important for each phase (based on practical experience). The workshop facilitators asked questions such as: *What is usually a challenge in this type of project? What type of methodology support do you need? What has used to work well?* All this to sharpen the focus of what is important for the project type and how a defined process can support it.
3. The workshop facilitators displayed a list of all RUP process elements using a video projector. A process element was a defined role, artifact or activity. The elements were ordered per RUP discipline. Starting at the top the group made decisions for each element whether to keep, remove or alter the element. The two previous steps was used as basis for taking decisions and was referred to during the selection process. However, this turned out to be a circumstantial process. The group and the workshop leaders agreed to only focus on *artifacts*, thus speeding up the process to a practical level. When an artifact was removed, this implicitly also indicated how roles and activities should be affected. An example of a artifact that was decided to be deselected is 'Capsule'. The RUP documentation explains that this is an artifact *"Used only for the design of real-time or reactive systems.."*, thus not relevant for the Mainstream project type described and discussed in step 1.

Step 3 was not finished by the end of the first day. One of the main reasons for this was that there was no RUP mentor present. Subsequently there was a lot of argument over what the different RUP concepts actually meant, and a lot of the time was spent searching for information. Another reason was that we initially tried to define artifacts, roles and activities; this took up a lot of time, thus it was decided to just focus on artifacts. Since the list was not finished at the end of the day, it was decided to spend a second day to finish the work. In the second day we only focused on artifacts and the company provided us with a RUP mentor. This time the process worked more fluently and we were able to finish the list of adapted RUP elements to mainstream projects.

C: Maturing the downsized RUP

Due to the composition of the members of the workshop, some disciplines were better covered than others. This sparked some discussion in the company on how to proceed. They found it necessary to involve more people to increase the information on certain disciplines, and it was decided that to increase the usefulness of the process it was necessary to run more iterations to gather experience from all the disciplines.

Having compiled the list of process elements the company continued the process by involving more of the employees. This to incorporate more relevant experiences and, not at least, to establish a common ownership. The focus turned from selecting/deselecting process elements at a very low level to focusing on best practices, in this case meaning to focus on vital project activities. Their next step was to define critical activities for each phase of RUP. This was done in a separate internal workshop. For each phase they held a discussion on what the critical activities were. When they agreed on an activity they found a descriptive name for it and proceeded to answer two questions: 1) What is accomplished by performing this activity? And 2) What is the risk of not performing this activity, or not performing it properly?

The name of the activity and the answer to the two questions was written on a piece of paper and post-it notes and put on a large paper that covered the wall. There was one such paper for each phase.

D: The initial documentation of the mainstream project activities

Having specialized RUP, or any other process for that matter, does not complete the job. The result must be brought out to the frontline people – the project leaders, the developers, the architects and so on. They must have the information at their fingertips in the actual situation of use in a form that makes them want to use it. There is a variety of practical ways of communication this information, from simple documents, to simple web-pages, to comprehensive hypertext documentation. Rational offers an electronic process guide that documents RUP in detail (RUP Online). This is a knowledge base with a web interface that describes roles, activities and artifacts (and templates for these – all arranged within the phases and disciplines of RUP. However, RUP online is comprehensive and may be more confusing than helpful to project members in need of specific project support. Any documentation of the process must reflect the modifications resulting from the specialization process.

Instead of using the tools from Rational, the company decided to establish a simple Wiki-web [10] with just-enough information and functionality to get the message out. This web does not resemble to the RUP-online documentation which holds a well of details. This Wiki can be seen as a common electronic whiteboard, where all users have more or less full access to the information and the rights to update it.. This Wiki Web is a company internal web-site that in simple terms describes the outcome of the workshops and the company internal process work. It explains the characteristics of the project type(s) so that the user can evaluate how well the variant suits the actual project and can also be used as a checklist to plan the project. The simple process documentation on the Wiki Web references RUP Online (web link) to lead the user to helpful descriptions and templates. A Wiki-Web also allows the users to add information thus being a dynamic process repository. One idea (not yet tested) is to store project experiences together with the process descriptions to offer later projects an insight into specific and relevant experience.

11.7.1 The Resulting Process Description

The resulting process documentation, presented trough the Wiki-web, is much simpler than we initially would think. It is more a guide into RUP than an independent complete process guide.

The process definition of the Mainstream type of projects is simply a list of critical activities where each activity is defined by (1) a title stating the purpose of the activity, (2) a short description, (3) the context of the activity, (4) reasons for why this is an important activity for this project type, (5) risks by omitting the activity, (6) a checklist for completion of the activity and (7) recommended problem solving approach. All these seven parts are presented on one page.

These activities are arranged with respect to the standard phases of RUP and also has some links to relevant information in RUP Online, e.g. to templates etc. This simple description is intentionally on a high level, omitting most of the details of RUP. The Wiki-web offers this information to all project members via the intranet. A separate area is created for each project where the project members document their best practices, templates used, comments to the process. In general, this is an experience reporting tool that communicates practical experiences for a given project type to others.

The case company has constituted a process group that continuously updates and refines the content of the Wiki based on real experiences being reported on the Wiki.

11.8 Evaluating

The company did from the beginning focus on project types. During the work described here, two different approaches were tried in order to define different types of projects. The bottom-up approach was tried first, and then the top-down approach. The bottom-up approach did not succeed as it became too complex to document a big amount of project experiences and identify a few common variants of RUP. During the workshops where this approach was tried, it was clear that the participants felt that the project types in some ways were defined already, but not given. The company had an informal definition of project types, not named ones, but with some consensus among the developers what these types were. In the workshops we tried to keep the entire focus on the characteristics of the project types, and the participants were not "allowed" to state types of projects. This approach clearly made the participants frustrated, and the approach did not bring up any defined project types based on the defined characteristics.

We did succeed with a top-down approach to defining a set of project types – starting by loosely naming typical types and then describe typical aspects trough a workshop. The participants were told to name three project types in the beginning, and this strict introduction seems to have helped the participants to reflect over what is really separating the different types of projects there were working on. The three types were relatively easy to identify and name. During the work these initial types were kept, and the belief that these were the important types grew. Even though the initial try with focus on project characteristics did not succeed, this attempt kept the focus on project characteristics during the whole work described here, and the participants were more conscious about what is a project type than the case might have been without the first try. The researchers therefore would like to recommend trying to keep focus on different aspects and characteristics of software projects.

During the work the focus has been on one type of projects only. The company did pick the type of project which was most important with respect to earnings and risk control, and the first attempt to tailor RUP was for this single type only. This focus seems to have been an important factor when it comes to the ability to tailor RUP. Having a common, well defined, mindset makes the decisions easier and the result simpler and more focused.

In this case study, a discussion of which tool to use for the documentation and deployment of the tailored RUP was postponed to a moment when the discussion about the content of the tailored RUP was in place. Adapting and documenting RUP or any other methodological framework is not done solely using a tool. The most crucial part of such a job is to involve a broad group of people having through experience with both the framework and – not at least – practical project work. The work in this case supports this presumption.

Employees in this company have knowledge of RUP above the average of what we have seen in analogous software development organizations in Norway. The work in the company shows that it is important to have a tailoring process that must be based on experience; it can be seen as a knowledge management, and documentation, process. Despite the company's knowledge of RUP, running such a process has not been easy and straight forward at all. The strategy has changed during the course of work based on new insights and achieved results (or lack of such).

11.9 Learning

Our motivation intentionally was to work together with the case company to adapt the RUP. We decided to try to keep it as simple and inexpensive as possible. The two authors that participated actively in the start worked with a small group from the company, thus reducing the total time spent. We also tried to use RUP as a heavy foundation by accepting the general characteristics of the method, such as the phases and the disciplines and go straight to the low-level details; the process elements. But this did not seem to be the best way. The process did become simpler and simpler as the work progressed. This helped the involved people keeping focus on what's most important; what type of process support is really needed in the projects based on experience. When starting out we intentionally did not take a standpoint with respect to *how* to document and disseminate the resulting process description. We looked into the suite of tools offered by Rational, but regardless of the rich features in those tools the company ended up with a very simple form of tool support for documentation and communication of the result, the Wiki web. In general it seems that the adaptation is best done as a simple, pragmatic process not as a heavily up-front planned and strictly managed process. It seems that the good old KISS-strategy once again have proven its superiority; Keep It Simple Stupid.

11.9.1 Some Specific Experiences from the Tailoring Workshops

Having good knowledge and experience is important to ensure sound decisions on how to adapt RUP. This however presupposes that such experience is available within the organization, which was the case in the project that this chapter is based on. If the overall knowledge of RUP is weak the group can be strengthened by hiring a RUP-mentor. The mentor is a certified expert that will be in position to answer questions and explain details of RUP.

Having a group working through the three steps of the initial workshop should take about one working day, given that the workshop leaders have prepared the work, the focus is on artifacts from a discipline point of view, and that there is a RUP mentor present to explain any uncertainties. To ensure a good result it is vital to include people with experience from all the disciplines of RUP.

Do not try to gather too much information in one single workshop. Concentrate on one issue at a time.

It is important to be patient; the outcome of the initial workshops was nothing but an altered list of RUP process elements. This list has to be matured and quality assured before it can be documented and put into use in projects.

11.10 Conclusion

We have presented a simple pragmatic method for adapting the RUP to a specific project type in a company. The method involves a series of workshops in which the key success factor seems to have been focus. Focus both through a specific project type, specific process elements and through phases or disciplines. Another key success factor is that a workshop consists of persons with the proper experience with regards to the focus.

The focus on a specific project type seems to have kept the participants on track throughout the adaptation process. It seems to have eased the process since everyone had a clear concept of what should be done in that particular project type. However, the benefits from making a project type adaptation as compared to making a project- or a company specific adaptation have yet to be evaluated.

The adaptation method has been a success in that the company has come up with a simple process for their most common project type, which has been made available for all employees. Whether this process becomes a success will be determined through further studies of the actual use patterns.

11.10.1 Further Research

Adoption of RUP: Fig. 11.1 shows some possible ways of tailoring RUP at different levels in a software developing organization. In this case study we have been following an organization which chose the project type adoption.

It is of interest to also follow more closely organizations selecting an organizational adoption, or a project adoption. The success and failure criteria in each case should be compared and analyzed.

Experiences from use of tailored RUP: In this case we did follow the process of tailoring and partly, documenting, a project type tailored RUP. We cannot say for sure if the tailoring has been successful until we have empirical results from the use of the tailored RUP. The next step in the research together with this company will be to collect experiences from the use of this instance of RUP.

Metrics: What kind of metrics should be applied when we are interested to measure the process of tailoring RUP in different organizations, and done in different ways? What kind of metrics should be applied when we try to evaluate the success of the use of the tailored RUP in different types of projects in different organizations? How to apply metrics when it comes to measure a software process is still an uncovered aspect of software process improvement, and we think that an association to a single process framework, like RUP, may ease the process of defining and validating metrics for software processes.

References

[1] Jacobson, I., Booch, G., and Rumbaugh, J. (1999) *The Unified Software Development Process*, (ed.) A.W. Longman. Reading: Addison Wesley Longman p. 463
[2] Krutchen, P. (2000) *The Rational Unified Process: An Introduction*. 2nd ed. Addison-Wesley p. 298
[3] Bergström, S. and Råberg, L. (2004) *Adopting the Rational Unified Process*. Addison-Wesley. p. 165–182
[4] Karlsson, F. Ågerfalk, P.J., and Hjalmarsson (2001) A. Method Configuration with Development Tracks and Generic Project Types. in *CAiSE/IFIP8.1 International Workshop in Evaluation of Modeling Methods in Systems Analysis and Design*. Interlaken, Switzerland
[5] http://www-1.ibm.com/support/docview.wss?uid=swg21158199
[6] http://www.m-w.com/dictionary.htm
[7] Nonaka, I. and Takeuchi, H. (1995) *The Knowledge-Creating Company*, Oxford University Press
[8] Avison, D. (1999) *Action Research*. Communications of the ACM, 42(1): p. 94–97
[9] Susman, G. and Evered, R. (1978) *An assessment of the scientific merits of action research*. Administrative Science, 23(4): p. 582–603
[10] http://www.atlassian.com/

12

A Workshop-Oriented Approach for Defining Electronic Process Guides - A Case Study

T. Dingsøyr, N.B. Moe, T. Dybå, and R. Conradi

Abstract: We introduce electronic process guides, and discuss their role in software engineering projects. We then present existing methods for constructing electronic process guides by defining a set of common processes for a company. Different approaches from the software engineering and management science are presented. We then go on to propose a new way of dealing with process description in software engineering: using process workshops as a tool to reach consensus on work practice. The main reason for this is to get realistic descriptions with accurate detail as well as company commitment in an efficient manner. We describe our workshop-oriented method to define processes, which we have used in small software companies, and show examples of results.

Keywords: electronic process guide, process workshop, process model, software process improvement

12.1 Introduction

The way we develop and maintain software, or the software process, has long been regarded as crucial for software quality and productivity (Lehman and Belady, 1985). Most quality systems and software process improvement initiatives prescribe recommended processes for the developers and organization to follow. We therefore need to describe the relevant processes.

In the 1990s there was a lot of work on defining formal and rather sophisticated process modeling languages, and associated tools for process execution and evolution. However, in spite of substantial efforts by academia and partly industry (Derniame et al.1999) and creation of several conference series (Oquendo 2003), the attitude was too formal to have a practical impact. In fact, most companies prefer rather simple process models – such as IDEF0 (National Institute of Standards and Technology 1993) proprietary ad-hoc formalisms (e.g., the one used for Rational Unified Process), or even quasi-formal diagrams using a document-producing tool like Word (Becker-Kornstaedt et al. 2001).

We can draw two lessons from this: Formal modeling of processes may easily be overdone and is anyhow not enough to ensure developer motivation and hence process conformance. Second, automated enactment should be used with great care.

A more practical approach to process work for companies, is to make such process descriptions available as electronic process guides (EPGs) on the company Intranet. Our recommendation is that the developers should be involved in such processes, both to work as recommended and to contribute to the process models. Otherwise, there will easily be a too large gap between the official process model and the actual process, leading to poor process conformance. This has happened in many organizations with elaborate quality systems, that are hardly respected by (or applicable for) the rank and file (Conradi and Dybå 2001). A balance must therefore be found between discipline (obeying formal routines) and creativity (Glass 1995) (actual development with much improvisation (Dybå 2000)).

This chapter reports on the experience with developing of an electronic process guide in a Norwegian medium-size company with rather strict requirements on their software processes. To increase process awareness by the developers, process workshops were run to collect experience that could lead to better process descriptions. This kind of participatory design has a strong Scandinavian work and research tradition.

The issue we would like to discuss in this chapter is our suggested method for organizing process workshops. Interesting questions are which organizing elements make a well-working process, and how the process can be designed to increase process guide usage in the future. We will describe how this was done in an example company, and discuss experiences from using this method, compare it to other possible approaches, and conclude with advice for organizing similar workshops.

Now, we present electronic process guides in further detail and then describe important issues in employee participation which we build on in designing process workshops. The rest of the chapter is organized as follows: Sect. 12.2 introduces the research method. Section 12.3 describes our workshop-oriented method to define software processes, which we have used in several small and medium-sized software companies. We present a case study of results from conducting process workshops in a satellite software company. Section 12.4 discusses findings from the case study in relation to existing theory, and Sect. 12.5 concludes the chapter.

12.1.1 Electronic Process Guides

Effectively disseminating process knowledge to process participants is crucial in any software process improvement effort. Process participants need effective guidance when process conformance is important, when a process changes frequently, and when new personnel join a project.

Traditionally, this has been the realm of large organizations, and the way of describing and communicating processes has focused on printed standards and handbooks. However, such handbooks are more often seen as dust collectors than software process improvement facilitators, and especially so in small and medium-sized companies.

For process guides to be useful, increasingly more software companies not only tailor their process guides to the specific needs of the company, but also make them available on the company's intranet. This way the traditional process handbook shifts from a bulky pile of paper to a flexible on-line structure allowing easy access to all relevant information by means of an electronic process guide (Scott et al. 2002).

A process guide can be seen as a structured, workflow-oriented, reference document for a particular process, and exists to support participants in carrying out the intended process (Kellner et al. 1998). Whether in the form of a printed handbook or an electronic version, a process guide should include the following basic elements:

- Activities: descriptions of "how things are done," including an overview of the activities, and details regarding each individual activity.
- Artifacts: details regarding the products created or modified by an activity, either as a final or intermediate result of the activity or as a temporary result created by one of the steps.
- Roles: details regarding the roles and agents involved in performing the activities.
- Tools and Techniques: details regarding the tools and techniques used to support or automate the performance of an activity.

A common way to describe processes is to describe process *entry, tasks, verification,* and *exit,* where *entry* and *exit* are criteria needed to be fulfilled and the *tasks* describe activities, roles, artifacts, tools, and techniques. This is commonly referred to as the ETVX model.

Based on these elements, Kellner et al (1998) have proposed a set of basic requirements and design principles for EPGs. Most importantly, an EPG should provide all the information elements and relationships contained in a good paper-based process guide. In addition, it should capitalize on diagrams, tables, and narrative to provide an effective user interface. Also, it should make extensive use of hyper-links to support flexible navigation and direct access to supporting information such as examples and templates.

However, the potential of EPG's can only be realized when key capabilities are not only adopted, but also infused across the organization. This is complicated by the fact that there is considerable scepticism among software developers to learn from and adhere to prescribed process models, which are often perceived as overly "structured" or implying too much "control" (Conradi and Dybå 2001). Therefore, we cannot expect such infusion of EPGs unless they are perceived as useful and easy to use in daily practice and consistent with the existing values, past experience, and needs of the software developers (F. Davis 1989; Venkatesh and Davis 2000).

12.1.2 Employee Participation

Conradi and Dybå (2001) showed the importance of employee participation during the development and introduction of formal software routines and that such routines must be supplemented by collaborative, social processes to promote effective infusion and organizational learning.

This insight is not new. Employee participation and the way people are treated, has been noted to be a crucial factor in organizational management and development ever since the famous productivity studies at Western Electric's Hawthorne plant in the 1920s (E Mayo 1933; E. Mayo 1945). The results of these studies started a revolution in management thinking, showing that even routine jobs can be improved if the workers are treated with respect.

Since then, participation and involvement has been one of the most important foundations of organization development and change (Cummings and Worley 2001; French and Bell 1999). Participation is also one of the fundamental ideas of Total Quality Mmanagement (Crosby 1979; Deming 2000; Juran 1992). Similarly, participation has always been a central goal and one of the pillars of organizational learning. For example, autonomous work groups (Trist 1981), quality circles (Ishikawa, 1990), survey feedback (Baumgartel 1959; Neff 1966), quality of work life programs (Davis 1977), search conferences (Emery and Purser 1996), and cultural analysis (Denison and Spreitzer 1991; Schein 1992) are all predicated on the belief that increased participation will lead to better solutions and enhanced organizational problem-solving capability.

What can be learned from these prior studies is that people tend to support what they have participated in creating, or to use Berger and Luckmann's (Berger and Luckmann, 1966) words: "it is more likely that one will deviate from programmes set up for one by others than from programmes that one has helped establish oneself."

An important aspect of participation is "codetermination," i.e. the direct participation of workers in decisions about what should best be done at their own level. Within the context of software development, no one is more expert in the realities of a software company's business with respect to the day-to-day details of particular technologies, products, and markets than the software developers and their first-line managers are. Hence, it is important to involve all those who are part of the software process, and have decisions made regarding the development of EPGs by those who are closest to the problem.

Consequently, and in order to get realistic descriptions with accurate detail as well as company commitment in an efficient manner, we involve all relevant employee groups in defining processes by using process workshops as a tool to reach consensus on work practice.

12.2 Method

The research reported in this chapter is from a large industrial research project, Software Process Improvement through Knowledge and Experience (SPIKE), where many companies cooperate with research institutions and universities in improvement activities. The collaboration is based on finding common improvement and learning goals, and working together to obtain the goals. The communication between contact persons in the companies and researchers is through meetings, telephone calls, and e-mail communication. The researchers usually stay two-day visits in the participating companies in order to also get into the informal arena in the company, and not just collaborate in official meetings.

This research method is a kind of action research (Greenwood and Levin 1998), where the researchers and participants from the companies had common goals: To improve software development, and learn from that experience. Together with the company, we discuss how improvement activities can be organized, and try it out in a cogenerative learning process. That the process is cogenerative means that both company "insiders" and researcher "outsiders" are able to reflect on actions performed. A communication arena is established with regular meetings between researchers and the quality responsible in the company. In this case, the process workshops were a solution suggested by researchers for a problem the quality department had: to improve documentation of the core processes of the company. We organized feedback-sessions after performing the process workshops for common learning.

Potential problems with this kind of research are that it can easily be biased, in that everyone is interested in reaching the goals that are set up. Thus, we do not know if the same results would be achieved with another set of researchers, with other people from the company, or with another company in the same situation. But this kind of research is a way to get interaction with companies in a way that would not be possible if it was not so much in the company's interest.

The case company was selected because they were putting much effort in software process improvement, and was thus a candidate for participation in the SPIKE project.

12.3 Defining Processes in a Medium-Size Company

We first describe the company where we carried out research, and then present our work with process workshops in this company.

12.3.1 A Satellite Software Company

Since the company was founded in 1984, they have delivered turnkey ground station systems, consultancy, feasibility studies, system engineering, training, and support. The company has been working with large development projects, both as a prime contractor and as a subcontractor.

Customers range from universities to companies like Lockheed Martin and Alcatel to governmental institutions like the European Space Agency and the Norwegian Meteorological institute. Most of the software systems that are developed are running on Unix, many on the Linux operating system.

The company possesses a stable and highly skilled staff, many with master's degrees in computer science, mathematics or physics, and have what we can describe as an "engineering culture." Approximately 60 people are working in the company, and the majority is working with software development. Projects are managed in accordance with quality routines fulfilling the European Space Agency PSS-05 standards and ISO 9001–2000.

The company had an extensive quality system, but the system was cumbersome to use because of the size – and because it existed partly on file and partly on paper. As a part of being certified according to ISO 9001–2000, the company decided to document all main processes in the company. We worked with the company in defining the processes for software development.

12.3.2 Defining Requirements for an EPG

We started out with an initial workshop. The goal of this workshop was to define the different existing project types in the company, and to decide the format and most important requirements for the process guide. The company defined four main project types, and they chose the most common one as a starting point for the following workshops. Product development was the most common project type, and the size of this project type was typically 1,000–4,000 work hours. Other project types was customer controlled development projects, delivery projects (integration of existing components, and configuration), maintenance projects, and studies. Typical activities for product development projects were either customizing an existing product for a customer, developing a new system for a customer, or an internal project with a mixture of new development and integration of existing products. After the project types were defined and product development was chosen as a starting point, the most important requirements were defined. The process guide should provide:

– Description of tasks for the most important roles in a project
– Checklists for each main process
– Templates for all documents produced
– Descriptions of best practice
– Access to all tools needed in the project (e.g., a requirement and a bug track system)

In addition to these "functional" requirements a few nonfunctional requirements were defined during the first workshop. The most important such requirements were that it should be: easy accessible, as simple as possible, and up to date.

12.3.3 Discussing Processes: The Process Workshop

We ran a total of six process workshops focusing on different parts of the development process. The workshops involved people from the market and quality department as well as the development unit.

In the first process workshop for product development, "initiation" was the one the company wanted to start with. The initiation process was defined to include "offer", "follow-up" and "blast off."

We followed the same pattern for each workshop, which we describe below with examples of output from the first workshop. See (Ahonen et al. 2002), for a discussion of a similar group process technique.

The workshops differed in length, but would usually last half a day. The researchers acted as moderators and secretaries. In addition to a meeting room, the workshop required a collection of yellow stickers in different colors, and walls that were covered with paper, where we could attach stickers and draw figures. A digital camera was useful to document the results of the workshop. We also found it useful to bring large process worksheets, based on the ETVX model: A sheet with boxes for input, activities, output, roles, and related documents involved in the process (see Fig. 12.2).

We defined process(es) in six steps and five substeps as shown in Fig. 12.1:

As the initiation of projects is an interface between different parts of the organization, it was important to bring together people from marketing, quality assurance, and the development department. We started the workshop by giving a

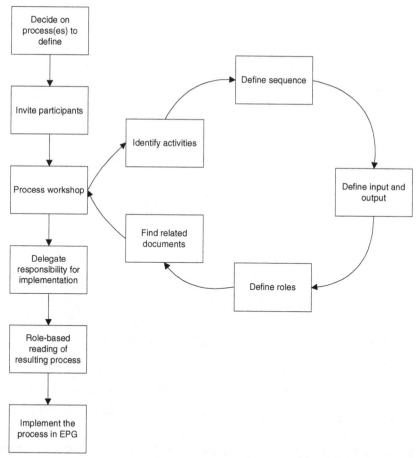

Fig. 12.1. Steps to define a process in a workshop

15-minute presentation of what we were going to do, and put a large sheet with a figure of the process worksheet (as in Fig. 12.2) on the wall – one for each process that would be discussed in the meeting.

For each subprocess we wanted to define, "offer," "follow-up," and "blast-off," we went through the substeps:

Identified activities. We brainstormed on the main activities of the process by using the KJ process (Scupin 1997) (after Japanese ethnologist Jiro Kawakita) and documented the result. The KJ is a creative group technique to organize and find relations between seemingly unrelated ideas. We did this as follows:

– We gave each participant a set of yellow stickers and a thick pen. We asked them to write suggestions for activities on each yellow sticker in large letters. People got time to document 5–10 ideas.
– We asked each participant to present her suggestions: Attach each sticker on a wall, and describe the activity. No-one was allowed to criticize or discuss the ideas at this point.

Fig.12.2. A process worksheet with input, activities, output, roles, and related documents defined

- Grouped the suggestions: The participants came forward to the wall and organized the yellow stickers into groups. We asked them to state why they chose to move the stickers.
- Formulated headings: We found new suitable headers that described the stickers in each group. The headings were formulated to make sense to people who have not participated in the workshop.
- We documented the diagram on the wall with groups and supporting activities on stickers.

During this work, several interesting discussions came up, and several important problems and misunderstandings were solved. Especially marketing and project managers had different views on initiation, but were able to agree on a common process during the workshop.

Because we wanted to get through three subprocesses in half a day, we used time boxing which limited discussion. However, we were able to produce an extensive material in the time slot for each subprocess.

The main activities identified in this step for the "blast-off" subprocess were:

- Appoint project manager
- Organize "Handover meeting"
- First project analysis
- Allocate resources
- Prepare for kick-off meeting
- Internal kick-off

Defined the sequence of the activities: We took the activities from the previous phase, made a sticker for each. Then, we placed them on the activities-field of the process worksheet, where time goes from left to the right. We found a suitable workflow between the activities.

Defined input and output: We found documents or artifacts that must be available to start the subprocess, and which documents that mark the end of the subprocess. We used stickers with other colors than for the activities to mark input and output, and attached them on the process worksheet on the wall together with the activities. Conditions that must be satisfied to begin or exit the subprocess can be described in checklists.

Defined roles. We brainstormed on which roles should contribute in each activity and found the following roles for the "blast off" phase: project manager, quality assurance, development responsible, technical responsible, product committee, bid manager, purchasing manager, logistics expert.

Related documents. We identified documents that either already existed in the company, or new documents that would be helpful in carrying out the activities. Such documents were templates, checklists, and good examples of input or output documents.

Fig. 12.3. A workshop participant adds an activity to a process worksheet

The researchers documented the process workshop by taking notes of stickers in different categories, and by the use of pictures (as in Fig. 12.3).

We found it helpful to ask the people who participated in the process workshop to read the result and comment on it (See (Shull et al. 2000) for an example of such a technique in requirements inspection). We assigned the most typical roles that were involved in the processes to people – and asked them to find if there was information that was lacking or irrelevant for this role in the description. This reading resulted in a number of modifications and clarifications on the process description.

Finally, two people in the company were responsible for making a draft process guide, based on the overall description of the processes which are developed in the workshop. Each activity was then described in much more detail than what appeared in the workshop minutes – The participants gave feedback on these before the processes were implemented in the process guide, as shown in Fig. 12.4.

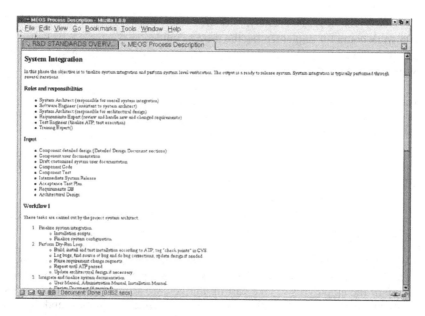

Fig. 12.4. A screenshot of a part of the resulting electronic process guide on the company Intranet

12.3.4 Following Work

After the first version of "initiation" was accepted and implemented in the process guide, the company was ready for the next workshop. After initiation it was natural to focus on product development. This process was defined to include the sub-processes: "specification," "elaboration," "component construction,"and "system integration." Also for these processes, input, activities, output, roles, and related documents involved in the process were defined.

After the two main processes, product development and initiation were defined, the company was ready to release the first version of the process guide. The enthusiasm was high after the workshops. It was therefore important to give the workshop participants feedback through a running system even if it was not complete. Waiting for the perfect and complete process guide would take too long and could kill the enthusiasm. While implementing and releasing the process guide, the company conducted process workshops on project closure, product release, delivery, and competence registration.

These seven first workshops had from 4–6 participants (researchers not included), and 20 persons (1/3 of the employees) from the company participated in one or more workshops. The workshops lasted from 2 h (workshop on format and requirements of the process guide) to 6.5 h. The participants did not need to prepare themselves before the workshops. The company used:

- 168 work hours for seven workshops
- 40 work hours on supplementary work after workshops
- 208 work hours for implementing the process guide
- 223 work hours for implementing project tracking tools in addition to the guide
- 38 work hours on documentation

The total cost of developing the first version of the process guide was 1049 work hours. The two researchers used 10 work hours each including preparation and supplementary work for each workshop.

12.4 Discussion

In this section, we would like to discuss our experience with conducting process workshops, and elaborate on strengths and weaknesses of applying such an approach.

We believe that participation and involvement is critical to achieve improvement in any organization, and see the process workshop as an arena which is open for many of the employees to take part in. Further, we see the process workshops as an arena where representatives from various departments can meet and discuss which will give participants a broader view of how work is conducted in the organization. Finally, we see the process workshop as an arena for collective reflection and learning, where employees can share experience on how they usually solve tasks, and discuss efforts to help them solve the tasks more efficiently.

It is not the intention in this paper to "prove" that process workshops are more suitable than other techniques in eliciting process descriptions. We do not yet have sufficient experience with the resulting process descriptions to investigate that issue. We will rather point out some elements that we noted when conducting the workshops which can be useful for other approaches in the future. However, we note the findings of Ahonen et al. (2002), who report that a similar workshop-technique for modeling software processes both increased the knowledge of the real process and identified points of improvement.

First, we noted that the people who participated in the workshops were contributing with many new perspectives on the processes. For example, one of the people in the quality department in the company had already made a draft version of a process description before organizing a workshop. He found that the workshop produced a number of activities, roles, and also input and output-documents that he did not think of himself.

The brainstorming sessions with yellow stickers worked well to get all participants involved in the process. We have experienced that software developers often can be quite introvert people; and the workshops gave them the opportunity to participate more actively in discussions. Using the stickers gives each participant approximately the same time to present experience.

The workshop provided an arena for cross-functional discussion in the company, and there were several discussions between for example the market and software development departments on how issues were to be handled. We think many clarifications were made that would not have appeared if it had not been for these workshops.

We were satisfied with using the simplified version of the ETVX "process worksheets" in the brainstorming sessions. Using the worksheet gave an easily understandable visual presentation of the results and the connection between different elements of the result. None of the participants in the workshops we organized said they found the ETVX sheets inappropriate.

During the sessions we used time boxing in order to generate ideas for all subprocesses and subprocess elements. Because of limited time, we had to stop some discussions to move to the next process element. In an organizational learning sense, one could argue that we should have had more space for free "dialogue," which would elicit more of the tacit knowledge from the people involved. However, using time boxing generated a "flow" in the workshop. We had the impression that none of the participants got bored or stopped engaging in discussions because the topic was irrelevant, which might have happened if we had allowed for more time.

Another aspect that gave a lot of feedback on the results was the role-based reading of the results of the workshop. Assigning roles to people was a good tool in discovering inconsistencies, for example that a role was missing in one subprocess description or that a document relevant to a role appeared in one subprocess as output and not as input in another subprocess later. It also gave us general feedback of the wording of the names of roles, documents, and activities.

We claim that the workshops provided an arena for participation which was consistent with existing values, past experience, and also with the needs of the company employees.

Further, the process workshops were fairly efficient in terms of resources spent to design the process guide. We do not think using other approaches such as process experts conducting interviews or purchasing existing "canned" processes would have come out cheaper for the company. Other approaches would also probably require more tailoring, and would not involve the employees to such a large degree. It would also put less focus on the learning aspects through reflection on own practice, which are evident in group-work.

On the basis of the workshops conducted, we can recommend other companies wanting to develop electronic process guides to organize a set of workshops using the brainstorming techniques, the ETVX sheets and the role-based review.

12.5 Conclusion and Further Work

From the previous discussion of how process workshops worked in the case study of the satellite software company we can conclude:

- Process workshops conducted in the way described provides an open forum for reflection and learning about own work methods.
- Process workshops are an efficient method for discussing and agreeing on a set of work processes.

Further work in this area will be to follow the usage and impact of this process guide in the satellite company. We would also like to further develop the process workshop by introducing other group-based techniques and methods. One possible future activity would be to focus more on the "verification" part of ETVX, which we think would be useful when processes are more established.

Acknowledgments

This work was conducted as a part of the SPIKE research project, supported by the Research Council of Norway. We are very grateful to our contact persons in the satellite company for providing a stimulating environment in the project and to the participants in the process workshops for a positive attitude towards new work methods.

References

Ahonen, J.J. Forsell, M., and Taskinen, S K. (2002) A Modest but Practical Software Process Modeling Technique for Software Process Improvement, Software Process Improvement and Practice, No. 1, Vol. 7, pp. 33–44

Baumgartel, H. (1959) Using Employee Questionnaire Results for Improving Organizations: The Survey 'Feedback' Experiment, Kansas Business Review, 12, pp. 2–6

Becker-Kornstaedt, U., Neu, H., and Hirche, G. (2001) Software Process Technology Transfer: Using a Formal Process Notation to Capture a Software Process in Industry, in V. Ambriola (Ed.), Proceedings from the Eight European Workshop on Software Process Technology (EWSPT'2001), pp. 63–76 Springer LNCS 2077

Berger, P.L. and Luckmann, T. (1966) The Social Construction of Reality: A Treatise in the Sociology of Knowledge, Harmondsworth: Penguin Books

Conradi, R. and Dybå, T. (2001) An Empirical Study on the Utility of Formal Routines to Transfer Knowledge and Experience. In V. Gruhn (Ed.), Proceedings of the European Software Engineering Conference 2001 (ESEC'2001) (pp. 268–276): ACM/IEEE CS Press

Crosby, P.B. (1979), Quality is Free: The Art of Making Quality Certain, NY: McGraw-Hill

Cummings, T.G. and Worley, C.G. (2001). Organization Development and Change, Cincinnati, Ohio: South-Western College Publishing

Davis, F. (1989), Perceived Usefulness, Perceived Ease of Use, and User Acceptance of Information Technology, MIS Quarterly, 13(3), 318–339.

Davis, L. (1977), Enhancing the Quality of Work Life: Developments in the United States. International Labour Review, 116(July–August), 53–65

Deming, E.W. (2000), Out of the Crisis. Cambridge, Massachusetts: The MIT Press (first published in 1982 by MIT Center for Advanced Educational Services)

Denison, D., and Spreitzer, G. (1991), Organizational Culture and Organizational Development: A Competing Values Approachl. In R. Woodman and W. Posmore (Eds.), *Research in Organizational Change and Development* (Vol. 5, pp. 1–22.). Greenwich, Connecticut: JAI Press

Derniame, J.-C., Kaba, B.A., and Wastell, D. (1999), *Software Process: Principles, Methodology, and Technology*: Springer Verlag LNCS 1500

Dybå, T. (2000), Improvisation in Small Software Organizations. *IEEE Software, 17*(September/October), pp. 82–87

Emery, M., and Purser, R.E. (1996), *The Search Conference*. San Francisco: Jossey-Bass

French, W.L. and Bell, C.H.J. (1999), *Organization Development: Behavioral Science Interventions for Organization Improvement*. Upper Saddle River, N J: Prentice-Hall

Glass, R.L. (1995), *Software Creativity*: Prentice Hall

Greenwood, D.J., and Levin, M. (1998). *Introduction to Action Research*: Sage Publications.

Ishikawa, K. (1990), *Introduction to Quality Control*. London: Chapman and Hall

Juran, J.M. (1992), *Juran on Quality by Design: The New Steps for Planning Quality into Goods and Services*. NY: Free Press

Kellner, M.I., Becker-Kornstaedt, U., Riddle, W.E., Tomal, J., and Verlag, M. (1998, 14–17 June). *Process Guides: Effective Guidance for Process Participants*. Paper presented at the Proceedings of the 5th International Conferenece on the Software Process: Computer Supported Organizational Work, Lisle, Illinois, USA

Lehman, M.M., and Belady, L.A. (1985), *Program Evolution – Processes of Software Change*: Academic Press

Mayo, E. (1933), *The Human Problems of an Industrial Civilization*. Boston: Harvard University Press

Mayo, E. (1945), *The Social Problems of an Industrial Civilization*. Boston: Harvard University Press

National Institute of Standards and Technology (1993), *The Standard for Integration Definition for Function Modelling (IDEF0)*

Neff, F.W. (1966), Survey Research: A Tool for Problem Diagnosis and Improvement in Organizations. In A. W. Gouldner and S. M. Miller (Eds.), *Applied Sociology* pp. 23–38. NY: Free Press

Oquendo, F. (2003, September 1–2). *Software Process Technology*, Paper presented at the Ninth International Workshop, EWSPT'2003, Helsinki, Finland

Schein, E.H. (1992), *Organizational Culture and Leadership*, San Francisco: Jossey-Bass

Scott, L., Carvalho, L., Jeffery, R., D'Ambra, J., and Becker-Koernstaedt, U. (2002), Understanding the use of an Electronic Process Guide, *Information and Software Technology, 44*, pp. 601–616

Scupin, R. (1997), The KJ Method: A Technique for Analyzing Data Derived from Japanese ethnology. *Human Organization, 56*(2), pp. 233–237

Shull, F., Rus, I., and Basili, V.R. (2000), How Perspective-Based Reading Can Improve Requirements Inspections. *IEEE Computer, 33*(7), pp. 73–79

Trist, E. (1981), *The Evolution of Socio-Technical Systems: A Conceptual Framework and an Action Research Program*, Toronto, Ontario: Ontario Quality of Working Life Center

Venkatesh, V., and Davis, F. (2000), A Theoretical Extension of the Technology Acceptance Model: Four Longitudinal Field Studies, *Management Science, 46*(2), pp. 186–204

13

An Empirical Investigation on Factors Affecting Software Developer Acceptance and Utilization of Electronic Process Guides

T. Dybå, N.B. Moe, and E.M. Mikkelsen

Abstract: *Objective*: Our objective is to perform an empirical investigation on factors affecting software developer acceptance and utilization of electronic process guides (EPGs) and to discuss the implications of the findings. *Rationale*: The potential benefits of EPGs can only be realized when key capabilities are not only adopted, but also infused across the organization. *Method*: We conducted a survey of 97 software developers in a medium-sized software company to test the importance of organizational support and four factors on the perceived attributes of using the EPG to its infusion. *Results*: The results showed that perceived usefulness is the fundamental driver in explaining current system usage and future use intentions, and furthermore, that perceived compatibility, perceived ease of use, and organizational support were the key determinants of perceived usefulness. *Conclusion*: This study advances our understanding of software developers' acceptance and utilization of EPGs in a voluntary setting. This way, software organizations can learn more about the determinants of successfully adopting and infusing EPGs and, accordingly, to take more appropriate actions.

13.1 Introduction

Effectively disseminating process knowledge to process participants is crucial in any software process improvement (SPI) effort. Process participants need effective guidance when process conformance is important, when a process changes frequently, and when new personnel join a project.

Traditionally, this has been the realm of large organizations, and the way of describing and communicating processes has focused on printed standards and handbooks. However, such handbooks are often of limited use as SPI facilitators, and especially so in small and medium-sized companies.

For process models to be useful, increasingly more software companies not only tailor their process models to the specific needs of the company, but also make them available on the company's intranet. This way the traditional process handbook shifts from a bulky pile of paper to a flexible on-line structure allowing easy access to all relevant information by means of an electronic process guide (EPG) [19, 25].

An EPG can be seen as a structured, workflow-oriented, reference document for a particular process, and exists to support participants in carrying out the intended process [18]. Whether in the form of a printed handbook or an electronic version, a process guide typically includes the following basic elements:

Activities: descriptions of "how things are done", including an overview of the activities and details regarding each individual activity.

Artifacts: details regarding the products created or modified by an activity, either as a final or intermediate result of the activity or as a temporary result created by one of the steps.

Roles: details regarding the roles and agents involved in performing the activities.

Tools and Techniques: details regarding the tools and techniques used to support or automate the performance of an activity.

Based on these elements, Kellner et al. [18] have proposed a set of basic requirements and design principles for EPGs. Most importantly, an EPG should provide all the information elements and relationships contained in a good paper-based process guide. In addition, it should capitalize on diagrams, tables, and narrative to provide an effective user interface. Also, it should make extensive use of hyper-links to support flexible navigation and direct access to supporting information such as examples and templates.

However, the potential of EPG's can only be realized when key capabilities are not only adopted, but also infused across the organization. This dichotomy between system availability and system use has been noted by Fichman and Kemerer [13], who distinguished between a firm's adoption of a technology and its assimilation of it. At the individual level, there is also a growing body of studies focusing on the determinants of technology acceptance and utilization (e.g. [8, 9, 20, 23, 31]).

New information technologies, such as an EPG, represent innovations for the potential adopters. Consequently, much of the research on individual adoption of information technologies derives its roots from the diffusion of innovation literature, in which individuals' perceived characteristics of innovating (PCI), among other factors, are posited to be significant influences on user acceptance ([20, 24]).

Other models that attempt to explain the relationship between user perceptions, attitudes, use intentions, and eventual system use include the technology acceptance model (TAM) [8, 9, 31], the theory of planned behavior (TPB) [3], and the model of personal computer utilization (MPCU) [30]. Recent work has focused on empirically testing these models to determine their relative explanatory power in explaining software developer acceptance of methodologies [23] and systems developer acceptance of object-oriented systems development [15].

This paper extends and integrates models from prior research by performing an empirical investigation to better understand the adoption and infusion of EPGs. We extend Riemenschneider et al.'s [23] comparison of TAM, PCI, TPB, and MPCU, by incorporating measures of organizational support and testing the full model of TAM. Also, we make a distinction between current use and future use intention and systematically examine the effects of perceptions and support on both outcomes.

In the next section, we present our proposed model, which comprises five independent and two dependent variables, and the corresponding research hypotheses. In Sect. 13.3, we provide an overview of the research context and subjects, the variables and measures, the data collection procedure, and the reliability and validity of the measurement scales used in the study. Sect. 13.4 presents the results of testing the hypothesis and exploring the relationships. Sect. 13.5 provides a discussion of the results, their implications, the limitations of the study, and suggests some directions for further research. Sect.13.6 provides some concluding comments.

13.2 Conceptual Model and Hypotheses

The research model to be empirically tested in this study is depicted in Fig. 13.1. The model derives its theoretical foundations by combining prior research in technology acceptance [8, 9, 31] with aspects of innovation diffusion theory [24] and empirically tested research on software developer acceptance of methodologies [23].

Using TAM as the starting point; the model includes additional constructs according to Riemenschneider *et al.*'s [23] findings. However, due to the voluntary nature of using the EPG within the company, we did not include voluntariness as a separate construct. In addition, we extended the model to include organizational support.

Organizational support and the extent of change agents' promotion efforts have been identified as an important factor in explaining an innovation's rate of adoption [24]. Furthermore, Iivari [17] found that increases in champion support are

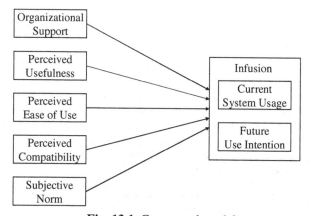

Fig. 13.1. Conceptual model

directly associated with increase in CASE tool usage. Also, coaching and support is mentioned as a key factor of success to facilitating and sustaining organizational learning and knowledge creation [21, 26]. There is therefore reason to believe that EPG infusion is helped by organizational support. Hence, we propose the following hypothesis:

H1: *Organizational support is positively associated with EPG usage and future use intentions.*

Perceived usefulness is defined as the degree to which a person believes that using a particular system would enhance his or her job performance [8]. Conceptually, this is similar to Rogers' [24] perceived relative advantage [20]. Within a software engineering context, software developers are generally reinforced for good performance by raises, promotions, bonuses, etc. This implies that an EPG with a high level of perceived usefulness is one for which a user believes that there is a positive user–performance relationship. There is also extensive research in the information systems (IS) community providing evidences of the effect of perceived usefulness on behavioral intention to use as well as on actual usage [8, 9,15,30,31]. This pattern has also been confirmed within the software engineering domain [23]. Thus, the ultimate reason that software developers exploit EPGs is that they find that the system improves their performance. Therefore, we hypothesize:

H2: *The perception of usefulness of the EPG is positively associated with EPG usage and future use intentions.*

Perceived ease of use refers to the degree to which a person believes that using a particular system would be free of effort [8]. This is, in reverse direction, similar to Rogers' [24] concept of complexity. Despite the insignificant role of perceived ease of use found by Riemenschneider *et al.* [23] regarding software developer acceptance of methodologies, perceived ease of use recurs in several studies as a significant determinant of adoption behavior (e.g. [1, 9, 30, 31]). This suggests that systems that are perceived to be easier to use and less complex have a higher likelihood of being accepted and used by potential users. Hence, we test the following hypothesis:

H3: *The perception of ease of use of the EPG is positively associated with EPG usage and future use intentions.*

Perceived compatibility was defined by Rogers [24] as the degree to which an innovation is perceived as being consistent with the existing values, needs, and past experience of potential adopters. Compatibility has thus been proposed to be positively related to the diffusion of innovations [24] and has also turned out to be a significant factor in explaining software developer acceptance of methodologies [23]. Thus, to the extent that compatibility is perceived positively, we have reason to believe that favorable attitudes toward using an EPG are likely. Therefore, we propose the following hypothesis:

H4: *The perception of compatibility of the EPG is positively associated with EPG usage and future use intentions.*

Subjective norm is the degree to which software developers think that others who are important to them think they should use the EPG. This suggests that perceived social pressure to perform the behavior will influence a person's intentions [3]. Although subjective norm was omitted from the original TAM, other studies have suggested its importance (e.g. [23, 29, 30, 31]). Furthermore, Venkatesh and Davis [31] and Hardgrave and Johnson [15] found that subjective norm had a positive direct effect on perceived usefulness. Thus, there is reason to believe that peers and managers may be able to influence a developer's acceptance and utilization of EPGs directly or indirectly through usefulness. Hence, we propose the following hypothesis:

H5: *The subjective norm of using the EPG is positively associated with EPG usage and future use intentions.*

Thus, in this study we consider five factors affecting software developer acceptance and utilization of EPGs, which have been selected based on the existing literature and company discussions.

13.3 Research Method

13.3.1 Study Context and Subjects

Study context. The context for this research is DNV Software, which is a medium-sized software company with approximately 150 employees in six organizational units. DNV Software is an independent business unit of Det Norske Veritas.

Established in 1864, DNV is an independent foundation with the objective of safeguarding life, property and the environment and is a major international provider of services for managing risk. DNV is an international company with about 5,800 employees in 300 offices in 100 different countries, and headquartered in Oslo, Norway. DNV operates in multiple industries internationally, but focuses on: Maritime, Oil & Gas, Process and Transportation (Rail and Automotive).

DNV Software's business idea is to deliver life-cycle centric solutions directly into the customer's value chain, with special focus on obtaining improved knowledge and workflow management. With 7 sales offices around the world, DNV Software has more than 3,000 clients within shipping, offshore and process industries in 55 countries.

A separate group within DNV Software, called Methods&Tools, is responsible for building competence on software development processes, methodology and supporting tools. Methods&Tools also has responsibility for coordinating the use of processes, methodologies and supporting tool across DNV Software projects based on reuse of knowledge and experience gained through continuous software process improvement. This responsibility includes the development and support of DNV Software's EPGs.

The EPGs are mainly supplementary to the company's work procedures based on ISO standards and, thus, of a voluntary nature.

The specific EPGs examined in this research consist of custom-created process models for the company's internal use, in the form of EPGs, to provide process directions for the complete software life cycle. The EPGs use fundamental concepts from the Capability Maturity Model (CMM), Microsoft Solution Framework (MSF) and Rational Unified Process (RUP).

Figure 13.2 shows a top-level view of a process model for software development projects. The model is scalable to both minor and larger assignments.

The EPGs are web-based and available through DNV Software's Intranet,

reflecting the company's best working practices. The model defines a series of work phase definitions providing activity descriptions, flow charts, guidelines, procedures, standards, checklists, and templates for deliverables. Verification and validation requirements and criteria for approval of project deliverables are included in the definition of milestones and decision points.

Sample. The characteristics of the sample are provided in Table 13.1. The educational level of the subjects is relatively high, with three quarters of the respondents (78.4%) holding a master's or doctoral degree. The average length of the respondents' job tenure at DNV was 7.4 years, while professional tenure (years of software development) was 10.6 years.

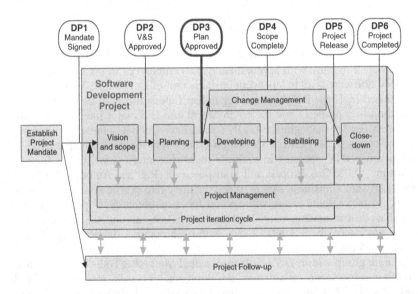

Fig. 13.2. Top-level view of one of DNV Software's Electronic Process Guides

Table 13.1. Sample characteristics

	mean	S.D.
years in the company	7.4	8.1
years of software development	10.6	8.1
	freq.	percent
highest completed education		
bachelor's degree	17	17.5
master's degree	60	61.9
doctoral degree	16	16.5
other	4	4.1
primary job function		
software development	63	64.9
quality/process development	7	7.2
project/line management	12	12.4
software support	5	5.2
software sales	5	5.2
other	5	5.2

13.3.2 Variables and Measures

Independent variables. Five independent variables were included in this study; organizational support, perceived usefulness, perceived ease of use, perceived compatibility, and subjective norm.

Organizational support was provided to the six organizational units of DNV Software according to separate agreements between the support team in Methods&Tools and the various operative units. It included activities related to pre-project support, on-going project support, and post-project support. Pre-project support included activities for training and detailed briefings for project personnel in the EPG and also included planning expertise and assisting individual projects with tailoring the EPG to the projects' environments and circumstances.

On-going project support included on-going consultation and tailoring to projects as they continued to use the EPG. It also included tracking and reporting progress, facilitating feedback meetings, and identifying and recommending improvement activities.

Post-project support comprised facilitation of post-project reviews and evaluation of the infusion to gather lessons learned regarding the deployment of the EPG as well as on the use of the EPG in the projects.

The extent of organizational support was measured by total number of hours provided to each of the six organizational units divided by the total number of employees in the respective departments to get the average number of hours of organizational support offered to each individual.

The questionnaire items for the four subjective scales for rating the perceived attributes of using the EPG were constructed using validated measurement scales from previous research, as discussed in Section 13.2. The *perceived usefulness* and *perceived ease of use* items came from the original Davis instrument [8] and Riemenschneider et al.'s items [23]. *Perceived compatibility* was adapted from Moor and Benbasat's short scale [20], while *subjective norm* items came from Venkatesh and Davis [31]. Review of the instrument within the company led to slight rewording of some items and the addition of one item in the perceived compatibility scale.

We used a 5-point Likert scale: "Strongly disagree", "Disagree", "Neither agree nor disagree", "Agree", and "Strongly agree" as the response format for rating all the perceived attribute of using the EPG.

Dependent variables. Two dependent variables were examined; current system usage, a measure of successful system implementation [9,11], and future use intentions, which reflect the likelihood that the system will be institutionalized in the future.

Current system usage was defined as the extent to which the EPG is used to support development tasks. Current system usage was operationalized and measured by adapting Sharma and Rai's [27] framework for assessing CASE usage for systems development.

Thus, we measured two dimensions of EPG usage: (1) *usage depth*, the proportion of life cycle phases being used and (2) *usage breadth*, the proportion of activities/projects using the EPG. For each task, EPG usage was measured on a scale of 0 to 4:

0: not used at all
1: used occasionally
2: used on a regular basis in a few activities/projects
3: used on a regular basis in most activities/projects
4: used on a regular basis in all activities/projects

The EPG usage level was computed as the ratio of the total usage score on development tasks and the maximum possible usage score on those tasks.

Future use intention was defined in terms of items that were adapted from standard scales such as those used by Riemenschneider *et al.* [23], Taylor and Todd [29], and Venkatesh and Davis [31].

As for the four independent variables of user perceptions, we used a 5-point Likert scale: "Strongly disagree", "Disagree", "Neither agree nor disagree", "Agree", and "Strongly agree" as the response format for rating the four items of future use intentions.

All subjective measurement scales are provided in the Appendix.

13.3.3 Data Collection Procedure

We conducted a survey of all prospective users of the EPG in the six organizational units of DNV Software. In total, 120 questionnaires were distributed and 97 usable responses were received, resulting in a good overall response rate of 81% [4]. Given this high response rate, no further analysis was done on the differences between respondents and non-respondents.

The questionnaire consisted of two parts. The first part asked for general background information related to the respondents' job tenure, professional tenure, educational level, and primary job function (Table 13.1).

The second part of the questionnaire was used to measure the depth and breath of EPG usage, future use intentions, and the perceived attributes of using the EPG. Thus, each respondent generated six scores; one for each of the four perceived attributes of using the EPG and one for each of the intention and usage measures (see Appendix).

13.3.4 Assessment of Reliability and Validity

Reliability refers to the consistency and stability of a score from a measurement scale. The reliability of the multiple-item measurement scales was evaluated by internal consistency analysis, using coefficient alpha [7]. Table 13.2 reports the number of items in each scale and the corresponding reliability coefficients. Alpha reliabilities ranged from 0.76 to 0.92, indicating acceptable internal consistency [22].

Three kinds of validity are of special concern for this research [12]; content validity, construct validity, and criterion-related validity.

Content validity has to do with the degree to which the scale items represent the domain of the concept under study. Content validity was, thus, built into the instrument from the outset through the choice of appropriate items from prior validated scales (e.g. from TAM and PCI).

Construct validity is an operational concept that examines whether the measurement scales represent and act like the attributes being measured. Assuming that the total score of a scale is valid, the extent to which an individual item measures the same thing as the total score is an indicator of the validity of that item. Hence, construct validity of the measurement scales was evaluated by principal components analysis with VARIMAX rotation. The factor loadings for each scale are summarized in Table 13.3.

The results show that the four independent variables captured 68.7% of the variance. As can be seen from the factor pattern matrix in Table 13.3, a simple four-factor structure emerged. No item loads highly on more than one factor. Furthermore, all items remaining in the four scales loaded together on the target factor, with the lowest loading being 0.46. Comrey [6] suggested that loadings in excess of 0.45 could be considered fair, those greater than 0.55 as good, those of 0.63 very good, and those of 0.71 as excellent. As the factor pattern shows, most loadings on the target factor are in the excellent range (15 out of 19), with only two loadings in the fair range. These results indicate that the various scales achieved a high degree of unidimensionality and, hence, construct validity.

Table 13.2. Coefficient Alpha of scales

construct	items	alpha
perceived usefulness	6	0.92
perceived ease of use	6	0.85
perceived compatibility	4	0.87
subjective norm	3	0.76
future use intention	4	0.85

Table 13.3. Principal components analysis with VARIMAX rotation

item	component 1 perceived usefulness	component 2 perceived ease of use	component 3 perceived compatibility	component 4 subjective norm
PU1	**0.81**	0.21	0.19	0.20
PU2	**0.87**	0.14	0.17	0.13
PU3	**0.80**	0.18	0.02	0.05
PU4	**0.76**	0.03	0.36	0.21
PU5	**0.81**	0.31	0.19	0.06
PU6	**0.70**	0.29	0.13	0.14
PEU1	0.07	**0.78**	0.07	0.12
PEU2	0.10	**0.74**	0.08	0.29
PEU3	0.21	**0.77**	0.06	0.08
PEU4	0.20	**0.86**	0.13	0.11
PEU5	0.28	**0.68**	0.11	0.06
PEU6	0.34	**0.46**	0.10	-0.25
PC1	0.15	0.28	**0.83**	0.11
PC2	0.04	-0.01	**0.83**	0.04
PC3	0.34	0.21	**0.77**	0.21
PC4	0.32	0.04	**0.73**	0.25
SN1	0.13	0.11	0.08	**0.88**
SN2	0.17	0.17	0.19	**0.80**
SN3	0.19	0.14	0.31	**0.52**
total eigenvalue	7.52	2.27	1.89	1.37
% of variance	39.59	11.94	9.92	7.22
cumulative %	39.59	51.53	61.45	68.67

Notes: The only restriction made for the factor solution was to retain components with eigenvalue > 1.

Thus, the four-factor structure emerged without restricting the number of factors in the solution.

Criterion-related validity is concerned with the degree to which the scales under study are related to an independent measure of the relevant criterion.

The criterion-related validity of the measurement instrument was evaluated by computing the multiple correlation (R) between the measures of the five independent variables and current system usage as well as future use intentions. The multiple correlation coefficients were 0.59 and 0.63 respectively and the corresponding adjusted R-square values were 0.31 and 0.36. Cohen [5] suggested that a multiple correlation coefficient of 0.14 corresponds to a small effect size, that coefficients of 0.36 correspond to a medium effect size, and that coefficients above 0.51 correspond to a large effect size. Since the values of both current system usage and future use intentions are above the threshold for a large effect size for the multiple correlation coefficients, we conclude that the independent variables have a high degree of criterion-related validity.

All quantitative analyses were conducted using Statistical Product and Service Solutions (SPSS).

Table 13.4. Variable means, standard deviations, and intercorrelations

variable	mean	S.D.	OS	PU	PEU	PC	SN	CSU	FUI
organizational support (OS)	13.24	12.11	1.00						
perceived usefulness (PU)	3.35	0.75	0.31***	1.00					
perceived ease of use (PEU)	3.10	0.60	0.12	0.51***	1.00				
Perceived compatibility (PC)	3.07	0.71	0.09	0.50***	0.35**	1.00			
Subjective norm (SN)	3.37	0.66	0.08	0.40***	0.33***	0.43***	1.00		
current system usage (CSU)	0.37	0.26	0.26**	0.56***	0.35***	0.38***	0.35***	1.00	
future use intention (FUI)	3.77	0.66	0.28**	0.60***	0.39***	0.23*	0.27**	0.46***	1.00

Notes: Pearson correlation coefficients are reported.
$*p < .05$ $**p < .01$ $***p < .001$ (one-tailed)

13.4 Results

Table 13.4 shows the means, standard deviations, and intercorrelations among the variables. Out of 21 correlations between the variables, four have a correlation coefficient larger than or equal to 0.5. The highest correlation (0.60) is between perceived usefulness and future use intention. The table shows that all bivariate correlations between each of the five independent variables and the two dependent variables, current system usage and future use intention, are significant, ranging from $r = 0.23$ $(p < 0.05)$ to $r = 0.60$ $(p < 0.001)$.

Table 13.5 shows the results of the regression procedures to test the joint contribution of the independent variables to the explanation of the relationships implied by Fig. 13.1. The table contains two regression equations: one with current system usage and the other with future use intentions as the dependent variables.

Consistent with much prior research, the results of current usage indicate that perceived usefulness ($\beta = 0.40$, $t = 3.43$, $p < 0.001$) is a strong and significant factor in explaining acceptance. However, none of the other four variables were significant in explaining current usage. The adjusted R-square was 0.31, thus explaining 31% of the variance in current usage.

Table 13.5. Regression analyses of current system usage and future use intentions

regression equation	adjusted R^2	Beta	t-value	hypothesis
CURRENT USAGE		0.11	1.19	H1
= OS +				
PU +		0.40	3.43***	H2
PEU +		0.06	0.59	H3
PC +		0.09	0.90	H4
SN	0.31	0.12	1.24	H5
USE INTENTIONS =		0.10	1.18	H1
OS +				
PU +		0.55	4.90***	H2
PEU +		0.13	1.29	H3
PC +		−0.11	−1.11	H4
SN	0.36	0.05	0.47	H5

Notes: Standardized betas are reported, ***$p < .001$

Similarly, the results for the likelihood of continued future usage suggests that the only relevant EPG characteristic is perceived usefulness ($\beta = 0.55$, $t = 4.90$, $p < 0.001$). This factor explained 36% of the variance in future use intentions.

However, the insignificance of organizational support, perceived ease of use, perceived compatibility, and subjective norm does not reflect their individual relationships with the dependent variables, as shown in Table 13.4, but instead indicates that in a multivariate context, they are not needed together with perceived usefulness to explain the variance in current usage and future use intentions. Therefore, we cannot determine the importance of the independent variables based solely on the derived variate, since relationships among the independent variables may "mask" relationships that are not needed for predictive purposes, but represent substantive explanatory findings nonetheless.

According to TAM, perceived usefulness is influenced by perceived ease of use [8,9]. Furthermore, Venkatesh and Davis [31] argued that the determinants of perceived usefulness have been relatively overlooked in the literature and that a better understanding of the determinants of perceived usefulness would enable us to design organizational interventions that would increase user acceptance and usage of new systems. Therefore, and in order to further investigate the factors affecting software developer acceptance and utilization of EPGs, we conducted stepwise regression analysis with perceived usefulness as the dependent variable.

As can be seen from Table 13.6, the results of this analysis shows that perceived ease of use ($\beta = 0.36$, $t = 4.17$, $p < 0.001$), organizational support ($\beta = 0.35$, $t = 4.16$, $p < 0.001$), and perceived compatibility ($\beta = 0.23$, $t = 2.90$, $p < 0.005$) were significant determinants of perceived usefulness. In total, these three factors explained 41% of the variance in perceived usefulness. The effect of subjective norm was not significant.

Furthermore, since we were specifically interested in examining the effect of organizational support on current system usage and future use intentions, we defined contrasted criterion groups based on the upper and lower third of the organizational support distribution. Thus, low support was defined as the lower third ($N = 32$) and high support was defined as the upper third ($N = 32$) of the distribution.

Table 13.6. Determinants of perceived usefulness

regression equation	adjusted R^2	beta	t-value
PU = OS +		0.35	4.13***
PEU +		0.36	4.17***
PC +	0.41	0.23	2.90**
SN		ns	

Notes: Standardized betas are reported.
**$p < 0.005$ ***$p < 0.001$,
ns = not significant

Table 13.7. Low organizational support versus high organizational support

	low support $(n = 32)$		high support $(n = 32)$		
	Mean	S.D.	Mean	S.D.	t-value
current system usage	0.31	0.26	0.46	0.27	2.21*
future use intention	3.64	0.72	4.05	0.51	2.61**

Notes: All t-tests are two-tailed.
*$p < 0.05$ **$p < 0.01$

The effect of organizational support was examined by testing the differences of the means between low and high organizational support using two-tailed t-tests. Results of these tests are summarized in Table 13.7. For each construct the table provides the mean score, standard deviation, and t-value.

Both variables showed a statistically significant difference between low and high support. Individuals in units receiving high organizational support reported a significantly greater extent of both current system usage ($t = 2.21$, $p < 0.05$) and future use intentions ($t = 2.61$, $p < 0.01$) than individuals in units receiving low organizational support.

In summary then, we find strong support for hypothesis 2, moderate support for hypotheses 1, 3, and 4, and weak support for hypothesis 5.

13.5 Discussion

A quantitative survey was performed to investigate factors affecting software developer acceptance and utilization of electronic process guides. The results showed that perceived usefulness was a strong and highly significant determinant of current system usage and future use intentions (Tables 13.4 and 13.5). This was as expected and is also in accordance with prior studies of IS development processes [15] and software engineering methodologies [23]. This suggests that perceived usefulness is a fundamental driver of both usage and use intentions and, thus, that the prospects for successfully infusing EPGs will be severely undermined if they are not regarded as useful by the developers.

Furthermore, the results showed that organizational support, perceived ease of use, perceived compatibility, and subjective norm did not directly impact a developer's usage or intention to use the EPG. Thus, the results suggests that software developers are primarily concerned about the usefulness of the EPG in facilitating the development process, with less regard for how easy it is to use, how much support they receive, or what others think they should do.

Although organizational support did not directly influence developers' use intentions and usage of the EPG, it had a sizable and significant effect on perceived usefulness (Table 13.6). This relationship indicates that the higher the level of organizational support, the more useful the EPG is perceived, and in turn, the more likely the developer will accept and utilize it. The insignificant direct effect of organizational support on use and use intentions is also consistent with prior research on the diffusion of software engineering techniques [14].

Likewise, perceived ease of use and perceived compatibility did not directly impact usage or use intentions. However, both factors showed a sizable and significant effect on perceived usefulness (Table 13.6). Prior research has also shown a strong relationship between perceived ease of use and perceived usefulness [15],[31], which suggests that the less effortful the EPG is to use, the more useful it is perceived and, thus, the more likely it will be accepted and utilized. In a similar vein, the more compatible the EPG is with how developers perform their work, the more useful they find it and the more they use it.

Subjective norm was neither significant in predicting the two dependent variables, current system usage and future use intentions, nor in predicting the key determinant of those variables; perceived usefulness. This is consistent with prior research in organizations in which system usage is voluntary [31], with prior studies that show that the direct effect of subjective norm on usage and use intentions subside over time with increased system experience [2], and with research on the acceptance of object-oriented systems development [15].

Thus, a major practical implication of this study is that it enables software managers to put in practice the elements of improvement and interventions that increase the likelihood of successful EPG infusion, e.g. by actively supporting new processes and their representations as EPGs in their respective organizations.

Another implication is that increased understandings of the determinants of perceived usefulness – organizational support, ease of use, and compatibility with existing work practices – enable process designers to make EPGs more acceptable to software developers. This could be done by involving key stakeholders and senior software developers in the development of the EPG, thereby attaining compatibility with existing values and work practices; by providing adequate training and feedback about using the EPG to ease its use; and by providing on-going consultation and tailoring to projects as they continue to use the EPG

In other words, the relationships between the factors affecting software developer acceptance and utilization of EPGs revealed by this study provide valuable insight to software managers and process designers in successful EPG influsion.

13.5.1 Limitations

Although we have discussed several implications of our results, the research reported here is not without its limitations. First, our study was limited to members of one overall organization, basically using the same system. While this means that variability is not due to the system in question, it does raise the issue of generalizability. The fact that respondents came from six different organizational units, each with its own culture and experience, using four EPG variants provides some support for the generalizability to other organizations. However, further research is needed to examine EPG usage in a wide variety of organizational settings.

Secondly, we relied upon self-reported system usage, which does not necessarily correlate with computer-recorded usage [28]. This suggests that future empirical studies should measure both self-reported system usage and computer-recorded usage. However, caution should be taken in interpreting "usage" since both self-reported system usage and computer-recorded usage refer to a view of knowledge as something that can be codified and explicitly stored in a database for easy access and use by anyone in the organization. This conception of process knowledge as something explicit and quantifiable draws a problematic distinction between knowledge as a tangible good and the use of that good in practice, which limits our ability to accurately measure usage, whether this usage is based on looking up a page at the company's intranet or whether it is based on the use of already internalized knowledge that does not require such explicit system usage.

Despite these limitations, we feel that this study contributes to the growing literature on empirical software engineering research and that it can provide a better understanding of the factors affecting software developer acceptance and utilization of EPGs.

13.5.2 Future Research

The results of this study point out a number of directions for future research. First, our model did not explain more than approximately one third (31% of current usage and 36% of future use intentions) of the variance in usage behavior, which means that approximately two thirds of variance in behavior is unexplained. In accordance with Taylor and Todd's [29] analysis of IT usage, this suggests a need for a broader exploration of factors beyond those suggested by traditional technology acceptance and innovation diffusion theories. Thompson et al. [30], for example, suggested that prior usage may be an important determinant, while Hartwick and Barki [16] showed that participation and involvement in the design process are related to usage and future use intentions.

Second, although our research focused on system usage as the primary outcome of interest, innovation research further distinguishes explicitly between various types of usage, including initial usage of the innovation and continued sustained usage [24]. Longitudinal research is, therefore, needed to explore these types of usage.

Finally, the results of the present study seem to be in line with Zelkowitz's [32] conclusion that there is a need to better understand the role that processes play in software development and to better understand how to package and transfer those processes as corporate assets. Further research should explore these issues, preferably using a multiple-case replication design.

13.6 Conclusion

This study focused on investigating factors affecting software developer acceptance and utilization of electronic process guides. Based on the results, it is reasonable to conclude that there exist a few factors that have a significant and positive effect on software developer acceptance and utilization of EPGs in a voluntary setting that complement Riemenschneider et al.'s [23] study, which was performed in a mandatory setting.

Also, a better understanding of the determinants of perceived usefulness can enable software managers to design organizational interventions that are capable of increasing user acceptance and usage of new systems.

To conclude, the results of this study should help managers and process designers by focusing attention on those factors in the organization that affect the successful adoption and infusion of EPGs.

Acknowledgments

This work was supported by the Research Council of Norway under Grant 156701/220. The authors wish to thank DNV Software and all respondents of the survey for their willingness to participate in the inquiries.

References

[1] Adams, D.A., Nelson, R.R., and Todd, P.A. (1992) Perceived Usefulness, Ease of Use, and Usage of Information Technology: A Replication, *MIS Quarterly*, Vol. 16, pp. 227–247

[2] Agarwal, R. and Prasad, J. (1997) The Role of Innovation Characteristics and Perceived Voluntariness in the Acceptance of Information Technologies, *Decision Sciences*, Vol. 28, pp. 557–582

[3] Ajzen, I. (1991) The Theory of Planned Behavior, *Organizational Behavior and Human Decision Processes*, Vol. 50, pp. 179–211

[4] Baruch, Y. (1999) Response Rate in Academic Studies - A Comparative Analysis, *Human Relations*, Vol. 52, No. 4, pp. 421–438

[5] Cohen, J. (1988) *Statistical Power Analysis for the Behavioral Sciences*, Second Edition, Hillsdale, New Jersey: Laurence Erlbaum

[6] Comrey, A. (1973) *A First Course on Factor Analysis*, London: Academic Press

[7] Cronbach, L.J. (1951) Coefficient Alpha and the Internal Consistency of Tests, *Psychometrica*, Vol. 16, pp. 297–334

[8] Davis, F. (1989) Perceived Usefulness, Perceived Ease of Use, and User Acceptance of Information Technology, *MIS Quarterly*, Vol. 13, No. 3, pp. 318–339

[9] Davis, F., Bagozzi, R., and Warshaw, P. (1989) User Acceptance of Computer Technology: A Comparison of Two Theoretical Models, *Management Science*, Vol. 35, No. 8, pp. 982–1003

[10] DeLone, W.H. and McLean, E.R. (1992) Information Systems Success: The Quest for the Dependent Variable, *Information Systems Research*, Vol. 3, No. 1, pp. 60–95

[11] DeLone, W.H. and McLean, E.R. (2003) The DeLone and McLean Model of Information Systems Success: A Ten-Year Update, *Journal of Management Information Systems*, Vol. 19, No. 4, pp. 9–30

[12] Dybå, T. (2000) An Instrument for Measuring the Key Factors of Success in Software Process Improvement, *Empirical Software Engineering*, Vol. 5, No. 4, pp. 357–390

[13] Fichman, R.G. and Kemmerer, C.F. (1993) Adoption of Software Engineering Process Innovations, *Sloan Management Review*, Vol. 34, No. 2, pp. 7–22

[14] Green, G.C. and Hevner, A.R. (2000) The Successful Diffusion of Innovations: Guidance for Software Development Organizations, *IEEE Software*, Vol. 17, No. 6, pp. 96–103

[15] Hardgrave, B.C. and Johnson, R.A. (2003) Toward an Information Systems Development Acceptance Model: The Case of Object-Oriented Systems Development, *IEEE Transactions on Engineering Management*, Vol. 50, No. 3, pp. 322–336

[16] Hartwick, J. and Barki, H. (1994) Explaining the Role of User Participation in Information System Use, *Management Science*, Vol. 40, No. 4, pp. 440–465

[17] Iivari, J. (1996) Why are CASE Tools Not Used?, *Communications of the ACM*, Vol. 39, No. 10, pp. 94–103

[18] Kellner, M.I., Becker-Kornstaedt, U., Riddle, W.E., Tomal, J., and Verlage M. (1998) Process Guides: Effective Guidance for Process Participants, *Proceedings of the Fifth International Conference on the Software Process: Computer Supported Organizational Work*, Lisle, Illinois, 14-17 June, pp. 11–25

[19] Moe, N.B., Dingsøyr, T., Dybå, T., and Johansen, T. (2002) Process Guides as Software Process Improvement in a Small Company, *Proceedings of the European Software Process Improvement Conference (EuroSPI'2002)*, Nürnberg, Germany, 18–20 September

[20] Moore, G.C. and Benbasat, I. (1991) Development of an Instrument to Measure the Perceptions of Adopting an Information Technology Innovation, *Information Systems Research*, Vol. 2, No. 3, pp. 192–222

[21] Nonaka, I. and Takeuchi, H. (1995) *The Knowledge-Creating Company: How Japanese Companies Create the Dynamics of Innovation*, NY: Oxford University Press

[22] Nunnally, J.C. and Bernstein, I.A. (1994) *Psychometric Theory*, Third Edition, NY: McGraw-Hill

[23] Riemenschneider, C.K., Hardgrave, B.C., and Davis, F.D. (2002) Explaining Software Developer Acceptance of Methodologies: A Comparison of Five Theoretical Models, *IEEE Transactions on Software Engineering*, Vol. 28, No. 12, pp. 1135–1145

[24] Rogers, E.M. (1995) *Diffusion of Innovations*, Fourth Edition, NY: The Free Press

[25] Scott, L., Carvalhoa, L., Jeffery, R., D'Ambra, J., and Becker-Kornstaedt, U. (2002) Understanding the Use of an Electronic Process Guide, *Information and Software Technology*, Vol. 44, pp 601–616

[26] Senge, P.M., Kleiner, A., Roberts, C., Ross, R., Roth, G., and Smith, B. (1999) *The Dance of Change: The Challenges of Sustaining Momentum in Learning Organizations*, NY: Currency/Doubleday

[27] Sharma, S. and Rai, A. (2000) CASE Deployment in IS Organizations, *Communications of the ACM*, Vol. 43, No. 1, pp. 80–88

[28] Straub, D.W., Limayem, M, and Karahanna-Evaristo, E. (1995) Measuring System Usage: Implications for IS Theory Testing, *Management Science*, Vol. 41, No. 8, pp. 1328–1342

[29] Taylor, S. and Todd, P. (1995) Understanding Information Technology Usage: A Test of Competing Models, *Information Systems Research*, Vol. 6, No. 2, pp. 144–176

[30] Thompson, R., Higgins, C., and Howell, J. (1991) Personal Computing: Toward a Conceptual Model of Utilization, *MIS Quarterly*, Vol. 15, No. 1, pp. 125–143

[31] Venkatesh, V. and Davis, F. (2000) A Theoretical Extension of the Technology Acceptance Model: Four Longitudinal Field Studies, *Management Science*, Vol. 46, No. 2, pp. 186–204

[32] Zelkowitz, M.V. (1996) Software Engineering Technology Infusion Within NASA, *IEEE Transactions on Engineering Management*, Vol. 43, No. 3, pp. 250–261.

Appendix 13: Operationalization of Constructs

Table 13.A.1. Likert scales

measure	construct
perceived usefulness	
PU1:	I find the PM useful in my job.
PU2:	using the PM improves my job performance.
PU3:	using the PM increases my productivity.
PU4:	using the PM enhances the quality of my work.
PU5:	using the PM makes it easier to do my job.
PU6:	the advantages of using the PM outweighs the disadvantages.
perceived ease of use	
PEU1:	learning to use the PM was easy for me.
PEU2:	I think the PM is clear and understandable.
PEU3:	using the PM does not require a lot of mental effort.
PEU4:	I find the PM easy to use.
PEU5:	the PM is not cumbersome to use.
PEU6:	using the PM does not take too much time from my normal duties.
perceived compatibility	
PC1:	the PM is compatible with the way I develop software.
PC2:	using the PM is compatible with all aspects of my work.
PC3:	using the PM fits well with the way I work.
PC4:	the PM is compatible with the way we organize our work.
subjective norm	
SN1:	people who influence my behavior think I should use the PM.
SN2:	people who are important to me think I should use the PM.
SN3:	co-workers think I should use the PM.
future use intention	
FUI1:	I intend to *increase* my use of the PM for work in the future.
FUI2:	I intend to *use* the PM in the future for my work.
FUI3:	given a choice, I would prefer *not to use* the PM in any future work.
FUI4:	I would like to *use* the PM in the future.

Table 13.A.2. Current system usage

currently, how would you assess *your* use of the PM in *your* activities/projects?	*not used* at all	used *occasionally*	used on a *regular* basis in a *few* activities/ projects	used on a *regular* basis in *most* activities/ projects	used on a *regular* basis in *all* activities/ projects
establish project mandate	☐	☐	☐	☐	☐
vision and scope	☐	☐	☐	☐	☐
planning	☐	☐	☐	☐	☐
developing	☐	☐	☐	☐	☐
stabilizing	☐	☐	☐	☐	☐
close-down	☐	☐	☐	☐	☐
change management	☐	☐	☐	☐	☐
project management	☐	☐	☐	☐	☐

14

Six Theses on Software Process Research

R. Conradi, A. Fuggetta, and M.L. Jaccheri

Abstract: There has been considerable research in technologies to support software processes since the late 1980s. Many process modeling languages have been devised, often with tools for editing and enactment of such models. The paper observes that much research have failed to have an industrial impact. The main reason is that software development is a creative and turbulent activity, so that only stable and well-known processes can be effectively modeled and enacted. The paper also points the analogy to workflow and coordination technologies.

Keywords: software process, software process modelling, software configuration management, workflow, software process improvement.

14.1 Introduction

Over the past two years the software process community has initiated and carried out a reaction on the purpose and scope of the research activities being carried out in the area. This has increased the awareness that there are many similarities between the problems and approaches of the software process technology community and those attacked by other research fields: software process improvement (SPI), information systems and workflow, databases, distributed technology, computer-supported cooperative work, groupware, and organizational and cognitive sciences. A number of events and initiatives have been launched to establish bridges and connections among these communities (DiNitto98; ISPW98; ICSP98; NSF98; RDP97; WAC99). These initiatives have reasonably demonstrated that it is urgent and mandatory (a) to fill the gaps among these different disciplines to develop a common baseline of concepts and principles, and (b) to jointly exploit the results that each community has independently produced. It is quite easy to state these goals. In practice, pursuing them is much more difficult than expected. This is due to a variety of reasons, the first one being the presence of several misconceptions and misunderstandings that still make it difficult to pursue an open and effective exchange of opinions and experiences. Being this just a position paper, we do not have the ambition of providing solid conceptual and technological contributions to solve these problems. Moreover, we will be purposely provocative, thus pushing the argument to its extreme. Indeed, our intention is just to provide a small contribution to further support the discussion and reaction of the community on the above issues. To achieve this goal, the paper proposed a few theses that represent and synthesize our understanding of the problem, based on the research and experimental work that we have accomplished over the past 8 years. Each thesis is briefly illustrated and justified. In addition, we proide a sketchy indication of the possible impacts that these theses might have on our research work.

14.2 Theses

Thesis 1 The problems and issues addressed by software process technology and workflow management are the same.
A detailed analysis of the objectives and scope of these two disciplines reveals an almost complete overlapping of themes and approaches. Both disciplines are interested in describing activities, roles, artifacts, tools, and (their respective) business rules. In both cases we need tools to support process modeling, analysis, enactment, monitoring, and measurement. In both cases we need to integrate and control "process-specific" tools such as compiler or information system components. Basically, each concern of software process technology can be mapped onto a similar one in the workflow area (and vice versa), including highly debated topics such as support to dynamic process change, inconsistency management, and exception handling. In general, we argue that there is growing evidence that software processes are just a particular class of processes/workflows. Consequently, we should not create artificial problems to justify a separate course of research activity. Rather, we should try to focus on how the experiences and technologies developed so far in these different areas can be jointly exploited to increase the quality and effectiveness of the technology we develop.

Thesis 2 Configuration management tools are "the real" Process-centered Software Engineering Environments (PSEEs).
If we look at the market of software engineering environments we would soon realize that the real PSEEs are configuration management systems such as Clear-Case/ClearGuide or PCMS. Organizations have coarse informal descriptions of their high level processes while they use CM systems to describe and enact their low level detailed processes. The peculiar characteristic of this class of systems is exactly their ability to describe a product, and to model and support/enact the process by which all software developers are supposed to manipulate the product. The software process technology community should recognize this fact and understand (1) why these systems are successful and (2) in which respect they are different from PSEEs and workflow management systems. The answer to the first question is that CM systems have tackled a problem that is really at the heart of any software development activity: product management. Moreover, they have automated very critical procedures, which would be unmanageable without a specific computerized support (see also Theses 3 and 4). Thus these tools have

succeeded in providing a solution that guarantees an unquestionable and decisive advantage to software developers. No serious software development organization would work without a CM environment. This is not true at all for most "canonical" PSEEs. As for the second question, we argue that the "process-centered" part of a configuration management environment (i.e., its component in charge of defining CM policies and procedures) exhibits most of the characteristics of typical production workflow systems. For instance, typical CM operations such as check-in and builds are characterized by a high degree of standardization and automation, and by a high volume of concurrent requests. Certainly, CM environments offer sophisticated mechanisms that are not considered at all by process/workflow systems. We should try to understand how to integrate typical workflow features with the product-oriented features of modern CM systems. Some work has been done by the community (see for example the features of environments such as Adele and EPOS).

Thesis 3 The significant factor that distinguish different classes technologies is not the process domain to which they are supposed to be applied (e.g., software development vs. information systems).
Rather, it is the nature of the activity being considered, e.g., repetitive and structured procedures vs. unstructured, creative, and cooperative ones. The workflow, groupware, and CSCW communities have recognized that any activity can be characterized according to its degree of structure and formalization. Ideally, we can draw an axis that represents the classes of processes/workflows we need to support. The two edges represent extreme situations. At one edge we have highly structured activities, characterized by a high degree of standardization, automation, and volumes. At the other edge, we have highly unstructured activities where the only thing we can specify is the behavioral characterization of participants. For instance, we can state the rules by which a videoconference is to be held (e.g., who can grant the right to speak), but we cannot and do not want to anticipate the order, nature, and concatenation of activities and operations carried out during the conference. This dichotomy has been used quite often to distinguish true workflow management systems from CSCW and groupware environments. Indeed, we do need to create integrated environment where the entire range of support can be implemented effectively. This means that we need to pursue (at least) three research topics. First, we need to understand how to characterize a specific process with respect to its degree of standardization. Second, we need to identify how to select among the available environments those that effectively address the needs of the process being studied. For instance, when and how is it convenient to use a groupware tool? What is the threshold in the degree of structuring of a process that indicates the need for a true workflow management system? Third, we need to integrate and jointly exploit the different environments and mechanisms that are today available. This problem has been already addressed in the community (see for instance the integration of SPADE and Imagine Desk, or the cooperative extensions to Oz), but certainly much work is still to be done.

Thesis 4 We have too often tried to model what can't be modeled, or is not worthwhile and useful to model.

To illustrate this thesis we will cite an example taken from the PDA (Personal Digital Assistant) market. A few years ago, Apple announced Newton, a revolutionary palmtop computer that provided personal assistance and that was able to recognize handwriting. The product never took off. Its handwriting recognition software was too complex and still unable to effectively recognize the handwriting of an individual. Moreover, it was pointlessly ambitious. Users do not really care about being enabled to write using their own handwriting. A few years later, US Robotics created a much simpler version of a Newton-like palmtop. Instead of offering a complete handwriting recognition program, it sports a very simple "graffiti" language, a sort of standard upper case based alphabet that can be easily learned and used by anyone in a few minutes. Palm Pilot is a leader in the market because of its simplicity and effectiveness. In software process research, we have been afflicted by a Newton-like syndrome. Quite often, we want to provide automatic support to activities that simply do not need to be supported "that far." For instance, while it is certainly useful to clearly describe the steps in a design method, it is purposeless to formally model it to support its detailed enactment (e.g., by indicating which steps in the method have to be carried out and in which order). Developers will never accept a tool that operates at that level of detail. Moreover, it would be useless. You can use a design method effectively only if you "know" it so deeply that it is part of your mental habit, and not just because "someone else" mandates what you are supposed to do at any time.

Thesis 5 Software Process Improvement (SPI) has the same nature of any other process improvement initiative.

Consistently, it should be based on the concepts, approaches, and techniques of rganizational and behavioral sciences. The SPI area includes all the activities related to standards (e.g., application of ISO 9000 to software processes), assessment methods (CMM and SPICE), metrics, and improvement paradigms (Quality Improvement Paradigm, QIP). It is our impression that while the CSCW community has paid much attention to the results and contributions of organizational, behavioral, and cognitive sciences, the SPI community has reused this kind of contributions only partially. For instance, SPI has produced methods (i.e., CMM, SPICE, Bootstrap) that make it possible to rank the maturity of an organization with respect to its technical ability (the "CMM key practices"). But these approaches have two limitations. First, they concentrate on specific technological issues and fail to provide a comprehensive and effective connection with general, organization-wise improvement problems. As an example, CMM is able to identify the need for establishing configuration management procedures, but it does not relate this to the general need of identifying the right organizational structure for a specific company/market/product context. Superimposing a configuration management policy to a wrong or inappropriate organization would worsen the situation. Second, methods such as the CMM do not provide concrete support for analysis and diagnosis of the problems afflicting a company. The only method offered by the CMM is the questionnaire, which provides just an evaluation score of technical-related practices. We argue that we, as software engineers, can learn a lot from the approaches and experiences of organizational and behavioral sciences. For instance, we should understand how to position assessment methods such as the CMM within the context of general approaches to organizational design and organization change management. If we do not do this, the risk is to "reinvent a (square) wheel" and to miss the opportunities of reusing available and consolidated results and guidelines.

Thesis 6 So far, we have substantially failed to demonstrate that SPT is useful. Also organizations still hesitate to adopt SPI methods.

Even if there is an increasing awareness that it is crucial to improve the software process, software developers do not consider SPT as a real and effective opportunity to achieve significant gains in their business. SPT is often considered too generic or esoteric to be really usable and effective. This is partially due to the motivations we have discussed so far in the previous theses. More in general, we believe that there is a general problem of credibility of the SPT research. Our environments are not used, and thus there is no industrial validation. Industry rather relies on simple project management tools, and use general process templates from a quality system (i.e., not instantiated process models) or guide their daily work. Also, SPI approaches are often just a collection of good generic principles, rather than operational and pragmatically pursuable methods, supported by practical cases, experiences, and scenarios. Many SPI frameworks, like QIP and CMM, have their origin in large organizations, and they have not yet been effectively scaled down to serve the majority of software-developing organizations. Organizations that pursue SPI initiatives may also be more motivated by bureaucratic needs (cf. ISO-9000 certification), rather than a real commitment to SPI. However, there is growing awareness and dedication in industry to pursue SPI, and in contributing to develop, adapt and validate existing SPI frameworks (cf. the ongoing ESPRIT ESSI program). We believe that we need to merge ideas from SPT, SPI, and the other technologies mentioned earlier. The goal must be to evaluate and "absorb" the contributions of the related disciplines working on these topics. For instance, using web-based SPT is expected to lower the threshold for computer-assisted process support and effective exploitation of experience databases as part of a quality system already in use. Only a substantial injection of "fresh air" can change the present course of actions, and renovate and boost the research in the process field.

14.3 Looking Ahead

The theses we have presented in this position paper are extreme and provocative positions and sometimes negatives. These are meant to stimulate the discussion and provide some elements to better direct and develop our research activity. The software process research community is at a critical turning point. This community can expand and progress if it will be able to face these issues and identify reasonable and convincing answers to address them.

References

[DiNitto98] Elisabetta Di Nitto and Alfonso Fuggetta, eds. Process Technology. Kluwer Academic Publisher, January 1998

[ICSP98]   5th International Conference on the Software Process, Illinois (USA), 1998. http://www.bell-labs.com/user/dep/prof/ispa/icsp5

[ISPW98]   11th International Software Process Workshop, Illinois (USA), 1998. http://www.bell-labs.com/user/dep/prof/ispa/ispw11/cfp.html

[RDP97]   International Workshop on Research Directions in Process Technology (RDP'97), Nancy, France, 1997.http://www.elet.polimi.it/fugetta/rdpt97.html

[WAC99]   1st International Conference on Work Activity Coordination, San Francisco, USA, 1999. http://www.cs.colorado.edu/wacc99

[NSF98]NSF Workshop on Workflow and Process Automation in Information Systems: State-of-the-Art and Future Directions, Athens, Georgia, USA, 1998. http://lsdis.cs.uga.edu/activities/NSF-workflow.

Section 4

Estimation Methods

Estimating development effort is a large challenge in the software industry. Most research has focused on models to support estimation processes, while most practice is based on expert opinion and judgement. Historical project data is useful in either case. Such data constitutes the basis for the initial development and local adaptation of models, and it supports experts on their judgments. The first article in this section reports a review of studies on expert estimation of software development effort. The second article describes the development and use of a repository of project data tailored to support effort estimation and risk analysis within a large company. The final article in this section reports a case study in another company that investigated applying use cases as the basis for effort estimation of large-scale, incremental development.

15. *Jørgensen, M. (2004)* "A Review of Studies on Expert Estimation of Software Development Effort", *Journal of Systems and Software,* 70 (1-2):37–60

16. *Jørgensen, M., Conradi, R., and Sjøberg, D. (1999)* "Reuse of software development experiences – a case study," *Telektronikk* (special issue on Software Quality in Telecommunication), Telenor, Oslo, 95(1):48–53

17. *Mohagheghi, P., Anda, B., and Conradi, R. (2005)* "Effort Estimation of Use Cases for Incremental Large-Scale Software Development," In Gruia-Catalin Roman, William G. Griswold, and Bashar Nuseibeh (Eds.): *Proc. 27th International Conference on Software Engineering (ICSE'2005),* St Louis, Missouri, USA, 15–21 May 2005, ACM/IEEE-CS Press, pp. 303–311.

15

A Review of Studies on Expert Estimation of Software Development Effort

M. Jørgensen

Abstract: This paper provides an extensive review of studies related to expert estimation of software development effort. The main goal and contribution of the review is to support the research on expert estimation, e.g., to ease other researcher's search for relevant expert estimation studies. In addition, we provide software practitioners with useful estimation guidelines, based on the research-based knowledge of expert estimation processes. The review results suggest that expert estimation is the most frequently applied estimation strategy for software projects, that there is no substantial evidence in favor of use of estimation models, and that there are situations where we can expect expert estimates to be more accurate than formal estimation models. The following twelve expert estimation "best practice" guidelines are evaluated through the review (1) Evaluate estimation accuracy, but avoid high evaluation pressure, (2) Avoid conflicting estimation goals, (3) Ask the estimators to justify and criticize their estimates, (4) Avoid irrelevant and unreliable estimation information, (5) Use documented data from previous development tasks, 6) Find estimation experts with relevant domain background and good estimation records, (7) Estimate top-down and bottom-up, independently of each other, (8) Use estimation checklists, (9) Combine estimates from different experts and estimation strategies, (10) Assess the uncertainty of the estimate, (11) Provide feedback on estimation accuracy and development task relations, and, (12) Provide estimation training opportunities. We found supporting evidence for all 12 estimation principles, and provide suggestions on how to implement them in software organizations.

Keywords: software development, effort estimation, expert judgment, project planning

15.1 Introduction

Intuition and judgment – at least good judgment – are simply analyses frozen into habit and into the capacity for rapid response through recognition. Every manager needs to be able to analyze problems systematically (and with the aid of the modern arsenal of analytical tools provided by management science and opera-

tions research). Every manager needs also to be able to respond to situations rap-idly, a skill that requires the cultivation of intuition and judgment over many years of experience and training. (Simon 1987)

In this paper we summarize empirical results related to expert estimation of software development effort. The primary goal and contribution of the paper is to support the research on software development expert estimation through an exten-sive review of relevant papers, a brief description of the main results of these papers, and the use of these results to validate important expert estimation guide-lines. Although primarily aimed at other researchers, we believe that most of the paper, in particular the validated guidelines, are useful for software practitioners, as well.

We apply a broad definition of expert estimation, i.e., we include estimation strategies in the interval from unaided intuition ("gut feeling") to expert judgment supported by historical data, process guidelines, and checklists ("structured esti-mation"). Our main criteria to categorize an estimation strategy as expert estima-tion is that the estimation work is conducted by a person recognized as an expert on the task, and that a significant part of the estimation process is based on a nonexplicit and nonrecoverable reasoning process, i.e., "intuition." Most estima-tion processes have both intuitive and explicit reasoning elements, as reported in the business forecasting study described in Blattberg and Hoch (1990). In fact, even formal software development estimation models may require expert esti-mates of important input parameters (Pengelly 1995), i.e., require nonexplicit and nonrecoverable reasoning. Estimation strategies where a formal model is at the core of the estimation process are, however, not the topic of this paper.

There are relatively few studies discussing software development effort expert estimation. For example, a search for estimation papers in the journals IEEE Transactions on Software Engineering, Journal of Systems and Software, Journal of Information and Software Technology, and Journal of Empirical Software En-gineering resulted in exactly 100 papers on software effort or size estimation[1]. Of these, only 17 (17%) include analyses or discussions of expert estimation; (Kusters 1990; Taff, et al. 1991; van Genuchten and Koolen 1991; Betteridge 1992; Goodman 1992; Abdel-Hamid, et al. 1993; Londeix 1995; Hughes 1996b; Höst and Wohlin 1997; Lederer and Prasad 1998; Ohlsson, et al. 1998; Chulani, et al. 1999; Myrtveit and Stensrud 1999; Verner, et al. 1999; Walkerden and Jeffery 1999; Mizuno, et al. 2000; Jørgensen and Sjøberg 2001a). Similarly, while there have been several surveys of software development effort estimation models (e.g., Mohanty 1981; Boehm 1984; Hihn and Habib-Agahi 1991b; Fairley 1992; Heemstra 1992; Walkerden and Jeffery 1997; Boehm and Sullivan 1999; Boehm, et al. 2000; Briand and Wieczorek 2002), we found only one survey on expert estimation research results (Hughes 1996a). Fortunately, there are many relevant studies on expert estimation in other domains, e.g., medicine, business, psychol-ogy, and project management. To evaluate, understand, and extend the software development expert estimation results, we therefore try to transfer selected expert estimation research results from other domains.

[1] Search conduced March 2002.

We have structured the large amount of empirical results around a discussion and empirical validation of twelve "best practice" expert estimation principles. The selection of those principles was based on three sources (1) What we have observed as best expert estimation practice in industrial software development projects, (2) The list of 139 forecasting principles described in Armstrong (2001d), and, (3) The nine software estimation principles described in Lederer and Prasad (1992). The selected 12 estimation principles do, of course, not cover all aspects of software development effort expert estimation. They provide, however, a set of principles that we believe are essential for successful expert estimation. Table 15.1 describes the topics and main result of each section of this paper.

15.2 Frequency of Use of Expert Estimation

Published surveys on estimation practice suggest that expert estimation is the dominant strategy when estimating software development effort. For example, the study of software development estimation practice at Jet Propulsion Laboratory reported in Hihn and Habib-Agahi (1991a) found that 83% of the estimators used "informal analogy" as their primary estimation techniques, 4% "formal analogy" (defined as expert judgment based on documented projects), 6% "rules of thumb", and 7% "models." The investigation of Dutch companies described in Heemstra and Kusters (1991) conclude that 62%, of the organizations that produced software development estimates, based the estimates on "intuition and experience" and only 16% on "formalized estimation models." Similarly, a survey conducted in New Zealand (Paynter 1996) reports that 86% of the responding software development organizations applied "expert estimation" and only 26% applied "automated or manual models" (an organization could apply more than one method). A study of the information systems development department of a large international financial company (Hill et al. 2000) found that *no* formal software estimation model was used. Jørgensen (1997) reports that 84% of the estimates of software development projects conducted in a large Telecom company were based on expert judgment, and Kitchenham et al. (2002) report that 72% of the project estimates of a software development company were based on "expert judgment." In fact, we were not able to find any study reporting that *most* estimates were based on formal estimation models. The estimation strategy categories and definitions are probably not the same in the different studies, but there is nevertheless strong evidence to support the claim that expert estimation is more frequently applied than model-based estimation. This strong reliance on expert estimation is not unusual. Similar findings are reported in, for example, business forecasting, see Remus, O'Connor et al. (1995) and Winklhofer et al. (1996).

There may be many reasons for the reported low use of formal software development effort estimation models, e.g., that software organizations feel uncomfortable using models they do not fully understand. Another valid reason is that, as suggested in our survey in Sect. 15.3, we lack substantial evidence that the use of formal models lead to more accurate estimates compared with expert estimation. The strong reliance on the relatively simple and flexible method of expert estimation is therefore a choice in accordance with the method selection principle

Table 15.1. Contents of Paper

section	description of Topic	main results
15.2	frequency of use of expert estimation	expert estimation is the dominant strategy when estimating software development effort
15.3	performance of expert estimation in comparison with estimation models	the design of the empirical studies comparing expert and model-based software development effort estimate seems to have had a strong impact on the results. It is not possible to conclude that expert estimation or estimation model, in general, are more accurate. However, expert estimates seems to be more accurate when there are important domain knowledge *not* included in the estimation models, when the estimation uncertainty is high as a result of environmental changes not included in the model, or when simple estimation strategies lead to relatively accurate estimates
15.4	reduce situational and human biases	empirical validation of the expert estimation principles:

15.5	support the estimation process	1. evaluate estimation accuracy, but avoid high evaluation pressure
		  2. avoid conflicting estimation goals
		  3. ask estimators to justify and criticize their estimates
		  4. avoid irrelevant and unreliable estimation information
		  5. use documented data from previous development tasks
		  6. find estimation experts with relevant domain background and good estimation records
		  7. estimate top-down and bottom-up, independently of each other.
		  8. use estimation checklists.
		  9. combine estimates from different experts and estimation strategies.
		 10. assess the uncertainty of the estimate.

15.6	provide feedback and training opportunities	11. provide feedback on estimation accuracy and task relations 12. provide estimation training opportunities
15.7	conclusions and further research	all 12 principles are based on empirical evidence. There is, however, still a need for more knowledge about how to apply them in various software estimation situations

described in "Principles of Forecasting" (Armstrong 2001c, pp. 374–375): "*Select simple methods unless substantial evidence exists that complexity helps. ... One of the most enduring and useful conclusions from research on forecasting is that simple methods are generally as accurate as complex methods.*" However, even if we had substantial evidence that the formal models led to, on average, more accurate estimates, this may not be sufficient for widespread use. Todd and Benbasat (2000), studying people's strategies when conducting decisions based on personal preferences, found that a decision strategy also must be easier to apply, i.e., demand less mental effort, than the alternative (default) decision strategy to achieve acceptance by the estimators. Similarly, Ayton (1998) summarizes studies from many domains where experts were resistant to replace their judgments with simple, more accurate decision rules.

15.3 Performance of Expert Estimation in Comparison with Estimation Models

We found 15 different empirical software studies comparing expert estimates with estimates based on formal estimation models. Table 15.2 briefly describes the designs, the results and the, from our viewpoint, limitations of the studies in a chronological sequence. We do not report the statistical significance of the differences in estimation accuracy, because most studies do not report them, and because a meaningful interpretation of significance level requires that (1) a population (of projects, experts, and estimation situations) is defined, and, (2) a random sample is selected from that population. None of the reported studies define the population, or apply random samples. The samples of projects, experts, and estimation situations are better described as "convenience samples." We use the term "expert" (alternatively, "software professional" or "project leader") in the description of the estimators, even when it is not clear whether the estimation situation, e.g., experimental estimation task, enables the expert to apply his/her expertise. Consequently, experts may in some of the studies be better interpreted as novices, even when the participants are software professionals and not students.

The results of the studies in Table 15.2 are not conclusive. Of the fifteen studies, we categorize five to be in favor of expert estimation (Studies 1, 2, 5, 7, and 15), five to find no difference (Studies 3, 4, 10, 11, and 13), and five to be in favor of model-based estimation (Studies 6, 8, 9, 12, and 14).

Interesting dimensions of the studies are realism (experiment versus observation), calibration of models (calibrated to an organization or not), and level of expertise of the estimator (students versus professionals). A division of the studies into categories based on these dimensions suggests that the design of the empirical studies has a strong impact on the result. All experiments applying estimation models not calibrated to the estimation environment (Studies 1, 2, 5, and 7) showed that the expert estimates were the most accurate. On the other hand, all experiments applying calibrated estimation models (Studies 10, 11, 12, and 13)

Table 15.2. Software Studies on Expert Estimation of Effort

Nr	references	designs of studies	results and limitations
1	(Kusters, et al. 1990)	experimental comparison of the estimation accuracy of 14 project leaders with that of estimation models (BYL and Estimacs) on one finished software project	the project leaders' estimates were, on average, more accurate than the estimation model. Limitations (1) The experimental setting, and (2) the estimation models were not calibrated to the organization
2	(Vicinanza, et al. 1991)	experimental comparison of the estimation accuracy of five software professionals with that of estimation models (function points and COCOMO) on ten finished software projects	the software professionals had the most and least accurate estimates, and were, on average, more accurate than the models. Limitation (1) The experimental setting. (2) the project information was tailored to the estimation models, e.g., no requirement specification was available, and (3) the estimation models were not calibrated to the organization
3	(Heemstra and Kusters 1991)	questionnaire based survey of 597 Dutch companies	the organizations applying function points-based estimation models had the same estimation accuracy as those *not* applying function points (mainly estimates based on "intuition and experience") on small and medium large projects, and lower accuracy on large projects. The use of function points reduced the proportion of very large (>100%) effort overruns. Limitations (1) the questionnaire data may have a low quality,[2] (2) the relationship is not necessarily causal, e.g., the organizations applying estimation models may be different to other organizations, and (3) response rate not reported.
4	(Lederer and Prasad 1992), (Lederer and Prasad 1993),	questionnaires based survey of 112 software organizations	the algorithmic effort estimation models did not lead to higher accuracy compared with "intuition, guessing, and personal memory." Limitations (1) the questionnaire data

[2] We include this comment on both studies applying questionnaires, because questionnaire studies typically have limited control over the quality of their data, see (Jørgensen 1995).

	(Lederer and Prasad 1998), (Lederer and Prasad 2000) (reporting the same study)		may have a low quality, (2) the relationship is not necessarily causal, e.g., the organizations applying estimation models may be different to other organizations, and (3) response rate of only 29%, i.e., potential biases due to differences between the organizations that answered and those that did not
5	(Mukhopadhyay, et al. 1992)	experimental comparison of the estimation accuracy of one expert with that of estimation models (case-based reasoning model based on previous estimation strategy of the expert, function points, and COCOMO) on five finished software projects	the expert's estimates were the most accurate, but not much better than the case-based reasoning estimation model. The algorithmic estimation models (COCOMO and function points) were the least accurate. Limitations (1) the experimental setting, (2) the algorithmic estimation models were not calibrated to the organization, and (3) only one expert
6	(Atkinson and Shepperd 1994)	experimental comparison of the estimation accuracy of experts (students?) with that of estimation models (analogy and function points) on 21 finished projects	one of the analogy-based estimation models provided the most accurate estimates, then the expert judgments, then the two other analogy based models, and finally, the function point based estimation model. Limitations (1) the experimental setting, and (2) missing information about the expert estimators and the models[3]
7	(Pengelly 1995)	experimental comparison of the estimation accuracy of experts (activity based estimates) with that of estimation models (Doty, COCOMO, function point, and Putnam SLIM) on and finished project	the expert estimates were the most accurate. Limitations (1) the experimental setting, (2) the estimation models were not calibrated to the organization, and (3) only one project was estimate
8	(Jørgensen 1997)	observation of 26 industrial projects, where five applied the function point estimation model, and 21 were based	the function point based estimates were more accurate, mainly due to avoidance of very large effort overruns. Limitations (1) most projects applying the function

[3] We were only able to locate a preliminary version of this paper (from one of the authors). It is possible that the final version provides more information about the expert estimation process.

Table 15.2. (*contd.*)

Nr	references	designs of studies	results and limitations
		on expert estimates (bottom-up-based estimates)	point model did also provided a bottom-up expert judgment-based effort estimate and combined these two estimates, and (2) the relationship is not necessarily causal, e.g., the projects applying an estimation model may be different from the other projects
9	(Niessink and van Vliet 1997)	observations of 140 change tasks of an industrial software system. Comparison of the original expert estimates with estimates from formal estimation models (function points and analogy)	the analogy based-model had the most accurate estimates. The expert estimates were more accurate than the function point estimates. Limitations (1) the expert estimates could impact the actual effort, the formal models could not, and (2) the formal models used the whole data set as learning set (expect the task to be estimated), the expert estimates had only the previous tasks
10	(Ohlsson, et al. 998)	observation of 14 student software projects developing the same software	the projects applying data from the experience database had no more accurate estimates than those which did not use the experience database. Estimation models based on previous projects with same requirement specification (analogy-based models) did not improve the accuracy. Limitations (1) the competence level of the estimators (students), and (2) the artificial context of student projects, e.g., not real customer
11	(Walkerden and Jeffery 1999)	experimental comparison of the estimation accuracy of 25 students with that of estimation models (analogy- and regression- based models) on 19 projects	the experts' estimates had the same accuracy as the best analogy based model and better than the regression-based and the other analogy-based models. Estimates based on expert selected analogies, with a linear size adjustment, provided the most accurate effort estimates. Limitations (1) the experimental setting, (2) the competence level of the estimators (students), and (3) the project information was tailored to the estimation models, e.g., no requirement specification was available
12	(Myrtveit and Stensrud 1999)	experimental comparison of the estimation accuracy of 68 software professionals with that of a combination	the models had the same or better accuracy than the combination of model and expert, and better accuracy than the unaided expert. Limitations (1) the experimen-

#	Reference	Description	Findings
		of expert estimates and models (analogy and regression), and models alone on 48 COTS projects (each participant estimated and project)	tal setting, and (2) the project information was tailored to the estimation models, e.g., no requirement specification was available
13	(Bowden, et al. 2000)	experimental comparison of students' ability to find "objects" as input to an estimation model in comparison with an expert system	there was no difference in performance. Limitations (1) the experimental setting, (2) the competence level of the estimators (students), and (3) study of input to effort estimation models, not effort estimation
14	(Jørgensen and Sjøberg 2002b)	observation of experts' ability to predict uncertainty of effort usage (risk of unexpected software maintenance problems) in comparison with a simple regression-based estimation model. Study based on interviews with 54 software maintainer before start and after completion of maintenance tasks	the simple regression model predicted maintenance problems better than software maintainers with long experience. Limitations (1) assessment of effort estimation uncertainty, not effort estimation
15	(Kitchenham, et al. 2002)	observations of 145 maintenance tasks in a software development organization. Comparison of expert estimates with estimates based on the average of two estimation methods, e.g., the average of an expert estimates and a formal model-based estimate. The actual projects estimates were also compared with the estimates from estimation models (variants of a regression + function point-based model) based on the observed maintenance tasks	there was no difference in estimation accuracy between the average-combined and the purely expert-based estimates. The expert estimates were more accurate than the model-based estimates. Limitations (1) the relationship is not necessarily causal, e.g., the project combining estimation methods may be more complex than the other projects, and (2) the expert estimates could impact the actual effort, the formal models could not[4]

[4] The authors conclude that the estimates did not impact the actual effort.

showed a similar or better performance of the models. The higher accuracy of the experts in the first experimental situation can be explained by the estimation models' lack of inclusion of organization and domain specific knowledge.[5] The similar or better accuracy of the models in the second experimental situation can be explained by the lack of domain-specific knowledge of the experts, i.e., in Studies 10, 11, and 13 the estimators were students, and in Study 12 the estimation information seems to have been at a, for the software professional, unfamiliar format.

Three of the studies (Studies 8, 9, and 14) where the model-based estimates were calibrated, *and* both expert and model estimates were applied by software projects, i.e., the five observational studies (Studies 3, 4, 8, 9, and 14), show results in favor of model-based estimation. The remaining two studies of that category (Studies 3 and 4), report similar accuracy of the models and the experts. A possible explanation for the similar or higher accuracy of model-based estimates of the observational studies is that the real-world model-based estimates frequently were "expert adjusted model estimates," i.e., a *combination* of model and expert. The model-based estimates of Study 8, for example, seem to be of that type. A typical "expert adjusted model estimation" process may be to present the output from the model to the experts. Then, the domain experts adjust the effort estimate according to what she/he believes is a more correct estimate. If this is the typical model-based estimation process, then the reported findings indicate that a combination of estimation model and expert judgment is better than pure expert estimates. More studies are needed to examine this possibility.

The above 15 studies are not conclusive, other than that there is no substantial evidence in favor of either model or expert-based estimates. In particular, we believe that there is a need for comparative studies including a description of the actual estimation models and actual expert estimation processes in real software effort estimation situations.

None of the studies in Table 15.2 were designed for the purpose of examining *when* we can expect expert estimation to have the same or better estimation accuracy compared with estimation models. This is however the main question. Clearly, there exist situations were the use of formal estimation models leads to more accurate estimates, and situations where expert estimation results in higher

---

[5] There is an on-going discussion on the importance of calibrating an estimation model to a *specific* organization. While the majority of the empirical software studies, e.g., Cuelenaere, et al. (1987), Marouane and Mili (1989), Jeffery and Low (1990), Marwane and Mili (1991), Murali and Sankar (1997), and Jeffery, Ruhe et al. (2000) report that calibration of estimation models to a specific organization led to more accurate estimates, the results in Briand et al. (1999) and Briand et al. (2000) suggest that use of multi-organizational software development project data were just as accurate. However, the results in Briand et al. 1999; and Briand et al. (2000) do not report from studies calibrating *general* estimation products. For example, the difference between the projects on which the original COCOMO model was developed (Boehm 1981) and projects conducted in the 1990s may be much larger than the difference between multi-organizational and organization specific project data. The evidence in favor of calibration of general estimation models in order to increase the estimation accuracy is, therefore, strong.

accuracy, e.g., the two types of experimental situations described earlier. To increase the understanding of when we can expect expert estimates to have an acceptable accuracy in comparison with formal estimation models, we have tried to derive major findings from relevant human judgment studies, e.g., time estimation studies, and describe the consistence between these findings and the software-related results. This turned out to be a difficult task, and the summary of the studies described in Table 15.3 should be interpreted carefully, e.g., some of the finings are rather vaguely formulated, and other researchers may interpret the results from the same studies differently.

An interesting observation is that the software development expert estimates are not systematically worse than the model-based estimates, such as the expert estimates in most other studied professions. For example, Dawes (1986) reports that the evidence against clinical expert judgment, compared with formal models, is overwhelming. Many of the studies described in Table 15.2, on the other hand, suggest that software development experts have the same or better accuracy as the formal estimation models. We believe that the two most important reasons for this difference in results are:

- The importance of specific domain knowledge (case-specific data) is higher in software development projects than in most other studied human judgment domains. For example, while most clinical diseases are based on stable biological processes with few, well-established diagnostic indicators, the relevant indicators of software development effort may be numerous, their relevance unstable and not well-established. For example, Wolverton (1974) found that: *"There is a general tendency on the part of designers to gold-plate their individual parts of any system, but in the case of software the tendency is both stronger and more difficult to control than in the case of hardware."* How much a particular project member tend to gold-plate, i.e., to improve the quality beyond what is expected by the customer, is hardly part of any estimation model, but can be known by an experienced project leader. According to Hammond et al. (1987) a "fit" between the type of estimation (human judgment) task and the selected estimation approach is essential, i.e., if a task is an expert estimation (intuition) inducing task, then the experts provide the most accurate estimates and when the task is a model estimation (analysis) inducing task then the models provided the most accurate estimates. As we interpret Hammond et al., many software development effort estimation tasks are expert estimation inducing tasks.
- The performance of the software development estimation models is poorer than estimation models in most other studied human judgment domains. For example, although there has been much research on the shape of the software "production function," i.e., relation between input and output parameters, for several years, no agreement has been reached. Dolado (2001), for example, investigated the relationship between software size and effort on 12 data sets using regression analysis and genetic programming. He reported that it was hard to conclude on a relationship between effort and size, and that we could only expect moderately good results of size-based estimation models. Currently, most software development effort estimation models are size-based.

Table 15.3. Expert versus Model Estimates

findings	strength of evidence	sources of evidence	consistence between the findings and the results described in software studies?
expert estimates are more accurate than model estimates when the experts possess (and efficiently apply) important domain knowledge not included in the estimation models. Model estimates are more accurate when the experts do *not* possess (or efficiently apply) important domain knowledge not included in the estimation models	strong	these findings are supported by "common sense," e.g., it is obvious that there exists important case-specific domain knowledge about software developers and projects that cannot be included in a general estimation model. The finding is also supported by a number of studies (mainly business forecasting studies) on the importance of specific domain knowledge in comparison with models, (see Lawrence and O'Connor 1996; Webby and O'Connor 1996; Johnson 1998; Mendes et al. 2001) for reviews on this topic. However, as pointed out by Dawes (1986), based on studies of clinical and business judgment, the correspondence between domain knowledge and estimation skills is easily overrated Meehl (1957) summarizes about 20 studies comparing clinical judgment with judgment based on statistical models. He found that the models had the same or better performance in all cases. The same negative result was reported by Dawes (1986). The results in favor of models seems to be less robust when the object to be estimated include human behavior, e.g., traffic safety (Hammond et al. 1987)	yes. all studies where the models were *not* calibrated to the organizational context and the estimators had domain knowledge (Studies 1, 2, 5, and 7) report that the expert estimates were more accurate. All studies were the estimators had little relevant domain knowledge (due to the lack of requirement specification, lack of experience or project information tailored to the estimation models), *and* the estimation models were calibrated to the organizational context (Studies 10, 11, 12, and 13) report that the models had the same or better performance

expert estimates are more accurate than model estimates when the uncertainty is low. Model estimates are more accurate when the uncertainty is high, e.g., when the project is much larger than previous projects

medium

the majority of studies (mainly business forecasting studies) support this finding, e.g., Braun and Yaniv (1992) Shanteau (1992) O'Connor et al. (1993) Hoch and Schkade (1996) and Soll (1996). However, a few studies suggest that uncertain situations favor expert judgment, e.g., the study described in Sanders and Ritzman (1991) on business related time series forecasting

mixed. study 3 reports that high uncertainty did *not* favor the use of (function point-based) estimation model. Similarly, Study 9 reports results suggesting that low uncertainty (homogeneous tasks) did not favor expert estimates compared with an analogy-based model. An investigation of the available studies on this topic suggests that high uncertainty favor the estimation models *only if* the uncertainty is included in the estimation model. If, however, a new software task is uncertain because it represents a new type of situation not included in model's learning data set, e.g., reflects the development of a project much larger than the earlier projects, then the models are likely to be less accurate. Similar results on how uncertainty impact the expert estimation performance are reported in Goodwin and Wright (1990) on time series forecasting

Table 15.3. (*contd.*)

findings	strength of evidence	sources of evidence	consistence between the findings and the results described in software studies?
experts use simple estimation strategies (heuristics) and perform just as well or better than estimation models when these simple estimation strategies (heuristics) are valid. Otherwise, the strategies may lead to biased estimates	strong	the results reported in Josephs and Hahn (1995) and Todd and Benbasat (2000), describing studies on time planning and general decision tasks, indicate that the estimation strategies used by unaided experts were simple, even when the level of expert knowledge was high. Increasing the time pressure on the estimators may lead the experts to switch to even simpler estimation strategies, as reported in the business forecasting study described in Ordonez and Benson III (1997). Gigerenzer and Todd (1999) present a set of human judgment studies, from several domains, that demonstrate an amazingly high accuracy of simple estimation strategies (heuristics). Kahneman et al. (1982), on the other hand studied similar judgment tasks and found that simple strategies easily led to biased estimates because the heuristics were applied incorrectly, i.e., they demonstrated that there are situations where the simple estimation strategies applied by experts are not valid. Unfortunately, it may be difficult to decide in advance whether a simple estimation strategy is valid or not	yes. the software development estimation experiment reported in Jørgensen and Sjøberg (2001b) suggests that the experts applied the so-called "representativeness heuristic", i.e., the strategy of finding the most similar previous projects without regarding properties of other, less similar, projects (see also discussion in Sect. 15.4.5). Most of the estimators applied a valid version of this, but some of them interpreted representativeness too "narrow," which lead to biased estimates. Similarly, Study 14 suggests that the low performance in assessing estimation uncertainty of experienced software maintainers were caused by misuse of the "representativeness heuristic"

Strong experts can be strongly biased and misled by irrelevant information, e.g., towards overoptimism. Estimation models are less biased

yes.

substantial evidence supports this finding, e.g., Kahneman et al. (1982) Blattberg and Hoch (1990) Lim and O'Connor (1996); Connolly and Dean (1997) Makridakis et al. (1998), p. 500–501; Whitecotton et al. (1998) and Hill et al. (2000) reporting results from various domains. In particular relevant are the studies on the "planning fallacy" (Kahneman and Tversky 1979), i.e., the studies on people's tendency to provide too optimistic prediction of own performance in spite of knowledge about their previous overoptimism. Buehler et al. (1997) summarize studies on possible cognitive and motivational reasons for the planning fallacy

the studies that describe expert and model estimates actually used by industrial software projects and report the size of the individual projects' effort overruns (Studies 3 and 8) suggest that the risk of large effort overruns was reduced when applying estimation models. The software development estimation results described in Jørgensen and Sjøberg (2001a) suggest that an early estimate based on little information strongly biased the re-estimation, although the estimators were told not to use the early estimate as input, i.e., irrelevant information strongly misled the estimators

On the other hand, we do *not* believe that the software development experts are more skilled estimators than experts in other domains. On the contrary, as reported in Jørgensen and Sjøberg (2001a) and Jørgensen and Sjøberg (2002b) the focus on learning estimation skills from software development experience seems to be very low.

Many of the shortcomings of expert estimation may be reduced when following well-documented estimation principles. In the following sections we present and discuss 12 expert estimation principles that have improvement of expert estimation as goal.

15.4 Reduce Situational and Human Biases

Lederer et al. (1990) describe a "rational" and a "political" model of the estimation process, based on interviews with 17 software managers. The rational model describes the estimation process as in most text-books on estimation, i.e., as a rational process with estimation accuracy as the only goal, while the political model describes the estimation process more as a "tug-of-war" with individual motives, differing goals, and power conflicts. While some of the biases resulting from a "tug-of-war" are situational, e.g., the wish to get a contract, others are more inherent human, e.g., the general need for positive feedback from other people. This section suggests six estimation principles aiming at reducing the size of situational and human biases:

- Evaluate estimation accuracy, but avoid high evaluation pressure.
- Avoid conflicting estimation goals.
- Ask the estimators to justify and criticize their estimates.
- Avoid irrelevant and unreliable estimation information.
- Use documented data from previous development tasks.
- Find estimation experts with highly relevant domain background and good estimation records.

A general framework for identifying and handling the situational and human biases is described in Meyer and Booker (1991), pp. 44–53.

15.4.1 Evaluate Estimation Accuracy, but Avoid High Evaluation Pressure

Several human judgment studies suggest that a high motivation for accuracy, for example when people feel personally responsible, perceive that the estimation task is very important or receive monetary rewards for accurate estimates, actually *decreases* the estimation accuracy (Sieber 1974; Armstrong, et al. 1975; Cosier and Rose 1977). Pelham and Neter (1995) suggest that this decrease in human judgment accuracy is mainly a problem in the case of difficult judgments, whereas high motivation for accuracy increases the estimation accuracy in cases with easy judgments. Their findings are consistent with the large number of studies on the effect of "evaluation apprehension," e.g., Sanders (1984). An increased awareness of being evaluated seems to increase the level of so-called "dominant responses" (instincts) on cost of reflective responses (Zajonc 1965), i.e., evaluation leads to more instinct and less reflection. That effect may be very robust, e.g., Zajonc et al. (1969) measured a decrease in performance by cockroaches completing a maze when other cockroaches were present. When reflections and analyses are important and the task is difficult, as in many software development estimation situations, a strong perception of evaluation may therefore lead to less accurate estimates.

These results are, at first sight, not consistent with the results reported from the empirical software development studies on this topic. For example, Lederer and Prasad (1998) report that the factor with the highest impact on the estimation accuracy was the use of the estimation accuracy in the evaluation of the performance of the software professionals. Similarly, the software estimation studies (Weinberg and Schulman 1974; Jørgensen and Sjøberg 2001a) found that inducing estimation accuracy as an important performance measure improved the estimation accuracy compared with situations where the projects were evaluated according to, e.g., time precision or quality.

The different findings are, in our opinion, not in conflict. There is no reason to believe that software professionals are different from other estimators, i.e., an increased perception of accuracy evaluation may easily lead to decreased estimation accuracy of software projects. However, evaluations may also lead to (1) the "self-fulfilling prophecy" effect of software effort estimates, e.g., that an over-optimistic initial estimate and a high focus on estimation accuracy lead to actions that make that estimate more realistic as reported in the software project simulation study Abdel-Hamid et al. (1999), and (2) an increase in "self-critical thinking" as in the study of first-job salary and exam results prediction of students reported in Shepperd et al. (1996). For example, when the accountability is high people may be motivated to spend more time and collect more relevant information to achieve an accurate estimate. The total effect of accuracy evaluation, therefore, depends on the strength of the pressure due to the accuracy evaluation, the flexibility of the work (determining the possible effect from the "self-fulfilling prophecy"), and the increased degree of "self-critical thinking" as a consequence of the evaluation. Software managers should focus on achieving the benefits from accuracy evaluation, while avoiding the disadvantages. In our opinion, this means that the estimation accuracy should be part of the projects' evaluation criteria, but that a strong pressure from accuracy accountability or reward/punishment should be avoided. In addition, means to ensure "self-critical thinking" should be introduced, e.g., through estimation checklists and described estimation processes.

15.4.2 Avoid Conflicting Goals

There are conflicting estimation goal in situations where the estimation process is impacted by other goals (evaluations) than the accuracy of the estimate. This section focuses on two important instances of conflicting estimation goals (1) the conflicts between "bid," "planned effort" and "most likely effort," and (2) the conflict between "wishful thinking" and "realism."

Jørgensen and Sjøberg (2001a) report that, frequently, there was no distinction between "bid", "planned effort" and "most likely effort" when estimating software development effort. Similar results, i.e., that the distinction between planning and estimation are "blurred", are reported in the time-estimation studies described in Edwards and Moores (1994) and Goodwin (1998). The decisions on "bid," "planned effort," and "most likely effort," however, have conflicting goals. A bid should, optimally, be low enough to get the job and high enough to maximize profit, the planned effort should enable a successful project and motivate to efficient work, and the estimate of the most likely effort should represent the most realistic use of effort. The conflict between these goals, together with the lack of separation of them, may hinder realism of the expert estimates. We have not found any software studies on the impact of this conflict on accuracy of effort estimate. However, applying common sense and the results described in the human judgment studies (Cosier and Rose 1977; Keen 1981; Buehler et al. 1997), where conflicting goals were reported to reduce the realism of the estimates, we believe that the evidence against mixing the goals of "bid," "planned effort," and "most likely effort" are fairly strong.

The results from many human judgment studies indicate that people get overoptimistic when predicting own performance, i.e., they have problems separating "wish" and "realism." A summary of these studies is described by Harvey (2001). Potential reasons for this over optimism, or "planning fallacy" (Kahneman and Tversky 1979), are the "I am above average"-bias (Klein and Kunda 1994), and the lack of distinction between "best case" and "most realistic case" (NewbyClark et al. 2000). A general phenomenon seems to be that the level of overoptimism increases with the level of control (Koehler and Harvey 1997), e.g., a software developer responsible for the whole task to be estimated is supposed to be more overoptimistic than a project leader that plans and supervises the work of other project members. This overoptimism may be difficult to reduce, and in Newby-Clark et al. (2000) it was found that the only effective method was to let someone other than the executing person predict the work. The same conclusion is reported in Harvey (2001): *"someone other than the person(s) responsible for developing and implementing a plan of action should estimate its probability of success."* Buehler et al. (1994) found that the cause of an increased realism, when estimating other peoples work, was the increase in use of previous experience, i.e., while estimating own work induces mental work on how to complete the task (construction), estimating other people's work induces reflections on how much effort similar tasks required (history reflections). Unfortunately, we have not been able to find any published software development estimation specific study on the topic of estimating own work or other people's work[6].

---

[6] In a recent, unpublished, study of 60 small and medium large software development tasks, we find supporting evidence for this difference between estimation own and other peoples work. The difference in level of over-optimism was significant, but not very large.

Similarly to the discussion in Sect. 15.4.1, there are advantages of estimating own work. For example, if there is a high level of flexibility in how to implement a software specification, then an initially overoptimistic estimate of own work may lead to actions that make the estimate more realistic. The decision whether to estimating own work or not may therefore be a trade-off between the potential advantages, e.g., higher motivation for low use of effort, and the disadvantages, e.g., the strong tendency of overoptimism. In situations where there are small opportunities for "self-fulfilling prophecies," e.g., when the flexibility of the project work is strongly limited, then the software developers should, optimally, *not* estimate their own work. In real projects, however, estimation of own work may be the only option, e.g., because there are no other experts on a particular task. In such cases, it is especially important to be aware of the typical overoptimism and apply the debiasing estimation principles described in this paper.

An illustrative example of a conflict between wishful thinking and realism when predicting own performance is described in Griffin and Buehler (1999): "*Canadians expecting an income-tax refund were asked to predict when they would complete and mail in their tax forms. These respondents had indicated that they typically completed this chore about 2 weeks before the due rate; however, when asked about the current year, they predicted that they would finish, on average, about 1 month in advance of the due date. In fact, only 30% of the respondents were finished by their predicted data - on average they finished, as usual, about 2 weeks before the deadline.*"

There are other, obviously unfortunate, variants of the conflict between "wishful thinking" and "realism," e.g., the "software estimation game" described in Thomsett (1996): "*Boss: Hi, Mary. How long do you think it will take to add some customer enquiry screens to the Aardvark System? Mary: Gee ... I guess about six weeks or so. Boss: WHAAT?!!!! That long?!!! You're joking, right? Mary: Oh! Sorry. It could be done perhaps in four weeks....*" This type of situation both puts an unfortunate pressure on the estimator and leads to conflicting goals, i.e., a conflict between "be realistic" and "please the manager."

Software professionals should learn to identify estimation goals different from accuracy, and try to avoid or at least reduce the impact from them. In particular, software professionals should learn to identify when a person has a particularly strong interest in the outcome, e.g., when a person strongly want the project to be started. In this kind of conflicting goals situation, the highly involved person cannot be expected to provide realistic estimates, even when she/he is the person with the longest and most relevant experience.

15.4.3 Ask Estimators to Justify and Criticize Their Estimates

Expert estimation of effort is frequently a "constructive" process. The estimators try to imagine how to build the software, which pieces that are necessary to develop and the effort needed to implement and integrate the pieces. Empirical results from human judgment studies suggests that this type of process easily lead the estimator into the mode of "confirming theories on how to complete the project", rather than "reject incorrect hypotheses and assumptions" (Brehmer 1980;

Koehler 1991). This means that the estimators' *confidence* in their estimates depend more on the amount of effort they spent working on it, than on the actual accuracy of the estimate. Justification and critique of own estimates may have several important advantages related to this problem. It may:

- Increase of the accuracy of the estimate, particularly in high uncertainty situations (Hagafors and Brehmer 1983)
- Lead to a more analytical estimation process and reduce the risk of using too simple estimation strategies (Hammond 1996)
- Improve the level of confidence in the estimate (Koriat et al. 1980) and
- Improve the compensation for missing information (Brenner et al. 1996).

All the above studies were general human judgment studies, e.g., studies based on real-world clinical judgment tasks, business tasks, or estimates of so-called "almanac quantities." We have found no published software development estimation study on this topic.

However, as part of an experiment conducted by the author of this paper, we asked 13 software professionals to estimate the effort they would need to implement a specified timeshift-swapping system for hospital nurses. When the effort estimates were completed, the estimators were asked to list reasons why their estimate could be wrong, i.e., a critique of their own estimates. The average number of reasons listed were 4.3, ranging from 2 to 8. Finally, the estimators were asked to consider a change of their original estimates in light of their critique. Nine out of the 13 software professionals increased their estimates of most likely effort, four of them more than 25%. The average increase in effort estimate was, however, only 10%, and four of the participants actually decreased their estimates. We had no opportunity to let the software professionals develop the software, i.e., we had no information about the realism of their estimates. However, the small, on average, adjustments suggested by our results mean that, although potentially helpful to improve estimation realism, we should not expect that justification and criticism improve the realism of estimates very much. If the initial estimate is hugely overoptimistic, a justification and critique may only improve the realism to some extent. A possible reason for this limited impact is described in Einhorn and Hogarth (1978), based on studies on clinical judgment and probability assessments. Estimators are typically not very skilled in searching for weakening information when evaluating their own estimates.

Inspite of the expected small impact on the realism of the estimate, we believe that justification and criticism are sound and low-cost elements of improvements of expert estimates.

15.4.4 Avoid Irrelevant and Unreliable Estimation Information

It is easy to accept that irrelevant and unreliable information should be avoided. However, we have yet to see a checklist or estimation process effectively implementing this estimation principle. This may reflect the belief that expert estimators are able to filter out irrelevant and unreliable information when facing it. There are, however, several human judgment studies that suggest that this is not always the case, and that expert estimates may be strongly impacted by irrelevant information, even when the estimators know that the information is irrelevant. For example:

- Whitecotton et al. (1998) report that people are just as good as models to provide financial forecasts when presented with the same highly relevant information, but less accurate when irrelevant information is included.
- Lim and O'Connor (1996) report from business related time series predictions that an adjustment of an estimate for new information was not sufficient when the initial estimate was highly inaccurate, i.e., that the unreliable initial estimate strongly impacted the subsequent estimates. The software development estimation study described by Abdel-Hamid et al. (1993) confirm this result.
- Tversky and Kahneman (1974) report, based on general knowledge tasks, that the estimators were impacted by irrelevant information, because it was included in the question, i.e., people may have an implicit tendency to regard information as important when it is presented in the same context as the estimation problem.
- Ettenson et al. (1987) report that domain experts (financial auditing) were better than novices to focus on the most relevant information, i.e., the experts applied less information compared with the novices. Selection of proper experts may, therefore, be important to avoid strong impact from irrelevant information.
- Jørgensen and Sjøberg (2002a) report that the information about the software development cost expected by the customer had a strong impact on the estimate even when the estimators were told that the customer knew nothing about the realistic costs and that the information should be regarded as irrelevant for the estimation task. More surprisingly, this impact from the customer expectation was strongly underestimated by the software professionals.

Consequently, it is may not be sufficient to warn against irrelevant information or instruct people to consider information as unreliable. The only safe approach seems to *avoid* irrelevant and unreliable information. For example, it may be difficult to provide realistic effort estimates if the customer expects an unrealistically low level of cost, and the estimator knows this. Then, the only safe option may be to find a new estimator, without that knowledge.

15.4.5 Use Documented Data from Previous Development Tasks

Use of documented data means that that the expert estimators have the opportunity to apply a more analytic estimation strategy and consequently, be less prone to human and situational biases. Benefits from use of documented software project data are reported by Lederer and Prasad (1992), who found that software project cost overruns were associated with lack of documented data from previous tasks, i.e., high reliance on "personal memory." Without documented data people seem to both overreact to immediate past information, as reported in the time series prediction study (Remus et al. 1995), and rely too much on the "representative-ness" estimation strategy, see the software development estimation study (Jørgensen and Sjøberg 2002b). The "representativeness" estimation strategy means, for example, that people use the actual effort of the *most* similar (most representative) recalled task as staring point for the estimate without regarding the distribution of effort of other similar tasks. This strategy works well when the most similar task is sufficiently similar, represents the typical use of effort on such tasks, and the estimation uncertainty is low. The strategy may, however, lead to inaccurate estimates when the need for adjustment is large, as illustrated in the business forecasting study (Blattberg and Hoch 1990), or the expected impact from the "regression toward the mean"[7] is high, as reported in the human judgment and software estimation studies (Kahneman and Tversky 1973; Nisbett and Ross 1980; Jørgensen 2002).

A similar argument for the importance of documented data is reported in the time usage estimation study (Kahneman and Lovallo 1993). That study claims that people tend to adopt an "internal" or "inside" perspective on the estimation task, when relying on their own memory, instead of documented data. This "inside" perspective leads to a concentration on case-specific planning and a neglect of "background" information, such as the distribution of completion times for similar projects or the robustness of the construction plan. An "inside" perspective may work well when the estimator has strongly relevant task experience and the situation does not induce biases, but may otherwise lead to a high degree of estimation inaccuracy. The results described in Kahneman and Lovallo (1993) may explain the reduction of high effort overruns from use of models reported in the software development estimation studies (Heemstra and Kusters 1991; Jørgensen 1997). The use of estimation models increases the use of historical data and, consequently, removes the potentially large biases from expert estimators' "inside view" and the use of the "representativeness" estimation strategy.

The software development estimation results reported in Walkerden and Jeffery (1999) indicate that a semiautomated use of documented data leads to the best estimation accuracy. They found, similar to the business forecasting results reported by Blattberg and Hoch (1990), that people were good at finding analogies, but did not adjust properly for large differences between the task to be estimated and the most similar tasks. A semiautomated process of using people to find the relevant analogues and a simple formula for adjustments for differences had the best estimation accuracy. If the need for adjustments is large, simple models supporting the adjustments seem to be especially important.

Overall, we believe that the potential benefits from use of documented data are similar to the potential benefits from use of estimation models, i.e., avoidance of very inaccurate estimates and reduction of human biases.

---

[7] The impact from "regression toward the mean" is based on the observation that high or low performance tends to be followed by more average performance, in particular when the variance (uncertainty) is high. This means, for example, that when the most similar task had an unusual high performance and the estimation uncertainty is high, then we should estimate effort closer to the average performance than the effort value of the most similar task (Jørgensen 2002).

15.4.6 Find Experts with Relevant Domain Background and Good Estimation Records

Recently we conducted an estimation survey of the estimation processes of 18 experienced software project leaders. Included in that survey was a question about how the project leaders selected experts to provide the effort estimates. While all the project leaders described that they emphasized domain and development experience, only four of them described that they applied information about the peoples' previous estimation accuracy, and only two that they tried to get information about the estimation process applied by the estimator. An underlying assumption of the selection of estimation experts was, as we interpreted it, that "the people most competent in solving the task should estimate it". While this assumption can be true, see Sanders and Ritzman (2001) for an overview of supporting expert judgment studies from various domains, we believe that the following refinements of the assumption are important:

- The relevance of experience is sometimes very "narrow," i.e., only applicable in very similar situations, see Skitmore et al. (1994) and Ericsson and Lehmann (1996) for overviews from different domains.
- Jørgensen and Sjøberg (2002b) report that software maintainers with application specific experience had fewer maintenance problems, but did *not* predict their own work more accurately. Similarly, Lichtenstein and Fischhoff (1977) report that the level of overoptimism when estimating the quality of their own answers on "general knowledge" questions was independent of the actual correctness of the answers, i.e., the level of expertise. These findings conflict those reported in statistical forecasting studies, e.g., Sanders and Ritzman (2001). An examination of the studies suggests that the explanation is the difference between involved and uninvolved estimators. While all the results described in Sanders and Ritzman (2001) are derived from studies where the estimators were uninvolved observers, the results described in Lichtenstein and Fischhoff (1977) and Jørgensen and Sjøberg (2002b) are from studies where own work was estimated. A large benefit from domain experience on estimation accuracy may, consequently, require that the estimator is an uninvolved observer.
- Klayman et al. (1999) report, based on tasks from several domains, that people get overconfident in the accuracy of their estimates when receiving a set of estimation tasks more difficult than what they usually get.
- Stone and Opel (2000) report that having estimation expertise is not the same as being skilled in knowing the uncertainty of an estimate. Their experiment, based on art history related judgment tasks, suggest that these two types of expertise require different types of feedback and training.

Consequently, we cannot safely assume that people knowing much about a task are good at estimating it, nor can we assume that people good at estimating are good at knowing how uncertain their estimates are. For this reason, there should be separate records on these three characteristics (know-how, know-how-much, and know-how-uncertain) for each individual. Knowing much about a task may, for example, be useful for the development of the work breakdown structure.

People with good estimation records should be consulted when estimating the most likely effort. People good at estimating uncertainty should be consulted when assessing the uncertainty of the estimate. These three skills are different and may require different estimators, training, and feedback, see Sect. 15.6.

15.5 Support the Estimation Process

There are many ways of supporting the experts' estimation processes. This section provides and discusses the expert estimation principles:

– Estimate both top-down and bottom-up, independently of each other
– Use estimation checklists
– Combine estimates from different sources
– Assess the uncertainty of the estimate

15.5.1 Estimate Both Top-Down and Bottom-Up, Independently of Each Other

There are different strategies of decomposing the estimation problem, e.g., phase-based decomposition, functionality-based decomposition, additive, multiplicative, or combinations of these types. Most studies support the, on average, improvement from decomposing an estimation problem, see for example the multidomain survey on this topic in MacGregor (2001). There are, however, studies that indicate no benefits of decomposition. For example, Connolly and Dean (1997) found that the estimation accuracy improved from software task decomposition in only one out of two experiments. Vicinanza et al. (1991) found that the expert applying a top-down (analogy)-based software development estimation process was more accurate than the experts relying on a decomposition-based process. Moløkken (2002) found that the software professionals applying a bottom-up software development estimation process were more overoptimistic than those applying a more top-down estimation process. Similarly, no benefits were found from applying the function point software development estimation model "bottom-up", instead of the common "top-down" application (Yau and Gan 1995). It is common sense that some tasks are too complex to understand and estimate as a whole, i.e., that decomposition is necessary to understand some problems. The results from the software estimation studies, however, suggest that there are potential problems with decomposing the software development estimation problem applying the "bottom-up" (additive decomposition) that are avoided through a top-down estimation process.

We suggest that a bottom-up estimation process, e.g., estimation of the activities described in a work breakdown structure (Tausworthe 1980), should be combined with a top-down estimation process, e.g., the process of estimating the project as a whole through comparison with similar completed projects. We believe that these two estimation processes should be conducted independently of each other, to avoid the "anchoring effect"[8], i.e., that one estimate gets strongly impacted by the other as reported in the software development effort study (Jørgensen and Sjøberg 2001a). If there are large deviations between the estimates provided by the different processes, and estimation accuracy is important, then more estimation information and/or independent estimation experts should be added. Alternatively, a simple average of the two processes can be applied (more on the benefits of different strategies of combining estimates in Sect. 15.5.3). Our belief in the usefulness of this "do-both" principle is based on the complementary strengths and weaknesses of top-down and bottom-up-based expert estimates as described in Table 15.4.

The claimed benefits and weaknesses in Table 15.4 are supported by results reported in, e.g., the software studies (Hill et al. 2000; Moløkken 2002). Buehler et al. (1994) report a study where the difference between instructing people to use their past experience, instead of only focusing on how to complete a task, reduced the level of overoptimism in time estimation tasks. This result supports the importance of applying a strategy that induces distributional (history-based) thinking, e.g., top-down estimation strategies. Perhaps the most important part of top-down estimation is *not* that the project is estimated as a whole, but that it encourages the use of history. Other interesting results on impacts from decomposition strategies include:

- Decomposition is not useful for low-uncertainty estimation tasks, only for high-uncertainty, as reported in several forecasting and human judgment studies (Armstrong et al. 1975; MacGregor 2001).

Table 15.4. Top-Down versus Bottom-Up

	top-down (as a whole)	bottom-up (decomposed)
strengths	more robust with respect to forgotten activities and unexpected events encourages "distributional" (history-based) thinking	leads to increased understanding of the execution and planning of the project (how-to knowledge)
weaknesses	does not lead to increased understanding of the execution and planning of the project depends strongly on the proper selection and availability of similar projects from memory or project documentation	easy to forget activities and underestimate unexpected events depends strongly on selection of software developers with proper experience does not encourage history-based criticism of the estimate and its assumptions

---

[8] *Anchoring: "the tendency of judges' estimates (or forecasts) to be influenced when they start with a 'convenient' estimate in making their forecasts. This initial estimate (or anchor) can be based on tradition, previous history or available data."* (Armstrong 2001b).

– Decomposition may "activate" too much knowledge (including nonrelevant knowledge). For this reason, predefined decompositions, e.g., predefined work breakdown structures, activating only relevant knowledge should be applied. The human judgment study reported in MacGregor and Lichtenstein (1991) supports this result.

In sum, the results suggest that bottom-up-based estimates only lead to improved estimation accuracy if the uncertainty of the whole task is high, i.e., the task is too complex to estimate as a whole, and, the decomposition structure activates relevant knowledge only. The validity of these two conditions is, typically, not possible to know in advance and applying both top-down and bottom-up estimation processes, therefore, reduces the risk of highly inaccurate estimates.

15.5.2 Use Estimation Checklists

The benefits of checklists are not controversial and are based on, at least, four observations:

– Experts easily forget activities and underestimate the effort required to solve unexpected events. Harvey (2001) provides an overview of forecasting and human judgment studies on how checklists support people in remembering important variables and possibilities that they would otherwise overlook.
– Expert estimates are inconsistent, i.e., the same input may result in different estimates. For example, experts seem to respond to increased uncertainty with increased inconsistency (Harvey 2001). Checklists may increase the consistency, and hence the accuracy, of the expert estimates.
– People tend to use estimation strategies that require minimal computational effort, at the expense of accuracy, as reported in the time estimation study described in Josephs and Hahn (1995). Checklists may "push" the experts to use more accurate expert estimation strategies.
– People have a tendency to consider only the options that are presented, and underestimate the likelihood of the other options, as reported in the "fault tree" study described in Fischhoff et al. (1978). This means that people have a tendency to "out of sight, out of mind." Checklists may encourage the generation of more possible outcomes.

Interestingly, there is evidence that checklists can bring novices up to an expert level. For example, Getty et al. (1988) describe a study were general radiologists were brought up to the performance of specialist mammographers using a checklist.

Although we have experienced that many software organizations find checklists to be one of their most useful estimation tools, we have not been able to find any empirical study on how different types of checklists impact the accuracy of software effort estimation. Common sense and studies from other domains leave, however, little doubt that checklists are an important means to improve expert estimation. An example of a checklist (aimed at managers that review software project estimates) is provided in Park (1996) (1) Are the objectives of the estimates clear and correct? (2) Has the task been appropriately sized? (3) Are the estimated cost and schedule consistent with demonstrated accomplishments on other projects? (4) Have the factors that affect the estimate been identified and explained? (5) Have steps been taken to ensure the integrity of the estimating process? (6) Is the organization's historical evidence capable of supporting a reliable estimate? (7) Has the situation changed since the estimate was prepared? This type of checklist clearly supports the estimation reviewer to remember important issues, increases the consistency of the review process, and "pushes" the reviewer to apply an appropriate review process.

A potential "by-product" of a checklist is the use of it as a simple means to document previous estimation experience. The aggregation of the previous estimation experience into a checklist may be easier to use and have more impact on the estimation accuracy compared with a large software development experience databases containing project reports and estimation data (Jørgensen et al. 1998).

15.5.3 Obtain and Combine Estimates from Different Experts and Approaches

When two or more experts provide estimates of the same task, the optimal approach would be to use only the most accurate estimates. The individuals' estimation accuracies are, however, not known in advance and a combination of several estimates has been shown to be superior to selecting only one of the available estimates. See Clemen (1989) for an extensive overview of empirical studies from various domains on this topic. The two software studies we were able to find on this topic are consistent with the findings from other domains. These studies report an increase in estimation accuracy through averaging of the individual estimate (Höst and Wohlin 1998) and group discussions (Jørgensen and Moløkken 2002). Based on the extensive evidence in favor of combining estimates the question should *not* be whether we should combine or not, but how?

There are many alternative combination approaches for software project estimates. A software project leader can, for example, collect estimates of the same task from different experts and then weight these estimates according to level of the experts' level of competence. Alternatively, the project leader can ask different experts to discuss their estimates and agree on an estimate. The choice of combination strategy and the benefits from combined estimates depend on a number of variables. The variables are, according to Hogarth's model (1978) (1) number of experts, (2) the individuals' (expected) estimation accuracy, (3) the degree of biases among the experts, and (4) the inter-correlation between the experts' estimates. A human judgment study validating Hogarth's model is described in (Ashton 1986). Our discussion on combination of estimates will be based on these four variables, and, a fifth variable not included in Hogarth's model[9] (5) the impact of combination strategy.

---

[9] This is no shortcoming of Hogarth's model, since his model assumes that the combined estimate is based on the *average* of the individual estimates.

Number of experts (1): The number of expert estimates to be included in the combined estimate depends on their expected accuracy, biases, and inter-correlation. Frequently, the use of relatively few (3–5) experts with different backgrounds seems to be sufficient to achieve most of the benefits from combining estimates, as reported in the study of financial and similar types of judgments described in Libby and Blashfield (1978).

The accuracy and biases of the experts (2+3): A documented record of the experts' previous estimation accuracy and biases is frequently not available or not relevant for the current estimation task. However, the project leaders may have informal information indicating for example the level of overoptimism or expertise of an estimator. This information should be used, with care, to ensure that the accuracy of the experts is high and that individual biases are not systematically in one direction.

The intercorrelation between the experts (4): A low intercorrelation between the estimators is important to exploit the benefits from combining estimates. Studies reporting the importance of this variable in business forecasting and software development estimation contexts are Armstrong (2001a) and Jørgensen and Moløkken (2002). A low intercorrelation can be achieved when selecting experts with different backgrounds and roles, or experts applying different estimation processes.

Combination process (5): There are several approaches of combining expert estimates. One may take the average of individual software development effort estimates Höst and Wohlin (998), apply a structured software estimation group process Taff et al. (991), select the expert with the best estimate on the previous task Ringuest and Tang (987), or apply the well-documented Delphi-process Rowe and Wright (2001). A comprehensive overview of combination strategies is described in Chatterjee and Chatterjee (1987). While the choice of combination strategy may be important in some situations, there are studies, e.g., the forecasting study described in Fisher (1981), that suggest that most meaningful combination processes have similar performance. Other human judgment and forecasting studies, however, found that averaging the estimates was the best combination strategy Clemen (1989), or that a group-based processes led to the highest accuracy (Reagan-Cirincione 1994; Henry 1995; Fischer and Harvey 1999). In Moløkken (2002) it is reported that a group discussion-based combination of individual software development effort estimates was more accurate than the average of the individual estimates, because the group discussion led to new knowledge about the interaction between people in different roles. Similar results, on planning of R&D projects, were found in Kernaghan and Cooke (1986) and Kernaghan and Cooke (1990). This increase in knowledge through discussions is an important advantage of group-based estimation processes compared with "mechanical" combinations, such as averaging. However, the evidence in favor of group-based combinations is not strong. For example, group discussion may lead to more biased estimates (either more risky or more conservative) depending on the group processes and the individual goals, as illustrated in the financial forecasting study described in Maines (1996).

In summary, it seems that the most important part of the estimation principle is to combine estimates from different sources (with, preferably, high accuracy and low inter-correlation), not exactly how this combination is conducted.

15.5.4 Assess the Uncertainty of the Estimate

Important reasons for the importance of assessing the uncertainty of an effort estimate are:

- The uncertainty of the estimate is important information in the planning of a software project (McConnel 1998).
- An assessment of the uncertainty is important for the learning from the estimate, e.g., low estimation accuracy is not necessarily an indicator of low estimation skills when the software development project work is highly uncertain (Jørgensen and Sjøberg 2002b).
- The process of assessing uncertainty may lead to more realism in the estimation of most likely software development effort. The software estimation study reported in Connolly and Dean (1997) supports this finding, but there are also contradictory findings, e.g., time usage estimation study described in Newby-Clark et al. (2000).

We recommend, similarly to the forecasting principles described by Armstrong (2001d), that the uncertainty of an estimate is assessed through a prediction interval. For example, a project leader may estimate that the most likely effort of a development project is 10,000 work-hours and that it is 90% certain (confidence level) that the actual use of effort will be between 5,000 and 20,000 work-hours. Then, the interval [5,000, 20,000] work-hours is the 90% prediction interval of the effort estimate of 10,000 work-hours.

A confidence level of $K\%$ should, in the long run, result in a proportion of actual values inside the prediction interval (hit rate) of $K\%$. However, Connolly and Dean (1997) report that the hit rates of students' effort predictions intervals were, on average, 60% when a 90% confidence level was required. Similarly, Jørgensen et al. (2002) report that the activity effort hit rates of several industrial software development projects were all less than 50%,[10] i.e., the intervals were much too narrow.

This type of overconfidence seems to be found in most other domains, see for example Alpert and Raiffa (1982), Lichtenstein et al. (1982), McClelland and Bolger (1994), Wright and Ayton (1994), and Bongaarts and Bulatao (2000). As reported earlier, Lichtenstein and Fischhoff (1977) report that the level of over-confidence was unaffected by differences in intelligence and expertise, i.e., we should *not* expect that the level of overconfidence is reduced with more experience. Arkes

---

[10] The industrial projects did not have a consistent use of confidence level, but, typically, let the estimators decide how to interpret minimum and maximum effort. Nevertheless, most meaningful interpretations of minimum and maximum effort should lead to higher hit rates than 40–50%.

(2001) gives a recent overview of studies from different domains on overconfidence, supporting that claim. Potential reasons for this overconfidence are:

- *Poor statistical knowledge.* The statistical assumptions underlying prediction intervals and probabilities are rather complex, see for example (Christensen 1998). Even with sufficient historical data the estimators may not know how to provide, for example, a 90% prediction interval of an estimate.
- *Estimation goals in "conflict" with the estimation accuracy goal.* The software professionals' goals of appearing skilled and providing "informative" prediction intervals may be in conflict with the goal of sufficiently wide prediction intervals, see for example the human judgment studies (Yaniv and Foster 1997; Keren and Teigen 2001) and our discussion in Sect. 15.4.1.
- *"Anchoring effect."* Several studies from various domains, (e.g., Kahneman, et al. 1982; Jørgensen and Sjøberg 2002a) report that people typically provide estimates influenced by an anchor value and that they are not sufficiently aware of this influence. The estimate of the most likely effort may easily become the anchor value of the estimate of minimum and maximum effort. Consequently, the minimum and maximum effort will not be sufficiently different from the most likely effort in high uncertainty situations.
- *"Tendency to overestimate own skills."* Kruger and Dunning (1999) found a tendency to overestimate one's own level of skill in comparison with the skill of other people. This tendency increased with decreasing level of skill. A potential effect of the tendency is that information about previous estimation inaccuracy of similar projects has insufficient impact on a project leaders uncertainty estimate, because most project leaders believe to be more skilled than average.

In total, there is strong evidence that the traditional, unaided expert judgment-based assessments of estimation uncertainty through prediction intervals are biased toward overconfidence, i.e., too narrow prediction intervals. An uncertainty elicitation process that seems to reduce the overconfidence in software estimation contexts is described in Jørgensen and Teigen (2002). This process, which is similar to the method proposed by Seaver et al. (1978), proposes a simple change of the traditional uncertainty elicitation process:

1. Estimates the most likely effort.
2. Calculate the minimum and maximum effort as fixed proportions of the most likely effort. For example, an organization could base these proportions on the NASA-guidelines (NASA 1990) of software development project effort intervals and set the minimum effort to 50% and the maximum effort to 200% of the most likely effort.
3. Decide on the confidence level, i.e., assess the probability that the actual effort is between the minimum and maximum effort.

Steps 2 and 3 are different from the traditional uncertainty elicitation process, where the experts are instructed to provide minimum and maximum effort values for a given confidence level, e.g., a 90% confidence level. The differences may appear minor, but include a change from "self-developed" to "mechanically" developed minimum and maximum values. Minimum and maximum values provided by oneself, as in the traditional elicitation process, may be used to indicate estimation skills, e.g., to show to other people that "my estimation work is of a high quality." Mechanically calculated minimum and maximum values, on the other hand, may reduce this "ownership" of the minimum and maximum values, i.e., lead to a situation similar to when experts evaluate estimation work conducted by other people. As discussed in Sect. 15.4.2, it is much easier to be realistic when assessing other peoples performance, compared with own performance. In addition, as opposed to the traditional process, there is no obvious anchor value that influences the prediction intervals toward overconfidence when assessing the appropriate confidence level of a mechanically derived prediction interval. Other possible explanations for the benefits of the proposed approach, e.g., easier learning from history, are described in Jørgensen and Teigen (2002). The proposed approach was evaluated on the estimation of a set of maintenance tasks and found to improve the correspondence between confidence level and hit rate significantly (Jørgensen and Teigen 2002).

An alternative elicitation method, not yet evaluated in software contexts, is to ask for prediction intervals based on low confidence levels, e.g., to ask a software developer to provide a 60% instead of a 90% prediction interval. This may reduce the level of overconfidence, because, as found by Roth (1993), people are generally better calibrated in the middle of a probability distribution than in its tails.

15.6 Provide Estimation Feedback and Training Opportunities

It is hard to improve estimation skills without feedback and training. Lack of estimation feedback and training may, however, be a common situation in software organizations (Hughes 1996a; Jørgensen and Sjøberg 2002b). The observed lack of feedback of software organizations means that it is no large surprise that increased experience did not lead to improved estimation accuracy in the studies (Hill et al. 2000; Jørgensen and Sjøberg 2002b). Similarly, many studies from other domains report a lack of correlation between amount of experience and estimation skills. Hammond (1996, pp. 278) summarizes the situation: *"Yet in nearly every study of experts carried out within the judgment and decision-making approach, experience has been shown to be unrelated to the empirical accuracy of expert judgments."*

Learning estimation skills from experience can be difficult (Jørgensen and Sjøberg 2000). In addition to sufficient and properly designed estimation feedback, estimation improvements may require the provision of training opportunities (Ericsson and Lehmann 1996). This section discusses feedback and training principles for improvement of expert estimates.

15.6.1 Provide Feedback on Estimation Accuracy and Development Task Relations

There has been much work on frameworks for "learning from experience" in software organizations, e.g., work on experience databases (Basili et al. 1994; Houdek et al. 1998; Jørgensen et al. 1998; Engelkamp et al. 2000) and frameworks for PostMortem (project experience) reviews (Birk et al. 2002). These studies do not, as far as we know, provide empirical results on the relation between type of feedback and estimation accuracy improvement. The only software study on this topic (Ohlsson et al. 1998), to our knowledge, suggest that outcome feedback, i.e., feedback relating the actual outcome to the estimated outcome, did not improve the estimation accuracy. Human judgment studies from other domains support this disappointing lack of estimation improvement from outcome feedback, see for example Balzer et al. (1989) Benson (1992) and Stone and Opel (2000). This is no large surprise, since there is little estimation accuracy improvement possible from the feedback that, for example, *"the effort estimate was 30% too low."* One situation were outcome feedback is reported to improve the estimation accuracy is when the estimation tasks are "dependent and related" and the estimator initially was under-confident, i.e., underestimated her/his own knowledge on general knowledge tasks (Subbotin 1996). Inspite of the poor improvement in estimation accuracy, outcome feedback is useful, since it improves the assessment of the uncertainty of an estimate (Stone and Opel 2000; Jørgensen and Teigen 2002). Feedback on estimation accuracy should, for that reason, be included in the estimation feedback.

To improve the estimation accuracy, several studies from various domains suggest that "task relation oriented feedback," i.e., feedback on how different events and variables were related to the actual use of effort, are required (Schmitt et al. 1976; Balzer et al. 1989; Benson 1992; Stone and Opel 2000). A possible method to provide this type of feedback is the use "experience reports" or "postmortem" review processes.

When analyzing the impacts from different variables on the use of effort and the estimation accuracy, i.e., the "task relation oriented feedback," it important to understand interpretation biases and the dynamics of software projects, e.g.,:

- The "hindsight bias," e.g., the tendency to interpret cause–effect relationships as more obvious after it happen than before, see Fischhof (1975) and Stahlberg et al. (1995) for general human judgement studies on this topic.
- The tendency to confirm rules and disregard conflicting evidence, as illustrated in the human judgement studies (Camerer and Johnson 1991; Sanbonmatsu et al. 1993) and our discussion in Sect. 15.4.3.
- The tendency to apply a "deterministic" instead of a "probabilistic" learning model. For example, assume that a software project introduces a new development tool for the purpose of increasing the efficiency and that the project has many inexperienced developers. The actual project efficiency turns out to be lower than that of the previous projects and the actual effort, consequently, becomes much higher than the estimated effort. A (naïve) deterministic interpretation of this experience would be that "new tools decrease the development

efficiency if the developers are inexperienced." A probabilistic interpretation would be to consider other possible scenarios (that did not happen, but could have happen) and to conclude that it seems to be more than 50% likely that the combination of new tools and inexperienced developers lead to a decrease in efficiency. This ability to think in probability-based terms can, according to Brehmer (1980), hardly be derived from experience alone, but must be taught. Hammond (1996) suggest that the ability to understand relationships in terms of probabilities instead of purely deterministic connections is important for correct learning in situations with high uncertainty.

- The potential impact of the estimate on the actual effort as reported in the software estimation studies (Abdel-Hamid and Madnik 1983; Jørgensen and Sjøberg 2001a), i.e., the potential presence of a"self-fulfilling prophecy." For example, software projects that overestimate the "most likely effort" may achieve high estimation accuracy if the remaining effort is applied to improve ("gold-plate") the product.
- The potential lack of distinction between "plan" and "estimate," see discussion in Sect. 15.4.2.
- The variety of reasons for high or low estimation accuracy, as pointed out in the industrial software estimation study (Jørgensen et al. 2002). Low estimation accuracy may, for example, be the results of poor project control, high project uncertainty, low flexibility in delivered product (small opportunity to "fit" the actual use of effort to the estimated), project members with low motivation for estimation accuracy, high project priority on time-to-market, "bad luck," or, of course, poor estimation skills.
- A tendency to asymmetric cause-effect analyses dependent on high or low accuracy, i.e., high estimation accuracy is explained as good estimation skills, while low estimation accuracy is explained as impact from external uncontrollable factors. Tan and Lipe (1997) found, in a business context, that: *Those with positive outcomes (e.g., strong profits) are rewarded; justification or consideration of reasons as to why the evaluatee performed well are not necessary. In contrast, when outcomes are negative (e.g. losses suffered), justifications for the poor results are critical. .... Evaluators consider controllability or other such factors more when outcomes are negative than when they are positive."*

In many human judgment situations with high uncertainty and unstable task relations, there are indications on that even task relation-oriented feedback is not sufficient for learning (Schmitt et al. 1976; Bolger and Wright 1994), i.e., the situations do simply not enable learning from experience. For this reason, it is important to recognize when there is nothing to learn from experience, as reported in the software estimation study (Jørgensen and Sjøberg 2000).

A problem with most feedback on software development effort estimates is that it takes too much time from the point-of-estimation to the point-of-feedback. This is unfortunate, since it has been shown that immediate feedback strongly improves the estimation learning and accuracy, as illustrated in the human judgment studies (Bolger and Wright 1994; Shepperd et al. 1996). Interestingly, Shepperd et al. (1996) also found that when the feedback is rapid, people with low confidence start to under-estimate their own performance, maybe to ensure that they will not be disappointed, i.e., there may be situations where the feedback can be *too* rapid too stimulate to realistic estimates. Although it is easy to over-rate the possibility to learn from feedback, it is frequently the only realistic opportunity for learning, i.e., even if the benefits are smaller than we like to believe, software organizations should do their best to provide properly designed estimation feedback.

15.6.2 Provide Estimation Training Opportunities

Frequently, real software projects provide too little information to draw valid conclusions about cause-effects (Jørgensen and Sjøberg 2000). Blocher et al. (1997) report similar results based on studies of people's analytical procedures. Blocher et al. attribute the cause-effect problems to the lack of learning about what would have happened if we had not done what we did, and the high number of alternative explanation for an event. Furthermore, they argue that learning requires the development of causal models for education, training, and professional guidance. The importance of causal domain models for training is supported by the human judgment results described in Bolger and Wright (1994). Similar reasons for learning problems, based on a review of studies on differences in performance between experts and novices in many different domains, are provided by Ericsson and Lehmann (1996). They claim that it is not the amount of experience but the amount of "deliberate training" that determines the level of expertise. They interpret deliberate training as "*individualized training activities especially designed by a coach or teacher to improve specific aspects of an individual's performance through repetition and successive refinement*". This importance of training is also supported by the review of human judgment studies described in Camerer and Johnson (1991), suggesting that while training had an effect on estimation accuracy, amount of experience had almost none.

We suggest that software companies provide estimation training opportunities through their database of completed projects. An estimation training session should include estimation of completed projects based on the information available at the point-of-estimation applying different estimation processes. This type of estimation training has several advantages in comparison with the traditional estimation training:

- Individualized feedback can be received immediately after completion of the estimates.
- The effect of not applying checklists and other estimation tool can be investigated on one's own estimation processes.
- The validity of own estimation experience can be examined on different types of projects, i.e., projects much larger than those estimated earlier.
- Reasons for forgotten activities or underestimated risks can be analyzed immediately, while the hindsight bias is weak.
- The tendency to be overconfidence can be understood, given proper coaching and training projects.

As far as we know, there are no reported studies of organizations conducting estimation training in line with our suggestions. However, the results from other studies, in particular those summarized in Ericsson and Lehmann (1996), strongly support that this type of training should complement the traditional estimation courses and pure "learning from experience."

15.7 Conclusions and Further Research

The two main contributions of this paper are:

- A systematic review of papers on software development effort expert estimation.
- An extensive examination of relevant human judgment studies to validate expert estimation "best practice" principles.

The review concludes that expert estimation is the dominant strategy when estimating the effort of software development projects, and that there is no substantial evidence supporting the superiority of model estimates over expert estimates. There are situations where expert estimates are more likely to be more accurate, e.g., situations where experts have important domain knowledge not included in the models or situations when simple estimation strategies provide accurate estimates. Similarly, there are situations where the use of models may reduce large situational or human biases, e.g., when the estimators have a strong personal interest in the outcome. The studies on expert estimation are summarized through an empirical evaluation of the twelve principles (1) evaluate estimation accuracy, but avoid high evaluation pressure, (2) avoid conflicting estimation goals, (3) ask the estimators to justify and criticize their estimates, (4) avoid irrelevant and unreliable estimation information, (5) use documented data from previous development tasks, (6) find estimation experts with relevant domain background and good estimation record, (7) estimate top-down and bottom-up, independently of each other, (8) use estimation checklists, (9) combine estimates from different experts and estimation strategies, (10) assess the uncertainty of the estimate, (11) provide feedback on estimation accuracy and task relations, and (12) provide estimation training opportunities. We find that there is evidence supporting all these principles and, consequently, that software organizations should apply them.

The estimation principles are to some extent based on results from other domains than software development, or represent only one type of software projects and experts. For this reason there is a strong need for better insight into the validity and generality of many of the discussed topics. In particular we plan to continue with research on:

- When to use expert estimation and when to use estimation models.
- How to reduce the over-optimism bias when estimating own work applying expert estimation.
- How to select and combine a set of expert estimates.
- The benefits of "deliberate" estimation training.

Acknowledgment

Thanks to professor in psychology at the University of Oslo, Karl Halvor Teigen, for his very useful suggestions and interesting discussions.

References

Abdel-Hamid, T.K. and Madnik, S.E. (1983) The Dynamics of Software Project scheduling, *Communications of the ACM*, 26(5), pp. 340–346

Abdel-Hamid, T.K., Sengupta, K., and Ronan, D. (1993) Software Project Control: An Experimental Investigation of Judgment with Fallible Information, *IEEE Transactions on Software Engineering*, 19(6), pp. 603–612

Abdel-Hamid, T.K., Sengupta, K., and Swett, C. (1999) The Impact of Goals on Software Project Management: An Experimental Investigation, *MIS Quarterly* 23(4), pp. 531–555

Alpert, M. and Raiffa, H. (1982) A Progress Report on the Training of Probability Assessors, *Judgment under Uncertainty: Heuristics and Biases* (Ed.), A. Tversky, Cambridge, Cambridge University Press, pp. 294–305

Arkes, H.R. (2001) Overconfidence in Judgmental Forecasting, *Principles of Forecasting: A Handbook for Researchers and Practitioners*, (Ed.), J.S. Armstrong, Boston, Kluwer Academic Publishers, pp. 495–515

Armstrong, J.S. (2001a) Combining Forecasts, *Principles of Forecasting: A handbook for researchers and practitioners*. (Ed.) J.S. Armstrong. Boston, Kluwer Academic Publishers, pp. 417–440

Armstrong, J.S. (2001b) The Forecasting Dictionary. *Principles of Forecasting: A Handbook for Researchers and Practitioners* (Ed.) J.S. Armstrong, Boston, Kluwer Academic, pp. 761–824

Armstrong, J.S. (2001c) Selecting Forecasting Methods, *Principles of Forecasting: A Handbook for Researchers and Practitioners* (Ed.) J.S. Armstrong, Boston, Kluwer Academic , pp. 365–386

Armstrong, J.S. (2001d) Standards and Practices for Forecasting, *Principles of Forecasting: A Handbook for Researchers and Practitioners*, (Ed.) J.S. Armstrong, Boston, Kluwer Academic , pp. 679–732

Armstrong, J.S., Denniston Jr., W.B., and Gordon, (1975) The Use of the Decomposition Principle in Making Judgments, *Organizational-Behavior-and-Human-Decision-Processes* 14(2), pp. 257–263

Ashton, R.H. (1986) Combining the Judgments of Experts: How Many and Which Ones? *Organizational Behaviour and Human Decision Processes* 38(3), pp. 405–414

Atkinson, K. and Shepperd, M. (1994) Using Function Points to Find Cost Analogies, *European Software Cost Modelling Meeting*, Ivrea, Italy

Ayton, A. (1998) How Bad is Human Judgment? *Forecasting with Judgment*(Ed.) G. Wright and P. Goodwin, NY, Wiley, pp. 237–268

Balzer, W.K., Doherty, M.E., and O'Connor, R.J. (1989) Effects of Cognitive Feedback on Performance, *Psychological Bulletin* 106(3), pp. 410–433

Basili, V., Caldierea, H., and Rombach, D. (1994) The Experience Factory, *Encyclopedia of Software Engineering*, (Ed.) J.J. Marciniak, Wiley, pp. 469–476

Benson, P.G. (1992) The Effects of Feedback and Training on the Performance of Probability Forecasters, *International Journal of Forecasting* 8(4), pp. 559–573

Betteridge, R. (1992) Successful Experience of Using Function Points to Estimate Project Costs Early in the Life-cycle, *Information and Software Technology*, 34(10), pp. 655–658

Birk, A., Dingsøyr, T., and Stalhane, T. (2002)Postmortem: Never Leave a Project Without it, *IEEE Software* 19(3), pp. 43–45

Blattberg, R.C. and Hoch, S.J. (1990) Database Models and Managerial Intuition: 50% model + 50% manager, *Management Science* 36, pp. 887–899

Blocher, E., Bouwman, M.J., and Daves, C.E. (1997) Learning from Experience in Performing Analytical Procedures, *Training Research Journal*, 3, pp. 59–79

Boehm, B., Abts. C., and Chulani. S. (2000) Software Development Cost Estimation Approaches - A Survey, *Annals of Software Engineering*, 10,pp. 177–205

Boehm, B. and Sullivan, K. (1999) Software Economics: Status and Prospects, *Information and Software Technology*, 41, pp. 937–946

Boehm, B.W. (1981) *Software Engineering Economics*, NJ, Prentice-Hall

Boehm, B.W. (1984) Software Engineering Economics, *IEEE Transactions on Software Engineering*, 10(1), pp. 4–21

Bolger, F. and Wright, G. (1994) Assessing the Quality of Expert Judgment: Issues and Analysis, *Decision Support Systems*, 11(1), pp. 1–24

Bongaarts, J. and Bulatao, R.A. (2000) *Beyond Six Billion: Forecasting the World's Population*, National Academy Press

Bowden, P., Hargreaves, M., and Langensiepen, C.S. (2000) Estimation Support by Lexical Analysis of Requirements Documents, *Journal of Systems and Software*, 51(2), pp. 87–98

Braun, P.A. and Yaniv, I. (1992) A Case Study of Expert Judgment: Economists' Probabilities versus Base-rate Model Forecasts, *Journal of Behavioral Decision Making*, 5(3), pp. 217–231

Brehmer, B. (1980) In One Word: Not from Experience., *Acta Psychologica*, 45, pp. 223–241

Brenner, L.A., Koehler, D.J., and Tversky, A. (1996) On the Evaluation of One-sided Evidence. *Journal of Behavioral Decision Making* 9(1), pp. 59–70

Briand, L.C., El Emam, K., Surmann, D., Wieczorek, I., and Maxwell, K.D. (1999) An Assessment and Comparison of Common Software Cost Estimation Modeling Techniques, *International Conference on Software Engineering*, Los Angeles, ACM, NY, pp. 313–323

Briand, L.C., Langley, T., and Wieczorek, I (2000) A Replicated Assessment and Comparison of Common Software Cost Modeling Techniques, *International Conference on Software Engineering*, Limerick, Ireland, ACM, NY, pp. 377–386

Briand, L.C. and Wieczorek, I. (2002) Resource Estimation in Software Engineering. *Encyclopedia of Software Engineering*, J.J. Marcinak, (Ed.) NY, Wiley

Buehler, R., Griffin, D., and MacDonald, H. (1997) The Role of Motivated Reasoning in Optimistic Time Predictions, *Personality and Social Psychology Bulletin*, 23(3), pp. 238–247

Buehler, R., Griffin, D., and Ross, M. (1994) Exploring the "Planning fallacy": Why People Underestimate their Task Completion Times, *Journal of Personality and Social Psychology*, 67(3), pp. 366–381

Camerer, C.F. and Johnson, E.J. (1991) The Process-Performance Paradox in Expert Judgment: How can Experts Know so Much and Predict so Badly? *Towards a General Theory of Expertise*, K. A. Ericsson and J. Smith, (Ed.), Cambridge University Press, pp. 195–217

Chatterjee, S. and Chatterjee, S. (1987) On Combining Expert Opinion, *American Journal of Mathematical and Management Sciences*, 7(3&4), pp. 271–295

Christensen, R. (1998) *Analysis of Variance, Design and Regression. Applied Statistical Methods*, Chapman & Hall/Crc

Chulani, S., Boehm, B., and Steece, B. (1999) Bayesian Analysis of Empirical Software Engineering Cost Models, *IEEE Transactions on Software Engineering*, 25(4), pp. 573–583

Clemen, R.T. (1989) Combining Forecasts: A Review and Annotated Bibliography, *International Journal of Forecasting*, 5(4), pp. 559–583

Connolly, T. and Dean, D. (1997) Decomposed versus Holistic Estimates of Effort Required for Software Writing Tasks, *Management Science* 43(7), pp. 1029–1045

Cosier, R.A. and Rose, G.L.(1977) Cognitive Conflict and Goal Conflict Effects on Task Performance, *Organizational Behaviour and Human Performance*,19(2), pp. 378–391

Cuelenaere, A.M.E., Genuchten, M.J.I.M., and Heemstra, F.J. (1987) Calibrating a Software Cost Estimation Model: Why and How, *Information and Software Technology*, 29(10), pp. 558–567

Dawes, R.M. (1986) Proper and Improper Linear Models, *International Journal of Forecasting*, 2, pp. 5–14

Dolado, J.J. (2001) On the Problem of the Software Cost Function, *Information and Software Technology*, 43(1), pp. 61–72

Edwards, J.S. and Moores, T.T. (1994) A Conflict between the Use of Estimating and Planning Tools in the Management of information systems. *European Journal of Information Systems* 3(2): 139–147.

Einhorn, H.J. and Hogarth, R.M. (1978). Confidence in judgment: Persistence of the illusion of validity. *Psychological review* 85(5): 395-416.

Engelkamp, S., Hartkopf, S., and Brössler, P. (2000) Project Experience Database: A Report Based on First Practical Experience, *PROFES*, Oulu, Finland, Springer Berlin Heidelberg New York, 204–215

Ericsson, K.A. and Lehmann, A.C. (1996) Expert and Exceptional Performance: Evidence of Maximal Adaptation to Task Constraints, *Annual Review of Psychology*, 47, pp. 273–305

Ettenson, R., Shanteau, J., and Krogstad, J. (1987) Expert Judgment: Is More Information Better, *Psychological Reports,* 60(1), pp. 227–238

Fairley, R.E. (1992) Recent Advantages in Software Estimation Techniques,*International Conference on Software Engineering*, Melbourne, Australia, pp. 382–391

Fischer, I. and Harvey, N. (1999) Combining Forecasts: What Information do Judges need to Outperform the Simple Average, *International Journal of Forecasting,* 15(3), pp. 227–246

Fischhof, B. (1975) Hindsight <> Foresight: The Effect of Outcome Knowledge on Judgement under Uncertainty, *Journal of Experimental Psychology: Human Perception and Performance,* 1, pp. 288–299

Fischhoff, B., Slovic, P., and Lichtenstein, S. (1978) Fault Trees: Sensitivity of Estimated Failure Probabilities to Problem Representation*Journal of Experimental Psychology: Human Perception and Performance,* 4(2), pp. 330–334

Fisher, G.W. (1981) When Oracles Fail – A Comparison of Four Procedures for Aggregating Subjective Probability Forecasts, *Organizational Behaviour and Human Performance,* 28(1), pp. 96–110

Getty, D.J., Pickett, R.M., D'Orsi, S.J., and Swets, J.A. (1988)Enhanced Interpretation of Diagnostic Images *Investigative Radiology,* 23, pp. 244–252

Gigerenzer, G. and Todd, P.M. (1999) *Simple Heuristics that make us Smart*, NY, Oxford University Press

Goodman, P.A. (1992) Application of Cost-Estimation Techniques: Industrial Perspective, *Information and Software Technology,* 34(6), 379–382

Goodwin, P. (1998) Enhancing Judgmental Sales Forecasting: The Role of Laboratory Research, *Forecasting with Judgment*, (Ed.) G. Wright and P. Goodwin, NY, Wiley, pp. 91–112

Goodwin, P. and Wright, G. (1990) Improving Judgmental Time Series Forecasting: A Review of the Guidance Provided by Research *International Journal of Forecasting,* 9, pp. 147–161

Griffin, D. and Buehler, R. (1999) Frequency, Probability, and Prediction: Easy Solutions to Cognitive Illusions? *Cognitive Psychology,* 38(1), pp. 48–78

Hagafors, R. and Brehmer, B. (1983) Does Having to Justify One's Judgments Change Nature of the Judgment Process? *Organizational Behaviour and Human Decision Processes,* 31(2), 223–232

Hammond, K.R. (1996) *Human Judgement and Social policy: Irreducible Uncertainty, Inevitable Error, Unavoidable Injustice,* NY, Oxford University Press

Hammond, K.R., Hamm, R.M., Grassia, J., and Pearson, T. (1987) Direct Comparison of the Efficacy of Intuitive and Analytical Cognition in Expert Judgment, *IEEE Transactions on Systems, Man, and Cybernetics,* 17(5), pp. 753–770

Harvey, N. (2001) Improving Judgment in Forecasting, *Principles of Forecasting: A Handbook for Researchers and Practitioners*, (Ed.) J.S. Armstrong. Boston, Kluwer Academic, pp. 59–80

Heemstra, F.J. (1992) Software Cost Estimation, *Information and Software Technology,* 34(10), pp. 627–639

Heemstra, F.J. and Kusters, R.J. (1991) Function Point Analysis: Evaluation of a Software Cost Estimation Model, *European Journal of Information Systems,* 1(4), pp. 223–237

Henry, R.A. (1995) Improving Group Judgment Accuracy: Information Sharing and Determining the Best Member, *Organizational Behaviour and Human Decision Processes,* 62, pp. 190–197

Hihn, J. and Habib-Agahi, H. (1991a) Cost Estimation of Software Intensive Projects: A Survey of Current Practices, *International Conference on Software Engineering,* IEEE Comput. Soc. Press, Los Alamitos, CA, pp. 276–287

Hihn, J. and Habib-Agahi, H. (1991b) Cost Estimation of Software Intensive Projects: A Survey of Current Practices, *International Conference on Software Engineering,* pp. 276–287

Hill, J., Thomas, L.C., and Allen, D.E (2000) Experts' Estimates of Task Durations in Software Development Projects, *International Journal of Project Management,* 18(1), pp. 13–21

Hoch, S.J. and Schkade, D.A. (1996) A Psychological Approach to decision Support Systems, *Management Science,* 42(1), pp. 51–64

Hogarth, R.M. (1978) A Note on Aggregating Opinions, *Organizational Behaviour and Human Performance,* 21(1), pp. 40–46

Houdek, F., Schneider, K. and Wieser, E., (1998) Establishing Experience Factories at DaimlerBenz an Experience Report, *International Conference on Software Engineering,* 19–25 April, Kyoto, Japan, IEEE CS Press pp. 443–447

Hughes, R.T. (1996a) Expert Judgement as an Estimating Method, *Information and Software Technology,* 38(2), pp. 67–75

Hughes, R.T. (1996b) Expert Judgement as an Estimation Method, *Information and Software Technology,* 38, pp. 67–75

Höst, M. and Wohlin, C. (1997) A Subjective Effort Estimation Experiment, *Information and Software Technology,* 39(11), pp. 755–762

Höst, M. and Wohlin, C. (1998) An Experimental Study of Individual Subjective Effort Estimations and Combinations of the Estimates, *International Conference on Software Engineering,* Kyoto, Japan, IEEE Comput. Soc, Los Alamitos, CA, pp. 332–339

Jeffery, D.R. and Low, G. (1990) Calibrating Estimation Tools for Software Development, *Software Engineering Journal,* 5(4), pp. 215–221

Jeffery, D.R., Ruhe, M., and Wieczorek, I. (2000) A Comparative Study of Two Software Development Cost Modeling Techniques Using Multi-Organizational and Company-Specific Data, *Information and Software Technology,* 42(14), pp. 1009–1016

Johnson, E.J. (1998) Expertise and Decision Under Uncertainty: Performance and Process, *The Nature of Expertise,* (Ed.) M.T.H. Chi, R. Glaser and M.J. Farr. Hillsdale, NJ, Lawrence Erlbaum, pp. 209–228

Josephs, R. and Hahn, E.D. (1995) Bias and Accuracy in Estimates of task Duration, *Organizational Behaviour and Human Decision Processes,* 61(2), pp. 202–213

Jørgensen, M. (1995) The Quality of Questionnaire Based Software Maintenance Studies, *ACM SIGSOFT – Software Engineering Notes,* 20(1), pp. 71–73

Jørgensen, M. (1997) An Empirical Evaluation of the MkII FPA Estimation Model, *Norwegian Informatics Conference*, Voss, Norway, Tapir, Oslo, pp. 7–18

Jørgensen, M. (2002) Software Effort Estimation by Analogy and "Regression Toward the Mean." To appear in: *Journal of Systems and Software*

Jørgensen, M., Moen, L., and Løvstad, N. (2002) Combining Quantitative Software Development Cost Estimation Precision Data with Qualitative Data from Project Experience Reports at Ericsson Design Center in Norway, *Proceedings of the Conference on Empirical Assessment in Software Engineering*, Keele, England, Keele University.

Jørgensen, M. and Moløkken, K. (2002) Combination of Software Development Effort Prediction Intervals: Why, When and How? *Fourteenth IEEE Conference on Software Engineering and Knowledge Engineering (SEKE'02)*, Ischia, Italy

Jørgensen, M. and Sjøberg, D. (2000) The Importance of not Learning from Experience, *European Software Process Improvement 2000 (EuroSPI'2000)*, Copenhagen, pp. 2.2–2.8

Jørgensen, M. and Sjøberg, D.I.K. (2001a) Impact of Effort Estimates on Software Project Work, *Information and Software Technology*, 43(15), pp. 939–948

Jørgensen, M. and Sjøberg, D.I.K. (2001b) Software Process Improvement and Human Judgement Heuristics, *Scandinavian Journal of Information Systems*, 13, pp. 99–121

Jørgensen, M. and Sjøberg, D.I.K. (2002a) The Impact of Customer Expectation on Software Development Effort Estimates, *Submitted to International Journal of Project Management*

Jørgensen, M. and Sjøberg, D.I.K. (2002b) Impact of Experience on Maintenance Skills, *Journal of Software Maintenance and Evolution: Research and practice*, 14(2), pp. 123–146

Jørgensen, M., Sjøberg, D.I.K., and Conradi, R. (1998) Reuse of Software Development Experience at Telenor Telecom Software, *European Software Process Improvement Conference (EuroSPI'98)*, Gothenburg, Sweden, 10.19–10.31

Jørgensen, M. and Teigen, K.H. (2002) Uncertainty Intervals versus Interval Uncertainty: An Alternative Method for Eliciting Effort Prediction Intervals in Software Development Projects, *Proceedings of: International conference on Project Management (ProMAC)*, Singapore, pp. 343–352

Jørgensen, M., Teigen, K.H., and Moløkken, K. (2002) Better Sure than Safe? Overconfidence in Judgment Based Software Development Effort Prediction Intervals, *Submitted to Journal of Systems and Software*

Kahneman, D. and Lovallo, D. (1993) Timid Choices and Bold Forecasts: A Cognitive Perspective on Risk Taking, *Management Science*, 39(1), pp. 17–31

Kahneman, D., Slovic, P., and Tversky, A. (1982) *Judgment under Uncertainty: Heuristics and Biases*, Cambridge, Cambridge University Press

Kahneman, D. and Tversky, A. (1973) On the Psychology of Prediction, *Psychological Review*, 80(4), pp. 237–251

Kahneman, D. and Tversky, A. (1979) Intuitive Predictions: Biases and Corrective Procedures, *TIMS Studies in Management Science*, 12, pp. 313–327

Keen, P.G.W. (1981) Information Systems and Organizational Change, *Social Impacts of Computing*, 24(1), pp. 24–33

Keren, G. and Teigen, K.H. (2001) Why is p=.90 Better than p=.70? Preference for Definitive Predictions by Lay Consumers of Probability Judgments, *Psychonomic Bulletin & Reviews*, 8(2), pp. 191–202

Kernaghan, J.A. and Cooke, R.A. (1986) The Contribution of the Group Process to Successful Project Planning in R&D Settings, *IEEE Transactions on Engineering Management*, 33(3), pp. 134–140

Kernaghan, J.A. and Cooke, R.A. (1990) Teamwork in Planning Innovative Projects: Improving Group Performance by Rational and InterPersonal Interventions in Group Process, *IEEE Transactions on Engineering Management*, 37(2), pp. 109–116

Kitchenham, B., Pfleeger, S.L., McColl, B., and Eagan, S. (2002) A Case Study of Maintenance Estimation Accuracy, To appear in: *Journal of Systems and Software*

Klayman, J., Soll, J.B., Gonzalez, V.C., and Barlas, S. (1999) OverConfidence: It Depends on How, What and Whom You Ask, *Organizational Behaviour and Human Decision Processes*, 79(3), pp. 216–247

Klein, W.M. and Kunda, Z. (1994) Exaggerated Self-Assessments and the Preference for Controllable Risks, *Organizational Behavior and Human Decision Processes*, 59(3), pp. 410–427

Koehler, D.J. (1991) Explanation, Imagination, and Confidence in Judgment *Psychological Bulletin*, 110(3), pp. 499–519

Koehler, D.J. and Harvey, N. (1997) Confidence Judgments by Actors and Observers, *Journal of Behavioral Decision Making*, 10(3), 221–242

Koriat, A., Lichtenstein, S., and Fischhoff, B. (1980) Reasons for Confidence, *Journal of Experimental Psychology: Human Learning and Memory*, 6(2), pp. 107–118

Kruger, J. and Dunning, D. (1999) Unskilled and Unaware of it: How Difficulties in Recognizing One's Own Incompetence Lead to Inflated Self-Assessments, *Journal of Personality and Social Psychology*, 77(6), pp. 1121–1134

Kusters, R.J. (1990) Are Software Cost-Estimation Models Accurate? *Information and Software Technology*, 32, pp. 187–190

Kusters, R.J., Genuchten, M.J.I.M., and Heemstra, F.J. (1990) Are Software Cost-Estimation Models Accurate? *Information and Software Technology*, 32(3), pp. 187–190

Lawrence, M. and O'Connor, M. (1996) Judgement or Models: The Importance of Task Differences, *Omega, International Journal of Management Science*, 24(3), pp. 245–254

Lederer, A.L., Mirani, R, Neo, B.S., Pollard, C., Prasad, J., and Ramamurthy, K. (1990) Information System Cost Estimating: A Management Perspective, *MIS Quarterly*, 14(2), pp. 159–176

Lederer, A.L. and Prasad, J. (1992) Nine Management Guidelines for Better Cost Estimating, *Communications of the ACM*, 35(2), pp. 51–59

Lederer, A.L. and Prasad, J. (1993) Information Systems Software Cost Estimating: A Current Assessment, *Journal of Information Technology,* 8(1), pp. 22–33

Lederer, A.L. and Prasad, J. (1998) A Causal Model for Software Cost Estimating Error, *IEEE Transactions on Software Engineering,* 24(2), pp. 137–148

Lederer, A.L. and Prasad, J. (2000) Software Management and Cost Estimating Error, *Journal of Systems and Software,* 50(1), pp. 33–42

Libby, R. and Blashfield, R.K. (1978) Performance of A Composite as A Function of the Number of Judges, *Organizational Behaviour and Human Performance,* 21(2), pp. 121–129

Lichtenstein, S. and Fischhoff, B. (1977) Do Those Who Know More Also Know More About How Much They Know? *Organizational Behaviour and Human Decision Processes,* 20(2), pp. 159–183

Lichtenstein, S., Fischhoff, B., and Phillips, L.D. (1982) Calibration of Probabilities: The State of the Art to 1980, *Judgment Under Uncertainty: Heuristics and Biases,* (Ed.) A. Tversky, Cambridge, Cambridge University Press

Lim, J.S. and O'Connor, M. (1996) Judgmental Forecasting with Time Series and Causal Information, *International Journal of Forecasting* 12(1), pp. 139–153

Londeix, B. (1995) Deploying Realistic Estimation (Field Situation Analysis). *Information and Software Technology,* 37(12), pp. 655–670

MacGregor, D.G. (2001) Decomposition for Judgmental Forecasting and Estimation, *Principles of Forecasting: A Handbook for Researchers and Practitioners,* (Ed.) J.S. Armstrong, Boston, Kluwer Academic, pp. 107–123

MacGregor, D.G. and Lichtenstein, S. (1991) Problem Structuring Aids for Quantitative Estimation, *Journal of Behavioral Decision Making,* 4(2), pp. 101–116

Maines, L.A. (1996) An Experimental Examination of Subjective Forecast Combination, *International Journal of Forecasting,* 12(2), pp. 223–233

Makridakis, S., Wheelwright, S.C., and Hyndman, R.J. (1998) *Forecasting: Methods and Applications,* NY, Wiley

Marouane, R. and Mili, A. (1989) Economics of Software Project Management in Tunisia: Basic TUCOMO, *Information and Software Technology,* 31(5), pp. 251–257

Marwane, R. and Mili, A. (1991) Building Tailor-Made Software Cost Model: Intermediate TUCOMO, *Information and Software Technology,* 33(3), pp. 232–238

McClelland, A.G.R. and Bolger, F. (1994) The Calibration of Subjective Probabilities: Theories and Models 1980–94, *Subjective Probability,* (Ed.) P. Ayton, Chichester, Wiley

McConnel, S. (1998) *Software Project Survival Guide,* Microsoft Press

Meehl, P.E. (1957) When Shall We Use Our Heads Instead of the Formula? *Journal of Counseling Psychology,* 4(4), pp. 268–273

Mendes, E., Counsell, S., and Mosley, N. (2001) *Measurement and Effort Prediction for Web Applications,* Springer Berlin Heidelberg New York, Germany

Meyer, M.A. and Booker, J.M. (1991) *Eliciting and Analyzing Expert Judgment: A Practical Guide*, Philadelphia, Pennsylvania, SIAM

Mizuno, O., Kikuno, T., Inagaki, K., Takagi, Y., and Sakamoto, K. (2000) Statistical Analysis of Deviation of Actual Cost from Estimated Cost Using Actual Project Data, *Information and Software Technology*, 42, pp. 465–473

Mohanty, S.N. (1981) Software Cost Estimation: Present and Future, *Software – Practice and Experience*, 11(2), pp. 103–121

Moløkken, K. (2002) Expert Estimation of Web-Development Effort: Individual Biases and Group Processes (Master Thesis). *Department of Informatics*, University of Oslo

Mukhopadhyay, T., Vicinanza, S.S., and Prietula, M.J. (1992) Examining the Feasibility of A Case-Based Reasoning Model for Software Effort Estimation, *MIS Quarterly*, 16(2), pp. 155–171

Murali, C.S. and Sankar, C.S. (1997) Issues in Estimating Real-Time Data Communications Software Projects, *Information and Software Technology*, 39(6), pp. 399–402

Myrtveit, I. and Stensrud, E. (1999) A Controlled Experiment to Assess the Benefits of Estimating with Analogy and Regression Models, *IEEE Transactions on Software Engineering*, 25, pp. 510–525

NASA (1990) *Manager's Handbook for Software Development* Goddard Space Flight Center, Greenbelt, MD, NASA Software Engineering Laboratory

Newby-Clark, I.R., Ross, M., Buehler, R., Koehler, D.J., and Griffin, D. (2000) People Focus on Optimistic Scenarios and Disregard Pessimistic Scenarios when Predicting Task Completion Times, *Journal of Experimental Psychology: Applied* 6(3), pp. 171–182

Niessink, F. and van Vliet, H. (1997) Predicting Maintenance Effort with Function Points, *International Conference on Software Maintenance*, Bari, Italy, IEEE Comput. Soc., Los Alamitos, CA, pp. 32–39

Nisbett, R.E. and Ross, L. (1980) *Human Inference: Strategies and Short Comings of Social Judgment*, Englewood Cliffs, NJ: Prentice-Hall

O'Connor, M., Remus, W., and Griggs, K. (1993) Judgmental Forecasting in Times of Change, *International Journal of Forecasting*, 9(2), pp. 163–172

Ohlsson, M.C., Wohlin, C., and Regnell, B. (1998) A project effort estimation study. *Information and Software Technology*, 40(14), pp. 831–839

Ordonez, L. and Benson III, L. (1997) Decisions Under Time Pressure: How Time Constraint Affects Risky Decision Making, *Organizational Behaviour and Human Decision Processes* 71(2): 121–140.

Park, R.E. (1996) A Manager's Checklist for Validating Software Cost and Schedule Estimates, *American Programmer*, 9(6), 30–35

Paynter, J. (1996) Project Estimation using Screenflow Engineering. *International Conference on Software Engineering: Education and Practice*, Dunedin, New Zealand, IEEE Comput. Soc. Press, Los Alamitos, CA, 150–159

Pelham, B.W. and Neter, E. (1995) The Effect of Motivation of Judgment depends on the Difficulty of the Judgment, *Journal of Personality and Social Psychology*, 68(4), pp. 581–594

Pengelly, A. (1995) Performance of Effort Estimating Techniques in Current Development Environments, *Software Engineering Journal*, 10(5), pp. 162–170

Reagan-Cirincione, P. (1994) Improving the Accuracy of Group Judgment: A Process Intervention Combining Group Facilitation, Social Judgment analysis, and Information Technology, *Organizational Behaviour and Human Decision Processes*, 58(2), pp. 246–270

Remus, W., O'Connor, M., and Griggs, K. (1995) Does Reliable Information Improve the Accuracy of Judgmental Forecasts? *International Journal of Forecasting*, 11(2), pp. 285–293

Ringuest, J.L. and Tang, K. (1987) Simple Rules for Combining Forecasts: Some Empirical Results, *Socio-Econ. Plann. Sci.*, 21(4), pp. 239-243

Roth, P.L. (1993) Research Trends in Judgment and Their Implications for the Schmidt-Hunter Global Estimation Procedure, *Organizational Behaviour and Human Decision Processes*, 54(2), pp. 299–319

Rowe, G. and Wright, G. (2001) Expert Opinions in Forecasting: The Role of the Delphi Process, *Principles of Forecasting: A Handbook for Researchers and Practitioners*, (Ed.) J.S. Armstrong, Boston, Kluwer Academic, pp. 125–144

Sanbonmatsu, D.M., Sharon, A.A., and Biggs, E. (1993) Overestimating Causality: Attributional Effects of Confirmatory Processing, *Journal of Personality and Social Psychology*, 65(5), pp. 892–903

Sanders, D.E. and Ritzman, L.P. (1991) On knowing When to Switch from quantitative to Judgemental Forecasts, *International Journal of Forecasting*, 11(6), pp. 27–37

Sanders, G.S. (1984) Self-Presentation and Drive in Social Facilitation, *Journal of Experimental Social Psychology*, 20(4), pp. 312–322

Sanders, N.R. and Ritzman, L.P. (2001) Judgmental Adjustment of Statistical forecasts, *Principles of Forecasting: A Handbook for Researchers and Practitioners*, (Ed.) J.S. Armstrong, Boston, Kluwer Academic, pp. 405–416

Schmitt, N., Coyle, B.W., and King, L. (1976) Feedback and Task Predictability as Determinants of Performance in Multiple cue Probability Learning Tasks, *Organizational Behaviour and Human decision processes*, 16(2), 388–402

Seaver, D.A., Winterfeldt von, D., and Edwards, W. (1978) Eliciting subjective Probability Distributions on Continuous Variables, *Organizational Behaviour and Human Decision Process*, 21(3), pp. 379–391

Shanteau, J. (1992) Competence in Experts: The Role of Task Characteristics, *Organizational Behaviour and Human Decision Processes*, 53(2), pp. 252–266

Shepperd, J.A., Fernandez, J.K., and Quellette, J.A. (1996) Abandoning Unrealistic Optimism: Performance Estimates and the Temporal Proximity of self-Relevant Feedback, *Journal of Personality and Social Psychology* 70(4), pp. 844–855

Sieber, J.E. (1974) Effects of Decision Importance on Ability to Generate Warranted Subjective Uncertainty, *Journal of Personality and Social Psychology*, 30(5), pp. 688–694

Simon, H.A. (1987) Making Management Decisions: The Role of Intuition and emotion, *Acad. Management Exec.* 1, pp. 57–63

Skitmore, R.M., Stradling, S.G., and Tuohy, A.P. (1994) Human Effects in early Stage Construction Contract Price Forecasting, *IEEE Transactions on Engineering Management*, 41(1), pp. 29–40

Soll, J.B. (1996) Determinants of Overconfidence and Miscalibration: The Roles of Random Error and Ecological Structure, *Organizational Behaviour and Human Decision Processes*, 65(2), pp. 117–137

Stahlberg, D., Eller, F., Maass, A., and Frey, D. (1995) We Knew it All Along: Hindsight Bias in Groups, *Organizational Behaviour and Human Decision Processes*, 63(1), pp. 46–58

Stone, Eric R and Opel, R.B. (2000) Training to improve calibration and discrimination: The effects of performance and environmental feedback, *Organizational Behaviour and Human Decision Processes*, 83(2), pp. 282–309

Subbotin, V. (1996) Outcome Feedback Effects on Under- and Overconfident Judgments (general knowledge tasks), *Organizational Behaviour and Human Decision Processes*, 66(3), pp. 268–276

Taff, L.M., Borchering, J.W., and Hudgins, J.W.R. (1991) Estimeetings: Development Estimates and A Front-end Process for A Large Project, *IEEE Transactions on Software Engineering* 17(8), pp. 839–849.

Tan, H.-T. and Lipe, M.G. (1997) Outcome Effects: The Impact of Decision process and Outcome Controllability, *Journal of Behavioral Decision Making*, 10(4), pp. 315–325

Tausworthe, R.C. (1980) The Work Breakdown Structure in Software Project management *Journal of Systems and Software*, 1(3), pp. 181–186

Thomsett, R. (1996) Double Dummy Spit and Other Estimating Games *American Programmer*, 9(6), pp. 16–22

Todd, P. and Benbasat, I, (2000) Inducing Compensatory information Processing Through Decision Aids that Facilitate Effort Reduction: An Experimental assessment, *Journal of Behavioral Decision Making*, 13(1), pp. 91–106

Tversky, A. and Kahneman, D. (1974) Judgment Under Uncertainty: Heuristics and Biases, *Science*, 185, pp. 1124–1131

van Genuchten, M. and Koolen, H. (1991) On the Use of Software Cost Models, *Information and Management*, 21, pp. 37–44

Verner, J.M., Overmyer, S.P., and McCain, K.W. (1999) In the 25 Years Sins The Mythical Man-Month What have We Learned About Project Management? *Information and Software Technology* 41, pp. 1021–1026.

Vicinanza, S.S., Mukhopadhyay, T., and Prietula, M.J. (1991) Software Effort Estimation: An Exploratory Study of Expert Performance, *Information systems Research*, 2(4), pp. 243–262

Walkerden, F. and Jeffery, D.J. (1997) Software Cost Estimation: A Review of Models, Process, and Practice, *Advances in Computers*, 44, pp. 59–125

Walkerden, F. and Jeffery, R. (1999) An Empirical Study of Analogy-Based software Effort Estimation, *Journal of Empirical Software Engineering*, 4(2), pp. 135–158

Webby, R.G. and O'Connor, M.J. (1996) Judgemental and Statistical Time Series Forecasting: A Review of the Literature, *International Journal of Forecasting,* 12(1), pp. 91–118

Weinberg, G.M. and Schulman, E.L. (1974) Goals and Performance in computer Programming. *Human Factors,* 16(1), pp. 70–77

Whitecotton, S.M., Sanders, D.E., and Norris, K.B. (1998) Improving Predictive Accuracy with a Combination of Human Intuition and Mechanical decision aids, *Organizational Behaviour and Human Decision Processes,* 76(3), pp. 325–348

Winklhofer, H., Diamantopoulos, A., and Witt, S.F. (1996) Forecasting Practice: A Review of the Empirical Literature and An Agenda for Future Research, *International Journal of Forecasting,* 12(2), pp. 193–221

Wolverton, R.W. (1974) The Cost of Developing Large-Scale Software, *IEEE Transactions on Software Engineering,* C-23(6), pp. 615–636

Wright, G. and Ayton, P. (1994) *Subjective Probability,* West Sussex, England, Wiley

Yaniv, I. and Foster, D.P. (1997) Precision and Accuracy of Judgmental Estimation, *Journal of Behavioral Decision Making,* 10, pp. 21–32

Yau, C. and Gan, L.-Y. (1995) Comparing the Top-Down and Bottom-Up Approaches of Function Point Analysis: A Case Study, *Software Quality Journal,* 4(3), 175–187

Zajonc, R.B. (1965) Social Facilitation, *Science,* 149 (Whole No. 3681), 269–274

Zajonc, R.B., Heingarner, A., and Herman, E.M. (1969) Social Enhancement and Impairment of Performance in the Cockroach, *Journal of Personality and Social Psychology,* 13(2), pp. 83–92

16

Reuse of Software Development Experiences – A Case Study

M. Jørgensen, R. Conradi, and D.Sjøberg

Abstract: In this paper we describe how Telenor Telecom Software (TTS) developed and implemented processes, roles and tools to achieve reuse of estimation and risk management experience, i.e. organizational learning. The results from the case study include:

- The development and introduction of an experience database integrated with the software development process – offering relevant experience 'just in time';
- Examples of types of experience useful for software developers;
- Recommendations on how to collect, package and distribute experience;
- Experience on roles and process to support reuse of software development experience.

Reprinted from Telektronikk (special issue on Software Quality in Telecommunication, Volume 95 (no.1), Magne Jørgensen, Reidar Conradi, Dag Sjøberg, " Reuse of software development experiences – a case study", pp. 48–53, Copyright © (1999), with permission from Telektronikk.

16.1 Introduction

The reported case study on reuse of software development experience was carried out in 1997–1998, supported by the national research project SPIQ (Software Process Improvement for better Quality). Among other things, the case study was motivated by the following challenges:

1. How can software development experience be efficiently shared between different development teams?
2. What types of experience are worth reusing?
3. What is the role of reuse of 'local' (context-dependent) experience compared with more 'global' (best practice) experience?

Our approach and results to help meeting these challenges, we believe, can be useful for other organizations facing similar challenges.

The remainder of the paper is organized as follows. Sect. 16.1.1 describes the research project SPIQ. Sect. 16.1.2 describes the organization studied. Sect. 16.2 describes and argues for approach chosen. Sect. 16.3 describes the results. Sect. 16.4 describes related work. Sect. 16.5 concludes, summarizes and suggests further work.

16.1.1 Software Process Improvement for Better Quality (SPIQ)

In April 1997, following a pre-project in 1996, the software process improvement project SPIQ was started. The program is sponsored by the Research Council of Norway (NFR) for at least three years. Its main goal is to

> "... increase the competitiveness and profitability of Norwegian IT industry through systematic and continuous process improvement ... "

The SPIQ project is based on the software process improvement principles of 'Total Quality Management', see for example [1], and the 'Quality Improvement Paradigm', see for example [2]. An important aspect of SPIQ is that it provides a means for the academia and the software industry to meet and discuss software improvement experiences and research results.

The work described in this paper has benefited from SPIQ in at least three ways:

1. The experience database design and results were discussed at the SPIQ meeings;
2. SPIQ has provided valuable research support;
3. SPIQ has financed parts of the Telenor Telecom Software's (TTS') internal work on 'reuse of experience'.

See http://www.fw.no/spiq/ for more information on SPIQ.

16.1.2 The Organization

TTS is split into five geographical locations and has more than 400 employees, most of them software developers. In other words, reuse of software development experience is an important but not trivial task. In 1995–1996 the company went through a 'Business Process Reengineering', see [3], resulting in a well documented, standardized software development process. The process descriptions and documents are available to all employees through the Intranet using an Internet browser.

The software development process used by the developers is called 'solution delivery' and is based on incremental delivery of software functionality in so-called 'time-boxes'. Each 'time-box' lasts 3–6 month, which provides good conditions for experience reuse, at least compared with organizations with a waterfall development model leading to projects with cycles of 1–2 years. The organization includes several support teams (development tool support team, measurement and estimation support team, test support team, quality team, etc.) for the development and maintenance processes. These teams turned out to be very important in the implementation of the process changes and collecting experience.

A recent, informal, in-house assessment (carried out by one of the authors of this paper) of the company, in accordance with the CMM framework, gave maturity levels on different key process areas between 2 and 4, i.e. TTS is a reasonably mature software development organization.

The company's software development process prescribes several steps motivated y the need for reuse of development experience: Each project should 1) be measured according to a measurement model, and 2) deliver an experience report when completed. The 'Measurement and Estimation Team' was allocated to carry out the measurements and the 'Quality Team' was the receiver of the experience reports.

We found that the project measurement and the experience reporting were to some extent carried out. However, there was not much systematic use of the information to improve the process. This observation was a major motive for our focus on reuse of experience in TTS.

16.2 The Approach

Our approach can be characterized as action science [4], which is a typical research method when studying industrial software development. Action science has advantages as well as disadvantages. The advantages are, for example, that action science may be the most efficient way to get:

– In-depth knowledge of software development organizations. This belief is e.g. supported by the learning model of [5], which focuses on the role of collecting concrete and context-dependent experience to support the learning process. According to this learning model only the lower levels of knowledge is context-independent and rule-based. In order to achieve higher levels of knowledge (being an expert) lots of context-dependent experience (local experience) has to be collected. *Our observations support this learning model. For example, while inexperienced project leaders asked for rule based methods regarding risk management, more experienced project leaders were more interested in how other projects had carried out their risk management activities.*

– Representative and realistic information on how terms and models important for meaningful reuse of experience are used. *For example, when we cooperated with the projected leaders on estimation of effort, we found a variety of interpretations of the term 'effort estimate'. This variety clearly reduced the potential for reuse of the effort estimation experience and data. Three major types of interpretations were found: Estimated effort means a) 'most likely effort'; b) 'the effort with the probability of 50 % not to exceed' (median); or c) 'the most likely effort + a (project dependent) risk buffer'.*

Disadvantages of action science are, on the other hand, that:

1. Action science studies are not carried out as strict experiments with control of the variables. Thus, a formal cause-effect relationship between the actions and the results cannot be established. In particular, the mixing of the participation and observer role makes objective analyses difficult. In addition, it is unlikely that anyone will (be able to) repeat the study to validate our observations.
2. There is no available observational language or theory to remove subjectivity and bias in the description of the observations. See for example the discussion of how the expectations impact the observational language in [6] – i.e. there is a danger of 'theory loaded observations'.

It is important to be aware of these disadvantages, but it should not stop anyone from carrying out studies like ours. Currently, action science (or similar methods) seems to be the only practical way of achieving in-depth 'real-world' results about software improvement. We believe, however, that more quantitative and experimental research on software processes should be the long-term goal of the software improvement research, leading to more general and objective knowledge. A more general discussion and comparison of research methods, particularly the role of case studies, can be found in [7].

Stimulated by the work at NASA-Software Engineering Laboratory on Experience Factory, see for example [8], and the opportunities we had at TTS, we started a search for 'pilots' where reuse of experience would improve the development process. Based on an informal analysis of the availability of information, availability of resources, time, probability of success, estimated cost and benefit, we decided to focus on the following two topics within the software development process:

- Estimation of software development effort
- Risk management.

A brief analysis gave that in order to support reuse of estimation and risk management experience, there was a need for

1. An experience reuse process, including new or modified role descriptions;
2. A supporting tool (the experience database);
3. Allocated experience reuse resources, both for implementing the experience reuse processes and for administrating the experience database.

16.3 The Results

This section describes the work and some of the results achieved in the period Spring 1997–Spring 1998. The organization continues to focus on experience reuse, i.e. the results and products are to some extent preliminary.

16.3.1 Manifestation of Experience

During the requirement analysis we soon discovered that the manifestation of experience can and should take many forms to be useful to the developers, such as:

- Quantitative and qualitative information that can be stored in traditional databases
- General tools implementing or based on 'best practice' within the organization
- Rule based systems (expert systems) reflecting expert experience and knowledge
- Pointers to people with useful experience (this may be the only way of 'representing' experience that cannot be articulated, i.e. tacit knowledge)
- Process descriptions on different levels and with different degrees of context dependence.

In addition, it was considered important that the experience database (the tool enabling the access to the stored experience) was available to all the developers at a low cost, integrated with the quality system, easy to use and easy to maintain.

16.3.2 Technical Platform

The technical platform chosen to meet these requirements was based on

- The organization's own Intranet. This made the experience database available to all the developers and well integrated with the organization's quality system
- A user interface based on a web browser with links to experience of different types. This removed the need for local installation
- An 'experience database' based on tables of data, spreadsheets, documents and rules implemented in executable programs, i.e. no traditional database.

Further, we decided to integrate the experience reuse support with the organization's process descriptions, i.e. from the relevant steps in the process descriptions we had links to useful information and tools in the experience database. The idea was to offer useful experience 'just in time'.

16.3.3 Reuse of Effort Estimation Experience

The effort estimation experience we offered was of the following types (linked to the relevant process steps):

Determine the Appropriate Estimation Model and Process

An 'expert system' recommending one or more estimation models was developed based on the collection and analysis of the experience of the organization's estimation experts. Following an analysis of whether formalized effort estimation is recommended or not, the expert system asks the user to answer nine questions. A simplified description of the questions and some implications of different answers are indicated in Table 16.1. The estimation models are briefly described in "Estimation Efforts" in Sect. 16.3.3. This expert system uses, in addition to the answers from the users, empirical data from TTS on the accuracy of the different estimation models, see Table 16.2, and the quality of the relevant historical data, i.e. a high degree of organizational dependent experience.

Table 16.1. Typical questions to and possible answers on estimation context

question	examples of implication
(1) will there be a high degree of infrastructure development and/or complex algorithms?	yes: FPA (function point analysis) based estimation is not recommended
(2) is the project context significantly different from previous TTS-projects?	yes: Previous experience (collected productivity data) will not be of much use. Normally, this excludes the use of FPA
(3) are most of the requirements described?	no: The work intensive estimation models ROPD (risk based, bottom-up estimation) and FPA are not worth the effort
(4) is a data model available?	no: The simplified FPA version (useful when developing an early estimate) cannot be used.
(5) does the delivery consist of many small, not logically connected changes/modules?	yes: FPA may not be useful
(6) will the effort to complete the project probably take more than six months?	no: FPA may require too much effort
(7) is the project willing to spend 1–2 man-days of effort for small projects (less than 12 man-months) and 2–4 man-days for larger projects?	no: ROPD or simplified FPA may be too work intensive
(8) will developers with experience from similar projects be available when estimating the effort?	no: ROPD requires a division of tasks into sub-tasks, i.e. without experience from similar projects ROPD can hardly be used
(9) will there be more than five deliveries similar to this one?	yes: If none of the standard estimation models are recommended, a tailored estimation model should be developed

Table 16.2. Accuracy of different estimation models

estimation model	TTS historical accuracy of model (average)
full function point analysis	± 15 % (mean magnitude of error)
simplified function point analysis	± 30 % (mean magnitude of error)
ROPD	± 20 % (mean magnitude of error)

Estimate Effort

Depending on estimation model, different types of experience data are available. Among others, the following estimation models and planning tools were supported by the experience database:

(a) MarkII Function Point Analysis (MkII FPA), see [9]. We improved and extended an existing spreadsheet implementing the MkII FPA estimation model. This estimation model takes as main input the estimated size of the functionality to be developed in function points.

Earlier we had analyzed data from more than 30 software development projects regarding how different variables, such as use of CASE tool, had had an impact on the development productivity, see [10]. This study indicated that the choice of development environment explained most of the productivity variance. Now we provided the estimator with historical data on previous projects similar to the current project. Table 16.3 shows some of the historical information that the estimator could make use of. The productivity is measured as UFP/w-h, unadjusted function points per work hour. Notice that the estimator has to predict a productivity category for his project, i.e. expert knowledge is still required.

(b) A bottom up, task and risk based estimation model was developed. This estimation model was supported with experience in the form of lists of 'tasks to remember' and suggestions on the effort distribution between the phases. Currently, there is ongoing work on how to improve the collection and reuse of historical data to support this bottom up, task and risk based estimation model, see [11]. We labeled this model *ROPD* (the Norwegian acronym for Risk Based Division into Sub-tasks).

(c) A risk analysis tool integrated in the estimation tools (or to be used separately) was developed. The risk analysis tool contains risk models, textual advice and guidelines based on previous experience. The content varies from a simple (but useful) checklist of tasks and risk factors to more sophisticated probability (beta-distribution) based risk models. Typically, the content was based on general frameworks and models, then adapted to the organization's needs according to expert knowledge and experience. This tool resulted in a probability based effort estimate and predictions such as "there is an 80% probability of not exceeding 3000 w-h of effort". It turned out that this type of probability based predictions were essential to introduce the distinction between planned and estimated effort in the organization. Similar to the results in [12] we found that probability based estimation had a positive impact on the realism in the effort estimates. Finally, pointers to the human estimation experts were provided.

Table 16.3. Suggestions of historical information in the tool

batch develo-pment	low prod.	medium prod.	high prod.	turbo prod.
cobol enviro-nment	0.05 UFP/w-h	0.10 UFP/w-h	0.20 UFP/w-h	0.30 UFP/w-h
powerbuilder environment	0.15 UFP/w-h	0.25UFP/w-h	0.50 UFP/w-h	0.70 UFP/w-h
on-line development	low prod.	medium prod.	high prod.	turbo prod.
cobol environment	0.07 UFP/w-h	0.15 UFP/w-h	0.20 UFP/w-h	0.30 UFP/w-h
powerbuilder environment	0.20 UFP/w-h	0.35UFP/w-h	0.70 UFP/w-h	1.00 UFP/w-h

16.3.4 Reuse of Risk Management Experience

Similar to the estimation support we linked our experience database to the risk management process. The experience database offers support through several tools to identify, analyze and manage software project risks. We interviewed several experienced project leaders in the organization to get the most relevant risk factors and the most relevant methods to reduce and control the risks. In addition, data from quality revisions were used to tailor the risk management support. Based on the collected information we developed:

- A 'TTS best practice' risk management process (extensions to the existing development process)
- A tool to identify, assess and store risk factors, and suggestions on how to reduce or control the risks
- A tool to visualize the risk exposure over time.

In many ways, what we did was to collect only a small fraction of the organization's knowledge about risk management. To become a learning organization the organization will need to continuously collect and distribute experience, i.e. new roles and a changed process are needed. Since systematic experience reuse in risk management has a short history in TTS, we found that we needed to start small in order to understand what sort of risk experience would be useful to collect.

16.3.5 Roles and Process

The studies and results described earlier in this paper resulted in the identification of needs for new roles and an increased focus on the implementation of the development process.

Roles

- An *'experience database administrator'* (a 'gardener') responsible for the availability and usability of the experience to be reused. This role may be split into two roles dividing the responsibility into a technical administrator and a content administrator. We suggest that the 'gardener' should be a part of the software process improvement team of the organization.
- Several *'process analysts'* responsible for analysis of information from each sub-process, such as the estimating process, the project management process or the testing process. The 'process analysts' is responsible for collecting and analyzing relevant information from completed projects and to generalize, tailor and package the useful experience.
- A network of *'support teams'* teaching and guiding the project leaders and members how to properly reuse the experience within each sub-process/topic.
- A *process owner* for the experience reuse process.

Notice the distinction between role and person. In a small organization a small team or (at least in theory) one single person may fill all these roles. Based on our experience at TTS, a critical minimum central effort to enable substantial reuse of estimation and risk management experience seems to be 2–3 man–years to fill the roles above.

Process

When we started our study, the organization did collect project data and it was mandatory to write experience reports, i.e., the process description had elements of experience reuse. However, the collected information was not systematically used to improve the processes. In other words, the process (or even more, the implementation of the process) had not had enough focus on the use of the collected information. Looking at other case studies of software process improvement, see for example [13], this seems to be a typical problem leading to graveyards of data and unused documents. In our opinion, this is a situation even worse than the situation where no data is collected and no reports written, and there is probably no more efficient way of destroying the respect for a measurement and experience report.

We believe that the current process description of TTS is sufficient to enable experience reuse, given sufficient resource to fill the experience reuse roles described earlier. For a more general experience reuse process and organization, see [8].

16.3.6 Benefits

An underlying initial hypothesis on experience reuse is, of course, that it has a long term benefit higher than the costs. Currently, we are not in the situation to decide whether this is true or not. We cannot validate the hypothesis, partly because it is too early, and partly because it is difficult to isolate the impact of our work from the impact of other parallel process improvement initiatives. However, even without a formal impact study we believe to see the following results of the experience reuse work:

- Improved estimation accuracy and more widespread use of the estimation models
- An increased focus on experience based risk management in the projects
- An acceptance in the organization for the need to collect and share experience.

In addition, we have made a number of interesting observations increasing the probability of successful reuse of experience in TTS, such as:

1. Currently, the experience reports written by the projects were of little use to other projects. This may indicate that without a clear model on how the experience will be reused, there is a great danger of reporting and collecting useless information.
2. The mere focus on reuse of experience had a positive impact on the 'improvement culture' in the organization. It would have been very interesting to carry out controlled experiments on how different actions impact the software improvement culture. An experimental design similar to the one described in 'Goals and performance in computer programming' [14] may be appropriate.

16.4 Related Work

The Experience Factory or EF [15, 16] is a framework for reuse of software life cycle experiences and products. EF relies on the Quality Improvement Paradigm [17] for continuous and goal-oriented process improvement, resembling the Shewhart/Deming Plan-Do-Check-Act cycle [18].

The EF framework prescribes an improvement organization inside a company, a kind of 'extended quality department'. This implies the "logical separation of project development (performed by the Project Organization) from the systematic learning and packaging of reusable experiences (performed by the Experience Factory)" [16]. The PERFECT EF framework extends this model by adding a third organizational component: the Sponsoring Organization, which uses the EF for strategic purposes [19].

Within the EF framework, the NASA Software Engineering Laboratory with its 275 developers has collected information about 150 projects in the period 1976–1996. The purpose is to record the effects of various software technologies (methods, tools, programming languages, QA techniques, etc.). However, NASA represents a special kind of stable and resourceful organization. It is a challenge to apply the EF ideas outside of NASA, i.e. to downscale it to companies with typically 10–30 developers, and where the EF roles are partly being played by the developers themselves. More applications of the EF framework in other contexts are therefore needed, see e.g. [19]. Our case study is a contribution in that respect.

16.5 Conclusions

"... (improvement) requires continual accumulation of evaluated experiences, in a form that can be effectively understood and modified, sorted in a repository of integrated experience models, that can be accessed/modified to meet the needs of the current project." [15]

In the introduction (Sect. 16.1) we asked the following questions:

1. *How can software development experience be efficiently shared between different development teams?*
2. *What types of experience is worth reusing?*
3. *What is the role of reuse of 'local' (context-dependent) experience compared with more 'global' (best practice) experience?*

Through our study we have contributed to the answers, but cannot claim to have the answers. Our main contribution may have been to give an in-depth example of how the questions/challenges were approached by TTS.

TTS has introduced a standardized development process documented on the web and made the processes available for all the software developers through the organization's Intranet. In many ways, this opens new possibilities for software development organizations. We have found that software development experience efficiently can be linked to the process steps and made available to all the developers in a very flexible way. However, the main challenges regarding becoming a learning organization and reusing experience is not the technology. We found that a lot of 'trial and error' and pragmatism is needed to find the useful experience and ways to formulate and spread this experience.

We found it useful to be very pragmatic regarding the manifestation of experience. For example, a very useful information in our experience database was the links to the experts having the required experience. Regarding the role of local (organization dependent) experience vs. best practice experience we found that the local experience made the best practice processes significantly more useful. In other words, optimal use of best practice processes seems to require collection and reuse of more local experience.

Achieving a learning organization is a formidable task. Senge claims that the following five disciplines are essential to creating learning organizations: *personal mastery, mental models, shared visions, team learning* and *systems thinking* [20]. An experience database like the one we have designed and implemented in TTS can serve as a basis for activities involved in all five disciplines. An experience database is also a useful means to agree on a common understanding of the current situation. "An accurate, insightful view of current reality is as important as a clear vision." [20]

Future work will address the major issue of how projects (contexts) should be characterized so that experiences collected in one project (context) are applicable to another project (context). How can we judge whether a project is sufficiently similar to (a subset of) the projects for which we have experience? The approaches described in [16] will be taken as a starting point.

Acknowledgments

The authors wish to thank the TTS employees Pål Woje, Geir Ove Espås, Majeed Hosseiney, Oddmar Aasebø and Tor Larsen for their enthusiasm and contribution to the work described in this paper.

References

[1] Deming, W.E. (1986) *Out of the Cris,* MIT Center for Advanced Engineering Study, Cambridge, MA, MIT Press

[2] Basili, V.R. (1985) Quantitative Evaluation of Software Engineering Methodology, in *Proceedings of the First Pan Pacific Computer Conference, Melbourne, Australia*

[3] Hammer, M. (1996) *Beyond Reengineering.* NY, Harper Collins

[4] Argyris, C. et al. (1985) *Action Science: Concepts, Methods and Skills for Research and Intervention,* San Francisco, CA, Joosey-Bass

[5] Dreyfus, H. and Dreyfus, S. (1986) *Mind Over Machine: the Power of Human Intuition and Expertise in the Era of the Computer,* NY, Free Press

[6] Goodman, N. (1951) *The Structure of Appearance,* Cambridge, MA, Harvard University Press

[7] Flyvebjerg, B. (1991) *Rationalitet og magt: det konkretes videnskap (bind I).* Copenhagen, Akademisk Forlag

[8] Basili, V.R. et al. (1992) The Software Engineering Laboratory: An Operational Software Experience Factory, in *Proceeding of the 14th International Conference in Software Engineering,* Melbourne, pp. 370–381

[9] Symons, C.R. (1993) *Software Sizing and Estimating, MkII FPA,* NY, Wiley

[10] Jørgensen, M. (1995) Empirical Evaluation of CASE Tool Efficiency, in *Proc. Sixth Int. Conf. on Applications of Software Measurement,* Orlando, pp. 207–230

[11] Schrader, T. (1998) *A Bottom-up Project Cost Estimation Method using Historic Data and a Standardized Work Breakdown Structure,* Trondheim, The Norwegian University of Science and Technology (Project Report)

[12] Conolly, T. and Dean, D. (1997) Decomposed versus Holistic Estimates of Effort Required for Software Writing Tasks, *Management Science,* 43(7), pp. 1029–1045

[13] Cusumano, M.A., Selby, R.W. (1996) *Microsoft Secrets,* London, Harper Collins Business, ISBN 0006387780

[14] Weinberg, G. and Shulman, E. (1974) Goals and Performance in Computer Programming, *Human Factors,* p. 16

[15] Basili, V.R. (1993) The Experience Factory and its Relationship to Other Improvement Paradigms, in I. Sommerville and M. Paul (eds.), *Proc. From ESEC'93, 4th European Software Engineering Conference,* Garmisch-Partenkirchen, Germany, September 1993, Springer Berlin Heidelberg New York, pp. 68–83 (Lecture Notes in Computer Science 717)

[16] Basili, V., Briand, L., and Thomas, W. (1994) Domain Analysis for the Reuse of Software Development Experiences, in *Proc. of the 19th Annual Software Engineering Workshop,* NASA/GSFC, Greenbelt, MD

[17] Basili, V.R. and Rombach, H.D. (1998) The TAME Project: Towards Improvement-Oriented Software Environments, *IEEE Transactions on Software Engineering,* 14(6), pp. 758–773

[18] Deming, W.E. (1982) *Quality, productivity, and competitive position.* Cambridge, Massachusetts Institute of Technology Center for Advanced Engineering Study, MA

[19] PERFECT Consortium (1996) *PIA Experience Factory, The PEF Model.* ESPRIT Project 9090, D-BL-PEF-2-PERFECT9090

[20] Senge, P.M. (1995) *The Fifth Discipline: the Art and Practice of the Learning Organization,* Currency/Doubleday

17

Effort Estimation of Use Cases for Incremental Large-Scale Software Development

P. Mohagheghi, B. Anda, and R. Conradi

Abatract: This paper describes an industrial study of an effort estimation method based on use cases, the Use Case Points method. The original method has been adapted to incremental development and evaluated on a large industrial system with modification of software from the previous release.

We modified the following elements of the original method (a) complexity assessment of actors and use cases, and (b) the handling of non-functional requirements and team factors that may affect effort. For incremental development, we added two elements to the method: (c) counting both all and the modified actors and transactions of use cases, and (d) effort estimation for secondary changes of software not reflected in use cases. We finally extended the method to: (e) cover all development effort in a very large system.

The method was calibrated using data from one release and it produced an estimate for the successive release that was only 17% lower than the actual effort. The study has identified factors affecting effort on large projects with incremental development. It also showed how these factors can be calibrated for a specific context and produce relatively accurate estimates.

Keywords: estimation, use cases, incremental development, management, cost estimation, life cycle, experimentation.

17.1 Introduction

Effort estimation is a challenge in every software project. The estimates will impact costs and expectations on schedule, functionality and quality. While expert estimates are widely used, they are difficult to analyze and the estimation quality depends on the experience of experts from similar projects. Alternatively, more formal estimation models can be used. Traditionally, software size estimated in the number of Source Lines of Code (SLOC), Function Points (FP) and Object Points (OP) are used as input to these models, e.g. COCOMO and COCOMO II [5].

Because of difficulties in estimating SLOC, FP or OP, and because modern systems are often developed using the Unified Modeling Language (UML), UML-based software sizing approaches are proposed. Examples are effort estimation methods based on use cases [11, 20], and software size estimation in terms of FP from various UML diagrams [22, 7].

The *Use Case Points* (UCP) estimation method introduced in 1993 by Karner estimates effort in person–hours based on use cases that mainly specify functional requirements of a system [11, 12]. Use cases are assumed to be developed from scratch, be sufficiently detailed and typically have less than 10–12 transactions. The method has earlier been used in several industrial software development projects (small projects compared to this study) and in student projects. There have been promising results and the method was more accurate than expert estimates in industrial trials [2, 3].

Recently, incremental or evolutionary development approaches have become dominant: requirements are covered (or discovered) in successive releases, and changing requirements (and software) is accepted as a core factor in software development. The Rational Unified Process (RUP) and agile methods like eXtreme Programming (XP) are examples. Each release of a software system may in turn be developed in iterations of fixed or variable duration, and be maintained for a while, before being replaced with a new release. Project management in these projects needs an estimation method that can estimate the effort for each release based on changes in requirements. Furthermore, software is built on a previous release that should be modified or extended.

This paper presents results of an empirical study on effort estimation of use cases in a large industrial system that is developed incrementally. We have adapted the UCP estimation method for complex use cases with modified transactions. The effort needed to modify a previous release was estimated by applying a formula from COCOMO II for modification of reused software and in the so-called Equivalent Modification Factor (EMF).

We concluded that use cases can predict the effort needed to realize a system, but the challenges are to define rules that account for the level of detail in use cases and how to estimate effort when software is incrementally updated. The accuracy of the estimates depends on many factors that are empirically set. Nevertheless, the method is rule-based, can be improved and be used as a supplement to expert estimates to produce early top-down estimates.

The study contributes in evaluating the UCP method for incremental development of a large system, identifying the factors that should be included in incremental effort estimation and those factors that impact estimation accuracy.

This paper is organized as follows. Section 17.2 presents the UCP method and the elements of the COCOMO method that are used in this study. Section 17.3 introduces the context. The research questions are formulated in Sect. 17.4. Section 17.5 presents the adapted UCP estimation method and Sect. 17.6 gives the estimation results. The results are further discussed in Sect. 17.7 and the research questions are answered in Sect. 17.8. Sect. 17.9 discusses relations to other work. Finally, the paper is concluded in Sect 17.10.

17.2 The Underlying Estimation Methods

17.2.1 The Use Case Points Estimation Method

A use case model defines the functional scope of the system to be developed. Attributes of a use case model may therefore serve as measures of the size and complexity of the functionality of a system. A recent study by Chen et al. on UML sizing metrics using 14 (small) eServices products showed that SLOC was moderately well correlated with the number of use cases, and that transactions in use cases can be used as measures of their complexity [8].

The Use Case Points (UCP) estimation method is an extension of the *Function Points Analysis* and *MK II Function Points Analysis* [21]. Table 17.1 gives a brief introduction of the six-step UCP method.

Table 17.1. The UCP estimation method

step	rule	output
1	classify actors: (a) simple, WF (Weight Factor) = 1 (b) average, WF = 2 (c) complex, WF = 3	unadjusted actor weights (UAW) = $\sum$ (#Actors * WF)
2	classify use cases: (a) simple – 3 or fewer transactions, WF = 5 (b) average – 4 to 7 transactions, WF = 10 (c) complex – more than 7 transactions, WF= 15	unadjusted use case weights (UUCW) = $\sum$ (#Use Cases * WF)
3	calculate the Unadjusted Use Case Point (UUCP).	UUCP = UAW + UUCW
4	assign values to the technical and environmental factors [0..5], multiply by their weights [−1..2] and calculate the weighted sums (TFactor and EFactor). Calculate TCF and EF as shown.	technical complexity factor (TCF) = 0.6 + (0.01 * TFactor) Environmental Factor (EF) = 1.4 + (−0.03 * EFactor)
5	calculate the adjusted Use Case Points (UCP).	UCP = UUCP * TCF * EF
6	estimate effort (E) in person-hours.	E = UCP * PHperUCP

In step 4, there are 13 *technical factors* (related to how difficult it is to build the system, e.g. distributed system, reusable code and changeability) and eight *environmental factors* (related to the efficiency of the project e.g. object-oriented experience and stable requirements). The weights and the formula for technical factors is borrowed form the Function Points method proposed by Albrecht [1]. Karner himself interviewed experienced personnel and proposed the weights for environmental factors. The formula for environmental factors is based on some estimation results.

In step 6, the adjusted Use Case Points (UCP) is multiplied by person-hours needed to implement each use case point (PHperUCP). The literature on the UCP method proposes from 20 to 36 PHperUCP [11, 18, 19].

Table 17.2 shows examples where the UCP method is applied to three projects in a company in Norway with 9–16 use cases each for new development. The application domain was banking. The system in this study is 20 times larger than the examples in Table 17.2 measured in use case points and 50 times larger in effort, something which motivates a modification of the method for larger systems.

17.2.2 The Constructive Cost Model (COCOMO)

The Constructive Cost Model (COCOMO) is a well-known estimation method developed originally by Barry Boehm in 1970s [5]. COCOMO takes software size and a set of factors as input and estimates effort in person-months. The basic equation in COCOMO is:

$$E = A * (Size)^B \tag{17.1}$$

In (17.1), E is the estimated effort in person-months, A is a calibration coefficient, *Size* may be in OP, FP or SLOC, and B counts for economy or diseconomy of scale. Economy of scale is observed if effort does not increase as fast as the size, because of e.g. using CASE tools. Diseconomy of scale is observed because of growing communication overhead and dependencies when the size increases. COCOMO suggests a diseconomy of scale by assuming $B > 1.0$.

Table 17.2. Some examples from [2]

project	UCP	estimated effort	actual effort	actual PHperUCP
A	138	2550	3670	26 6
B	155	2730	2860	18 5
C	130	2080	2740	21 1

COCOMO also includes various cost drivers that fall out of the scope of this paper. COCOMO assumes an incremental model of development, but the effort is estimated for the whole project.

One challenge in estimation of incrementally developed software is to estimate the degree of change between releases. This is earlier studied in the context of maintenance. Eick et al. [10] reported that during maintenance of a 100 Million LOC system, 20–30% of source code is added or deleted every year, with a slightly decreasing change rate over time. Another study by Lehman et al. reported that 60–80% of software modules are modified in the beginning of the maintenance phase, but this rate is again reduced over time [13]. It is interesting to evaluate these results when software is both maintained and is significantly evolved between releases.

Another challenge is to consider modification of software delivered in a previous release to integrate new functionality, improve quality, restructure, and correct bugs and other "secondary" changes. Boehm et al. write that there are non-linear effects involved in module interface checking (when k out of m software modules are modified), which occurs during design, coding, integration and testing of modified code [5]. The same conditions apply in incremental or evolutionary development. Only effort for software understanding may be less, since development is done by the same organization and with relatively stable staff.

COCOMO II includes a model to estimate *Equivalent new kilo Source Lines of Code* (ESLOC) from *Adapted kilo Source Lines of Code* (ASLOC, size of the reused software) for software reuse [6]. The model is shown in Fig. 17.1.

ESLOC = ASLOC * AAM,
where
AAM = 0.01 * [AA + AAF *{1 + (0.02 * SU * UNFM)}],   *for*
 AAF < = 50 *or*
AAM = 0.01 * [AA + AAF + (SU * UNFM)], *for* AAF > 50
and
AAF = (0.4 * DM + 0.3 * CM + 0.3 * IM).

The abbreviations stand for:
AAM = Adaptation Adjustment Modifier
AA = Assessment and Assimilation factor, [0..8]
AAF = Adaptation Adjustment Factor
SU = Software Understanding factor, [10 (self-descriptive code)..50 (obscure code)]
UNFM = programmer's unfamiliarity with software, [0 (completely familiar)..1 (completely unfamiliar)]
DM = percentage of Design Modification
CM = percentage of Code Modification
IM = percentage of the original Integration effort required to integrate the adapted software into an overall product

---

Fig. 17.1. COCOMO II model for estimating cost of software reuse

If software is reused without modification (black-box reuse), the only cost of reuse is related to assessment and assimilation. The cost will increase with the modification degree. Note that the adaptation cost can exceed 100%. i.e. reuse may cost more than developing from scratch if the cost of assessment or understanding is high or if the reused software is highly modified. These factors are necessarily subjective quantities. In [6], the above model is used to develop a cost estimation model for product line development.

COCOMO has also an extension for software maintenance, predicting maintenance effort as a function of initial development effort, the annual change traffic and an adjustment factor that reflects the difference between development and maintenance. This model may be used for maintenance of each release in incremental development (with mainly corrective changes). New requirements are usually forwarded to future releases.

17.3 The Company Context

The system in this study is a large distributed telecom system developed by Ericsson. It is characterized by multi-site development, development for reuse (almost 60% of software components are shared with another product) and several programming languages (C, Erlang, Perl and Java). The software size of the latest release in this study is more than 450 KSLOC (Kilo SLOC), or about 1000 KSLOC measured in equivalent C code.

The software process is an adaptation of RUP. Each release typically has 5–7 iterations, and the duration of iterations is 2–3 months. Until now, five main releases of the system are delivered to the market. The architecture is component-based with most components built in-house. Ericsson organizations in different countries have been involved in development, integration and testing of releases.

At the highest level, requirements are defined by use cases and supplementary specifications (for non-functional requirements e.g. availability, security and performance). The use case model in the study contains use case diagrams modeled in Rational Rose, showing actors and relations between use cases, while flows are described in textual documents called *use case specifications*. Each use case specification includes:

- One or several main flows that are complex and each have several transactions
- One or several alternative flows
- A list of parameters and constraints, such as counters and alarms
- Possible exceptional flows. These describe events that could happen at any time and terminate a flow. Exceptional flows are described in a table, which gives the event that triggers an exceptional flow, action and the result
- Use cases may *extend* or *include* other use cases

Each release may contain new use cases. Usually, previous use cases and use case specifications are also modified or extended with new or modified transactions, actors, flows or parameters. What is new or modified in each use case is marked with bold and blue font in the use case specification, not distinguishing between these two types of changes. In the remainder of this paper, we will use the terms use case specification and use case interchangeably.

17.4 Motivation of the Study and Research Questions

In this system, expert estimates are used in different phases of every release in an inside-out style: effort is estimated for activities such as design, coding and some testing in a bottom-up style, and the total effort is estimated by multiplying the above estimated effort by an *Overhead Factor* (OF). OF varies between 1.0 and 2.5 in different estimates based on project characteristics and the time of estimation. The reasons behind this factor are that activities like system test tend to fill whatever time available, and the size of some activities such as project management is proportional to the size of the system.

Expert estimates done by technical staff tend to be over-optimistic. The UCP method can, on the other hand, be applied also by non-technical staff and is rule-based, allowing improvement. We consequently decided to extend and evaluate this estimation method. Already when the UCP method was introduced to the project leaders to get their permission for the study, it was considered interesting. A project leader used it in addition to expert estimates by considering the amount of changes in use cases compared to the previous release.

We have formulated the following research questions for this study:

RQ1. Does the UCP method scale up for a large industrial project?

RQ2. Is it possible to apply the UCP method to incremental changes in use cases?

RQ3. How can effort to modify software from a previous release be estimated?

RQ4. Does the method produce reasonable results in this industrial setting?

The UCP method has earlier been tested only on small projects and with development from scratch.

17.5 The Adapted UCP Estimation Method

17.5.1 Overview of the Adapted Method

This section describes how the UCP method has been modified. The new rules are summarized in Table 17.3, with the same abbreviations as in Table 17.1 and as described below.

Table 17.3. The adapted UCP estimation method

step	rule	output
1	1.1. classify all actors as average, WF = 2. 1.2. count the number of new/modified actors.	UAW= #Actors*2 modified UAW (MUAW) = #New or modified actors * 2
2	2.1. since each transaction in the main flow contains one or several transactions, count each transaction as a single use case. 2.2. count each alternative flow as a single use case. 2.3. exceptional flows, parameters, and events are given weight 2. Maximum weighted sum is limited to 15 (a complex use case). 2.4. included and extended use cases are handled as base use cases. 2.5. classify use cases as: (a) simple – 2 or fewer transactions, WF = 5 (b) average – 3 to 4 transactions, WF = 10 (c) complex – more than 4 transactions, WF= 15 2.6. count points for modifications in use cases according to Rules 2.1–2.5 to calculate the modified unadjusted use case weights (MUUCW).	unadjusted use case weights (UUCW) = $\sum($ #Use Cases * WF) $+\sum($ #use case points for exceptional flows and parameters from 2.3) MUUCW = $\sum$ (#new/modified use cases * WF) $+\sum($ points for new/modified exceptional flows and parameters)
3	3.1. calculate UUCP for all software. 3.2. calculate Modified UUCP (MUUCP).	UUCP = UAW + UUCW MUUCP=MUAW + MUUCW
4	assume average project.	TCF = EF = 1
5	5.1. calculate adjusted use case points (UCP). 5.2. calculate adjusted modified UCP (MUCP).	UCP = UUCP MUCP = MUUCP
6	6.1. estimate effort for new/modified use cases. 6.2. estimate effort for secondary changes of software. 6.3. estimate total effort.	$E\_primary$= MUCP * PHperUCP $E\_secondary$ = (UCP - MUCP) * EMF * PHperUCP E = $E\_primary$ + $E\_secondary$

Step 1. Actors. An actor may be a human, another system or a protocol. Since the classification has little impact on the final estimation result, all actors are assumed to be average. Modified actors are also counted as the Modified Unadjusted Actor Weights (MUAW).

Step 2. Counting the UUCW and MUUCW. We started to count the Unadjusted Use Case Weights (UUCW) for Release 1 using the method described in Sect. 17.2.1. All use cases in this study would be classified as complex. Nevertheless, the total use case points would be still very low for all the 23 use cases (23 * 15 = 345 UUCW). But these use cases are much larger and more complex than in previous studies. Therefore we decided to break use cases down into smaller ones (not the use case specifications, but only in counting) as described in Rules 2.1 and 2.2. Rewriting use cases is too time-consuming while counting flows and transactions is an easy task.

Use cases should then be classified. Applying step 2 in Table 17.1 led to most use cases being classified as simple (66%), and very few as complex. However, the complexity of transactions does not justify such distribution.

An example of a use case called *Connect* is given in Fig. 17.2. It has one main flow with three transactions (*M1*, *M2*, and *M3*) and one alternative flow with one transaction (*A1*). Note that each transactions may in turn include several

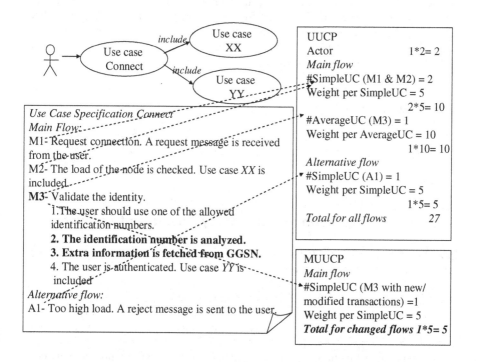

Fig. 17.2. Counting UUCP and MUUCP for a use case called *Connect*

(sub)transactions. Here, *M1* is described in one transaction, but it includes verifying that the received message is according to the accepted protocols. *M2* refers to an included use case. *M3* has four transactions where none of these is a single transaction and includes another use case as well. Therefore, we classified the use cases according to Rule 2.5. So *M1*, *M2*, and *A1* would be classified as simple use cases, while *M3* would be an average one.

In Rule 2.6, modified transactions or parameters are counted. In Fig. 17.2, two transactions in *M3* are modified or are new (in bold text) and are classified as a new simple use case. Thus this use case is modified by 5/27 = 0.19.

Karner proposed not counting so-called included and extended use cases, but the reason is unclear. We have applied the same rules to all the use cases. However, these are counted only once (like other use cases).

Step 3. Counting UUCP. The Unadjusted Use Case Points (UUCP) are calculated; once for all use cases (in Rule 3.1) and once for modifications (in Rule 3.2).

Step 4. TCF and EF. Assigning values to technical and environmental factors are usually done by experts or project leaders, based on their judgment [2]. The impact of the Technical Complexity Factor (TCF) is small and it does not cover all the non-functional requirements either. We have therefore handled this otherwise, as described in step 6. The Environmental Factor (EF) is not relevant in this case as there are few changes to this factor from one release to another. However, this factor does have a large impact on the estimate and we have accounted for omitting it by using a high PHperUCP. Dropping these factors is also suggested in other cost models [13].

Step 5. The adjusted UCP and MUCP will be equal to the unadjusted ones since TCF and EF are set to 1.

Step 6. We assume that there are two mechanisms that consume effort in our model: *E_primary* estimates effort for realizing new and modified use cases, while *E_secondary* estimates effort for *secondary changes* as described later. The total estimated effort is the sum of these.

17.5.2 Effort Estimation for Secondary Changes of Software

In addition to changes related to functionality estimated in *E_primary*, there are several other reasons for why software is modified:

1. Perfective functional changes not specified in use cases. Functionality is also enhanced and improved in each release by initiating so-called change requests after requirement freeze. There may also be ripple effects of changes in use cases.
2. Perfective non-functional changes. Quality attributes are improved between releases (performance, security, reliability etc.), but these changes are not reflected in use cases. A study of change requests for four releases of the same

system showed that 44% of change requests were issued to improve quality attributes [16]. Improving quality attributes is usually achieved by modifying software that is already implemented.

3. Corrective changes. Some effort is spent on modifying software to correct detected defects.
4. Preventive changes to improve design and reduce software decay also consume effort. Also note that preventive changes to improve file structure or to reduce dependencies between software modules may later impact quality attributes such as maintainability.

We decided to use the model described in Fig. 17.1 as a first trial to estimate effort for secondary modifications by a so-called *Equivalent Modification Factor* (*EMF*). For our model, in the simplest form we propose:

− AA (Assessment and Assimilation) = 2%, we assume low search, test and evaluation effort for software developed in-house.
− SU (Software Understanding) = 30% for moderate understandable software.
− In [16], we reported that source code is approximately modified by 55% between releases, and this can be used as mean value for CM (Code Modification percentage).
− DM (Design Modification percentage) is usually less than CM and is set to 30% here, which is close to the mean value of changes in use cases (23–31% counted in use case points).
− IM (Integration effort percentage) is set to be 65%, i.e. slightly over CM [6].
− UNFM (Unfamiliarity with software) = 20% for mostly familiar with code.

The above values give AAF (Adaptation Adjustment Factor) = 48%. Thus, EMF (AAM in Fig. 17.1) will be equal to 56%. The reason for renaming the factor is to distinguish between modification of software from a previous release and systematic software reuse in COCOMO II. We have not found any empirical studies that evaluated such a factor in incremental development. This factor gives equivalent UCP for secondary modifications.

In Rule 6.2, we multiply EMF with the size of use case points that are not modified or new. Alternatively, we could multiply it with SLOC from the previous release and use (17.1) to estimate effort for this part. Since we wanted to evaluate the UCP method, we used use case points also in this step.

17.6 Estimation Results

The estimation method was modified based on the use cases and effort of one release (called Release 1 here building on Release 0) and was later tested on the successive release (called Release 2). Release 2 was the latest release of the system at the time of this study.

Of the 23 use cases in Release 1, seven use cases were not modified, one use case was new, while 15 use cases were modified. We broke down the use cases,

Table 17.4. No. of use cases in each class

	release 1	release 2
simple use case	170	95
average use case	83	100
complex use case	35	59
sum use cases	*288*	*254*
modified simple use case	57	81
modified average use case	18	16
modified complex use case	2	11
sum modified use cases	*77*	*108*

inserted the number of transactions, actors, exceptions and parameters in spread-sheets in Microsoft Excel, counted the use case points and estimated the effort following the rules in Table 17.3. Table 17.4 shows that after break-down of the use cases (UC) we ended up with 288 use cases in Release 1.

Table 17.4 also shows data for Release 2, which had 21 use cases: two use cases were not modified, one use case was new, while 18 were modified. Note that three use cases are missing in Release 2 (the sum should be 24). Two use cases were merged in other use cases, while one use case is removed from our analysis since development was done by another organization and we do not have data on effort here.

We decided to compensate for not counting the environmental factors and for the large number of complex use cases, by using the maximum used number of PHperUCP that is 36. Nevertheless, the estimates were almost half the actual effort spent in Release 1 for all activities. Therefore we compared our estimates with the projects in Table 17.2 with respect to what the estimates should cover.

For projects *A* and *B* in Table 17.2, estimates have been compared with the total effort after the construction of use case models. These projects' effort distribution is very different from this system, as shown in Tables 17.5 and 17.6. The *Other* column in Table 17.5 covers deployment and documentation, while in Table 17.6 it covers configuration management, software process adaptation, documentation and travel. Effort distribution profiles will of course vary depending on environment and technologies. In our case, Development before System Test (use case modeling, analysis and design, coding, module testing and use case testing added by Ericsson) counts for half the total effort.

The existing estimation method in the company estimates effort needed for Development before System Test and multiplies this by an Overhead Factor (OF) to cover all project activities. We concluded that the 36 PHperUCP covers only Development before System Test. Based on empirical data presented in Table 17.6, it should be multiplied by approximately 2 to estimate the total effort.

Table 17.5. Percentages of actual effort spent in different activities in example projects in Table 17.2

project	development before system test	system test	project management	other
A	80%	2%	13%	5%
B	63%	7%	27%	3%

Table 17.6. Percentages of actual effort spent in different activities in Release 1 and 2 in this study

release	development before system test	system test	project management	other
1	50%	25%	10%	15%
2	55%	19%	11%	15%

For confidentiality reasons, we cannot give the exact figures for the estimates and the actual effort. However, our UCP estimates were 21% lower for Release 1 and 17% lower for Release 2 than the actual effort, the latter being around 100 person–years; i.e. fairly accurate for large projects (all use cases used in the estimation are actually implemented).

For comparison, the effort to develop the first release was 2–3 times this number. The expert estimates for Release 2 were 35% lower than the actual effort, and thus the adapted UCP method had lower relative error than expert estimates.

The effort for estimating each release was approximately two person-days, but we spent also a few days initially on modifying the method. The method was easy to learn, but assigning values to factors and deciding classification rules need access to experts, empirical data and guidelines for writing use cases.

17.7 Discussion of the Results

We consider the data on effort as reliable and we have had access to all the use cases. The estimation was done by us: the first author was an employee of Ericsson at the time of this study and the second author had previous experience with the UCP method. Although the method was presented to a few project leaders, we could not involve them in the adaptation work due to internal reorganizations.

The adapted UCP method produced reasonable estimates with the following changes divided in three groups:

1. *Generic changes that should be considered in every project (modified the UCP method):*
   (a) Size and the level of detail in use cases. There is no standard way of writing use cases. We broke each use case down to several smaller ones to compensate for the size and we modified the classification rules, justified by the complexity of transactions.

(b) Technical and environmental factors. These factors are incorporated in PHperUCP, OF and EMF. Since the method is adjusted to the context and is used on successive releases of the same system, these factors are redundant.

2. *Changes specific to incremental development (added to the UCP method):*
   (c) Incremental modification of use cases. We estimated effort for new and modified transactions, actors or parameters to estimate effort for primary changes.
   (d) The Equivalent Modification Factor (EMF). This factor is used to estimate equivalent use case points for modification of software from a previous release or secondary changes, including perfection of quality attributes. It is set to 56% in this study.

3. *Changes specific to the development organization (extended the UCP method):*
   (e) The Overhead Factor (OF). We used the largest value of PHperUCP proposed by other studies, i.e. 36. It covered effort for use case modeling, analysis and design, coding, module testing and use case testing; i.e. Development before System Test. OF is used to estimate the total effort based on the effort for Development before System Test. This empirically derived factor is set to 2.

An alternative to OF would be to use 72 PHperUCP. We chose to add this factor to the method to highlight the diseconomy of scale in large projects and the impact of effort distribution profile on the estimation method. EMF, PHperUCP and OF rely on empirical observations and our judgments, and can be subject of further adjustments.

All estimation methods are imprecise, because the assumptions are imprecise. The method was adapted using data from one release, but it gave even better results for the successive release. Each estimate should also come with a range, starting with a wider range for early estimates. Use cases are updated in the early requirement specification stage, which gives a range of $0.67 - 1.5$ estimated effort according to COCOMO [5].

The impact of $E\_secondary$ is large on the total estimated effort (65% in Release 1 and 55% in Release 2). In addition to portions of the software affected by changed use cases, the rest of the software is also modified to improve quality, and there are in general change requests and defect reports that were not pre-planned. Parts of the software may become more stable after a few releases or be used in a black-box style without modification, so that $E\_secondary$ decreases. But software also decays and there is cost related to re-factoring and redesign.

When releases are normally planned in relatively constant intervals, a planned release will take approximately the same effort as the previous one. The question is then whether all the planned use cases can be implemented by available resources and whether the project has taken into account the impact of secondary changes. Therefore, the method is still useful.

17.8 Answers to Research Questions

Four research questions were presented in Sect. 17.4. We answer these as follows:

RQ1. Does the UCP method scale up for a large industrial project?
It did when we broke down the use cases as reflected in Rules 2.1-2.5 in Table 17.3. One alternative is to include examples of typical use cases in the method, such as those defined in [9].

RQ2. Is it possible to apply the UCP method to incremental changes in use cases?
Yes. Rules 1.2, 2.6, 3.2, and 6.1 in Table 17.3 show how to estimate effort for changes in use cases.

RQ3. How can effort to modify software from a previous release be estimated?
We used the COCOMO II formula for adapted software, calculated EMF and applied it on use case points for the rest of the software. The EMF may be adjusted to the context.

RQ4. Does the method produce reasonable results in this industrial setting?
The adapted UCP method fitted well into the adapted RUP process and produced reasonable results. The method is cheap and understandable.

17.9 Related Work

Work in effort estimation for *ab initio* software development has been reported since the mid-1960s. Work has also been done to predict effort needed for software maintenance, see [17] for an overview. Different models use the history or a prediction of change impact (as the number of modules, FP, modification requests, SLOC or change traffic) as input. Maintenance or evolution in these models is unplanned changes to software after ab initio development, applicable e.g. to each release of a system in incremental development.

Carbone et al. propose combining data from use case diagrams, class diagrams and state diagrams in an automated tool for effort estimation [7]. The method has a *Fast* estimation when there are few details in these diagrams and a *Serious* estimation later. There are many factors that should be set empirically, it depends on an OO paradigm for modeling and design, and incremental development is not discussed. The authors also present earlier work, basically based on class diagrams.

Ashman suggests predicting effort for implementing each use case in person-days and summing up these to estimate effort for an iteration [4]. The predictions are expert opinions rather than rule-based. He makes two observations that are applicable also to our model. Firstly, a use case encompasses a discrete and significant proportion of a system's functionality. Therefore it is easier to estimate effort using these large functional chunks. Secondly, it is possible to compare the estimated and actual effort at the end of each iteration (or each release in our case) and tune the model to fit the project.

An important question is whether multiple estimation techniques should be applied to achieve a better result. MacDonell et al. have compared three estimation methods on effort data of a medical records information system [15]. They observed that the best method varies from one study to another. Since they could not define *a priori* which technique is best for each case, a combination of techniques is recommended.

17.10 Conclusion

An effort estimation method based on use cases has been adapted and tested on a large industrial system with incremental changes in use cases. One main assumption is that use cases may be used as a measure of the size of a system, and that changes in these may be used as a measure of changes in functionality between releases. Generally, predicting the size of a software system in SLOC or FP in early phases is as difficult as predicting the needed effort, while use cases are written early. For changes not reflected in use cases, an additional model is used.

The method does not depend on any tools (although there are tools for the original UCP method), paradigms or programming languages, and can promote high quality use cases. The method is cheap, transparent and easy to understand. The method is also suitable when development is being outsourced.

The main contributions of the study are:

- Discussing how to adapt the UCP method for a large industrial system and to a specific context. The proposed changes for breaking down use cases and new classification rules were necessary since use cases are written with different level of details in different projects. Future work may provide some example use cases that may be used for calibrating classification rules to a context. For a model to scale up, additional factors such as a higher value of PHperUCP and the Overhead Factor (OF) may also be necessary.
- Adapting the UCP method for incremental development. Two mechanisms of effort consumption are identified: (a) primary changes reflected in changes in use cases, and (b) secondary changes or modification of software from a previous release as a ripple effect of primary changes, unplanned changes and improvements in quality attributes.
- Identifying the impact of effort distribution profile on estimation results, reflected in the Overhead Factor (OF).

Use case diagrams are usually available before other UML diagrams, but have variable level of details. A challenge is to define some standards for these. Furthermore, use cases essentially express functional requirements. The influence of non-functional requirements should be included in the technical factors, the number of PHperUCP or as the estimated effort for secondary changes.

There are few empirical studies on estimation of incrementally developed systems. The UCP method showed flexibility in adapting to the context, but there are many context-dependent factors in the original method and in our extensions of it.

Future studies can help to understand the degree of modification in incremental development of a system (use cases, code and integration costs), and how the method works on other types of systems.

Acknowledgements

The study was performed in the INCO project (INcremental and COmponent-based Software Development), a Norwegian R&D project in 2001–2004 [http://www.ifi.uio.no/~isu/INCO/]. It was part of the first author's PhD study, which was performed in Ericsson, Grimstad- Norway. We thank Ericsson for the support.

References

[1] Albrecht, A.J. (1979) Measuring Application Development Productivity, in *Proceedings of the IBM Applic. Dev. Joint SHARE/GUIDE Symposium,* Monterey, CA, pp. 83–92

[2] Anda, B., Dreiem, D., Sjøberg, D.I.K., Jørgensen, M. (2001) Estimating Software Development Effort Based on Use Cases – Experiences from Industry, in *M. Gogolla, C. Kobryn (Eds.): UML 2001 – The Unified Modeling Language. Modeling Languages, Concepts, and Tools, 4th Int'l Conference.* Springer Berlin Heidelberg New York LNCS 2185, pp. 487–502

[3] Anda, B. (2002) Comparing Effort Estimates Based on Use Cases with Expert Estimates, in *Proceedings of Empirical Assessment in Software Engineering (EASE 2002)* (Keele, April 8–10, 2002), 13 p

[4] Ashman, R. (2004) Project Estimation: A Simple Use-Case-Based Model *IT Pro*, 6, 4 (July/August 2004), pp. 40–44

[5] Boehm, B., Clark, B., Horowitz, E., Westland, C., Madachy, R., Selby, R.(1995) Cost Models for Future Software Life Cycle Processes: COCOMO 2.0. *USC Center for Software Engineering*, http://sunset.usc.edu/publications/TECHRPTS/1995/index.html

[6] Boehm, B., Brown, W., Madachy, R., Yang, Y. (2004) Software Product Line Cycle Cost Estimation Model, in *Proceedings of the ACM-IEEE Int'l Symposium on Empirical Software Engineering (ISESE 2004)* (Redondo Beach CA, 19–20 August, 2004), IEEE-CS Order No. P2165, pp. 156–164

[7] Carbone, M. and Santucci, G. (2002) Fast&Serious: A UML Based Metric for Effort Estimation, in *Proceedings of the 6th ECOOP Workshop on Quantitative Approaches in Object-Oriented Software Engineering (QAOOSE'02)* (Spain, June 11, 2002), 12 p

[8] Chen, Y., Boehm, B.W, Madachy, R., and Valerdi, R. (2004) An Empirical Study of eServices Product UML Sizing Metrics, in *Proceedings of the ACM-IEEE Int'l Symposium on Empirical Software Engineering (ISESE 2004)* (Redondo Beach CA, pp.19–20, August 2004), IEEE-CS Order No. P2165, pp. 199–206

[9] Cockburn, A. (2000) *Writing Effective Use Cases*, Addison-Wesley ISBN 0-201-70225-8

[10] Eick, S.G., Graves, T.L., Karr, A.F., Marron, J.S., and Mockus, A. Does Code Decay? Assessing the Evidence from Change Management Data, *IEEE Trans. Software Engineering*, 27(1): 1–12, Jan. 2001

[11] Karner, G. (1993) *Metrics for Objectory*, Diploma thesis, University of Linköping, Sweden. No. LiTH-IDA-Ex-9344:21

[12] Karner, G. (1993) *Resource Estimation for Objectory Projects*, Objective Systems SF AB (copyright owned by *Rational Software)*

[13] Kemerer, C.F. (1987) An Empirical Validation of Software Cost Estimation Models, *CACM*, 30, pp. 416–429

[14] Lehman, M.M., Perry, D.E., and Ramil, J.F. (1998) Implications of Evolution metrics on Software Maintenance. In *Proceedings of the Int'l Conference on Software Maintenance (ICSM 1998)*,16–20 Nov, 1998, Bethesda, Maryland, USA, IEEE-CS Press, pp. 208–217

[15] MacDonell, S.G. and Shepperd, M.J. (2003) Combining Techniques to Optimize Effort Predictions in Software Project Management, *Journal of Systems and Software*, 66, pp. 91–98

[16] Mohagheghi, P. and Conradi, R. (2004) An Empirical Study of Software Change: Origin, Impact, and Functional vs. Non-Functional Requirements. in *Proceedings of the ACM-IEEE International Symposium on Empirical Software Engineering (ISESE 2004)* (Redondo Beach CA, 19–20 August 2004), IEEE-CS Order No. P2165, pp. 7–16

[17] Ramil, J.F. and Lehman, M.M. (2000) Metrics of Software Evolution as Effort Predictors – A Case Study, in *Proceedings of the Int'l Conference on Software Maintenance (ICSM 2000)*, IEEE-CS Press, pp. 163–172

[18] http://www.processwave.net/, July 2004

[19] Schneider, G. and Winters, J.P. (1998) *Applying Use Cases, a Practical Guide*, Addison-Wesley

[20] Smith, J. (1999) The Estimation of Effort Based on Use Cases, *Rational Software*, White paper

[21] Symons, P.R. (1991) *Software Sizing and Estimating MK II FPA (Function Point Analysis)*,Wiley

[22] Uemura, T., Kusumoto, S., and Inoue, K. (1999) Function Point Measurement tool for UML Design Specification, in *Proceedings of the 6th Int'l IEEE Software Metrics Symposium*, IEEE-CS Press, pp. 62–69

Section 5

Empirical Studies in OO and Component-based Systems

Object-oriented programming and component-based development are two core paradigms in modern software development. This section reports three studies in these areas. The first article reports a comprehensive case study in ABB on the use of UML, the de facto standard in industry for modelling object-oriented systems. The second article reports a survey conducted in Norway, Germany and Italy on the use of commercial off-the-shelf software (COTS) in industrial projects. The last article reports a controlled experiment, with both professional Java consultants and students as participants, to test the effect of two different control styles on the maintainability of object-oriented software.

18. *Anda, B.C.D., Hansen, K., Gullesen, I., and Thorsen H.K., (2005)* "Experiences from Using a UML-based Development Method in a Large Organisation," accepted for *Empirical Software Engineering*, per September p 36. (in this book).

19. *Li, J., Conradi, R., Slyngstad, O.P.N., Bunse, C., Khan, U., Torchiano, M., and Morisio M., (2005)* "An Empirical Study on Off-the-Shelf Component Usage in Industrial Projects," In Frank Bomarius and Seija Komi-Sirviö (Eds.): *Proc. 6th International Conference on Product Focused Software Process Improvement (PROFES'2005)*, 13–16 June, Oulu, Finland Finland, Springer LNCS 3547, pp. 54–68.

20. *Arisholm E., and Sjøberg, D.I.K. (2004)* "Evaluating the Effect of a Delegated versus Centralized Control Style on the Maintainability of Object-Oriented Software," *IEEE Transactions on. Software Engineering*, 30(8):521–534, August. 2004.

18

Experiences from Introducing UML-based Development in a Large Safety-Critical Project

B. Anda, K. Hansen, I. Gullesen, and H.K. Thorsen

Abstract: UML and UML-based development methods have become de facto standards in industry, and there are many claims for the positive effects of modelling object-oriented systems using methods based on UML. However, there is no reported empirical evaluation of UML-based development in large, industrial projects. This paper reports a case study in ABB, a global company with 120,000 employees, conducted to identify immediate benefits as well as difficulties and their causes when introducing UML-based development in large projects.

ABB decided to use UML-based development in the company's system development projects as part of an effort to enable certification according to the IEC 61508safety standard. A UML-based development method was first applied in a large, international project with 230 system developers, testers and managers. The goal of the project was to build a new version of a safety-critical process control system. Most of the software was embedded. The project members were mostly newcomers to the use of UML.

Interviews with 16 system developers and project managers at their sites in Sweden and Norway were conducted to identify the extent to which the introduction of UML-based development had improved their development process. The interviewees had experienced improvements with traceability from requirements to code, design of the code, and development of test cases as well as in communication and documentation. These results thus support claims in the literature regarding improvements that may be obtained through the use of UML. However, the results also show that the positive effects of UML-based development were reduced due to (1) legacy code that it was not feasible to reverse engineer into UML, (2) the distribution of requirements to development teams based on physical units and not on functionality, (3) training that was not particularly adapted to this project and considered too expensive to give to project members not directly involved in development with UML, and (4) a choice of modelling tools with functionality that was not in accordance with the needs of the project.

The results from this study should be useful in enabling other UML adopters to have more realistic expectations and a better basis for making project management decisions.

18.1 Introduction

Companies that adopt UML-based development aim to improve their development process and gain, for example, easier communication within the project, improved design of the code, and improved documentation and thus easier future maintenance.

In general, there are high costs involved in introducing new software development methods and risks of failure if the method is not adapted. Therefore, there is a need for case studies to increase knowledge about consequences of project managerial decisions in the context of UML-based development, and about which improvements are realistic in different project contexts.

This paper reports a case study conducted on a large development project in the Swedish–Swiss global company ABB. The goal of the project was to create a new version of a safety-critical process control system based on several existing systems. The development took place at four sites in three countries; and 230 developers, testers and managers were involved, of whom approximately 100 used a UML-based development method themselves or read and applied UML documents. Most of them were newcomers to such development. Most of the software was embedded, while the rest was for the Windows platform. There were approximately 1,000 requirements for this system. The company decided to adopt UML-based development and a method was developed in-house to enable certification according to the IEC 61508 safety standard [14]. Previously, there had been no common methodology for the analysis and design of software in the company.

Interviews were conducted with 16 project managers and developers in the project, who represented different sites, different kinds of development and different roles in the project. The interviews were analyzed according to principles from grounded theory, [25], to ensure that the interviewees' opinions were conveyed systematically. The interviews showed that UML-based development improved traceability, communication, design, documentation and testing, but it was recognized in this project that the improvements were not as great as they could have been, due to difficulties with the use of UML, in particular regarding (1) choice of diagram to use in specific situations, (2) the interfaces between different models, and (3) the level of detail in the models. The results further showed that these difficulties were, at least partially, caused by project decisions with respect to the reverse engineering of legacy code, distribution of requirements to teams, training and mentoring, and choice of modelling tools.

Despite the widespread adoption of UML, there are few reported empirical studies on the effects of UML-based development. A survey of 5,453 scientific articles published in 12 leading software engineering journals and conferences in the decade from 1993 to 2002, identified 113 controlled experiments in which individuals or teams performed one or more software engineering [24]. Four of the experiments investigated different aspects of the use of UML [6, 19, 20, 29]. The first investigates the construction of use case models, the second and third investigate the comprehension of UML diagrams, while the fourth compares the concepts of UML with those of two other formalisms. In addition, the usability of UML-diagrams have been investigated in the context of a student project [2], and experiences of applying UML in the development of embedded systems have been reported in [21]. To the authors' knowledge this is the only empirical evaluation of UML adoption in a large-scale industrial project.

Within ABB, the constraints of the safety standard meant that the teams had to apply the UML-based method rigorously and produce all the required models. Hence, this project represented a rare opportunity to investigate the effects of

UML-based development. The main contribution of this paper is, therefore, that it describes improvements and challenges when adopting UML-based development in an industrial environment. Such information may be beneficial to other companies adopting UML.

The remainder of this paper is organized as follows. Section 18.2 describes the company, the project and the ABB UML method. Section 18.3 describes the research method. Section 18.4 describes the results with respect to improvements. Section 18.5 describes the results with respect to challenges in the project. Section 18.6 discusses the scope and validity of the results. Section 18.7 concludes and describes plans for future work.

18.2 UML-Based Development in the ABB Project

This Section describes the company, the project and the UML-based development method that was applied in the project.

18.2.1 ABB

ABB is a global company that operates in around 100 countries and employs approximately 120,000 people. It is a leader in power and automation technologies, and develops software and hardware for these markets. The company has a large number of development projects, the majority of which require the development of embedded software (with special hardware included).

ABB's safety products must be certified according to the international standard IEC 61508 in order to be used in plants or installations where the processes used can be dangerous to humans or damage the environment. This standard is becoming a requirement for the process industry and in discrete manufacturing. It is a life-cycle standard and includes requirements pertaining to the methodology of software development.

Before the start of the project reported in this paper there was little common streamlining of software development in the company; a large number of different methods, programming languages and software tools were used. ABB hoped that the introduction of UML-based development would lead to improvements in requirements handling and traceability, improved design of code, fewer defects in the product and reduced overall costs of development.

18.2.2 The Project

The goal of the project was to develop a new version of a safety-critical system based on several existing systems. The system was to be installed at several locations. Each installation would program its own logic on top of the system delivered by ABB, which is not modified at the installations.

The workforce comprised approximately 230 people located at four sites: two in Sweden, one in Norway and one in Germany. Approximately 100 people were involved in development with UML. The UML-based development method was used at the first three sites. Some of the developers and all the product managers were domain experts. ABB relies on having domain expertise in-house because they sell a complete product to its customers. Safety certifiers, UML experts, quality managers and peer developers (also with domain knowledge) reviewed the UML models at predefined *gates* in the development process. The development was organized in teams, while testing was mostly done by specialized testers. The team members were mostly newcomers to the use of UML, although some were experienced.

This software project is ABB's most ambitious project regarding quality assurance in that it followed the requirements of IEC 61508. To ensure that the software operates at a certain minimum safety integration level (SIL level), this standard strongly recommends the use of semi-formal development methods. Consequently, a UML-based development method (the ABB UML method), which qualifies as a semi-formal method according to IEC 61508, was developed by the company [26, 27]. In addition, the system components are SIL certified, which implies that the software parts of the components must implement (parts of) the safety requirements so that the whole component can be SIL-certified. These requirements were derived from the requirements for the safety level before the total set of requirements was distributed to the development teams. Thus, from the point of view of the development teams, there was little difference between the safety-related requirements and the functional requirements.

The existing systems consisted of 3–4 million lines of code and there were approximately 1,000 requirements for this version; one third of which concerned satisfying safety requirements, while the remainder consisted of requirements for new functionality from the product management.

The size of the requirements varied from a small design requirement to a communication protocol. Figure 18.1 shows one example of a requirement for functionality and one for safety, respectively. Teams were set up and requirements were distributed among teams based on physical units, experience with these units and on which teams had available resources. There was no initial grouping of requirements to logical units of functionality. Each team was responsible for producing a set of documents with UML models.

C and C++ were used in the software implementation. UML version 1.3 and Rational Rose was used for modelling. UML-based development is, in general, being used increasingly in embedded development and much of the software was embedded. [15].

The project consisted of several sub-projects. The three sub-projects that developed safety software and applied the ABB UML method are described briefly below.

Sub-project A, the largest one, developed software based on a comprehensive existing code base. This includes code running both on a Windows PC platform and on an embedded 32 bit RISC processor. The developers on this project were mainly located in Sweden at site 1, but some work was done in Norway.

req. id	definition:	pri: 1	SIL ≥ 2
SR- DGN- 034	MEMORY INTEGRITY VERIFICATION all volatile memory shall be tested cyclically to support the diagnostic coverage achieved with the used 1oo2 memory architecture.	stability: stable	source: technical management
		Req. Type: safety function	
	Motivation: this is necessary in order to detect dormant failures also in unused areas of the memory. This is one of the necessary measures to enable use of (limited) dynamic memory allocation. NOTE: With either "double memory" or "double and inverted" storage in single memory architectures, low effectiveness will be sufficient (stuck-at faults). In this case, the cycle-time requirement is based on EN 298, i.e. considered as a second fault that has to be detected within 24 h.		
req. id	Definition:	pri: 1	SIL ≥ 2
PR- DLV- 033	ENHANCED CPU2R PROCESSOR MODULE There shall be a enhanced CPU2R, PM865, processor module with necessary functionality for SIL 2 certification, available.	stability: stable	source: product management
		req. type: System Architecture, HW	
	motivation: market requirement to meet the requirements for SIL 2 with the safety controller. In addition, to reach an SIL 3 classification of the safety system when used together with the SM in a 1oo2 structure, this module must comply fully with the applicable requirements for SIL 2. *Note:* This processor module shall be based on the PM864.		

Fig. 18.1. Examples of requirements

- Sub-project B developed hardware and embedded software for a 32 bit RISC processor. The project was divided into two teams: the hardware team, which dealt with electronic and mechanical design, and the software team. This sub-project had no existing systems to relate to. It was mainly located in Sweden at site 2.

- Sub-project C developed C code in the form of embedded software for a 16 bit processor. This sub-project was the only one that generated code automatically from their UML models. This sub-project had no existing systems to relate to. It was located in Norway.

18.2.3 The ABB UML Method

ABB has an existing methodological framework into which UML-based development was introduced. The overall ABB development method follows closely a traditional V-model for development with ten major phases, each of which has a corresponding test, verification or validation counterpart. The method is used together with the ABB Gate model for projects, which defines the milestones for decision making in a project [1].

The goal of the ABB UML method is to cover the lower part of the V-model, from requirements analysis to functional testing. The first time the method was used, emphasis was mostly on analysis and design. The relations between the V-model, the Gate model and the ABB UML method are shown in Fig. 18.2. G0 ...G6 refers to the gates of the Gate model and indicate when these are passed.

The ABB UML method was developed internally. It was not based on any particular method for UML-based development, but those responsible for it had experience with development based on UML, and were familiar with basic literature on such development, for example [4, 7, 10]. The main reason why UML-based development was chosen as a basis for a semi-formal development method was the good tool support for modelling with UML. The ABB UML method is generic and thus had, at its inception, no particular relevance to the specifics of software development in ABB. The company's plan was to start with a basic method and develop it in response to experience gained from the projects in which it is used.

The ABB Gate Model stipulates that project documents should be reviewed at specific milestones in the project. As a consequence, the ABB UML method is document-driven. The development process is centred on two documents: the *description of function* (DOF), which describes the results of the requirements analysis, and the *design description* (DD). There were predefined templates for these documents. The UML models were inserted into these documents automatically, using Rational Rose and Rational SoDA.[1] The models are reviewed only as part of the documents.

The ABB UML method prescribes the use of use cases, sequence diagrams, deployment diagrams and class diagrams. The use of state chart diagrams and activity diagrams is optional. The method provides guidelines for the requirements analysis of both software and hardware, guidelines for the design of software, and guidelines for using Rational Rose. In addition, there are guidelines aimed specifically at satisfying the safety standard [11]. Iterations are encouraged within each phase, and the phases in the development project should, to some extent, be conducted in parallel; that is, the analysis phase does not need to be completed before starting on the design phase or on the implementation. The ABB UML method (framed in Fig. 18.2) was the subject of evaluation in this case study, not the complete V model. The steps of the ABB UML method are shown in Appendix A.

---

[1] Information about both tools can be found at www.rational.com.

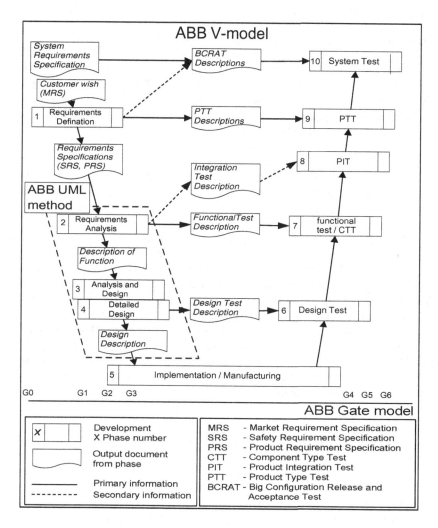

Fig. 18.2. Development in ABB

18.3 Research Method

The overall research method applied here is a case study [28]. Case studies can be exploratory, descriptive or explanatory. This case study can best be characterized as exploratory due to the lack of previous case studies on UML-based development. Case studies are most suitable for investigating research questions of the types *what, how* and *why*. In this study, we investigate *how* the company's development process was improved by adopting UML-based development, *what* particular difficulties were encountered with the use of UML and provide some explanations for *why* these difficulties occurred.

18.3.1 Data Collection

ABB wanted the opinions of the project members on the ABB UML method. Interviews were conducted with 16 people who had experience with the ABB UML
method in the project. The authors selected the interviewees so that all the sites,
subprojects and roles in the project were represented. Table 18.1 shows the distribution of the interviewees. Sub-project B was the only one involving hardware
and software development and so we included interviewees concerned with both
aspects of development. ABB did not have sufficiently detailed historical data
from previous projects that could be used in the assessment of this project and to
supplement the interviews.

All the developers interviewed had applied the ABB UML method. Two of the
managers had also done some development and applied the method, while others
had reviewed project documents that contained UML. Some of the interviewees
had had positive experiences when applying UML in previous projects, but those
projects were smaller than the project under study and did not have the same
safety requirements. Most interviewees, however, had no particular expectations
regarding the ABB UML method at the start of the project, but applied it because
they had to in order to satisfy the safety standard. The interviewees' experience in
ABB varied from approximately two years to more than 25 years.

The interview guide was developed by the authors. The interviews were semi-
structured, based on the interview guide shown in Appendix B, but adapted to
each interviewee. The aim was to encourage the interviewees to speak freely about
the different aspects of the project and the ABB UML method. Each interview
lasted from 30 to 50 min, and was conducted by two researchers not employed by
ABB (the first and fourth authors).

Table 18.1. Distribution of interviewees

project\site	Norway	Sweden site 1	Sweden site 2	total
sub-project A	2 developers	1 proj. manager 3 developers		6
sub-project B			1 proj. manager s/w 1 developer s/w 1 proj. manager h/w 1 developer h/w	4
sub-project C	1 proj. manager 1 developer			2
overall project	1 manager 1 quality manager 1 system architect	1 quality manager		4
total	7	5	4	16

18.3.2 The Analysis Procedure

The interviews were taped and transcribed before analysis. The interviewees had backgrounds that varied enormously. Consequently, not all of the questions in the interview guide were answered by all the interviewees. Some of the questions were open-ended and were answered differently by the different interviewees. It is, therefore, not feasible to report answers on the individual questions. Instead, the transcribed interviews were analyzed according to the principles of grounded theory [25], as well as on advice in the literature on the analysis of interviews [8, 22]. There is no standard way of analyzing in-depth interviews, and papers seldom describe in detail how such analysis is done [13]. Consequently, we had to identify for ourselves a suitable way of doing the analysis in this case. We decided to do it in the following steps:

1. Identify categories for coding. The categories are shown in Appendix C. There are categories for the following: interviewees' expectations, experience and training, possible improvements, opinions about project characteristics, and difficulties related to the use of UML. The categories are based on the interview guide and on experience gained from the actual interviews. The categories related to improvements are based principally on the expectations that ABB had when the method was introduced, and the categories related to project characteristics are the results of project decisions that could cause problems.
2. Code the interviews. All the relevant sentences in the interviews were coded according to one or more categories. The interviewees often expressed themselves in many words, so some of the sentences from the interview were simplified to facilitate the rest of the analysis.

Several iterations of steps 1 and 2 were performed, in order to identify an appropriate set of categories.

3. Sort the sentences. All sentences related to possible improvements were sorted into descriptive (describing the area), positive (supporting an improvement) and negative (opposing an improvement). With respect to the sentences about difficulties with UML and problematic project challenges there were only sentences describing these as problematic.
4. Check background of interviewees. The varying backgrounds of the interviewees meant that not all of them had experience with each topic. Hence, for improvements within the specific topics, we examined who of the interviewees had experience that would enable them to have an opinion. For project characteristics, we examined who had found each characteristic to be problematic.
5. Identify relationships. Relationships were identified between project characteristics and difficulties related to the use of UML. A project characteristic was considered to be one cause of a UML problem if it was explicitly mentioned as such or the two were mentioned together in the interview in a way that strongly indicated a relationship.

18.4 Improvements in the Development Process

We have refined ABB's expectations for improvement in the different areas:

A1: Traceability, defined as support for the construction of models that enables traceability from requirements to code.
A2: Communication, defined as ease of discussing design and implementation both within the development teams and in reviews.
A3: Design, defined as support for design activities as well as perceived structural properties of the code.
A4: Documentation, defined as documentation of code for the purpose of passing reviews (gates) as well as expected future maintainability.
A5: Testing, defined as ease of making functional test cases and their coverage.
A6: Development costs.

The positive and negative sentences related to each of the areas were used to establish the extent to which there were improvements. Not all the interviewees mentioned potential improvements in all areas. There are several reasons for this. One interviewee was the manager for the whole safety project and did not have opinions on specific aspects of the development process, but had opinions on documentation and costs. For three of the interviewees, this was their first project in ABB. Hence, they did not have opinions on whether there were improvements.

The only exception was with respect to documentation, because they had read the documentation of previous projects. In addition, one of the interviewees had not been involved in testing, two had not been deeply involved in development and had no opinions on design and traceability, and three had worked in small teams that had not been involved in reviews and could not have opinions about communication.

Table 18.2 shows the interviewees' opinions related to A5 about testing. Each row represents the opinion(s) of one interviewee. Five of the interviewees had only positive opinions, while six had both positive and negative opinions, although mostly positive. Table 18.3 shows the results of the coding of the interviews with respect to the different areas for improvement. The table shows how many of the interviewees mentioned each of the areas, how many had only positive opinions, and how many had only negative opinions.

Most of the interviewees with both positive and negative opinions were, however, mostly positive as in the example in Table 18.2. Table 18.3 shows improvements on all aspects except development costs, which were considered to have increased due to the introduction of UML-based development. The interviewees had, however, also experienced difficulties with all aspects. Table 18.2 is a summary of how and the extent to which each aspect was improved.

Table 18.2. Opinions on testing

positive	Negative
the analysis and design models are input to testing and that works quite well, that is, it has led to a better focus on completeness	the UML models are too large and detailed to be used effectively
it has been easy to make test cases, and the results of the tests are good	there were uncertainties about how to test and how to document the tests
the test cases were planned already during analysis. We did not do that before	
test cases were defined early and in a structured manner. This job, which would normally be big, took only one day. Testing has revealed higher quality in terms of fewer errors[a]	
we detect more errors now[a]	
it is much easier to write the functional test cases when we have use cases	the use cases are often too detailed and then the test cases get too detailed as well
we have used sequence diagrams in the testing. We have detected errors that we would not have detected otherwise	
the testers should now know how to write test specifications because they are based on UML	I am not certain that the testers always apply use cases and sequence diagrams in testing
the use of UML has had a positive effect on the number of defects[a]	the testers have not been trained in UML and consequently do not use the UML-diagrams as input as much as they should
we use the UML models to generate test cases. It is now a lot easier than before to identify which test cases must be run after an update	
working with UML in a structured manner provided a better basis for testing	I do not think that this has led to a large difference with respect to testing since we did not succeed very well in the earlier phases

[a]The different sub-projects had different amounts of defects

Table 18.3. Results on possible improvements

improvement	Mentioned by	only positive	only negative
A1: Traceability	10	3	2
A2: Communication	9	5	3
A3: Design	10	5	2
A4: Documentation	16	8	3
A5: Testing	11	5	0
A6: Costs	12	0	12

Traceability. The method was considered to give good support for tracing from requirements to code and vice versa. This represented an improvement compared with the previous situation with only textual descriptions of analysis and design, and it helped ensure that all requirements were implemented. The interviewees had struggled somewhat with the tool to make it accept external references to the textual requirements. The large amount of legacy code, of which large parts were not reverse engineered, means that not all the code in the product can be traced back to the requirements.

Design of the code. The use of the ABB UML method dictated a greater focus on design than had been the case previously. The interviewees thought that people had come to realize the importance of designing before coding, which realization had resulted in an improved design. Previously, a prototype would often evolve into code, while now the development is more top-down, and a design framework is available before coding starts. In particular, the interviewees considered that the use of sequence diagrams forced them to design thoroughly. Some found, however, that there was not sufficient support in the method for combining top-down and bottom-up development, something which was necessary when many building blocks were already available in the form of hardware components or legacy code.

Documentation. This project was better documented, both in terms of quantity and quality, than previous software development projects in ABB. The documents now had a more unified structured with respect to content, and the interviewees found it easier to read them because of the common structure. The interviewees thought that more software developers can learn UML than learn to express themselves well in English. In addition, several of the interviewees emphasized that the developers found it more fun to make diagrams than to write textual documentation; hence, they produced more a comprehensive set of analysis and design documents. The interviewees found use cases and sequence diagrams to be particularly useful. They had, however, experienced difficulties with the format of the documents due to problems with the templates, such as which parts of the UML models were automatically inserted into the documents and the numbering of the sections in the documents. The documents were also often very large because the project members found it difficult to know how much context they should include in their models in order to describe their own part. Some documents, for example, contained several hundred pages describing only one piece of functionality. Some interviewees from sub-projects A and B, the sub-projects which did not generate code from the UML models, thought that they spent too much effort on producing documentation during the project that would be outdated when the product was finished. Those who generated code automatically also reverse engineered their code to update their models and did not experience this problem.

Testing. The development of test cases became quicker and easier when the UML models were available, and the coverage of the test cases had improved. On the negative side, the large amount of detail in the UML models made them difficult to use as input to testing. Not all the testers had received training in UML, which meant that they could not easily apply the UML-based test cases, and consequently these were used less often in testing than they could have been.

Costs. There were, of course, costs related to learning a new method. The introduction of a new method also led to much rework. For example, some of the interviewees rewrote the *description of function* several times, due to a revised understanding of the nature of use cases. The amount of detail in the analysis models meant that these sometimes had to be updated later in the project. The interviewees had also expended a great deal of effort on discussing how to best apply UML, both within the teams and in the reviews. In addition, the reviews were considered to have taken more time because the documents were produced with a new method. The interviewees found it difficult to estimate how much the introduction of UML-based development had cost in terms of extra effort, but several of them guessed that it had doubled the effort on the project. The interviewees thought, however, that there might be improvements with respect to costs on future projects, when they could benefit from the documentation made on this project and the team members would be more experienced.

18.5 Challenges in the Project

The previous section showed that the interviewees had experienced several improvements to their development process as a consequence of introducing UML-based development, but also that difficulties with using UML, in combination with characteristics of the project that were the results of project management decisions, had caused difficulties and thus had reduced the possible positive effects of introducing such a development method. This section describes the difficulties experienced by the interviewees, the project characteristics that were considered to cause most problems and how these characteristics affected the use of UML.

18.5.1 Project Characteristics and their Consequences

The interviewees mentioned four characteristics of the project that contributed to the difficulties with using UML and that had led to problems with obtaining the desired improvements. These characteristics were the consequences of project

Table 18.4. Opinions on aspects of the project

project characteristics	mentioned by	comment
legacy code	6	mentioned by all people from sub-project A, which was the project that had to integrate with legacy code.
org. of req. and teams	5	mentioned by those with the most experience or interest in UML-based development.
training and mentoring	10	mentioned mostly by those who had received in-house training and had a positive attitude to the method.
Tool	10	mentioned by interviewees from most of the project

management decisions made because of budget and timing constraints in the project: (1) it was considered too costly to reverse engineer into UML the large amount of legacy code that the project had to modify and integrate with, (2) the requirements were distributed to the teams based on physical, and not functional, units of the system, (3) it was considered too costly to provide thorough training for all people involved in the project, (4) the choice of tools for the modelling process possessed functionality that was not in accordance with the needs of the project. Table 18.4 shows how many of the interviewees described difficulties with the four project attributes. The table also describes the interviewees who mentioned the characteristics.

Legacy code

Reverse engineering of the complete existing code base before the start of the project was considered too difficult, and consequently too expensive. The ABB UML method stipulates that the parts of the existing code that will integrate with the new code should be reverse engineered into UML models. It also stipulates that interfaces should be identified in these models and that modelling of the new system should use these interfaces, but there is little support on how to actually do this in the method. UML-based development methods mostly assume development from scratch, and to the authors' knowledge, there is little methodological support for using UML when modifying existing, non-object-oriented systems, even though it is often necessary and also recommended to introduce UML into an existing production environment [23]. The interviewees described the problems related to the large amount of legacy code that was not reverse engineered, and the consequences of these problems. An example of statements about integration with, and modification of, legacy code is given in Table 18.5. Each row relates the opinion of one interviewee.

Table 18.5. Statements related to having legacy code

those who had to integrate with legacy code had a much tougher job using this method than had those who developed from scratch, because we have not succeeded in reverse engineering all of the system; for example, not the parts that were very C-oriented. This means that we often did not have UML interfaces in the existing code, and it was necessary with so many adaptations in the code to integrate the new parts that we felt that we might as well document and test

the person I worked with implemented new functionality in the existing code and met bigger problems than I, who developed from scratch, did. He had a new part, modelled in UML. To realize it, the old code had to be changed almost every second line. Then it was difficult to view the old system as a black box

we experienced problems because we added to functionality that was not functionally documented, and to design properly, for example, using a state diagram, you need an existing design that builds on a state diagram. For the most part, the legacy code was not designed in such a way

the main problem was having existing code that should be modified. It was necessary to know which parts of the old system should be included in the models in order to describe the new part correctly. I believe it would have been much easier if we had developed from scratch. Reverse engineering resulted in very large design documents where only a small part was useful when modelling the new functionality

we added new functionality to an existing, complex software system that was badly documented. In addition, the templates and guidelines that we used were not adapted to integration with legacy code

We modelled against a system that was not object-oriented. There were not, for example, always classes or interfaces in the old code that we could use, so we had to simulate that there were interfaces at the points where we needed them.

Figure 18.3 shows the interviewees' opinions about the consequences of having to deal with a large amount of legacy code. Each statement from the interviewees is categorized to clarify the relationships. The main consequences were the following:

- Difficulties with identifying which parts of the architecture implemented which parts of the functionality, and how the new requirements related to the existing functionality. This created difficulties when distributing requirements to teams.
- Both developers and reviewers had difficulties with abstracting away from the code in analysis and design when they knew the existing code well. This contributed to analysis and design models with too much detail.

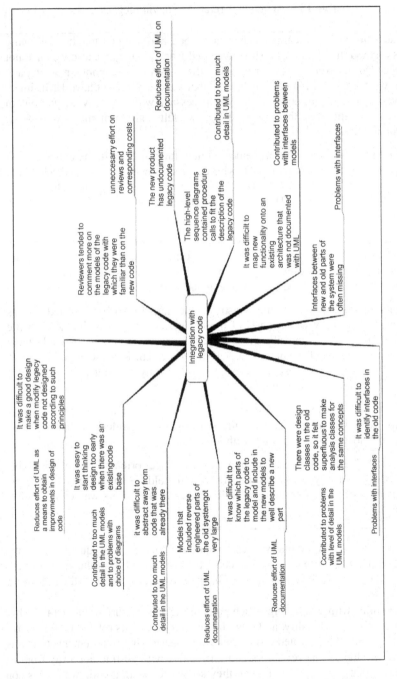

Fig. 18.3. Consequences of modifying legacy code

- Difficulties with identifying clear-cut interfaces to the old code that could be used in the new models. It was necessary to know the old code well in order to know how much of it had to be modelled to document the new part well.
- General problems with obtaining benefits with respect to design when applying UML because they had to know, and adapt to, the existing code.

Organization of Requirements and Teams

The distribution of requirements to teams was mostly done before beginning to use the ABB UML method. It was done based on physical units, previous experience and on which teams had available resources. There were approximately 1000 requirements for the new system, but these were not organized hierarchically. The ABB UML method states that identical functionality should be identified and separated out as included use cases, but there was no organized activity of identifying similar functionality over several teams; nor was there any activity on integrating the different models and ensuring unified interfaces. Figure 18.4 shows the interviewees' opinions about the consequences of not organizing and distributing requirements to teams based on functionality and not organizing cooperation among teams that were developing functionality that interacted with the functionality being developed by other teams. The main consequences were the following:

- The focus was often on physical components as such and not on functionality.
- Related functionality was not always distributed to the same team, meaning that it was often difficult to map requirements to use cases.
- One analysis model did not necessarily correspond to a logical part of the system. Hence, it was difficult to integrate different models, and in some cases there was overlapping functionality in different models.

Training and Mentoring

Most of the developers were novices at modelling with UML when starting to work on this project. Otherwise, they were well-qualified developers (most holding the equivalent of an MSc degree) and with several years experience at ABB. They were familiar with both the V-model and Gate model. At the start of the project, they attended courses of two to five days that covered UML syntax, Rational Rose tools and the ABB UML method. A special team, the UML team, was set up to help the rest of the project with the use of UML, which included responsibility for developing templates and for reviewing documents, with particular focus on the correct use of UML. The number of people in the UML team varied from three to five over the course of the project.

The interviewees reported that there had been too little training because managers, reviewers and testers, who did not themselves develop, did not receive training even though they had to read and understand the models. Some of them

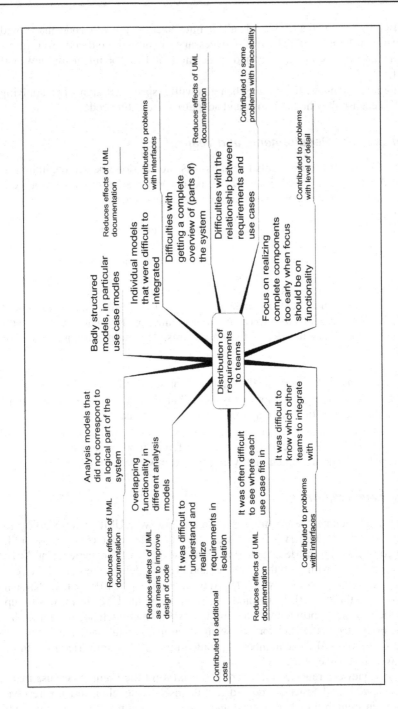

Fig. 18.4. Consequences of unsystematic distribution of requirements to teams

also had roles that required them to motivate and teach others to use UML correctly. Developers who started on the project after the courses did not receive the same training as the others.

There were also problems reported with the training they received. The interviewees said that the courses focused too much on UML syntax and too little on the ABB UML method and semantics of diagrams and constructs. There were not enough practical exercises on using the tools and it was not made clear what should actually be achieved by modelling. It was considered necessary, but not sufficient, to master the syntax in order to apply UML successfully. The courses were developed for the project, but not adapted to the specific context.

The interviewees believed that the UML team was not sufficiently qualified, and did not have sufficient authority, to guide the total use of UML in the project. The reason was that the members of the UML team lacked the necessary experience with both development and UML. At the beginning of the project there were some senior developers in the team, but these were considered too important for the rest of the project to be given time to spend on the UML team. The members of the UML team did not receive additional training in UML-based development. Figure 18.5 shows the interviewees' opinions on the consequences of these problems. The main consequences were these:

- It was not well understood how to apply the concepts of actors and use cases in the context of embedded development.
- There were large differences in how the different teams applied UML and the method.
- Those who had attended courses often expected to be able to use the course material directly in the development, but this caused difficulties since the material was not adapted to the project context.
- The templates that were used in the project were not sufficiently adapted to the project context.
- The project members did not always use UML-models when they could have used them. UML-models were, for example, not always applied as input to making test cases.

Tools used in Modelling and Documenting

Some of the interviewees believed that Rational Rose lacked stability, but they were mostly satisfied with its functionality. Rational Rose SoDA was used to produce documents automatically from the models in Rational Rose; that is, the models were inserted into predefined Word-templates. The interviewees reported that it was difficult to create documents with an acceptable layout when the models were inserted into documents automatically. For example, the developers were unable to set the text fonts in the UML-models in Rational Rose, and they did not succeed in controlling the numbering of the sections in the documents. Therefore, they had to make quite a lot of changes to the automatically generated documents, and consequently it was costly to make changes in the models because this implied generating new documents.

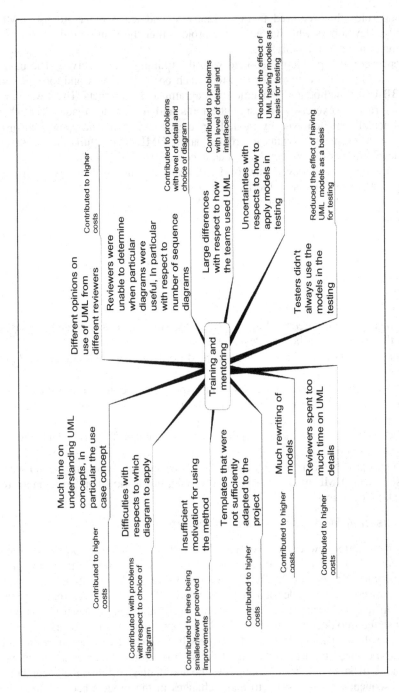

Fig. 18.5. Consequences of insufficient training and mentoring

In addition, the interviewees thought that Rational Rose may also have contributed somewhat to the low level of detail in the high-level sequence diagrams because Rational Rose facilitates in the sequence diagrams, the use of classes and methods that have already been defined in class diagrams.

18.5.2. Difficulties with Using UML

The previous section described project decisions that caused problems with applying UML and thus reduced the effect of introducing UML-based development. The interviewees mentioned three main difficulties with applying UML: (1) the choice of diagram to use in a specific situation, (2) the interfaces between models, and (3) the level of detail in the models. Table 18.6 shows how many of the interviewees mentioned problems with each of the aspects.

Choice of Diagrams

Some interviewees reported problems with the choice of diagram to apply. They found that there was too much focus on use cases and sequence diagrams in the ABB UML method, and thought that activity diagrams could be more useful early in analysis when few actual objects have been identified. More use of activity diagrams could have contributed to deterring the focus on detailed classes. The interviewees had, however, focused on making the UML models that were compulsory in the ABB UML method, since they did not feel that they had a good enough grasp of the goal of applying each of the models to choose when to apply which. The lack of insight into exactly what each model should express also meant that the interviewees found it difficult to know when it was necessary to supplement the models with text and when the models were self-contained.

Interfaces

The interviewees had experienced large problems with interfaces between models describing different, but interacting, parts of the system. Well-described interfaces were considered vital for understanding where each part fits in and to get an overview of the system, but most of the interviewees found that the interfaces were either missing or too detailed.

High-level interfaces were in the form of actors. In addition to actors that were external to the whole system, such as operators and hardware devices, the ABB UML stipulates that subsystems should be considered as actors for each other. These subsystems could be legacy code or other subsystems being developed in

Table 18.6. Results on difficulties with UML

UML aspect	mentioned by
choice of diagram	6
interfaces	10
level of detail	10

parallel. An actor mostly interacts with a subsystem in several places. In the modelling process, such low-level interfaces were marked with the symbol o. Such interfaces were gradually substituted with actual function calls when these were established. The interviewees had experienced several problems:

- For interfaces in the form of *actors that were not human users* it was more difficult to identify them and how they would interact with the system than for those actors that represented human users.
- Interfaces in *the legacy code* posed difficulties because the legacy code was only partially reverse engineered into UML models. Consequently, there were often few interfaces in the old code that could be used directly.
- Interfaces in *subsystems that were developed in parallel* also posed problems. The ABB UML method stipulates that the people responsible for the different subsystems should communicate about the exact nature of the interface. However, this was often difficult because the different subsystems were developed according to different schedules and some subsystems were developed mostly bottom-up, based on existing components, while others were developed top-down. The interviewees also reported that they did not have a good grasp of how to group use cases into subsystems, something that also contributed to the interfaces between the subsystems not being clear-cut.

Level of Detail

Examples of statements about level of detail in the models are given in Table 18.7. Each row relates the opinion of one interviewee. The main problems were these:

Table 18.7. Problems related to level of detail in the UML models

the embedded software interfaces hardware devices. Hardware developers are used to starting by specifying a number of registers that bits will be flipped in and out of. They do not think in terms of functionality to request or provide. This attitude leads to models that are too detailed; for example, high-level sequence diagrams showing actual function calls, and design models that were too large and complex and thus difficult to use
it was difficult to decide on the level of detail for the use cases. For example, do we need two or 20 use cases to describe the problem? We found out that it was easier to pass reviews with fewer use cases
it was difficult to understand the use case concept and to describe the correct use cases. We ended up with too much design in our use cases and our high-level sequence diagrams. This was, to a great extent, because we were describing a physical component of the system and found it difficult to start at a high level of abstraction. The difference between analysis and design was not clear
use cases can be described in a number of different ways, all of which are correct. In practice the development, and consequently the descriptions of the models, are always a mixture of top-down and bottom-up; that is, between describing functionality and considering the components of which a system will consist

Table 18.7. *(Contd.,)*

there were large differences between the level of detail of the use cases of the different teams. Some made only one large use case for a large function that could have been split up, while others made a large amount of use cases and a complex use case model for functions that were quite simple

we made more sequence diagrams than we actually needed in the analysis because the reviewers intended there to be a sequence diagram for each use case flow, regardless of how well that flow was described in the use case. The reviewers were unable to see when a sequence diagram would be useful and when it would not

we thought about code when we were supposed to focus on functionality. I think we should have made more effort to stay at a higher level of abstraction

we had large difficulties with our high-level classes. Since we already had implementation classes in the legacy code, we thought it quite was useless to have to invent some high-level classes

our UML models were often too detailed. During design we were constrained by our use cases and high-level sequence diagrams, since these were so detailed and included design

the design models have become very detailed. There is too much information in them and they are up to three hundred pages long

- The teams had started to think about code when the focus should have been on functionality. Both the use cases and the high-level sequence diagrams were considered to be too detailed, because they often included the same functions as the code.
- It was difficult to decide how to divide functionality into use cases and to decide how many sequence diagrams should be made for each use case.
- The distinction between analysis and design was not clear. The analysis models included design details and were consequently often difficult to use in the design, because they constrained the design models.

18.6 Scope and Validity of the Results

This section describes the scope and validity of the case study reported in this paper.

18.6.1 Scope of the Results

This case study was conducted on a large, distributed development project with a great deal of legacy code. The project included development of embedded software as well as software for the Windows platform. The project members were mostly newcomers to the use of UML. In the authors' opinion, most of the experiences gained from this project are relevant for other large projects that introduce UML-based development. There are, however, a number of aspects particular to this project.

- Much of the software to be developed was real-time and embedded. The ABB UML method was not particularly tailored to this kind of development. Only one of the interviewees stated, however, that he missed particular real-time features. Object-oriented modelling and UML-based development may be less suited for development of embedded software because the concepts of actors and use cases are more difficult to apply to a system where there is not so much external communication and because many of the objects are established in advance.
- The ABB UML method was applied within an overall development process with focus on the acceptance of project documents at predefined gates in the development project. This meant that the documents with the UML models, and not the models themselves, were subject to review. Many of the interviewees had experienced difficulties with the format of these documents, and that may have overshadowed their opinions on UML-based development as such.
- The requirements were well-defined before the application of the ABB UML method. The safety requirements were derived from IEC 61508. Most of the functional requirements were the result of the system's relations to hardware artifacts, while some of them were responses to the needs of users of the system, such as process operators and engineers. This meant that the functional requirements were mostly independent of users' needs and abilities to define requirements. Use cases are claimed to be particularly useful for eliciting and elaborating functional requirements, but such activities were not part of this project, and use case modelling may, therefore, have been considered less useful than it would have been if such activities had been included.
- The use cases were constructed solely by developers who were also domain experts. ABB develops products for sale, and consequently there were no clients involved in the development process. This probably contributed to the low level of detail in the use case models.
- The teams had worked in a very vertical way, mostly with one team being responsible for analysis, design and coding. The benefits of analysis and design with UML may have been greater if the analysis and/or design models had been handed over to other teams for further elaboration. In addition, in practice, not all steps of the ABB UML method were necessarily followed by all teams. Absolute conformance to a development method is, however, seldom observed in software development projects [9], and in this case the safety constraints forced the developers to produce all the UML-models stipulated by the ABB UML method.

ABB chose UML-based development because of good tool support. We believe that the project would have experienced many of the same improvements and challenges if they had chosen another modelling language and method as a basis for their improvement initiative. However, we do believe that there are some matters that are particular to UML-based development. The use of use case diagrams may lead to a focus on the overall system rather than on the individual parts. The packages in Rational Rose may also have contributed to an awareness of each team working on a part of a larger system. In this case, the system to be constructed was too large and complex to easily provide an overall picture of its functionality. Many of the difficulties reported in the interviews were related to problems with describing models and their interfaces in such a way that they could provide an overview of the system. These difficulties may have been lessened if a method for analysis and design had been used that had less focus on overall functionality and more on detailed design.

18.6.2 Validity of the Results

The results of this study are based on interviews with the project participants, and our measures are their perceived improvements and problems. The interviewees were selected to represent different parts of the project and they all had experience with using UML on the project. The people present at the interviews (the first and fourth author) were not employed by ABB, and the interviewees were guaranteed anonymity. The impression of the interviewers is that the interviewees spoke freely. The conduct of interviews and confidentiality issues are discussed further in [12] which is, among others, based on the experiences from the interviews conducted in ABB.

With respect to validity of results based on interviews there are, in particular, two aspects of validity to consider [18]:

- Descriptive validity, that is, whether the interviewees' opinions are rendered correctly. In this case, the interviews were transcribed, based on tapes, by the research assistant who had been present at, but not directly involved in, the interviewing. The analysis was based on these transcribes.
- Interpretive validity, that is, whether the interviews are correctly interpreted. In this case, the interviewees spoke very informally, and ten of the interviewees were Swedish. Consequently, it was necessary to translate and rewrite the transcriptions somewhat before the coding of the interviews. It is possible that the meaning of some individual sentences may have been altered slightly in this process. The categories used in the analysis are the result of several iterations on coding the interviews, and previous iterations also included other categories for coding that were discarded because very few sentences in the interviews were coded according to them. These categories were requirements analysis, the method description and the syntax of UML in relation to improvements, project decisions and difficulties with UML, respectively. Three project members, who had not been interviewed, also read through and verified a draft of this paper.

There are few empirical studies on UML-based development with which to compare our results. Nevertheless, some of our results are supported by the results reported in a paper with lessons learned from developing embedded software [21]. That paper also reports improved communication, in particular between software and systems engineers, due to the introduction of UML-based development, as well as challenges with respect to describing interfaces between UML models. Our results are also supported by the results from a study on the introduction of object-oriented development [17]. The experiences reported in that paper also emphasize the need for sufficient training, reverse engineering of legacy code, and adequate distribution of subsystems to teams, as well as the economic challenges involved in these activities in projects working on a tight schedule. Furthermore, some of our results are supported by the results from a study on the usability of UML diagrams [2]. That study also revealed difficulties with understanding the concept of use cases and describing them with appropriate detail, as well as with modelling interface objects in class diagrams. Difficulties with level of detail in use case models have been mentioned, for example, in [3, 5, 16].

18.7 Conclusions and Future Work

This paper reports the results of a case study on adopting UML and an associated UML-based development method in a large, international development project in ABB. This project developed a new version of a safety-critical process control system. Much of the work was concerned with modifying existing systems. The project was carried out by several teams located at four sites in three countries. The UML-based development method had been developed in-house in ABB, and before the introduction of this method, there was no common method in the company for the analysis and design of software.

Data was collected through interviews with 16 developers and managers. Principles from grounded theory were used in the analysis of the interviews.

The interviewees had obtained several immediate improvements as a consequence of introducing a UML-based development method. These were improved traceability of requirements to code, improved communication within the development teams (and to some extent in the reviews), improved design of the code, quicker development of test cases and better coverage of these, and a product that was better documented than were previous products. The interviewees also stated that there had been difficulties related to obtaining these improvements and also that development costs had increased due to the adoption of UML. When applying UML, the interviewees had experienced difficulties with choosing an appropriate diagram in a specific situation, interfaces between different models, and with the level of detail in the models. There were four decisions made at the start of the project that the interviewees identified as having caused problems with the use of UML. These were related to lack of reverse engineering of legacy code, unsystematic distribution of requirements to teams, insufficient training and mentoring, and choice of modelling tools.

Despite the widespread use of UML in industry, there has been little evaluation of UML-based development in industrial projects. In the authors' opinion, this study thus represents a contribution to the body of knowledge regarding benefits and challenges involved in adopting UML-based development that should provide valuable input to the development of a theory in the field as well as to practitioners. The ABB UML method has also been changed, partly based on the results from this study.

The following activities are in progress, or are planned, in order to further evaluate the use of UML-based development in ABB. First, a questionnaire, with questions based on the results of the interviews, has been distributed to the participants in the project to investigate specific aspects of the development process in more detail. Second, project documents from the project, in the form of UML-documents, review reports and test reports are being analyzed, to identify what changes were made to the analysis models and what caused these changes to be made. Third, more case studies on the adoption, adaptation and use of UML-based development in various types of projects are needed to better understand how such development should be applied to improve software development processes.

Acknowledgements

We acknowledge all the employees of ABB in Sweden and Norway who participated in the interviews and their managers. We thank Lionel Briand for valuable comments on the case study, and we also thank Hans Christian Benestad, Vigdis By, Dag Sjøberg, Marek Vokác, Ray Welland, Chris Wright and the anonymous reviewers for their comments on a previous version of the paper. The reported work was funded by The Research Council of Norway through the industry project SPIKE (Software Process Improvement based on Knowledge and Experience).

References

[1] ABB Gate Model for Product Development 1.1 tech. report 9AAD102113, ABB/GP-PMI, Västerås, Sweden, 2001

[2] Agarwal, R. and Sinha, A.P. (2003) Object-Oriented Modeling with UML: A Study of Developers' Perceptions, Communications of the ACM, Vol. 46, No. 9, pp. 248–256

[3] Armour, F. and Miller, G. (2000) *Advanced Use Case Modelling*, Addison-Wesley

[4] Booch, G., Rumbaugh, J., and Jacobson, I. (1998) *The Unified Modeling Language User Guide*, Addison-Wesley

[5] Cockburn, A. (2000) *Writing Effective Use Cases*, Addison-Wesley

[6] Cox, K. and Phalp, K. (2000) Replicating the CREWS Use Case Authoring Guidelines Experiment, *Empirical Software Engineering*, Vol. 5, No. 3, pp. 245–267

[7] Douglass, B.P. (2004) *Real Time UML: Advances in the UML for Real-Time Systems*, 3rd Edition, Addison-Wesley, Boston, MA

[8] Eisenhardt, K.M. (1989) Building Theories from Case Study Research, *Academy of Management Review*, Vol. 14, No. 4, pp. 532–550

[9] Fitzgerald, B. (1997) The Use of Systems Development Methodologies in Practice: A Field Study, *Information Systems Journal*, Vol. 7, pp. 201–212

[10] Fowler, M. (2003) UML Distilled, *A Brief Guide to the Standard Object Modelling Language,* 3rd edition, Addison-Wesley

[11] Hansen, K.T. and Gullesen, I. (2002) Utilizing UML and Patterns for Safety Critical Systems, in Jürjens et al. (eds.): Critical Systems Development with UML, number TUM-I 0208 in TUM technical report, UML'02 Satellite Workshop Proceedings

[12] Hove, S.E. and Anda, B. (2005) Experiences from Conducting Semi-Structured Interviews in Empirical Software Engineering Research, Accepted for presentation at Metrics 2005

[13] Huberman, A.M. and Miles, M.B. (2002) *The Qualitative Researcher's Companion*, SAGE, Inc., Thousand Oaks, CA

[14] IEC 61508: Functional safety of electrical/electronic/programmable electronic safety-related systems. 1998. (http://www.iec.ch/)

[15] Jürjens, J. (2003) Developing Safety-Critical Systems with UML, *Proceedings 6th International Conference on the Unified Modeling Language (UML 2003)*, edited by Stevens, P. *et al.*, pp. 360–372, Springer Berlin Heidelberg New York, LNCS 2863

[16] Kulak, D. and Guiney, E. (2000) *Use Cases: Requirements in Context*, Addison-Wesley

[17] Malan R., Coleman, D., and Letsinger, R. (1915) Lessons from the Experiences of Leading-Edge Object Technology Projects in Hewlett-Packard, *Proceedings OOPSLA 1995*, pp. 33–46

[18] Maxwell, J.A. (1992) Understanding and Validity in Qualitative Research, *Harvard Educational Review*, Vol. 62, No. 3, pp. 279–300

[19] Otero, M.C. and Dolado, J.J. (2002) An Initial Experimental Assessment of the Dynamic Modelling in UML, *Empirical Software Engineering*, Vol. 7, No. 1, pp. 27–47

[20] Peleg, M. and Dori, D. (2000) The Model Multiplicity Problem: Experimenting with Real-Time Specification Methods, *IEEE Transactions on Software Engineering*, Vol. 26, No. 8, pp. 742–759

[21] Pettit, R.G. (2004) Lessons Learned Applying UML in Embedded Software Systems Designs, *Proceedings of the Second IEEE Workshop on Software Technologies for Future Embedded and Ubiquitous Systems (WSTFEUS'04)*, pp. 75–79, Vienna, Austria

[22] Seaman, C.B. (1999) Qualitative Methods in Empirical Studies in Software Engineering, *IEEE Transactions on Software Engineering*, Vol. 25, No. 4, pp. 557–572

[23] Selic, B. (2003) The Pragmatics of Model-Driven Development. *IEEE Software*, Vol. 20, No. 5, pp. 19–25

[24] Sjøberg, D.I.K. *et al.* (2005) A Survey of Controlled Experiments in Software Engineering, To appear in *IEEE Transactions on Software Engineering*

[25] Strauss, A. and Corbin, J. (1998) *Basics of Qualitative Research: Techniques and Procedures for Developing Grounded Theory*, 2nd edition, SAGE, Inc., Thousand Oaks, CA

[26] The ABB Instruction (2001) Software and Hardware Development

[27] The ABB Guideline (2003) Guideline for Use of Semi-Formal Methods in Software and Hardware Design

[28] Yin, R. (2003) *Case Study Research: Design and Methods*, 3rd edition, SAGE, Inc., Thousand Oaks, CA

[29] Zendler, A. *et al.* (2001) Experimental Comparison of Coarse-Grained Concepts in UML, OML and TOS, *The Journal of Systems and Software*, Vol. 56, No. 4, pp. 21–30

Appendix 18.A – Brief Description of the ABB UML Method

The requirements analysis phase of the ABB UML method:

R1. Identify actors and use cases, and document them
Actors are the system's external interfaces. Humans, timers, sensors, or anything else that interacts with the system, can be an actor. For a use case diagram in a subsystem, other (interacting) subsystems should also be defined as actors.
  Use cases:
  – Define the system as seen from the actors' point of view.
  – Represent the different usage of the system and system services.
  – Capture the requirements.
  A use case is always initiated by an actor.

R2. Group use cases and actors into subsystems
  There should be strong cohesion within the subsystems and a weak coupling between the subsystems.

R3. Refine the use cases and identify dependencies
  If some use cases show common behaviour at specific points, and this commonality can be extracted without disturbing the main functionality, it can be factored out as a separate use case and included in the diagrams from which they were extracted using the <<include>> stereotype. If some use cases have behaviour that can be seen as additions to, or variations of, normal behaviour, such forms of behaviour can be factored out as separate use cases and included in the use cases from which they were extracted using the <<extend>> stereotype. The different possible extension points are listed inside the lower half of the use case, and each <<extend>> is marked with the connecting extension point.

The analysis phase of the ABB UML method:

A1. Describe flow of events inside the use case (textual)
  Describe each use case with the normal flows of events inside the use cases (each use case has at least one normal flow of events). Then capture the exceptional flows of events for each use case. This is done in several iterations.

A2. Create high-level sequence diagrams
  High-level sequence diagrams should be used to show the dynamics between the objects involved in the use case and the actors interfacing them, for both normal and exceptional flows of events. Objects of type inclusionPoint with the names of the included use cases, and objects of type extensionPoint with the <<extend>> names take the included and extended sequence diagrams' roles. Only objects with 'focus of control' or actors may initiate messages. A base use case transfers 'focus of control' to the object to which it sends a synchronous message, but it keeps the 'focus of control' if the message is

asynchronous. An object that receives a message gains "focus of control". Information contained in objects must be placed there by another object before it can be extracted, and it originates in an actor outside the system.

A3. Define interfaces between use cases in different subsystems
There are interfaces between the subsystems. In the use case diagrams there are dependency arrows from the use cases to their interfaces. The exact messages included in the interfaces are identified by those responsible for the subsystems that interact.

A4. Describe the activities in the use case in an activity diagram (Optional)
Activity diagrams should show the different activity states of the use case, for both normal and exceptional flows of events.

A5. Create high-level class diagrams
Identify high-level classes. A high-level class describes the commonality between similar objects in the sequence diagrams and defines the structure and behaviour for each object in the class. Assign objects to the correct classes. The interactions between the objects in the sequence diagrams help to identify the operations in the classes. The different messages will identify operations in the class of the receiving object. Find the information contents necessary to process each message in the sequence diagrams. This information will end up as attributes in the class of the receiving object.
The high-level class-diagram should show associations between the classes.

A6. Update sequence diagrams with correct high level class and operation names
When high-level class diagrams are made, the mapping back to the sequence diagrams must be done. Mark out in which technology the high-level class would be implemented (SW, VHDL, HW). These distinctions will be used when we start to build the component view.

The Detailed Design phase of the ABB UML Method (Note that the hardware developers did no detailed design):
Detail design (SW)
The goal of this phase is to realize the high-level classes with implementation class diagrams and to group the classes in components. The detailed class diagrams include relations between classes, operations and attributes. State transition diagrams may be used in the process of elaborating the class diagrams.
The detailed classes are connected to the high-level classes through a "realize" association. In this context, it makes sense to expose operation signature details for the high level classes.
The classes with strong coupling are typically candidates for a component, as are classes with the same implementation technology. When classes with strong coupling but different implementation technology are distributed to different components, an interface must be made to take care of the classes.

Appendix 18.B – Interview Guide

1. What is your professional background?
2. Can you describe your role in the project?
3. How well did you know UML and UML-based development at the start of this project?
4. What were your expectations when starting to use UML and the ABB UML method; what benefits and costs did you expect?
5. Have you previously worked on similar projects, with or without UML, so that you can compare experiences from that project with this one?
6. What are your opinions about the training you received?
7. With whom did you cooperate on the use of UML?
8. Did you have to adapt the ABB UML method in any way to the needs of the part of the system that you were modelling?
9. What is your experience with the different diagrams, use cases, sequence diagrams, class diagrams etc.?
10. Were there parts of the systems that you had problems modelling using UML?
11. How did you find the reviews?
12. Who are the receivers of the UML-models that you produce, apart from the reviewers?
13. What kinds of interface did your code have to other UML models or to existing code and how do you think you succeeded in modelling those interfaces?
14. What were, in your opinion, the costs involved in applying UML and the ABB UML method and what were the benefits?
15. Do you have any experience with maintenance of systems that are documented using UML?
16. Is there anything that you would have done differently if you could start all over again?
17. How would you rate the ease of comprehension of the UML models that you have read?
18. Do you believe that you can identify good use of UML; do you have any specific criteria?

Appendix 18.C – Categories for Coding of the Interviews

Background:
Expectations
Experience
Training (which)
Activities (in the project)

Possible improvements:
Traceability
Communication, Reviews
Design
Documentation
Test, Defects
Costs

Project characteristics:
Training, Mentoring (opinions)
UML team
Legacy code
Organization (of requirements and teams)
Tools, Templates

Use of UML:
Interfaces
Level of detail, Abstraction level
Choice of diagrams

19

An Empirical Study on Off-the-Shelf
Component Usage in Industrial Projects

J. Li, R. Conradi, O.P.N. Slyngstad, C. Bunse, U. Khan, M. Torchiano, and
M. Morisio

Abstract: Using OTS (Off-The-Shelf) components in software projects has become increasing popular in the IT industry. After project managers opt for OTS components, they
can decide to use COTS (Commercial-Off-The-Shelf) components or OSS (Open Source
Software) components instead of building these themselves. This paper describes an empirical study on why project decision-makers use COTS components instead of OSS components, or vice versa. The study was performed in form of an international survey on
motivation and risks of using OTS components, conducted in Norway, Italy and Germany.
We have currently gathered data on 71 projects using only COTS components and 39 projects using only OSS components, and five using both COTS and OSS components. Results
show that both COTS and OSS components were used in small, medium and large software
houses and IT consulting companies. The overall software system also covers several
application domains. Both COTS and OSS were expected to contribute to shorter time-to-
market, less development effort and the application of newest technology. However, COTS
users believe that COTS component should have good quality, technical support, and will
follow the market trend. OSS users care more about the free ownership and openness of the
source code. Projects using COTS components had more difficulties in estimating selection
effort, following customer requirement changes, and controlling the component's negative
effect on system security. On the other hand, OSS user had more difficulties in getting the
support reputation of OSS component providers.

19.1 Introduction

Due to market requirements concerning cost and time-to-market, software developers are searching for new technologies to improve their projects with respect to
these qualities. Software components promise to have a positive impact on software reuse, resulting in time and cost efficient development. Therefore, software
developers are using an increasing amount of COTS (Commercial-Off-The-Shelf)
and OSS (Open Source Software) components in their projects. Although both
COTS and OSS component are claimed to save development effort, they are still
very different. COTS components are owned by commercial vendors, and their

users normally do not have access to the source code of these components. On the other hand, OSS components are provided by open source communities. Thus, they offer full control on the source code [15].

When planning a new software project, project decision makers need to decide whether they should buy a COTS component, or acquire an OSS component if it was decided to use OTS components. To make such a decision, it is important to investigate previous projects using such components and summarize the relevant decision-making processes and project results.

The study presented in this paper has investigated 71 finished software projects using only COTS components and 39 projects using only OSS components. It compared the COTS components with the OSS components in three dimensions: (1) who is using OTS components, (2) why project members decide to use them, and (3) what were the results of using them.

The remainder of this paper is organized as follows: Section 19.2 presents some previous studies on benefits and risks of using OTS components. Section 19.3 describes the research design applied. Section 19.4 presents the collected data, whereby the discussion of results is given in Sect. 19.5. Finally, conclusions and future research are presented in Sect. 19.6.

19.2 Previous Studies on OTS Component

COTS components promise faster time-to-market and increased productivity of software projects [1]. At the same time, COTS software introduces many risks, such as unknown quality of the COTS components, which can be harmful for the final product, or economic instability of the COTS vendor who may terminate maintenance support [2]. Furthermore, the use of OSS in industrial products is growing rapidly. The basic idea behind open source is very simple: When programmers can read, redistribute, and modify the source code for a piece of software, the software evolves. People improve it, people adapt it, and people fix bugs. And this can happen at a speed that, if one is used to the slow pace of conventional software development, seems astonishing [15].

OSS has many proposed advantages [3]: *OSS is usually freely available for public download. The collaborative, parallel efforts of globally distributed developers allow much OSS to be developed more quickly than conventional software. Many OSS products are recognized for high reliability, efficiency, and robustness.* Despite its wide appeal, OSS software faces a number of serious challenges and constraints. *The popularity of OSS increases the risk that so-called net-negative-producing programmers will become involved. Many software tasks, such as documentation, testing, and field support are lacking in OSS projects. If developers produce or sell a product, which integrates OSS as source code, they may need the licensor's permission. Otherwise, the licensor might claim for damages or force them to end the product's further development, delivery and sale [4].* Furthermore, many common perceptions about OSS need further empirical clarification. For example, there is still no empirical evidence that OSS fosters faster system growth [10]. There is also no strong evidence that OSS is more modular than closed source software [10].

Some previous studies have investigated the process of using COTS components in software development, such as COTS component selection [5] and COTS-based development processes [6]. Other studies have investigated how to use OSS software in product development [4], such as mission-critical development [11] and information system infrastructure development [12]. Although these studies present recommendations on how to integrate COTS or OSS component into the final product, few studies have investigated a higher level question: Why should I use COTS components instead of OSS components, or vice versa?

19.3 Research Design

This study is the second phase of a systematic study on process improvement and risk management in OTS based development. We started from a pre-study focused on COTS components, which was performed in the form of structured interviews of 16 COTS projects in Norwegian IT companies [9]. This study presented in this paper extended the pre-study in two dimensions. First, it included OSS components because they represent an alternative to COTS components. Second, this study included samples from Norway, Italy and Germany. In addition, the sample was selected randomly instead of on convenience as in the pre-study.

19.3.1 Research Questions

To investigate the motivation of using OTS components, we first want to know who is using OTS components. Therefore, the first research question is:

RQ1: *What are the commonalities and differences in profiles on projects using COTS components vs. those using OSS components?*
After we know who is using OTS components, we want to know why they decided to use OTS components. Thus, the second research question is:

RQ2: *What are the commonalities and differences in the motivation of projects using COTS components vs. those using OSS components?*
After we know who and why, we need to know the possible problems of using OTS components. We intended to investigate whether the current motivation and expectations of using OTS components are proper or not. Therefore, the third research question is:

RQ3: *What are the commonalities and differences in possible risks (problems) of projects using COTS components vs. those using OSS components?*

19.3.2 Research Method

In this study, we used a questionnaire to collect data, organized in six sections:

1. Background questions to collect information on the company, and respondents.
2. Background information concerning projects, such as development environment, application domain, and non-functional requirements emphasis.
3. The motivation of using OTS components.
4. The specific motivation of using COTS or OSS components.
5. Information relevant to process improvement and risk management in OTS component-based development.
6. Detailed information about one specific OTS component used in the actual project.

19.3.3 Concepts used in this Study

Concepts used in this study are listed in the first page of the questionnaire, for example:

− *Component*. Software components are program units of independent production, acquisition, and deployment that can be composed into a functioning system. We limit ourselves to components that have been explicitly decided either to be built from scratch or to be acquired externally as an OTS-component. That is, to components that are not shipped with the operating system, not provided by the development environment, and not included in any pre-existing platform.
− *OTS component* is provided (by a so-called provider) from a COTS vendor or the OSS community. The components may come with certain obligations, e.g. payment or licensing terms. An OTS component is not controllable, in terms of provided features and their evolution and is mainly used as closed source, i.e. no source code is usually modified.

19.3.4. Data Collection

Sample Selection. The unit of this study is a completed software development project. The projects were selected based on two criteria:

− The project should use one or more OTS components
− The project should be a finished project, possibly with maintenance, and possibly with several releases.

We used random selection to gather representative samples in three European countries:

− In Norway, we gathered a company list from the Norwegian Census Bureau (SSB) [7]. We included mostly companies which were registered as IT companies. Based on the number of employees, we selected the 115 largest IT companies (100 biggest IT companies plus 15 IT departments in the largest 3 companies in five other sectors), 150 medium-sized software companies (20–99 employees), and 100 small-sized companies (5–19 employees) as the original contacting list.

- In Italy, we first got 43,580 software companies from the yellow pages in the phone book. We then randomly selected companies from these. For these randomly selected companies, we read their web-site to ensure they are software companies or not. 196 companies were finally clarified as software companies, and were used as the original contact list.
- In Germany, we selected companies from a list coming from an organization comparing to the Norwegian Census Bureau. We then used the existing IESE customer database to get contact information of relevant IT/Software companies, in line with the Norwegian selection.

Data collection procedure. The final questionnaire was first designed and pre-tested in English. It was then translated into the native language of the actual country and published on the SESE web tool at Simula Research Lab [8]. Possible respondents were first contacted by telephone. If they had suitable OTS-based projects and would like to join our study, a username and password was sent to them, so that they could log into the web tool to fill in the questionnaire (they can also use a paper version). The average time to fill in the questionnaire is between 20 to 30 minutes.

19.3.5 Data Analysis

According to the focus of the different research questions, we used different data analysis methods:

- For RQ1, we analyzed the distribution of the variables.
- For RQ2, we want to see both the commonalities and differences of variables. To compare differences, we first used box-plots to show the median and distribution of the variable. We then compared the mean difference of variables. S.S. Stevens classified "permissible" statistical procedures [18] according to four main scales: nominal, ordinal, interval and ratio scale [19]. For the ordinal scales, the permissible statistics included median, percentiles, and ordinal correlations. Mean and standard deviations are allowed for interval and ratio scales. In our study, although the scale of our data is Likert scales, we also compared the mean value of different variable to see if they are significant different. A number of reasons account for this analysis: First, Spector [20] showed that people tend to treat categories in Likert scales as equidistant, regardless of the specific categories employed. Second, using parametric tests for scales that are not strictly interval does not lead, except in extreme cases, to wrong statistical decisions [21]. Third, D.J.Hand concluded that *restrictions on statistical operations arising from scale type are more important in model fitting and hypothesis testing contexts that in model generation or hypothesis*

generation contexts. In the latter, in principle, at least, anything is legitimate in the initial search for potentially interesting relationship [22]. Although we used a t-test to compare the mean difference, the intention of this study is still model generation and hypothesis generation. We therefore believe that it is permissible to treat Likert-scales items as leading to interval scales measurements that can be analyzed with parametric statistics.
– For RQ3, we used the same analysis method as in RQ2.

19.4 Research Results

Although the data collection is still on-going in Germany and Italy, we have gathered results from 115 projects (47 from Norway, 25 from Italy, and 43 from Germany). In these 115 projects, 71 used only COTS components, 39 used only OSS components, and five used both COTS and OSS components. In this study, we discarded the projects using both COTS components and OSS component, because they will confound the results and cover only 4% of the total projects.

Most respondents of the 110 projects, which used either COTS components or OSS components, have a solid IT background. More than 89% of them are IT managers, project managers, or software architects. More than 88% of them have more than 2 year experiences with OTS-based development. All of them have at least a bachelor degree in informatics, computer science, or telematics.

19.4.1 Answers to RQ1 – Who is Using OTS Components

To answer RQ1, we designed two sub-questions:

– RQ1.1: What are the commonalities and differences in profiles of the companies and projects using COTS components vs. using OSS components?
– RQ1.2: What are the commonalities and differences in emphasis in projects using COTS component vs. using OSS components?

Results are coming from projects in several domains, as showed in Fig. 19.1. The distribution of company size and the companies' main business area are shown in Fig. 19.2 and Fig. 19.3.

For RQ1.2, we listed some possible characteristics of the actual system:

– Time-to-market
– Effort (cost)
– Reliability
– Security
– Performance
– Maintainability
– New functionality (first launch in the market)
– Improved functionality (over competitors)

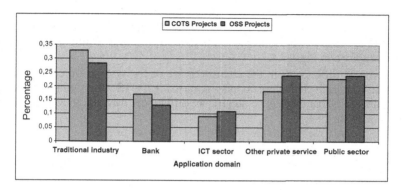

Fig. 19.1. Distribution of the application domain of the final system

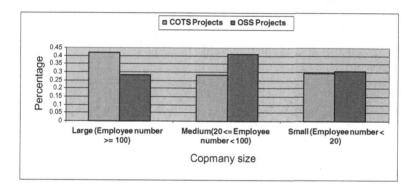

Fig. 19.2. Distribution of company size

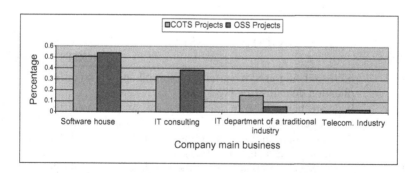

Fig. 19.3. Distribution of companies' main business areas

Respondents were asked to answer "do not agree at all", "hardly agree", "agree somewhat", "agree mostly", "strongly agree", or "do not know". We assign an ordinal number from 1 to 5 to the above alternatives (5 means strongly agree). The results are shown in Fig. 19.4.

To compare differences in the characteristics of the system, we compared the mean values of each characteristic in systems using COTS vs. systems using OSS. The results show that there is no significant difference. Answers to RQ1 are summarized in Table 19.1.

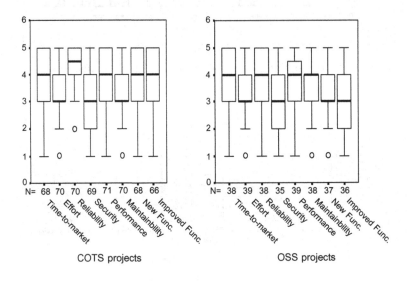

Fig. 19.4. The emphasis on characteristics of the system

Table 19.1. Answers to research question RQ1

research question	commonalities (COTS and OSS)	differences (COTS vs. OSS)
RQ 1.1	both are being used in systems of several application domains (see Fig.19.1).	no difference
RQ 1.1	both are being used in small, medium, and large IT companies (see Fig.19.2)	no difference
RQ 1.1	software house and IT consulting companies are the main users (see Fig.19.3)	no difference
RQ 1.2	both systems emphasis on time-to-market, reliability, and performance (see Fig. 19.4)	no difference

19.4.2 Answers to RQ2 – Why was it Decided to use OTS Components?

To answer RQ2, we designed three sub-questions:

- RQ2.1: What were the differences of users' general expectations on COTS components vs. OSS components?
- RQ2.2: What were the specific motivations of using COTS components?
- RQ2.3: What were the specific motivations of using OSS components?

For RQ2.1, we gathered some common expectations of using OTS components from our pre-study [9] and from literature reviews [1, 3]:

- Shorter time-to-market
- Less development effort/cost
- Less maintenance effort/cost
- Larger market share
- Compliance with industrial standards
- Keeping up with the newest technology
- Better system reliability
- Better system security
- Better system performance.

We used the same format and measurement as RQ1.2. The results are shown in Fig.19.5.

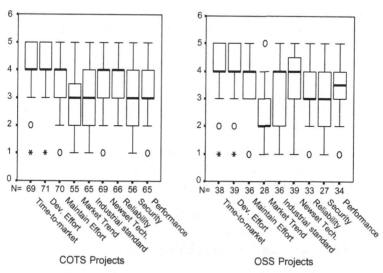

Fig. 19.5. The general expectations of using OTS components

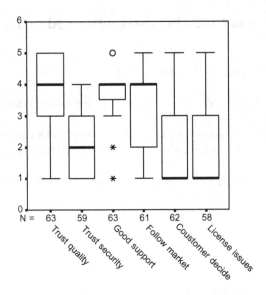

Fig.19.6. Specific motivation of using COTS components

We used SPSS 11.0 to compare the mean values of each motivation of using COTS vs. using OSS. The results show that there is no significant difference.

For RQ2.2, we gathered some specific motivations of using COTS components:

- Reduce risk of bad quality, because components were paid for
- Reduce risk of poor security, because source code was closed/unavailable
- Provider could give adequate technical support
- Provider may provide give components following market trends
- It was decided by customer
- Political reasons (company policy, licensing conditions).

The results of RQ2.2 are shown in Fig.19.6.

For RQ2.3, we gathered some specific motivations of using OSS components:

- Reduce risk of provider going out of business
- Reduce risk of provider changing market strategies
- Reduce risk of selected components evolving into an unwanted direction
- Component can be acquired for free
- Source code is available and can easily be changed
- It was decided by the customer
- Political reasons (company policy, licensing conditions).

The results of RQ2.3 are shown in Fig. 19.7.

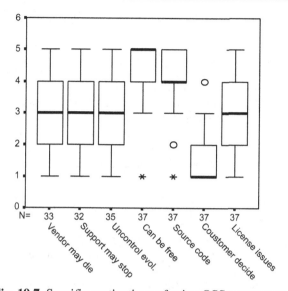

Fig. 19.7. Specific motivations of using OSS components

Table 19.2. Answers to research question RQ2

research question	commonalities (COTS and OSS)	differences (COTS vs. OSS)
RQ 2.1	both COTS and OSS users expect that the components can contribute to shorter time-to-market, less development effort, less maintenance effort, and newest technology (see Fig.19.5)	No difference
RQ 2.2	COTS users believe that paid software will give good quality and will follow market trends. They also believe that the COTS vendor will provide good technical support (see Fig.19.6).	
RQ 2.3	the main motivations of using OSS are that code could be acquired for free, source code is available, and to avoid the possible vendor support risk (see Fig. 19.7).	

Answers to research question RQ2 are summarized in Table 19.2.

19.4.3 Answers to RQ3 – What were the Results of using OTS Components

To answer RQ3, we formulized 15 possible risks (as showed in Table 19.3) on OTS-based development.

We asked respondents to fill in whether these problems had actually happened in the investigated project or not. We used the same measurement as RQ1.2. The results are shown in Fig. 19.8.

Table 19.3. Possible risks in OTS based development

phase	ID	possible risks
project plan phase	R1	the project was delivered long after schedule [13].
	R2	effort to select OTS components was not satisfactorily estimated [14].
	R3	effort to integrate OTS components was not satisfactorily estimated [13].
requirements Phase	R4	requirement were changed a lot [14].
	R5	OTS components could not be sufficiently adapted to changing requirements [14].
	R6	it is not possible to (re)negotiate requirements with the customer, if OTS components could not satisfy all requirements [9].
component integration phase	R7	OTS components negatively affected system reliability [4, 16].
	R8	OTS components negatively affected system security [4, 15, 16].
	R9	OTS components negatively affected system performance [16].
	R10	OTS components were not satisfactorily compatible with the production environment when the system was deployed [16].
system maintenance and evolution	R11	it was difficult to identify whether defects were inside or outside the OTS components [14].
	R12	it was difficult to plan system maintenance, e.g. because different OTS components had asynchronous release cycles [13].
	R13	it was difficult to update the system with the last OTS component version [13].
provider relationship management	R14	provider did not provide enough technical support/ training [4, 13].
	R15	information on the reputation and technical support ability of provider were inadequate [4, 13].

To compare differences, we compared the mean values of each risk in projects using COTS vs. projects using OSS. The significant results (P-value < 0.05) are shown in the following Table 19.4.

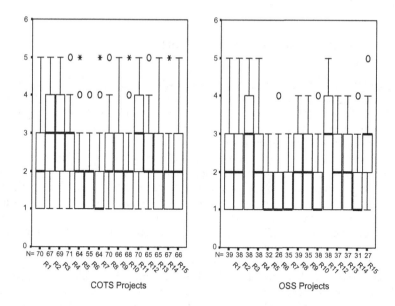

Fig. 19.8. Existing Problems in projects using COTS components vs. projects using OSS components

Table 19.4. The mean differences of three risks between COTS projects and OSS projects (Independent Samples *T*-Test without considering equal variances)

risk	mean difference(COTS - OSS)	significance (2-tailed)
R2	0.54	0.033
R5	0.39	0.027
R8	0.50	0.014
R15	-0.56	0.033

Answers to research question RQ3 are summarized in Table 19.5.

Table 19.5. Answers to research question RQ3

research question	commonalities (COTS and OSS)	differences (COTS vs. OSS)
RQ 3	common risk is that it is difficult to estimate the integration effort and to identify whether the defects are inside the component or outside.	COTS users had a higher risk on estimating the selection effort, following requirement changes, and controlling COTS components' negative effect on security. OSS users had a higher risk on getting the information of providers' support reputation.

19.5 Discussion

19.5.1 Comparison with Related Work

By analyzing all activities normally performed when integrating OTS components, Giacomo [24] concluded that the OSS component is not completely different from the COTS component. Our results show that both COTS and OSS components were used in projects and companies with similar profiles. Software houses and IT consulting companies were their main users.

COTS and OSS components promise shorter time-to-market and increased productivity [1]. Some previous studies claim that OTS components are generally more reliable than in-house built components, because they have been used by different users in different environments. Our results confirm that both COTS and OSS components were used in projects with emphases on time-to-market, reliability, and performance. In addition, the key motivations of using OTS components were to save development time and effort, and to get newest technology.

A COTS component generally is a black-box and is provided by the commercial vendor. Our results show that COTS users believe that the paid component should have good quality and good technical support. However, our results show that they were not more satisfied in reliability and performance of the components than OSS users. On the other hand, COTS users had more difficulties in controlling the components' negative security effects than OSS users. Some previous studies have argued that OSS software is more secure than COTS because its code can be reviewed by a huge number of coders. Our results give further support on this conclusion. In addition, our data shows that COTS users had more difficulties in estimating the selection effort and following requirement changes than OSS users. The possible reason is that COTS users cannot access the source code of the components. It is therefore difficult for them to review the source code and perform necessary changes when necessary.

OSS components are generally provided by an open source community with source code. Our results show that the main motivation of using OSS components is the open and possible free code, which can be changed if necessary. Although OSS user did not have commercial support contract with OSS component providers, they were not less satisfied on the technical support than COTS users. However, we need to explain this fact carefully. The reason might be that OSS users would like to read and change the code themselves, instead of asking for help, as we found in the key motivations of using OSS.

Holck et al. [23] concluded that a major barrier on using OSS in industrial project is the customer's uncertainty and unfamiliarity with OSS vendor relationship. Our data showed that OSS users were less satisfied on knowing OSS provider's technical support reputation. How to establish credible and mutually acceptable combinations of OSS delivery and procurement models therefore needs future research.

19.5.2 Possible Treats to Validity

Construct validity. In this study, most variables and alternatives are taken directly, or with little modification, from existing literature. The questionnaire was pre-tested using a paper version by 10 internal experts and 8 industrial respondents. About 15% questions have been revised based on pre-test results.

Internal validity. We have promised respondents in this study a final report and a seminar to share experience. The respondents were persons who want to share their experience and want to learn from others. In general, we think that the respondents have answered truthfully.

Conclusion validity. This study is still on-going. More data will be collected from Germany and Italy. A slightly larger sample will be gathered to give more significant statistical support on the conclusions of this study.

External validity. We used different random selection strategies to select samples in different countries. It is because the limited availability of the necessary information. In Italy, the information of the official organization as a national "Census Bureau" in Norway and Germany is not available. The samples had to be selected from "yellow pages". The method problems by performing such a survey in three countries will be elaborated in a future paper. Another possible limitation is that our study focused on fine-grained OTS components. Conclusions may be different in projects using complex and large OTS products, such as ERP, Content management systems, and web service in general.

19.6 Conclusion and Future work

This paper has presented preliminary results of a state-of-the practice survey on OTS-based development in industrial projects. The results of this study have answered three questions:

- RQ1: Who is using OTS components?
  Both COTS and OSS components were used in projects with similar profiles. There is also no difference on the profiles of companies using COTS or OSS components.
- RQ2: Why was it decided to use OTS components?
  The main motivation of using either COTS or OSS component was to get shorter time-to-market, less development effort, and to get newest technology. COTS users have bigger trust in the COTS quality and COTS vendor support ability. Possible free source code is the key motivation of OSS users. OSS users prefer to have access the source code so that they can revise it when necessary.
- RQ3: What are the possible problems of using OTS components?
  It was more difficult for COTS component users to follow requirement changes than OSS users. It is also more difficult for COTS users to estimate the selection effort and to control COTS components' negative effect on system security. OSS users were more uncertain on OSS provider support reputation than COTS users.

Results of this study have shown state-of-the-practice data. The next step is to do a follow up qualitative study to investigate the cause-effects of the conclusions of this study. We have held a seminar at OSLO in Feb. 2005 and preliminary investigated possible cause-effects of our results with participants of this study and other industrial colleagues. The next step is to do a larger qualitative study with personal interviews to further study these cause-effect assumptions.

Acknowledgements

This study was partially funded by the INCO (INcremental COmponent based development) project [17]. We thank the colleagues in these projects, and all the participants in the survey

References

[1] Voas, J. (1998) COTS Software – the Economical Choice? *IEEE Software*, 15(2), pp. 16–19

[2] Voas, J. (1998) The challenges of Using COTS Software in Component-Based Development, *IEEE Computer*, 31(6), pp. 44–45

[3] Fitzgerald, B. (2004) A Critical Look at Open Source, *IEEE Computer*, 37(7), pp. 92–94

[4] Ruffin, M. and Ebert, C.(2004) Using Open Source Software in Product Development: A Primer, *IEEE Software*, 21(1), pp. 82–86

[5] Brownsword, L., Oberndorf, T., and Sledge, C. (2000) Developing New Processes for COTS-Based Systems, *IEEE Software*, 17(4), pp. 48–55

[6] Lawlis, P.K., Mark, K.E., Thomas, D.A., and Courtheyn, T. (2001) A Formal Process for Evaluating COTS Software Products, *IEEE Computer*, 34(5), pp. 58–63

[7] SSB (Norwegian Census Bureau) (2004): http://www.ssb.no

[8] SESE web tool (2004): http://sese.simula.no

[9] Li, J., Bjørnson, F.O., Conradi, R., and Kampenes, V.B. (2004) An Empirical Study of Variations in COTS-based Software Development Processes in Norwegian IT Industry, *Proc. of the 10th IEEE International Metrics Symposium*, Chicago, September, 2004, IEEE CS Press (2004), pp. 72–83

[10] Paulson, J.W., Succi, G., and Eberlein, A. (2004) An Empirical Study of Open-Source and Closed-Source Software Products, *IEEE Transactions on Software Engineering*, 30(4), pp. 246–256

[11] Norris, J.S.(2004) Missioin-Critical Development with Open Source Software, *IEEE Software*, 21(1), pp. 42–49

[12] Fitzgerald, B. and Kenny, T.(2004) Developing an Information Systems Infrastructure with Open Source Software, *IEEE Software*, 21(1), pp. 50–55

[13] Rose, L.C.(2003) Risk Management of COTS based System Development, Cechich, A., Piattini, M., Vallecillo, A. (Eds.), Component-Based Software Quality – Methods and Techniques, LNCS Vol. 2693. Springer Berlin Heidelberg New York, pp. 352–373

[14] Boehm, B.W., Port, D., Yang, Y., and Bhuta, J.(2003) Not All CBS Are Created Equally COTS-intensive Project Types, *Proc. of the 2nd International Conference on COTS-Based Software Systems*, Ottawa, Canada, February 2003, LNCS Vol. 2580. Springer Berlin Heidelberg New York pp. 36–50

[15] Open Source Initiative (2004): http://www.opensource.org/index.php

[16] Padmal V. (2003) Risks and Challenges of Component-Based Software Development, *Communications of the ACM*, 46(8), pp. 67–72

[17] INCO project description, 2000, http://www.ifi.uio.no/~isu/INCO

[18] Stevens, S.S. (1951) Mathematics, Measurement, and Psychophysics, in S.S.Stevens (Ed.) *Handbook of Experimental Psychology*, NY, Wiley

[19] Stevens, S.S (1946) On the Theory of Scales of Measurement, Vol. 103. *Science* pp. 677–680

[20] Spector, P. (1980) Ratings of Equal and Unequal Response Choice Intervals, *Journal of Social Psychology*, Vol. 112 , pp.115–119

[21] Velleman, P.F. and Wilkinson L.(1993) Nominal, Ordinal, Interval, and Ratio Typologies Are Misleading, *Journal of the American Statistician*, 47(1), pp. 65–72

[22] Hand, D.J. (1996) Statistics and Theory of Measurement, *Journal of the Royal Statistical Society: Series A (Statistics in Society)*, 159(3), pp. 445–492

[23] Holck J., Larsen, M.H., and Pedersen, M.K. (2005) Managerial and Technical Barriers to the Adoption of Open Source Software, *Proc. of the 4th International Conference on COTS-Based Software Systems*, Bilbo, Spain, February, 2005, LNCS Vol. 3412, Springer Berlin Heidelberg New York, pp. 289–300

[24] Giacomo, P.D. (2005) COTS and Open Source Software Components: Are They Really Different on the Battlefield? *Proc. of the 4th International Conference on COTS-Based Software Systems*, Bilbo, Spain, Vol. 3412. Springer Berlin Heidelberg New York, pp. 301–310

20

Evaluating the Effect of a Delegated versus Centralized Control Style on the Maintainability of Object-Oriented Software

E. Arisholm and D.I.K. Sjøberg

Abstract: A fundamental question in object-oriented design is how to design maintainable software. According to expert opinion, a delegated control style, typically a result of responsibility-driven design, represents object-oriented design at its best, whereas a centralized control style is reminiscent of a procedural solution, or a "bad" object-oriented design. This paper presents a controlled experiment that investigates these claims empirically. A total of 99 junior, intermediate and senior professional consultants from several international consultancy companies were hired for one day to participate in the experiment. To compare differences between (categories of) professionals and students, 59 students also participated. The subjects used professional Java tools to perform several change tasks on two alternative Java designs that had a centralized and delegated control style, respectively.

The results show that the most skilled developers, in particular the senior consultants, require less time to maintain software with a delegated control style than with a centralized control style. However, more novice developers, in particular the undergraduate students and junior consultants, have serious problems understanding a delegated control style, and perform far better with a centralized control style.

Thus, the maintainability of object-oriented software depends, to a large extent, on the skill of the developers who are going to maintain it. These results may have serious implications for object-oriented development in an industrial context: having senior consultants design object-oriented systems may eventually pose difficulties unless they make an effort to keep the designs simple, as the cognitive complexity of "expert" designs might be unmanageable for less skilled maintainers.

Keywords: design principles, responsibility delegation, control styles, object-oriented design, object-oriented programming, software maintainability, controlled experiment.

20.1 Introduction

A fundamental problem in software engineering is to construct software that is easy to change. Supporting change is one of the claimed benefits of object-oriented software development.

The principal mechanism used to design object-oriented software is the *class*, which enables the encapsulation of attributes and methods into logically cohesive abstractions of the world. Assigning responsibilities and collaborations among classes can be performed in many ways. In a *delegated control* style, a well-defined set of responsibilities are distributed among a number of classes [31]. The classes play specific roles and occupy well-known positions in the application architecture [32, 33]. Alternatively, in a *centralized control* style, a few, large "control classes" co-ordinate a set of simple classes [31]. According to object-oriented design experts, a delegated control style is easier to understand and change than is a centralized control style [4, 15, 31–33].

One of the major goals of a responsibility-driven design method is to support the development of a delegated control style [31–33], that is, the design of a delegated control style is one of its prescribed principles. The empirical study in [25] confirms that a responsibility-driven design process may result in a delegated control style. That study also suggests that a data-driven design approach (adapted from structured design to the object-oriented paradigm) results in a centralized control style because one controller class is assigned the responsibility of implementing the business logic of the application, using data from simple "data objects".

In a use-case driven design method, as advocated in most recent UML textbooks, one of the commonly prescribed principles is to assign one (central) control class to coordinate the sequence of events described by each use-case [17, 18]. However, a question not explicitly discussed in the UML textbooks is *how much* responsibility the control class should have in the design of maintainable software. At one extreme, the control class might only be responsible for *initiating* the use-case and communicating with boundary (interface) classes, while the real work is delegated to entity (business) classes, which in turn collaborate to implement the business logic and flow of events of the use-case. In this case, use-case driven design would resemble responsibility-driven design, with a delegated control style. At the other extreme, the control class might implement the actual business logic and flow of events of a use-case, in which case the entity classes function only as simple data structures with "get" and "set" methods. In this case, use-case driven design would resemble data-driven design, with a centralized control style.

To compare the maintainability of the two control styles, the authors of this paper previously conducted a controlled experiment [2]. For the given sample of 36 undergraduate students, the delegated control style design required significantly more effort to implement the given set of changes than did the alternative centralized control style design. This difference in change effort was primarily due to the difference in the effort required to understand how to perform the change tasks.

It is evident that the expert recommendations and the results of our previous experiment run counter to each other. It might be that a delegated control style provides better software maintainability for an expert, while a centralized control style might be better for novices. Novices may struggle to understand how the objects in a delegated control style actually collaborate to fulfil the larger goals of an application. Differences in "complexity" of object-oriented designs may be explained by the cognitive models of the developers [26]. Thus, the degree of maintainability of a software application depends not only on attributes of the software artefact itself, but also on certain cognitive attributes of the particular developer whose task it is to maintain it. This factor seems to be underestimated by the object-oriented experts; neither is it investigated in most controlled experiments evaluating object-oriented technologies. Consequently, the main research question we attempt to answer in this paper is the following: For the target population of junior, intermediate and senior software consultants with different levels of education and work experience, which of the two aforementioned control styles is easier to maintain?

We conducted an experiment with a sample of 99 Java consultants from eight consultancy companies, including the major, partly international, companies Cap Gemini Ernst & Young, Ementor, Accenture, TietoEnator and Software Innovation. To compare differences between (categories of) professionals and students, 59 students also participated. The treatments were the same two alternative designs given in the previous pen-and-paper student experiment [2]. The experimental subjects were assigned to the two treatments using a between-subjects randomized block design.

To increase the realism of the experiment [16, 24, 29], the subjects used their usual Java development tool instead of pen and paper. The professionals were located in their usual work offices during the experiment, the students in their usual computer lab. The subjects used the Simula Experiment Support Environment [3] to receive the experimental materials, answer questionnaires and upload task solutions. Each subject spent about one work day on the experiment. As in ordinary programming projects, the companies of the consultants were paid to participate. The students received individual payment.

The remainder of this paper is organized as follows. Section 20.2 outlines fundamental design principles of object-oriented software. Section 20.3 describes existing empirical research that evaluates object-oriented design principles. Section 20.4 describes the design of the controlled experiment. Section 20.5 presents the results. Section 20.6 discusses threats to validity. Section 20.7 concludes.

20.2 Delegated Versus Centralized Control in Object-Oriented Designs

This section describes the concepts underlying the object of study, that is, the two control styles evaluated in the experiment. The two control styles are each illustrated by one example design, which examples are also the design alternatives used as treatments in our experiment.

20.2.1 Relationships between Design Properties, Principles and Methods

To clarify the concepts studied in this paper, we distinguish between *design properties*, *design principles* and *design methods*. Object-oriented design properties characterize the resulting design. Examples are *coupling* [8] and *cohesion* [7]. Object-oriented design principles prescribe "good" values of the design properties. Examples are *low coupling* and *high cohesion,* as advocated in [14, 22]. Object-oriented design methods prescribe a sequence of activities for creating design models of object-oriented software systems.[1] Examples are responsibility-driven design [32], data-driven design [25, 27, 30] and use-case driven design [17, 18]. Ideally, design methods should support a set of (empirically validated) design principles.

20.2.2 Delegated versus Centralized Control Style

The control styles studied in this paper are depicted in Fig. 20.1. According to the terminology defined in [31], delegated and centralized control styles embody two radically different principles for assigning responsibilities and collaborations among classes. A delegated control style is described as follows:

> A delegated control style ideally has clusters of well defined responsibilities distributed among a number of objects. Objects in a delegated control architecture tend to coordinate rather than dominate. Tasks may be initiated by a coordinator, but the real work is performed by others. These worker objects tend to both 'know' and 'do' things. They may even be smart enough to determine what they need to know, rather than being plugged with values via external control. To me, a delegated control architecture feels like object design at its best...
>
> Wirfs-Brock [31]

In contrast, a centralized control style typically consists a central object (Fig. 20.1), which is responsible for the initiation and coordination of all tasks:

> A centralized control style is characterized by single points of control interacting with many simple objects. The intelligent object typically serves as the main point of control, while others it uses behave much like traditional data structures. To me, centralized control feels like a "procedural solution" cloaked in objects...
>
> Wirfs-Brock [31]

---

[1] The existing literature provides no clear distinction between object-oriented *analysis* and object-oriented *design*. Consequently, the process we define as object-oriented design may include activities that also might be referred to as object-oriented analysis. However, in this paper, such a distinction is not important.

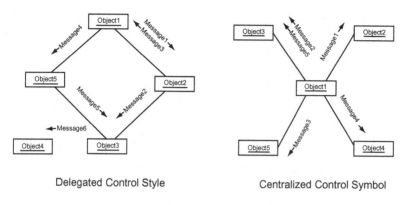

Delegated Control Style   Centralized Control Symbol

Fig. 20.1. Delegated versus Centralized Control Style

20.2.3 Example – The Coffee-Machine Design Problem

This section illustrates the two control styles, using two alternative example designs of the coffee-machine design problem. These designs were discussed at a workshop on object-oriented design quality at OOPSLA'97 [19] and are described in two articles in C/C++ User's Journal [15]:

> This two-article series presents a problem I use both to teach and test OO design. It is a simple but rich problem, strong on "design," minimizing language, tool, and even inheritance concerns. The problem represents a realistic work situation, where circumstances change regularly. It provides a good touch point for discussions of even fairly subtle designs in even very large systems...

> Cockburn [15]

The initial problem statement was as follows:

> You and I are contractors who just won a bid to design a custom coffee vending machine for the employees of Acme Fijet Works to use. Arnold, the owner of Acme Fijet Works, like the common software designer, eschews standard solutions. He wants his own, custom design. He is, however, a cheapskate. Arnold tells us he wants a simple machine. All he wants is a machine that serves coffee for 35 cents, with or without sugar and creamer. That's all. He expects us to be able to put this little machine together quickly and for little cost. We get together and decide there will be a coin slot and coin return, coin return button, and four other buttons: black, white, black with sugar, and white with sugar.

> Cockburn [15]

The two alternative designs discussed in [15] are, we believe, good examples of a centralized and a delegated control style, respectively. Table 20.1 shows the classes and their assigned responsibilities for the two alternative designs. The first design, referred to as the Centralized Control (CC) design in this paper (denoted "Mainframe design" in [15]), consists of seven classes. The second design, referred to as the Delegated Control (DC) design in this paper (denoted "Responsibility-Driven Design" in [15]), consists of 12 classes.

Table 20.1. Overview of the two design alternatives

	CC	DC
coffee-machine	initiates the machine; knows how the machine is put together; handles input	initiates the machine; knows how the machine is put together; handles input
cashbox	knows amount of money put in; gives change; answers whether a given amount of credit is available	knows amount of money put in; gives change; answers whether a given amount of credit is available
frontpanel	knows selection; knows price of selections, and materials needed for each; coordinates payment; knows what products are available; knows how each product is made; knows how to talk to the dispensers	knows selection; coordinates payment; delegates drink making to the Product
product		knows its recipe and price
product register		knows what products are available
Recipe		knows the ingredients of a given product; tells dispensers to dispense ingredients in sequence
dispensers	controls dispensing; tracks amount it has left	knows which ingredient it contains; controls dispensing; tracks amount it has left
dispenser register		knows what dispensers are available
ingredient.		knows its name only
output	knows how to display text to the user	knows how to display text to the user
input	knows how to receive command-line input from the user	knows how to receive command-line input from the user
main	initializes the program	initializes the program

In both designs, the *FrontPanel* class acts as a "control class" for the use-case "Make Drink". However, the number and type of responsibilities assigned to the *FrontPanel* class are different in the two designs. In the CC design, the *FrontPanel* is responsible for most tasks: it knows the user selection, the price of each type of coffee and how each type of coffee is made. To make a specific type of coffee, the *FrontPanel* calls the *dispense* method of various *Dispenser* objects in an *if–then–else* structure. In the DC design, the *FrontPanel* just *initiates* the use case, and delegates the control of how a given type of coffee is made to a *Product*, which knows its price and *Recipe*. In turn, the *Recipe* is responsible for knowing the *Ingredients* of which a product consists, but has no knowledge about pricing. Cockburn [15] assessed the CC design as follows:

> Although the trajectory of change in the mainframe approach involves only one object, people soon become terrified of touching it. Any oversight in the mainframe object (even a typo!) means potential damage to many modules, with endless testing and unpredictable bugs. Those readers who have done system maintenance or legacy system replacement will recognize that almost every large system ends up with such a module. They will affirm what sort of a nightmare it becomes.

Furthermore, Cockburn [15] assessed the DC design as follows:

> The design we come up with at this point bears no resemblance to our original design. It is, I am happy to see, robust with respect to change, and it is a much more reasonable "model of the world." For the first time, we see the term "product" show up in the design, as well as "recipe" and "ingredient." The responsibilities are quite evenly distributed. Each component has a single primary purpose in life; we have avoided piling responsibilities together. The names of the components match the responsibilities.

Thus, the DC design has a distinctly delegated control style, whereas the CC design has a distinctly centralized control style. According to Cockburn [15], most novices (students) come up with the CC type of design. However, most experts would probably agree that the DC design is, as Cockburn argues, a more maintainable solution to the coffee-machine design problem.

20.3 Related Empirical Studies

In one of the few field experiments comparing alternative object-oriented technologies, a data-driven and a responsibility-driven design method were compared [25]. Two systems were developed based on the same requirements specification; using the data-driven and the responsibility-driven design method, respectively. The results suggest that the responsibility-driven design method results in a delegated control style, whereas the data-driven design method results in a centralized control style. Structural attribute measures (defined in [12]) of the two systems were also collected and compared. Based on the measured values, the authors suggested that use of the responsibility-driven design method resulted in higher quality software than did use of the data-driven design method, because the responsibility-driven software system had less coupling and higher cohesion than did the data-driven software system. We believe it may be premature to draw such conclusions. Whether the design measures used in the experiment actually measured "quality" was not evaluated by means of direct measurement of external quality attributes.

Nevertheless, there *is* a growing body of results that indicates that class-level measures of structural attributes, such as coupling and cohesion, can be reasonably good predictors of product quality (see survey in [5]), which supports the conclusions in [25]. However, most of these metrics validation studies have been case studies, and so there is a lack of control that limits our ability to draw conclusions regarding cause-effect relationships [20, 21]. One notable exception was a controlled experiment that investigated whether a "good" design (adhering to Coad and Yourdon's design principles [14]) was easier to maintain than was a "bad" design [6, 9]. The results suggest that reducing coupling and increasing cohesion (as suggested in Coad and Yourdon's design principles) improve the maintainability of object-oriented design documents. However, as pointed out by the authors, the results should be considered preliminary, primarily because the subjects were students with little programming experience.

A controlled experiment to assess the changeability (i.e., change effort and correctness) of the example coffee-machine designs described in Sect. 20.2.3 is reported in [2]. Thirty-seven undergraduate students were divided into two groups in which the individuals designed, coded and tested several identical changes to one of the two design alternatives. The subjects solved the change tasks using pen and paper. Given the argumentation described in Sect. 20.2, the results were surprising in that they clearly indicated that the delegated control design requires significantly more change effort for the given set of changes than does the alternative centralized control design. This difference in change effort was primarily due to the difference in effort required to *understand* how to perform the change tasks. Consequently, designs with a delegated control style may have higher cognitive complexity than have designs using a centralized control style. No significant differences between the two designs were found with respect to correctness.

In summary, more empirical studies are needed to evaluate principles of design quality in object-oriented software development. The control style of object-oriented design represents one such fundamental design principle that needs to be studied empirically. Related empirical studies provide no convincing answers as to how the control style of object-oriented design affects maintainability. The field experiment reported in [25] lacks validation against external quality indicators. The results of the experiments in [2, 6] contain apparent contradictions. Furthermore, both experiments used students as subjects solving pen-and-paper exercises. A major criticism of such experiments is their lack of realism [16, 24], which potentially limits our ability to generalize the findings to the population about which we wish to make claims, that is, professional programmers solving real programming tasks using professional tools in a realistic development environment. An empirical study reported in [26] reveals substantial differences in how novices, intermediates and experts perceive the difficulties of object-oriented development. These results are confirmed by a controlled experiment in which, among other things, a strong interaction between the expertise of the subjects and type of task was identified during object-oriented program comprehension [10]. Consequently, the results of the existing empirical studies are difficult to generalize to the target population of professional developers.

20.4 Design of Experiment

The conducted experiment was a replication of the initial pen-and-paper student experiment reported in [2]. The motivation for replicating a study is to establish an increasing range of conditions under which the findings hold, and predictable exceptions [23]. A series of replications might enable the exploratory and evolutionary creation of a theory to explain the observed effects on the object of study. In this experiment, the following three controlled factors were modified, compared with the initial experiment:

More representative sample of the population. The target population of this experiment was professional Java consultants. To obtain a more representative sample of this population, we hired 99 junior, intermediate and senior Java consultants from eight software consultancy companies. To compare differences between (categories of) professionals and students, 59 undergraduate and graduate students also participated. Descriptive statistics of the education and experience of the sample population are given in [1].

More realistic tools. Professional developers use professional programming environments. Hence, traditional pen-and-paper based exercises are hardly realistic. In this experiment, each subject used a Java development tool of their own choice, e.g., JBuilder, Forte, Visual Age, Visual J++ and Visual Café.

More realistic experiment environment. The classroom environment of the previous experiment was replaced by the offices in which each developer would normally work. Thus, they had access to printers, libraries, coffee, etc. as in any other project they might be working on. The students were located in one of their usual computer labs.

20.4.1 Hypotheses

In this section, the hypotheses of the experiment are presented informally. The hypotheses reflect the expectation that there is an *interaction* between the programming experience and the control style of an object-oriented design. We expect experienced developers to have the necessary skills to benefit from "pure" object-oriented design principles, as reflected in a delegated control style. Based on the results of the previous experiment [2], we expect novice developers to have difficulties understanding a delegated control style, and to thus perform better with a centralized control style. There are two levels of hypothesis: one that compares the control styles for all subjects, and another that compares the relative differences between the developer categories. The null-hypotheses of the experiment are as follows:

HO_1 – The Effect of Control Style on Change Effort. The time spent on performing change tasks on the DC design and CC design is equal.

HO_2 – The Effect of Control Style on Change Effort for Different Developer Categories. The difference between the time spent on performing change tasks on the DC design and CC design is equal for the five categories of developer.

HO_3 – The Effect of Control Style on Correctness. The number of correct solutions for change tasks on the DC design and CC design is equal.

HO_4 – The Effect of Control Style on Correctness for Different Developer Categories. The difference between the number of correct solutions for change tasks on the DC design and CC design is equal for the five categories of developer.

In Sect. 20.4.5, the variables of the study are explained in more detail, and HO_1, HO_2, HO_3 and HO_4 are reformulated, the first two in terms of a GLM model, the second two in terms of a logistic regression model.

20.4.2 Design Alternatives Implemented in Java

The coffee-machine design alternatives described in Sect. 20.2.3 were used as treatments in the experiment. The two designs were coded using similar coding styles, naming conventions and amount of comments. Names of identifiers (e.g., variables and methods) were long and reasonably descriptive. UML sequence diagrams of the main scenario for the two designs were given to help clarify the designs. The sequence diagrams are provided in [1].

20.4.3 Programming Tasks

The programming tasks of the experiment consisted of six change tasks: a training task, a pre-test task and four (incremental) coffee machine tasks ($c1$–$c4$). To support the logistics of the experiment, the subjects used the web-based Simula Experiment Support Environment (SESE) [3] to answer an experience questionnaire, download code and documents, upload task solutions and answer task questionnaires. The experience questionnaire, detailed task descriptions and change task questionnaire are provided in [1]. Each task consisted of the following steps:

1. Download and unpack a compressed directory containing the Java code to be modified. This step was performed only prior to task $c1$ for the coffee-machine design change tasks ($c1$–$c4$) since these change tasks were based on the solution of the previous task.
2. Download task descriptions. Each task description contained a test case that each subject used to test the solution.

3. Solve the programming task using the chosen development tool.
4. Pack the modified Java code and upload it to SESE.
5. Complete a task questionnaire.

Training Task
For the training task, all the subjects were asked to change a small program so that it could read numbers from the keyboard and print them out in reverse order. The purpose of this task was to familiarize the subjects with the steps outlined above.

Pre-test Task
For the pre-test task, all the subjects implemented the same change on the same design. The change consisted of adding transaction log functionality in a bank teller machine, and was not related to the coffee-machine designs. The purpose of this task was to provide a common baseline for comparing the programming skill level of the subjects. The pre-test task had almost the same size and complexity as the subsequent change tasks $c1$, $c2$ and $c3$ combined.

Coffee-Machine Tasks
The change tasks consisted of four incremental changes to the coffee-machine:

c1. *Implement a coin return-button.*
c2. *Introduce bouillon as a new drink choice.*
c3. *Check whether all ingredients are available for the selected drink.*
c4. *Make one's own drink by selecting from the available ingredients.*

20.4.4 Group Assignment

A randomized block experimental design was used; each subject was assigned to one of two groups by means of randomization and blocking. The two groups were *CC* (in which the subjects were assigned to the CC design) and *DC* (in which the subjects were assigned to the DC design). The blocks were "undergraduate student", "graduate student", "junior consultant", "intermediate consultant" and "senior consultant". Table 20.2 shows the distribution of the categories of subject in the different groups.

Table 20.2. Subject Assignment to Treatments using a Randomized Block Design

	CC	DC	Total
Undergraduate	13	14	27
Graduate	15	17	32
Junior	16	15	31
Intermediate	17	15	32
Senior	17	19	36
Total	78	80	158

20.4.5 Execution and Practical Considerations

To recruit the professional developers, several companies were contacted through their formal sales channels. A contract for payment and a time schedule were then agreed upon. The companies were paid normal consultancy fees for the time spent on the experiment by the consultants (five to eight hours each). Seniors were paid more than intermediates, who in turn were paid more than juniors. A project manager in each company selected the subjects from the company's pool of consultants.

To recruit the students, graduate and undergraduate students at the Department of Informatics at University of Oslo were contacted through email. The students were paid a fixed amount for participating.

The experiment was conducted in 12 separate sessions on separate days (one or more sessions in each of the nine companies, and one session for the students). All the subjects in a given session were co-located at the same company site. The subjects could only take breaks or make telephone calls *between* change tasks. During each session, one or several researchers were present on the site at all times, to ensure that the subjects followed our requests and to assist them in case of technical problems.

We wanted the subjects to perform the tasks with satisfactory quality in as short a time as possible, because most software engineering jobs induce a relatively high pressure on tasks to be performed. However, if the time pressure placed on the participatory subjects is too high, the quality of the task solution may be reduced to the point where it becomes meaningless to use the corresponding task times in subsequent statistical analyses. The challenge is therefore to place realistic time pressure on the subjects. The best way to deal with this challenge depends to some extent on the size, duration and location of an experiment [28]. In this experiment, we used the following strategy:

– Instead of offering an hourly rate, we offered a "fixed" honorarium based on an estimation that the work would take five hours to complete. We told the subjects that they would be paid for those five hours independently of the time they would actually need. Hence, those subjects who finished early (e.g., in two hours) were still paid for five hours. We employed this strategy to encourage the subjects to finish as quickly as possible and to discourage them from working slowly in order to receive higher payment. However, in practice, once the five hours had passed, we told those subjects who had not finished that they would be paid for additional hours if they completed their tasks. The students received a fixed payment equivalent to eight hours salary as a teaching assistant, regardless of the actual time spent:
– The subjects were allowed to leave when they finished. Those who did not finish had to leave after eight hours.
– The subjects were informed that they were not all given the same tasks to reduce the chances that they would, for competitive reasons, prioritize speed over quality.
– The last task (*c4*) was not included in the analysis, because in our experience, the final change task in an experiment needs special attention as a result of potential "ceiling effects". If the last task is included in the analyses, it is difficult

to discriminate between the performance of the subjects regarding effort and correctness. Subjects who work fast may spend more time on the last task than they would otherwise. Similarly, subjects who work slowly may have insufficient time to perform the last task correctly. Consequently, the final change task in this experiment was not included in the analysis. Thus, the analysis of effort is not threatened by whether the subjects actually managed to complete the last task, while at the same time the presence of the large task helped to put time pressure on the subjects during the experiment. Pilot experiments were conducted to ensure that it would be very likely that all subjects would complete tasks *c1-c3* within a time span of maximum eight hours. As shown in Sect. 20.5, only two out of 158 subjects did not complete all the tasks.

We (the researchers) and the subjects signed a confidentiality agreement stating that we guaranteed that all the information about the subjects' performance should be kept strictly confidential. In particular, no information would be given to the company or to the individuals themselves about their own performance. The subjects guaranteed that they would not share information about the experiment with their colleagues, either during or after the experiment.

20.4.6 Analysis Model

To test the hypotheses, a regression-based approach was used on the unbalanced experiment design. The variables in the models are described later.

Dependent Variables

Log(Effort). the total effort in Log(minutes) to complete the change tasks. Before starting on a task, the subjects wrote down the current time. When the subjects had completed the task, they reported the total effort (in minutes) for that task. The first author of this paper double-checked the reported times using time stamps reported by the SESE tool. The variable *Effort* was the combined total effort to complete the change tasks. Thus, non-productive time between tasks was not included. A log-transformation of the effort data gave an almost perfect normal distribution.

Correctness. a binary correctness score with value 1 if all the change tasks were correctly implemented and 0 if at least one of these tasks contained serious logical errors.

Each change task solution was reviewed by an independent consultant with a PhD in computer science who lectures on testing at the University of Oslo. He was not informed about the hypotheses of the experiment. To perform the correctness analysis, he first developed a tool that automatically unpacked and built the source code corresponding to each task solution (uploaded to SESE by the subjects). In total, this corresponds to almost 1,000 different Java programs. Then, each solution was tested using a regression test script. For each test run, the difference between the *expected* output of the test case (this test output was given to the subjects as part of the task specifications) and the *actual* output generated by each program was computed. The tool also showed the complete source code as well as the source code differences between each version of the program delivered by each subject, to identify exactly how they had changed the program to solve the change task. To perform the final grading of the task solutions, a web-based grading tool was developed that enabled the consultant to view the source code, the source code difference, the test case output and the test case difference. He gave the score *correct* if there were no, or only cosmetic, differences in the test case output, and no serious logical errors were revealed by manual inspection of the source code; otherwise he gave the score *incorrect*. The consultant performed this analysis twice to avoid inconsistencies in the way he had graded the task solutions. Completing this work took approximately 200 hours.

Controlled Factors

Design – the main treatments of the experiment; that is, the factors DC and CC.
Block – the developer categories used as blocking factors in the experiment; that is, the factors Undergraduate, Graduate, Junior, Intermediate and Senior. For the professional consultants, a project manager from each company chose consultants from the categories "junior", "intermediate" and "senior" according to how they usually would categorize (and price) their consultants. Potential threats caused by this categorization are discussed further in Sect. 20.6.1.

Covariates

Log(Pre_Dur) – the (log-transformed) effort in minutes to complete the pre-test task. The individual results of the pre-test can be used as a covariate in the models to reduce the error variance caused by individual skill differences.

Model Specifications

For the hypotheses regarding effort, a generalized linear model (GLM) approach was used to perform a combination of analysis of variance (ANOVA), analysis of covariance (ACOVA) and regression analysis [13]. For the hypotheses regarding correctness, a logistic regression model was fitted using the same (GLM) model terms as for effort, that is, including dummy (or indicator) variables for each factor level and combinations of factor levels [13].

The models are specified in Table 20.3. Given that the underlying assumptions of the model are not violated, the presence of a significant model term corresponds to rejecting the related null-hypothesis. Model (1) was used to test hypotheses HO_1 and HO_2. Model (2) was used to test hypotheses HO_3 and HO_4. In addition, model (3) was included to test the hypothesis on effort restricted to those subjects with correct solutions. Thus, model (3) represents an alternative way to assess the effect of the design alternatives on change effort. Since the subjects with correct solutions no longer represent a random sample, the covariate *Log(Pre_Dur)* was included to adjust for skill differences between the groups. Furthermore, since the covariate is confounded with *Block*, it is no longer meaningful to include *Block* in model (3).

Table 20.3. Model Specifications

model	Response	model term	primary use of model term
(1)	log(effort)	design	test $H0_1$ (effort main effect)
		block	assess the effect of different developer categories on effort
		design* block	test $H0_2$ (effort interaction)
(2)	correct	design	test $H0_3$ (correctness main effect)
		block	assess the effect of different developer categories on correctness
		design* block	test $H0_4$ (correctness interaction)
(3)	log(effort)	design	alternative test of $H0_1$ for subjects with correct solutions
		log(pre_effort)	covariate to adjust for programming skill differences
		log(pre_effort)*design	test on homogeneity of slopes

The final specification of the models must take place after the actual analyses because the validity of the underlying model assumptions must be checked against the actual data. For example, we determined that a log-transformation of effort was necessary to obtain models with normally distributed residuals, which is an important assumption of GLM. Furthermore, the inclusion of insignificant interaction terms may affect the validity of the coefficients and p-values (and the resulting interpretation) of other model terms. Insignificant interaction terms are therefore candidates for removal from the model. Whether insignificant terms should actually be removed depends on whether the reduced model fits the data better than the complete model. This is explained further in Sect. 20.5.

20.5 Results

This section describes the results of the experiment. In Sect. 20.5.1, descriptive statistics of the data are provided to illustrate the size and direction of the effects of the experimental conditions. In Sect. 20.5.2, the hypotheses outlined in Sect. 20.4.1 are tested formally using the statistical models described in Sect. 20.4.6. Finally, in Sect. 20.5.3, we draw some general conclusions by interpreting both the descriptive statistics and the results from the formal hypothesis tests.

20.5.1 Descriptive Statistics

Table 20.4 shows the descriptive statistics related to the main hypotheses of the experiment. Two of the 158 subjects in the experiment did not complete all the tasks, as indicated by column N^*. The columns *Mean* to *Max* show the descriptive

Table 20.4. Descriptive statistics of change effort (in min) and correctness (in %)

block	design	N	N*	mean	std	min	q1	me dian	q3	max	cor rect %
undergraduate	CC	13	0	79	30	45	56	81	87	161	62
	DC	14	0	108	63	23	73	88	151	267	29
		27	0	94	51	23	60	84	99	267	44
graduate	CC	15	0	65	23	23	49	60	85	105	80
	DC	17	0	73	37	23	52	63	85	173	65
		32	0	69	31	23	51	63	85	173	72
junior	CC	16	0	95	32	39	76	95	114	170	63
	DC	15	0	110	46	60	71	102	127	217	33
		31	0	102	39	39	72	100	122	217	48
intermediate	CC	17	0	107	49	51	72	91	133	215	65
	DC	14	1	101	46	54	63	92	127	202	40
		31	1	104	47	51	69	91	126	215	53
senior	CC	16	1	103	62	35	64	75	135	253	76
	DC	19	0	71	38	31	40	61	95	169	74
		35	1	86	52	31	51	67	111	253	75
total	CC	77	1	91	44	23	60	83	101	253	69
	DC	79	1	91	48	23	60	77	120	267	50
		156	2	91	46	23	60	82	105	267	59

statistics of the change effort (in minutes to solve change tasks c1+c2+c3). The column *Correct* shows the percentage of the subjects that delivered correct solutions for all three tasks. The *Total* row shows that the mean time required to perform the tasks was 91 m for both the CC and DC design. Furthermore, 69% of the subjects delivered correct solutions on the CC design, but only 50% did on the DC design.

However, there are quite large differences between the different *categories* of developer, especially when comparing undergraduate and junior developers with graduate students and senior professionals. The apparent interaction between developer category and design alternative is illustrated in Fig. 20.2. For example, the undergraduate students spent on average about 30% less time on the CC design than on the DC design (79 min vs 108 min). They were also much more likely to produce correct solutions on the CC design than on the DC design (62% vs 29%). This indicates that, for undergraduate students, the CC design is easier to change than is the DC design. This picture is reversed when considering the seniors: they spent on average about 30% *more* time on the CC design than on the DC design (103 min vs 71 min). For the seniors, there is no difference in correctness for the two design alternatives (76% for the CC design v 74% for the DC design). This indicates that, for senior developers, the DC design is easier to change than is the CC design. The graduate students, juniors and intermediates seem to benefit from using the CC design when considering both change effort and correctness, although the differences between the control styles are much smaller than for the undergraduate students and seniors.

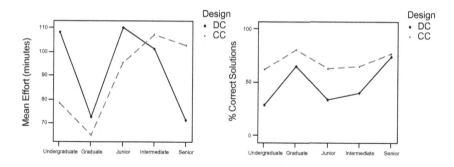

Fig. 20.2. Interaction plots of mean effort and correctness

20.5.2 Hypothesis Tests

The results of testing the hypotheses on change effort are shown in Table 20.5. Residual analyses of the model indicate that the assumptions of the GLM model are not violated (further details are provided in [1]).

There is insufficient evidence to reject the null-hypothesis HO_1, that is, we cannot conclude that there is a difference in change effort between the two design alternatives (*Design*, $p = 0.964$). By contrast, the results identify significant differences in change effort for the five developer categories (*Block*, $p = 0.001$). A post-hoc Tukey's pairwise comparison of differences in the mean of the developer categories show that, overall, the graduate students were faster than juniors ($p = 0.0027$) and intermediates ($p = 0.0034$). There were no significant differences between any other pair of categories.

Regarding the hypotheses about the interaction between design and developer category, HO_2, there is insufficient support for rejecting the null-hypothesis (*Design*Block*, $p = 0.133$). In light of the descriptive statistics, this was somewhat surprising, because the relative difference in change effort between the design alternatives is still considerable for *some* categories of developer, and in opposite directions. Since we did not have a clear hypothesis about how much experience would be required to benefit from the DC design, the analysis model including all developer categories in the interaction term is quite conservative. Only large interaction effects between several of the categories would result in a significant model term. Consequently, we performed a post-hoc analysis based on model 1, but included only two developer categories: subjects with "high experience", which included the seniors and intermediates, and subjects with "low experience", which included the undergraduates, graduates and juniors. In this case, the interaction term was significant ($p = 0.028$). We emphasize that this is an exploratory analysis, because the experience level was not set a priori, but was instead set on the basis of the actual data.

Table 20.5. GLM model (model 1) for Log(effort) (hypotheses HO$_1$ and HO$_2$)

```
factor type   levels   values
design fixed  2        DC CC
block  fixed  5        undergraduate Graduate Junior Intermediate
                       Senior
```

analysis of variance for log(effort), using adjusted SS for tests

source	DF	Seq SS	Adj SS	Adj MS	F	P
design	1	0.0310	0.0004	0.0004	0.00	0.964
block	4	4.0454	3.9932	0.9983	4.84	0.001
design*Block	4	1.4788	1.4788	0.3697	1.79	0.133
error	146	30.1090	30.1090	0.2062		
total	155	35.6642				

term	Coef	SE Coef	T	P
constant	4.39952	0.03657	120.31	0.000
design				
DC	0.00166	0.03657	0.05	0.964
block				
graduate	-0.25945	0.07224	-3.59	0.000
junior	0.16559	0.07303	2.27	0.025
intermediate	0.15855	0.07326	2.16	0.032
senior	-0.08006	0.06999	-1.14	0.255
design*Block				
DC*Graduate	0.3012	0.07224	0.42	0.677
DC*Junior	0.05869	0.07303	0.80	0.423
DC*Intermediate	-0.02752	0.07326	-0.38	0.708
DC*Senior	-0.17024	0.06999	-2.43	0.016

The results of testing the hypotheses on correctness are shown in Table 20.6. The results clearly show that the subjects are much less likely to produce correct solutions on the DC design than on the CC design (*Design*, odds-ratio = 0.40, p = 0.009), all other conditions being equal. The null-hypothesis HO$_3$ is rejected. Furthermore, graduate students and seniors are much more likely to produce correct solutions (odds-ratios 3.42 and 4.03, respectively) than are the other developer categories. The interaction term *Design*Block* was removed from the logistic regression model because the coefficients were far from significant and reduced the goodness of fit. Hence, there is insufficient statistical evidence to reject HO$_4$. We cannot conclude that the CC design improves correctness for only *some* categories of developers. On the basis of the evidence collected, it improves correctness for all the categories. The goodness-of-fit tests for the model in Table 20.6 show a high correlation between the observations and the model estimates. Thus, the underlying model assumptions of logistic regression are not violated.

Finally, Table 20.7 shows the results of the analysis of covariance model on Log(Effort) for the subjects who managed to produce correct solutions. The results show that the change effort is much less for the DC design than for the CC design (*Design*, p = 0.003). Thus, those subjects who actually manage to understand the DC design sufficiently well to produce correct solutions also use less time than those who produce correct solutions on the CC design. As can be seen from the descriptive statistics (Table 20.4) and from the logistic regression model of correctness (Table 20.6), these subjects are overrepresented by senior consultants and graduate students. Residual analyses of the model indicate that the assumptions of the GLM model are not violated. See details in [1].

Table 20.6. Logistic regression model (model 2) for correctness (hypotheses $H0_3$ and $H0_4$)

```
response information

variable  value          count
correct   1                 94   (event)
          0                 64
          Total            158

logistic regression table
odds          95% CI
predictor            Coef     SE Coef         Z     P      Ratio    Lower
Upper
constant           0.2403     0.4330       0.55 0.579
design
 DC               -0.9154     0.3483      -2.63 0.009      0.40     0.20
0.79
block
 graduate          1.2307     0.5667       2.17 0.030      3.42     1.13
10.39
 junior            0.1342     0.5422       0.25 0.805      1.14     0.40
3.31
 intermediate      0.3196     0.5386       0.59 0.553      1.38     0.48
3.96
 senior            1.3941     0.5606       2.49 0.013      4.03     1.34
12.10

log-likelihood = -97.814
test that all slopes are zero: G = 17.675, DF = 5, P-Value = 0.003
goodness-of-fit tests
method               Chi-Square     DF      P
pearson                  1.526       4    0.822
deviance                 1.486       4    0.829
hosmer-Lemeshow          1.500       6    0.959
```

Table 20.7. Change effort for subjects with correct solutions

```
factor      type levels values
design      fixed      2 DC CC

analysis of variance for log(Effort), using adjusted SS for tests

source              DF     seq SS     adj SS     adj MS        F      P
log(pre_Effort)      1     3.2835     3.1802     3.1802    24.06  0.000
design               1     1.2421     1.2421     1.2421     9.40  0.003
error               91    12.0275    12.0275     0.1322
total               93    16.5531

term                Coef     SE Coef        t        p
constant          2.9912     0.2622      11.41   0.000
log(pre_Effort) 0.32893     0.06706       4.91   0.000
design
 DC              -0.11628    0.03793      -3.07   0.003
```

20.5.3 Summary of Results

This section summarizes the results by considering both the descriptive statistics (which describe the results of the specific sample population) and the hypotheses tests (which indicate the extent to which the results can be generalized to the target population) with regard to both effort and correctness.

Based on the formal hypothesis tests, the results suggest that there is no difference in change effort between the two designs when considering all subjects, regardless of whether they produced correct solutions or not (model 1). The descriptive statistics indicate large relative differences between two specific categories of developer (undergraduate student versus senior consultant), but there is insufficient support for an interaction effect between the design alternatives and the given developer categories with regard to effort ($p = 0.133$). However, a post-hoc analysis conducted on the basis of the actual data still suggests that there is an interaction effect between a more coarse-grained variable "experience" and change effort ($p = 0.028$).

All developer categories are more likely to produce correct solutions on the CC design than on the DC design (model 2). There is no support for an interaction effect between design alternatives and the developer category with regard to correctness. However, the effect size of design on correctness is very large for the undergraduate students and junior developers, who clearly have serious difficulty in producing correct solutions on the DC design, whereas the effect size of design is negligible for the seniors.

When only considering those subjects who managed to produce correct solutions (probably the most skilled subjects, because the subjects with correct solutions also used, on average, considerably *less* time than did subjects with incorrect solutions), the DC design seems to require less effort than does the CC design (model 3).

In summary, when considering both effort and correctness in combination, the results suggest the following conclusions. Only senior consultants seem to have the necessary skills to benefit from the DC design. The graduate students also perform well on the DC design, but they perform even better on the CC design. The CC design favors the less skilled developers, over-represented by undergraduate students and junior developers. There are no clear indications in either direction for the intermediate developers.

20.6 Threats to Validity

This paper reports an experiment with a high degree of realism compared with previously reported controlled experiments within software engineering. Our goal was to obtain results that could be generalized to the target population of professional Java consultants solving real programming tasks with professional development tools in a realistic work setting. This is an ambitious goal, however. For example, there is a trade-off between ensuring realism (to reduce threats to *external* validity) and ensuring control (to reduce threats to *internal* validity). This section discusses what we consider to be the most important threats to the validity of this experiment.

20.6.1 Construct Validity

The construct validity concerns whether the independent and dependent variables accurately measure the concepts we intend to study.

Classification of the Control Styles

An important threat to the construct validity in this experiment is the extent to which the actual design alternatives that were used as treatments ("delegated" versus "centralized" control styles) are representative of the concept studied. There is no operational definition to classify precisely the control style of object-oriented software; a certain degree of subjective interpretation is required. Furthermore, when considering the extremes, the abstract concepts of a centralized and delegated control style might not even be representative of realistic software designs. Still, some software systems might be "more centralized than" or "more delegated than" others.

Based on expert opinions in [15] and our own assessment of the designs, it is quite obvious that the DC design has a more delegated control style than the CC design. However, it is certainly possible to design a coffee-machine with an even more centralized control style than the CC design (e.g., a design consisting of only one control class and no entity classes whatsoever), or a more delegated control style than the DC design. We chose to use as treatments example designs developed by others [15]. We believe these treatments constitute a reasonable trade-off between being clear representatives of the two control styles, and being realistic and unbiased software design alternatives.

Classification of Developers

Someone who is considered as (say) an intermediate consultant in one company might be considered (say) a senior in another company. Thus, the categories are not necessarily representative of the categories used in every consultancy company. A replication in other companies might therefore produce different results with respect to how the variable *Block* affects change effort and correctness. However, as seen from the results, the *Block* factor representing the categories is a significant explanatory variable of change effort and correctness, and, as expected, senior consultants provided better solutions in a shorter time than did juniors and undergraduate students. Thus, for the purpose of discriminating between the programming skill and experience of the developers, the classification was sufficiently accurate.

Measuring Change Effort

The effort measure was affected by noise and disturbances. Some subjects (in particular the professionals) might have been more disturbed or have taken longer breaks than did others. For example, senior consultants are likely to receive more telephone calls because they typically have a central role in the projects in which they would normally participate. To address this possible threat, we instructed the consultants not to answer telephone calls or talk to colleagues during the experiment. The subjects were also instructed to take their lunch break only *between* two change tasks. At least one of the authors of this paper was present at the company site during all experiment sessions and observed that these requests were followed to a large extent. The monitoring functionality of SESE [3] also enabled us to monitor the progress of each subject at all times, and follow up if we observed little activity. Similar measures were applied during the student experiment session.

Measuring Correctness

The dependent variable *Correct* was binary, and indicated whether the subjects produced functionally correct solutions on *all* the change tasks, thus producing a working final program. As described in Sect. 20.4.6, a significant amount of effort was spent on ensuring that the correctness scores were valid. More complex measures to identify the *number* of programming faults or the *severity* of programming faults were also considered. However, such measures would necessarily be more subjective, and hence more difficult to use in future replications than the adopted "correct" "not correct" score.

Effort and Correctness as Indicators of Maintainability

An important issue is whether one of the designs, after being subject to the changes, would be more "maintainable", or in general, have higher "quality" than the other design, for certain categories of developer. We believe that the effort spent when performing the changes, and the achieved correctness, represent two important indicators of the maintainability of the two control styles. However, due to the limited number and duration of tasks, they only indicate short-term maintainability. For example, the results reported in [2] suggest that the change tasks on the CC design result in higher coupling and require more lines of code to be changed than do the change tasks on the DC design. As argued in [2], these internal attributes indicate that the DC design might be more structurally stable in the long run, but we will still not really know what the consequences would be regarding the actual costs of maintaining the software, unless new experiments are performed. Thus, this is a threat to construct validity that also has consequences for the external validity of this experiment.

20.6.2 Internal Validity

The internal validity of an experiment is the degree to which conclusions can be drawn about the causal effect of the controlled factors on the experimental outcome.

Differences in Settings between Developer Categories

To improve external validity, the setting of the experiment should be as realistic as possible [28, 29]. Thus, the students in this experiment were situated in a computer lab; the professional consultants in a normal work environment. Furthermore, each developer was permitted to use a Java development environment of their own choice. Most of the students used Emacs and Javac, whereas the professionals used a variety of professional integrated development environments. Finally, there were differences in payment between students and professionals. We cannot rule out the possibility that these differences in settings are confounding factors regarding a direct comparison of the performance of students versus professionals.

However, the primary goal of this experiment was to compare *relative* differences of the effect the two control styles, for which all categories of student and professional developer were evenly distributed across the two design alternatives. Furthermore, there were no differences in setting *within* each developer category. Hence, these differences in setting were not included as additional covariates in the models described in Sect. 20.4.6. For example, although the students and professionals used different tools, the distribution of tools was quite even across the two design alternatives and within each developer category. In this particular case, we also checked the extent to which the chosen development tool affected the performance of the subjects, by including *DevelopmentTool* as a covariate in the models described in Sect. 20.4.6. The term was not a significant explanatory variable for effort ($p = 0.437$) or correctness ($p = 0.347$). Another possibility would have been to use only one specific tool, to completely eliminate variations due to different tools as a possible confounding factor. However, that would introduce other threats, related, for example, to tool learning effects.

In summary, we believe it is unlikely that the main results described in this paper, that is, the relative comparison of the effect of the two design alternatives for different categories of developer, are threatened by differences in setting.

20.6.3 External Validity

The question of external validity concerns "[the] populations, settings, treatment variables and measurement variables [to which] this effect [can] be generalized" [11].

Scope of Systems and Tasks

Clearly, the two alternative designs in this experiment were very small compared with "typical" object-oriented software systems. Furthermore, the change tasks were also relatively small in size and duration. However, the change task questionnaires received from the participants after they had completed the change tasks indicate that the *complexity* of the tasks was quite high. Nevertheless, we cannot rule out the possibility that the observed effects would be different if the systems and tasks had been larger.

The scope of this study is limited to situations in which the maintainers have no prior knowledge of a system. It is possible that the results do not apply to situations in which the maintainers are also the original designers. As also discussed in Sect. 20.6.1, a related issue is whether the short-term effects observed in this experiment are representative of long-term maintenance. It is possible that the effects we observed are due principally to the higher cognitive complexity of a delegated control style, and that even less skilled maintainers will eventually pass the learning curve of a delegated control style to the extent that they can benefit from it.

Fatiguing effects

Despite our effort to ensure realism, the experiment is still not completely representative of a "normal day at the office". In a normal work situation, one might be able to take longer breaks and in general be less stressed and tired than in an experimental setting. We cannot rule out the possibility that such fatiguing effects might introduce a bias for one of the control styles.

Representativeness of Sample

An important question for this experiment is whether the professional subjects were representative of "professional Java consultants". Our sample included consultants from major international software consultancy companies. A project manager was hired from each company to, among other things, select a representative sample of their consultants for the categories "junior", "intermediate" and "senior". The selection process corresponded to how the companies would usually categorize and price consultants. Hence, in addition to experience and competence, availability was also one of the selection criteria. Thus, it could be the case that the "best" professionals were underrepresented in our sample, since it is possible that they had already been hired by other companies. Fortunately, we observed that, on many occasions, the project managers took busy consultants off their current projects to participate in the experiment.

20.7 Conclusions

The degree of maintainability of a software application depends not only on attributes of the software itself, but also on certain cognitive attributes of the particular developer whose task it is to maintain it. This aspect seems to be underestimated by expert designers. Most experienced software designers would probably agree that a delegated control style is more "elegant", and a better object-oriented representation of the problem to be solved, than is a centralized control style. However, care should be taken to ensure that future maintainers of the software are able to understand this (apparently) elegant design. If the cognitive complexity of a design is beyond the skills of future maintainers, they will spend more time, and probably introduce more faults, than they would with a (for them) simpler but less "elegant" object-oriented design.

Assuming that it is not only highly skilled experts who are going to maintain an object-oriented system, a viable conclusion from the controlled experiment reported in this paper is that a design with a centralized control style may be more maintainable than is a design with a delegated control style. These results are also relevant with regard to a use-case driven design method, which may support both control styles: it is mainly a question of how much responsibility is assigned to the control class of each use case.

Although an important goal of this experiment was to ensure realism, by using a large sample of professional developers as subjects who are instructed to solve programming tasks with professional development tools in a normal office environment, there are several threats to the validity of the results that should be addressed in future replications. Increasing the realism (and thereby external validity) reduced the amount of control, which introduced threats to internal validity. For example, we allowed the developers to use a development tool of their own choice. Another possibility would have been to use only one specific tool, to eliminate variations due to different tools as a possible confounding factor. However, that would introduce other threats, related, for example, to tool learning effects. Thus, we believe that this reduction in control is a small price to pay considering that the improved realism of this experiment allows us to generalize the results beyond that which would be possible in a more controlled laboratory setting with students solving pen-and-paper tasks. Still, whether the results of this experiment generalize to realistically sized systems and tasks is an open question. Consequently, the most important means to improve the external validity of the experiment is to increase the size of the systems and the tasks. Furthermore, the results might be different in situations where less skilled maintainers successfully perform a sufficient number of tasks to pass the learning curve of a delegated control style.

The results of this experiment are surprising in a further way. For the given tasks, the graduate students performed very well, and outperformed junior and intermediate consultants. One reason could be that the project managers selected low-skilled consultants for the experiment. However, contrary to this, the project managers confirmed that they also included their best people, and on many occasions took them off their current projects to participate in the experiment. A more likely reason is that graduate students, because of the stringent selection process for admission to Masters programmes, are better than relatively inexperienced professionals. Another possibility is that formal training in object-oriented programming is more important than work experience. Both hypotheses are, to some extent, supported by the descriptive statistics presented in [1]: the seniors are more likely to have completed graduate studies than are the juniors and intermediates. Both the seniors and graduate students have more credits in computer science courses than have the undergraduate students, juniors and intermediate consultants. In future studies, we will attempt to explore these complex interactions among the underlying characteristics (such as programming experience in specific languages, work experience and education) to better explain the observed variations in programmer performance.

Acknowledgements

We thank Lionel Briand, Magne Jørgensen, Vigdis By Kampenes, Ray Welland, Chris Wright and the anonymous reviewers for their valuable contributions to this paper. We thank KompetanseWeb for their excellent support on the SESE tool. Gunnar Carelius provided valuable support during the preparation and quality assurance of the experimental materials in SESE. Are Magnus Bruaset did an outstanding job on the testing and qualitative assessment of the Java solutions delivered by the subjects. We thank the students at the University of Oslo for their participation, and the staff at the Department of Informatics in the same university for their technical support. Finally, this paper would not have been possible without the consultants and project managers who participated from the following companies: Accenture, Cap Gemini Ernst & Young, Ementa, Ementor, Genera, Objectnet, Software Innovation, Software Innovation Technology and TietoEnator.

References

[1] Arisholm, E. and Sjøberg, D.I.K. (2003) "A Controlled Experiment with Professionals to Evaluate the Effect of a Delegated versus Centralized Control Style on the Maintainability of Object-Oriented Software," *Simula Research Laboratory Technical Report 2003-6* (http://www.simula.no/~erika)

[2] Arisholm, E., Sjøberg, D.I.K., and Jørgensen, M. (2001) "Assessing the Changeability of two Object-Oriented Design Alternatives – A Controlled Experiment," *Empirical Software Engineering*, Vol. 6, No. 3, pp. 231–277

[3] Arisholm, E., Sjøberg, D.I.K., Carelius, G.J., and Lindsjørn, Y. (2002) A Web-based Support Environment for Software Engineering Experiments, *Nordic Journal of Computing*, Vol. 9, No. 4, pp. 231–247

[4] Beck, K. and Cunningham, W. (1989) A Laboratory for Teaching Object-Oriented Thinking, *SIGPLAN Notices*, Vol. 24, No. 10, pp. 1–6

[5] Briand, L. and Wuest, J. (2002) Empirical Studies of Quality Models in Object-Oriented Systems, *Advances in Computers*, Vol. 59, pp. 97–166

[6] Briand, L., Bunse, C., and Daly, J.W. (2001) A Controlled Experiment for Evaluating Quality Guidelines on the Maintainability of Object-Oriented Designs, *IEEE Transactions on Software Engineering*, Vol. 27, No. 6, pp. 513–530

[7] Briand, L.C., Daly, J., and Wust, J. (1998) A Unified Framework for Cohesion Measurement in Object-Oriented Systems, *Empirical Software Engineering*, Vol. 3, No. 1, pp. 65–117

[8] Briand, L.C., Daly, J.W., and Wust, J. (1999) A Unified Framework for Coupling Measurement in Object-Oriented Systems, *IEEE Transactions on Software Engineering*, Vol. 25, No. 1, pp. 91–121

[9] Briand, L.C., Bunse, C., Daly, J.W., and Differding, C. (1997) An Experimental Comparison of the Maintainability of Object-Oriented and Structured Design Documents, *Empirical Software Engineering*, Vol. 2, No. 3, pp. 291–312

[10] Burkhardt, J.-M., Detienne, F., and Wiedenbeck, S. (2002) Object-Oriented Program Comprehension: Effect of Expertice, Task and Phase, *Empirical Software Engineering*, Vol. 7, No. 2, pp. 115–156

[11] Campell, D.T. and Stanley, J.C. (1963) *Experimental and Quasi-Experimental Designs for Research*, Rand McNally and Company

[12] Chidamber, S.R. and Kemerer, C.F. (1994) A Metrics Suite for Object-Oriented Design, *IEEE Transactions on Software Engineering*, Vol. 20, No. 6, pp. 476–493

[13] Christensen, R. (1998) *Analysis of Variance, Design and Regression*: Chapman & Hall/CRC Press

[14] Coad, P. and Yourdon, E. (1991) *Object-Oriented Design*, First edition, Prentice-Hall

[15] Cockburn, A. (1998) The Coffee Machine Design Problem: Part 1 & 2, *C/C++ User's Journal*

[16] Glass, R.L. (1994) "The Software Research Crisis," *IEEE Software*, Vol. 11, No. 6, pp. 42–47

[17] Jacobson, I., Booch, G., and Rumbaugh, J. (1999) *The Unified Software Development Process*: Addison-Wesley.

[18] Jacobson, I., Christerson, M., Jonsson, P., and Overgaard, G. (1992) *Object-Oriented Software Engineering*, Addison-Wesley

[19] Keller, R.K., Cockburn, A., and Schauer, R. (1997) Object-Oriented Design Quality: Report on OOPSLA'97 Workshop #12, *Proc. OOPSLA'97 Workshop on Object-Oriented Design Quality, http://www.iro.umontreal.ca/~keller/Workshops/OOPSLA97*

[20] Kitchenham, B., Pickard, L., and Pfleeger, S.L. (1995) Case Studies for Method and Tool Evaluation, *IEEE Software*, Vol. 12, No. 4, pp. 52–62

[21] Kitchenham, B.A. (1996) Evaluating Software Engineering Methods and Tools, Part 1: The Evaluation Context and Evaluation Methods, *ACM Software Engineering Notes*, Vol. 21, No. 1, pp. 11–15

[22] Lieberherr, K.J. and Holland, I.M. (1989) Assuring Good Style for Object-Oriented Programs, *IEEE Software*, Vol. 6, No. 5, pp. 38–48

[23] Lindsay, R.M. and Ehrenberg, A.S.C. (1993) The Design of Replicated Studies, *The American Statistician*, Vol. 47, No. 3, pp. 217–228

[24] Potts, C. (1993) Software Engineering Research Revisited, *IEEE Software*, Vol. 10, No. 5, pp. 19–28

[25] Sharble, R.C. and Cohen, S.S. (1993) The Object-Oriented Brewery: A Comparison of two Object-Oriented Development Methods, *Software Engineering Notes*, Vol. 18, No. 2, pp. 60–73

[26] Sheetz, S.D. (2002) Identifying the Difficulties of Object-Oriented Development, *Journal of Systems and Software*, Vol. 64, No. 1, pp. 23–36

[27] Shlaer, S. and Mellor, S. (1998) *Object-Oriented Systems Analysis: Modeling the World in Data*, Yourdon Press

[28] Sjøberg, D.I.K., Anda, B., Arisholm, E., Dybå, T., Jørgensen, M., Karahasanovic, A., and Vokác, M. Challenges and Recommendations when Increasing the Realism of Controlled Software Engineering Experiments, in *Empirical Methods and Studies in Software Engineering, ESERNET, 2001–2002* R. Conradi and A.I. Wang, (Eds.): *Lecture Notes in Computer Science 2765*, Springer Berlin Heidelberg New York, pp. 24–38

[29] Sjøberg, D.I.K., Anda, B., Arisholm, E., Dybå, T., Jørgensen, M., Karahasanovic, A., Koren, E., and Vokác, M. (2002) Conducting Realistic Experiments in Software Engineering, *Proc. ISESE'2002 (First International Symposium on Empirical Software Engineering), October 3–4, 2002*, pp. 17–26

[30] Tockey, S., B. Hoza, B., and Cohen, S. (1990) Object-Oriented Analysis: Building on the Structured Techniques, *Proc. Software Improvement Conference*

[31] Wirfs-Brock, R.J. (1994) Characterizing your Application's Control Style, *Report on Object Analysis and Design*, Vol. 1, No. 3

[32] Wirfs-Brock, R.J. and Wilkerson, B. (1989) Object-Oriented Design: A Responsibility Driven Approach, *SIGPLAN Notices*, Vol. 24, No. 10, pp. 71–75

[33] Wirfs-Brock, R.J., Wilkerson, B., and Wiener, R. (1990) *Designing Object-Oriented Software*, Prentice-Hall

Author List

Bente C. D. Anda
Simula Research Laboratory, P.O. Box 134, NO-1325 Lysaker, Norway.
E-mail: bentea@simula.no

Erik Arisholm
Simula Research Laboratory, P.O. Box 134, NO-1325 Lysaker, Norway.
E-mail: erika@simula.no

Finn Olav Bjørnson
Department of Computer and Information Science, Norwegian University of Science and Technology (NTNU), NO-7491 Trondheim, Norway.
E-mail: bjornson@idi.ntnu.no

Christian Bunse
Fraunhofer IESE, Fraunhofer-Platz 1, D-67663 Kaiserslautern, Germany.
E-mail: Christian.Bunse@iese.fraunhofer.de

Reidar Conradi
Department of Computer and Information Science, Norwegian University of Science and Technology (NTNU), NO-7491 Trondheim, Norway and Simula Research Laboratory, P.O.BOX 134, NO-1325 Lysaker, Norway.
E-mail: Reidar.Conradi@idi.ntnu.no

Torgeir Dingsøyr
SINTEF ICT, NO-7465 Trondheim, Norway.
E-mail: torgeir.dingsoyr@sintef.no

Tore Dybå
SINTEF ICT, NO-7465 Trondheim, Norway and Simula Research Laboratory, P.O.BOX 134, NO-1325 Lysaker, Norway.
E-mail: tore.dyba@sintef.no

Alfonso Fuggetta
CEFRIEL – Politecnico di Milano, Via Fucini 2, I-20133 Milano, Italy.
E-mail: Alfonso.Fuggetta@polimi.it

Ingolf Gullesen
ABB Corporate Research Center, P.O. Box 90, NO–1375 Billingstad, Norway.
E-mail: ingolf.gullesen@no.abb.com

Kai Hansen
ABB Corporate Research Center, P.O. Box 90, NO–1375 Billingstad, Norway.
E-mail: kai.hansen@no.abb.com

Geir Kjetil Hanssen
SINTEF ICT, NO-7465 Trondheim, Norway.
E-mail: geir.k.hanssen@sintef.no

Maria Letizia Jaccheri
Department of Computer and Information Science, Norwegian University of
Science and Technology (NTNU), NO-7491 Trondheim, Norway.
E-mail: letizia@idi.ntnu.no

Magne Jørgensen
Simula Research Laboratory, PO Box 134, NO-1325 Lysaker, Norway.
E-mail: magne.jorgensen@simula.no

Amela Karahasanović
Simula Research Laboratory, P.O. Box 134, NO-1325 Lysaker, Norway.
E-mail: amela@simula.no

Umair Khan
Fraunhofer IESE, Fraunhofer-Platz 1, D-67663 Kaiserslautern, Germany.
E-mail: khan@iese.fraunhofer.de

Barbara A. Kitchenham
National ICT Australia, Locked Bag 9013, Alexandria, NSW 1435, Australia.
E-mail: barbara.kitchenham@nicta.com.au

Jingyue Li
Department of Computer and Information Science, Norwegian University of
Science and Technology (NTNU), NO-7491 Trondheim, Norway.
E-mail: Jingyue.Li@idi.ntnu.no

Edda M. Mikkelsen
DNV Software, NO-1322 Høvik, Norway.
E-mail: Edda.Mikkelsen@dnv.com

Nils Brede Moe
SINTEF ICT, NO-7465 Trondheim, Norway.
E-mail: nils.b.moe@sintef.no

Parastoo Mohagheghi
Department of Computer and Information Science, Norwegian University of Science and Technology (NTNU), NO-7491 Trondheim, Norway.
E-mail: parastoo@idi.ntnu.no

Maurizio Morisio
Dip. Automatica e Informatica, Politecnico di Torino, Corso Duca degli Abruzzi, 24, I-10129 Torino, Italy
E-mail: maurizio.morisio@polito.it

Emil André Røyrvik
SINTEF Industrial Management, NO-7465 Trondheim, Norway.
E-mail: Emil.Royrvik@sintef.no

Dag Ingar Kondrup Sjøberg
Simula Research Laboratory, P.O. Box 134, NO-1325 Lysaker, Norway.
E-mail: Dag.Sjoberg@ifi.uio.no

Odd Petter N. Slyngstad
Department of Computer and Information Science, Norwegian University of Science and Technology (NTNU), NO-7491 Trondheim, Norway.
E-mail: oslyngst@idi.ntnu.no

Hanne Kristin Thorsen
Department of Informatics, University of Oslo, P.O. Box 1080 Blindern, NO-0316 Oslo, Norway and Simula Research Laboratory, P.O. Box 134, NO-1325 Lysaker, Norway.
E-mail: hannekt@ifi.uio.no

Marco Torchiano
Dip. Automatica e Informatica, Politecnico di Torino, Corso Duca degli Abruzzi, 24, I-10129 Torino, Italy.
E-mail: marco.torchiano@polito.it

Tor Ulsund
Geomatikk AS, Otto Nielsens vei 12, N-7052 Trondheim, Norway.
E-mail: tor.ulsund@geomatikk.no

Marek Vokáč
Simula Research Laboratory, P.O. Box 134, NO-1325 Lysaker, Norway.
E-mail: marekv@simula.no

Hans Westerheim
SINTEF ICT, NO-7465 Trondheim, Norway.
E-mail: hans.westerheim@sintef.no

Keyword Index